TOM **TAYLOR** DANIELE **DI NICUOLO** WALTER **BAIAMONTE**

SEVEN SECRETS ™

Published by

BOOM! STUDIOS™

LOGO DESIGN
GRACE PARK

SERIES DESIGNER
MICHELLE ANKLEY

COLLECTION DESIGNER
CHELSEA ROBERTS

ASSISTANT EDITOR
GWEN WALLER

EDITOR
DAFNA PLEBAN

**BOOM!
STUDIOS**

SEVEN SECRETS Vol. 1, April 2021. Published by BOOM! Studios, a division of Boom Entertainment, Inc. Seven Secrets is 2021 © & ™ Tom Taylor. Originally published in single magazine form as SEVEN SECRETS No.1-6, 2020, 2021 © & ™ Tom Taylor. All rights reserved. BOOM! Studios™ and the BOOM! Studios logo are trademarks of Boom Entertainment, Inc., registered in various countries and categories. All characters, events, and institutions depicted herein are fictional. Any similarity between any of the names, characters, persons, events, and/or institutions in this publication to actual names, characters, and persons, whether living or dead, events, and/or institutions is unintended and purely coincidental. BOOM! Studios does not read or accept unsolicited submissions of ideas, stories, or artwork.

BOOM! Studios, 5670 Wilshire Boulevard, Suite 400, Los Angeles, CA, 90036-5679. Printed in China. First Printing.

ISBN: 978-1-68415-706-8 eISBN: 978-1-64668-250-8

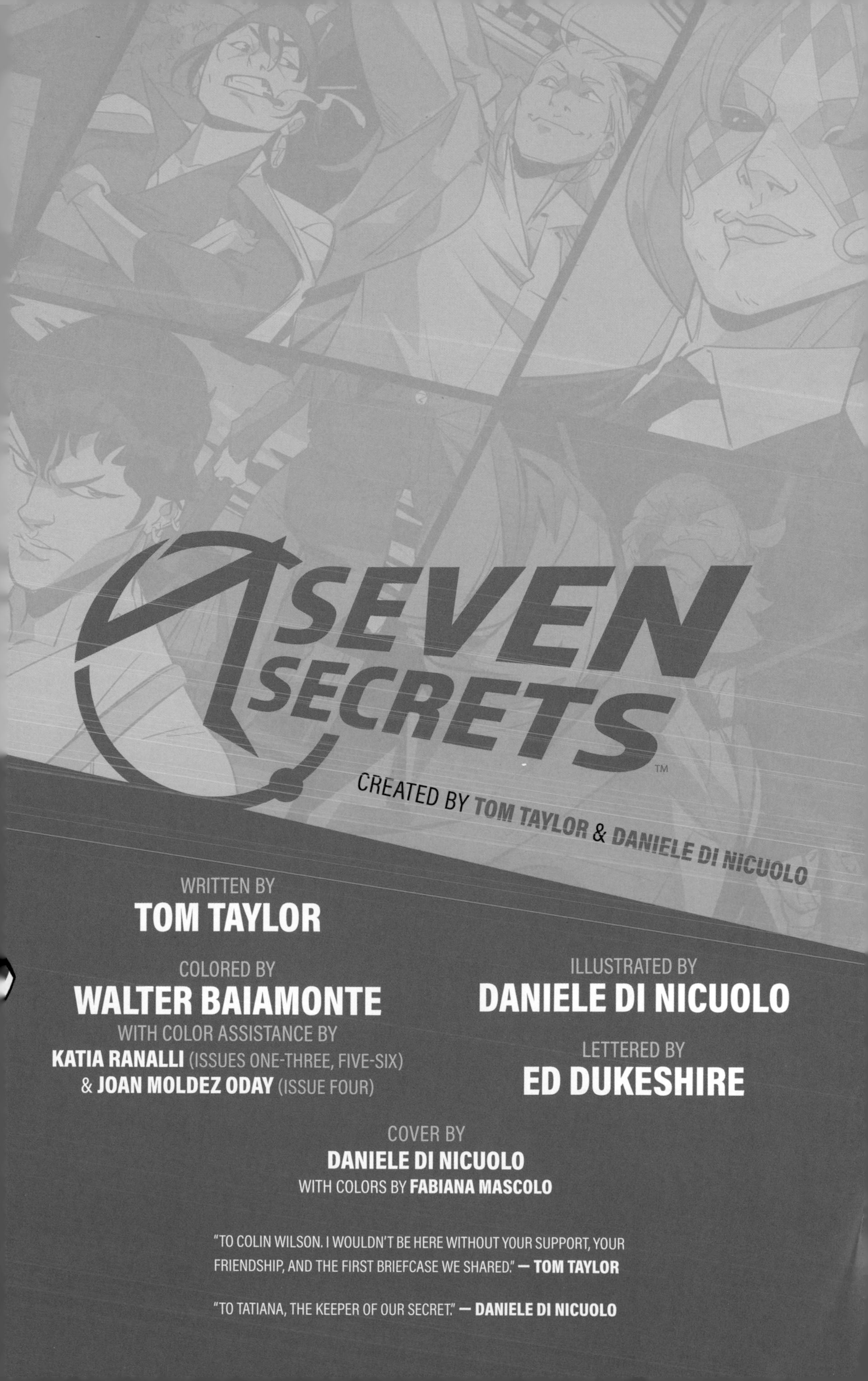

SEVEN SECRETS™

CREATED BY **TOM TAYLOR** & **DANIELE DI NICUOLO**

WRITTEN BY
TOM TAYLOR

COLORED BY
WALTER BAIAMONTE
WITH COLOR ASSISTANCE BY
KATIA RANALLI (ISSUES ONE-THREE, FIVE-SIX)
& **JOAN MOLDEZ ODAY** (ISSUE FOUR)

ILLUSTRATED BY
DANIELE DI NICUOLO

LETTERED BY
ED DUKESHIRE

COVER BY
DANIELE DI NICUOLO
WITH COLORS BY **FABIANA MASCOLO**

"TO COLIN WILSON. I WOULDN'T BE HERE WITHOUT YOUR SUPPORT, YOUR FRIENDSHIP, AND THE FIRST BRIEFCASE WE SHARED." — **TOM TAYLOR**

"TO TATIANA, THE KEEPER OF OUR SECRET." — **DANIELE DI NICUOLO**

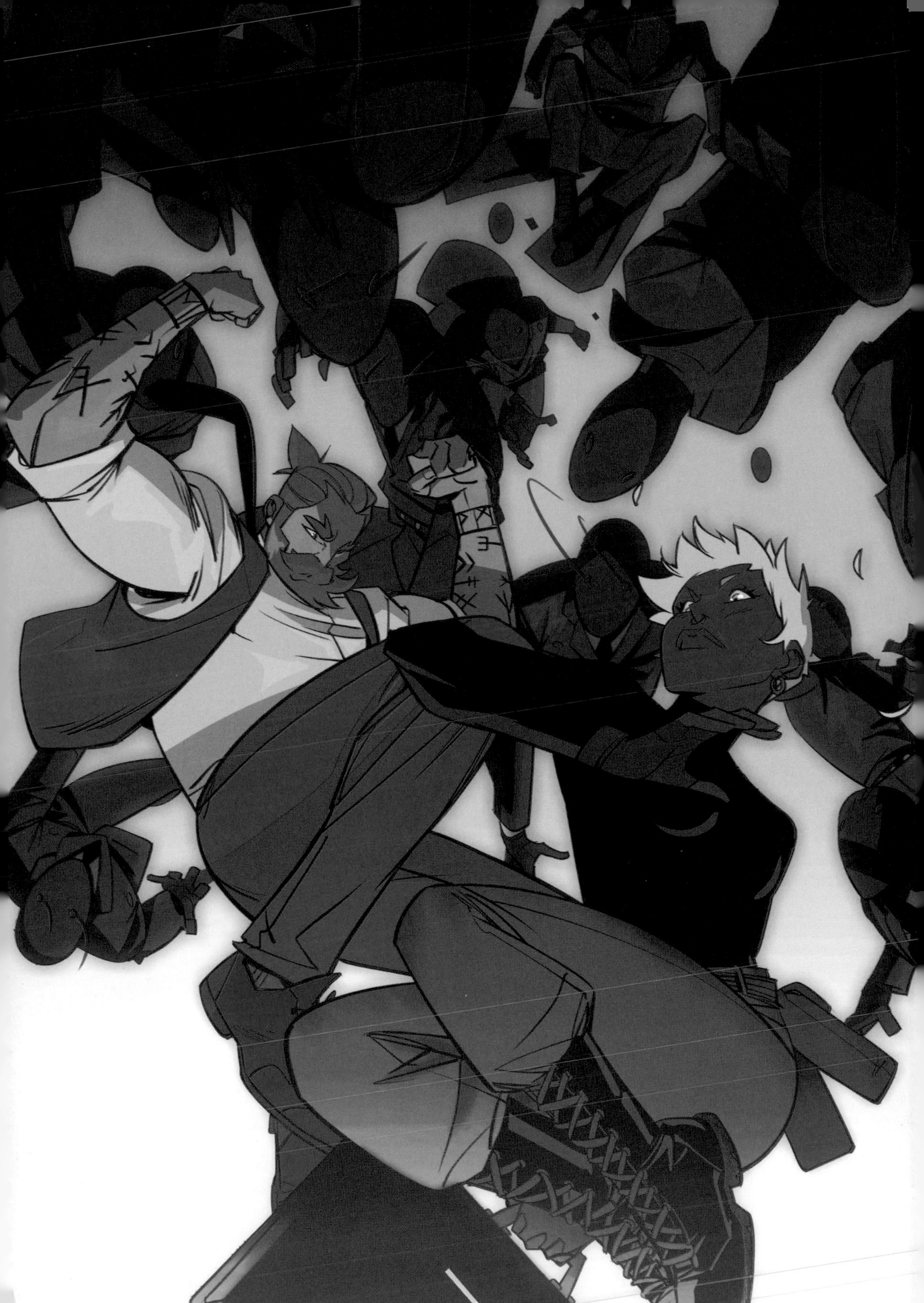

CHAPTER ONE

DANIELE DI NICUOLO WITH COLORS BY **WALTER BAIAMONTE** ISSUE ONE COVER

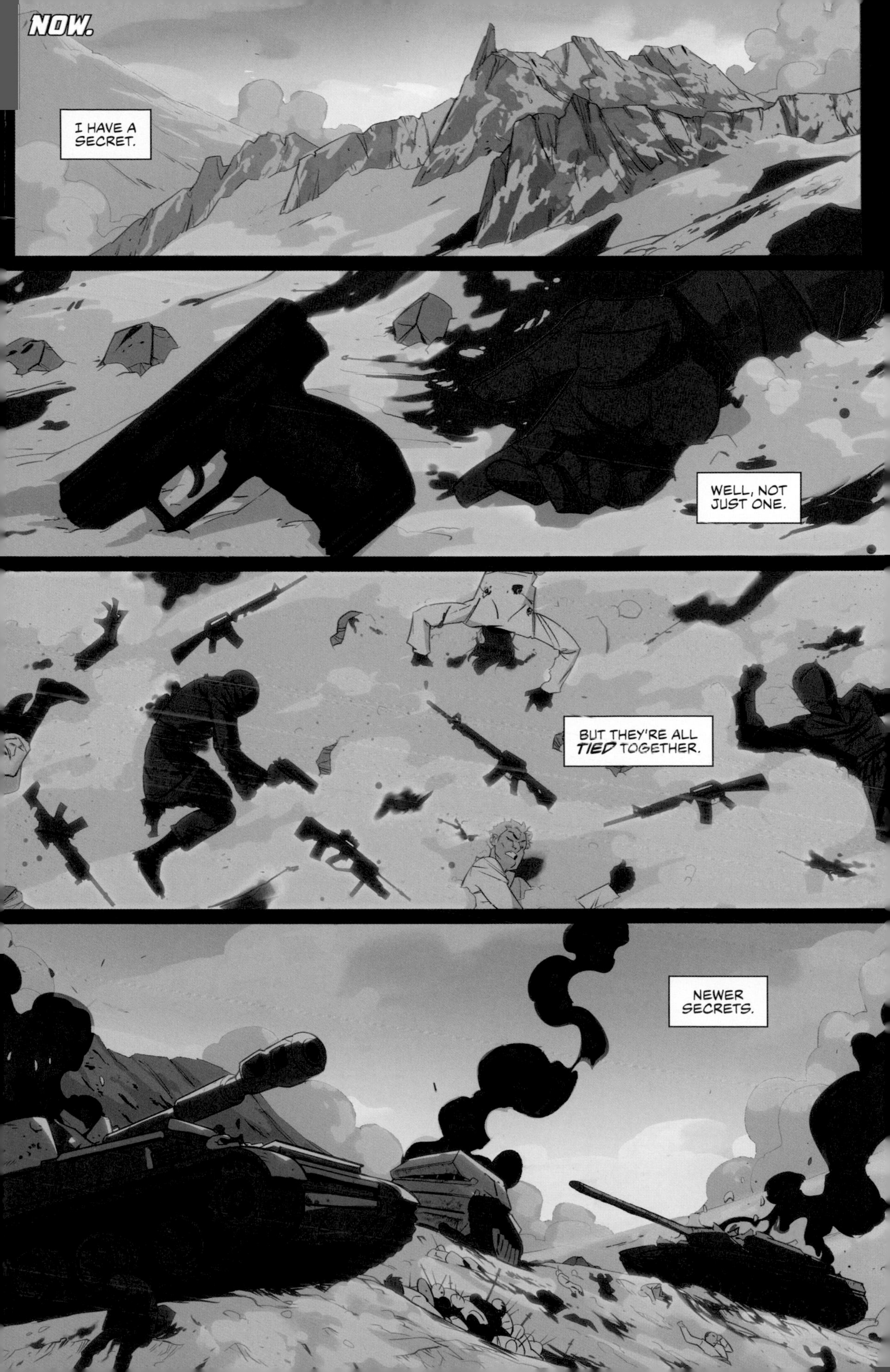
NOW.
I HAVE A SECRET.
WELL, NOT JUST ONE.
BUT THEY'RE ALL TIED TOGETHER.
NEWER SECRETS.

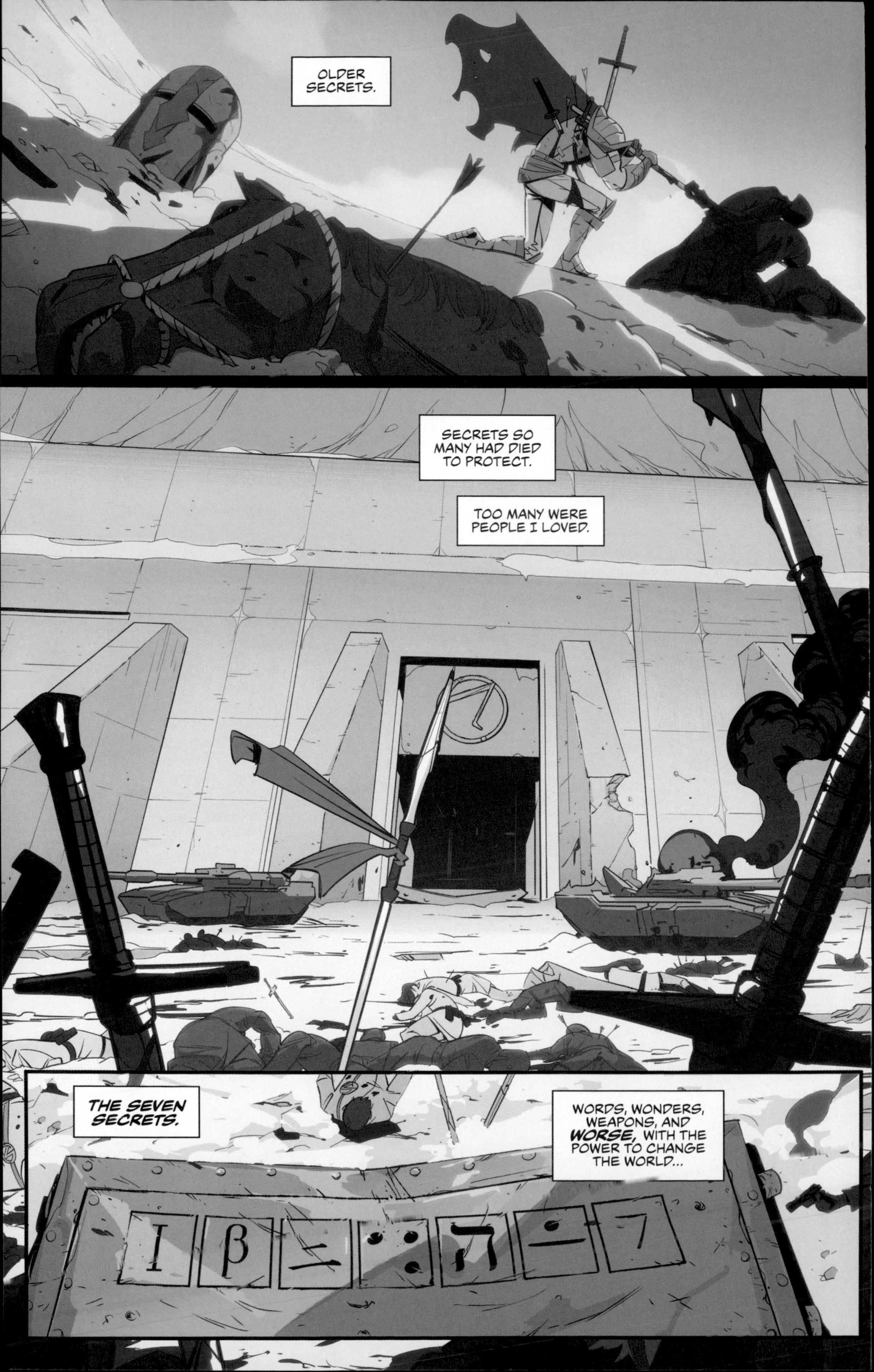
OLDER SECRETS.
SECRETS SO MANY HAD DIED TO PROTECT.
TOO MANY WERE PEOPLE I LOVED.
THE SEVEN SECRETS.
WORDS, WONDERS, WEAPONS, AND WORSE, WITH THE POWER TO CHANGE THE WORLD...

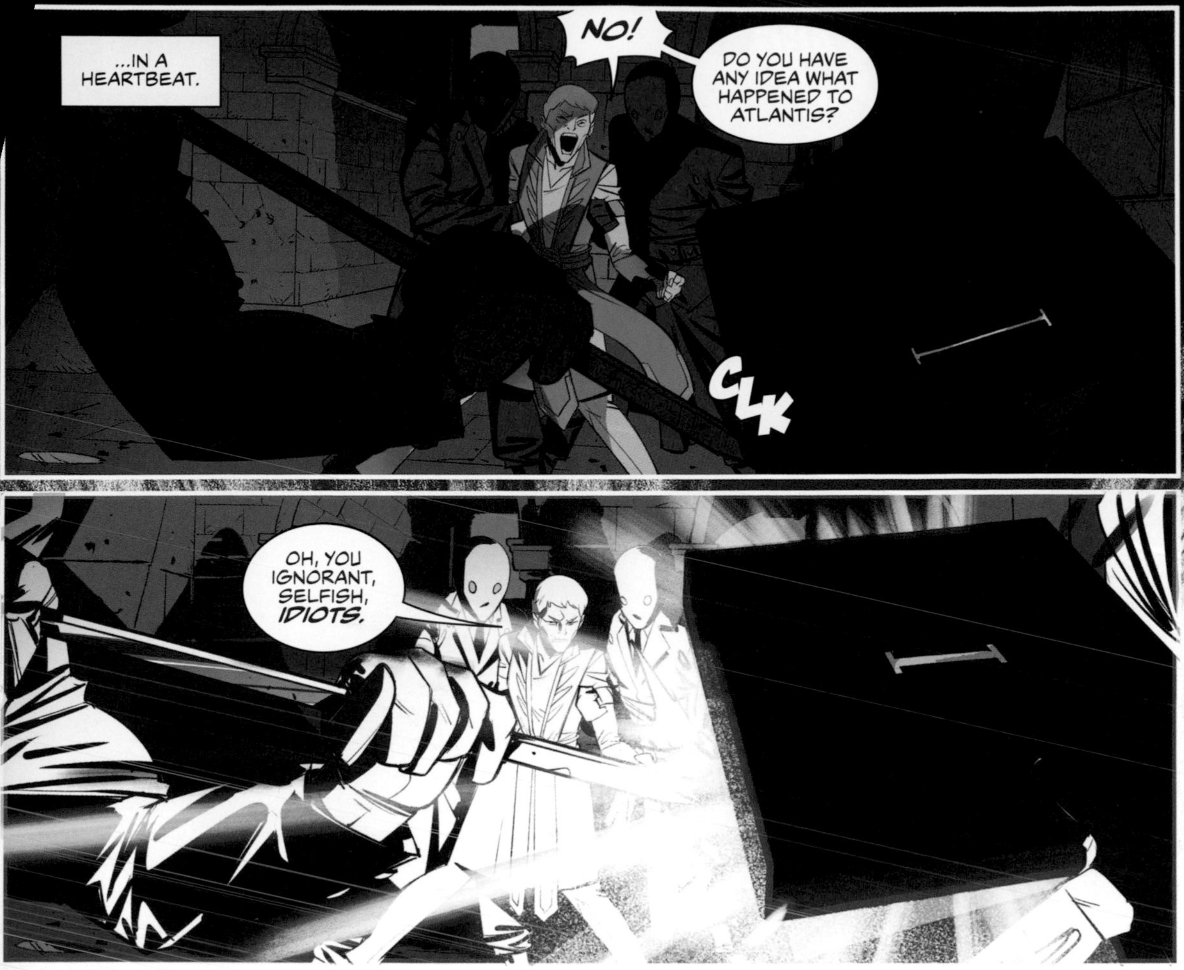
...IN A HEARTBEAT.
NO!
DO YOU HAVE ANY IDEA WHAT HAPPENED TO ATLANTIS?
CLK
OH, YOU IGNORANT, SELFISH, IDIOTS.

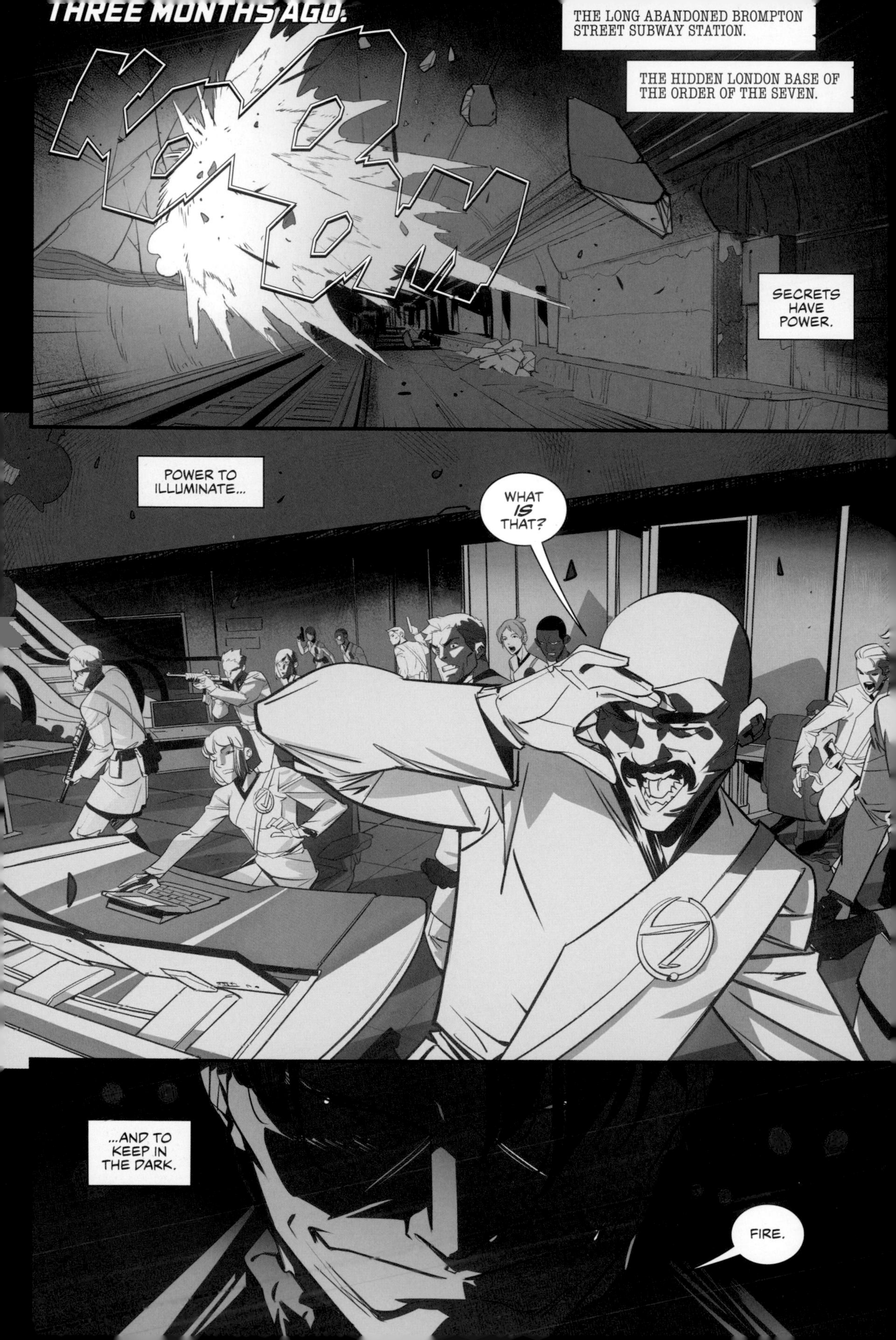
THREE MONTHS AGO:
THE LONG ABANDONED BROMPTON STREET SUBWAY STATION.
THE HIDDEN LONDON BASE OF THE ORDER OF THE SEVEN.
KA-BOOM
SECRETS HAVE POWER.
POWER TO ILLUMINATE...
WHAT IS THAT?
...AND TO KEEP IN THE DARK.
FIRE.

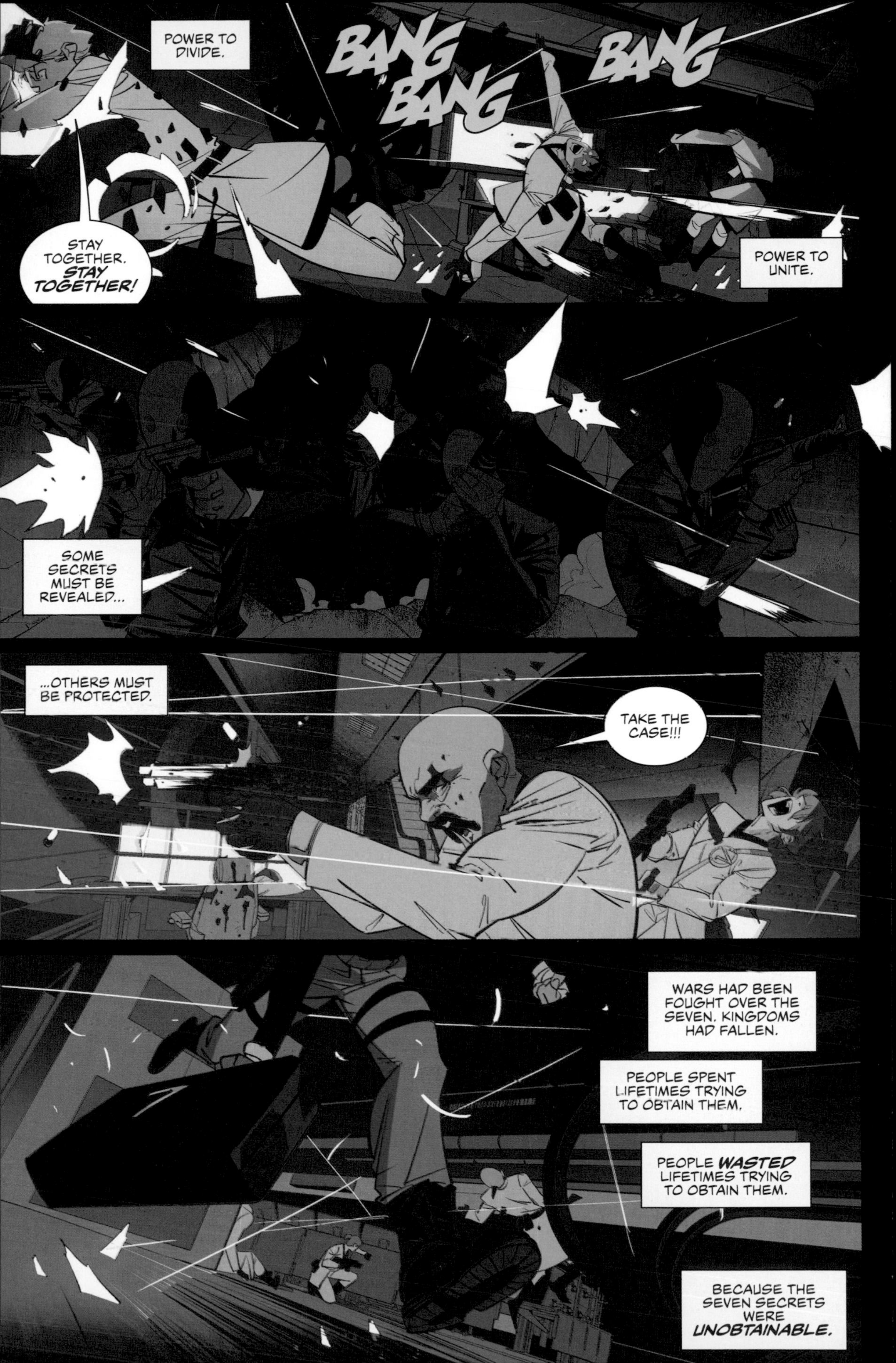
POWER TO DIVIDE.
BANG BANG
BANG
STAY TOGETHER. *STAY TOGETHER!*
POWER TO UNITE.
SOME SECRETS MUST BE REVEALED...
...OTHERS MUST BE PROTECTED.
TAKE THE CASE!!!
WARS HAD BEEN FOUGHT OVER THE SEVEN. KINGDOMS HAD FALLEN.
PEOPLE SPENT LIFETIMES TRYING TO OBTAIN THEM.
PEOPLE *WASTED* LIFETIMES TRYING TO OBTAIN THEM.
BECAUSE THE SEVEN SECRETS WERE *UNOBTAINABLE.*

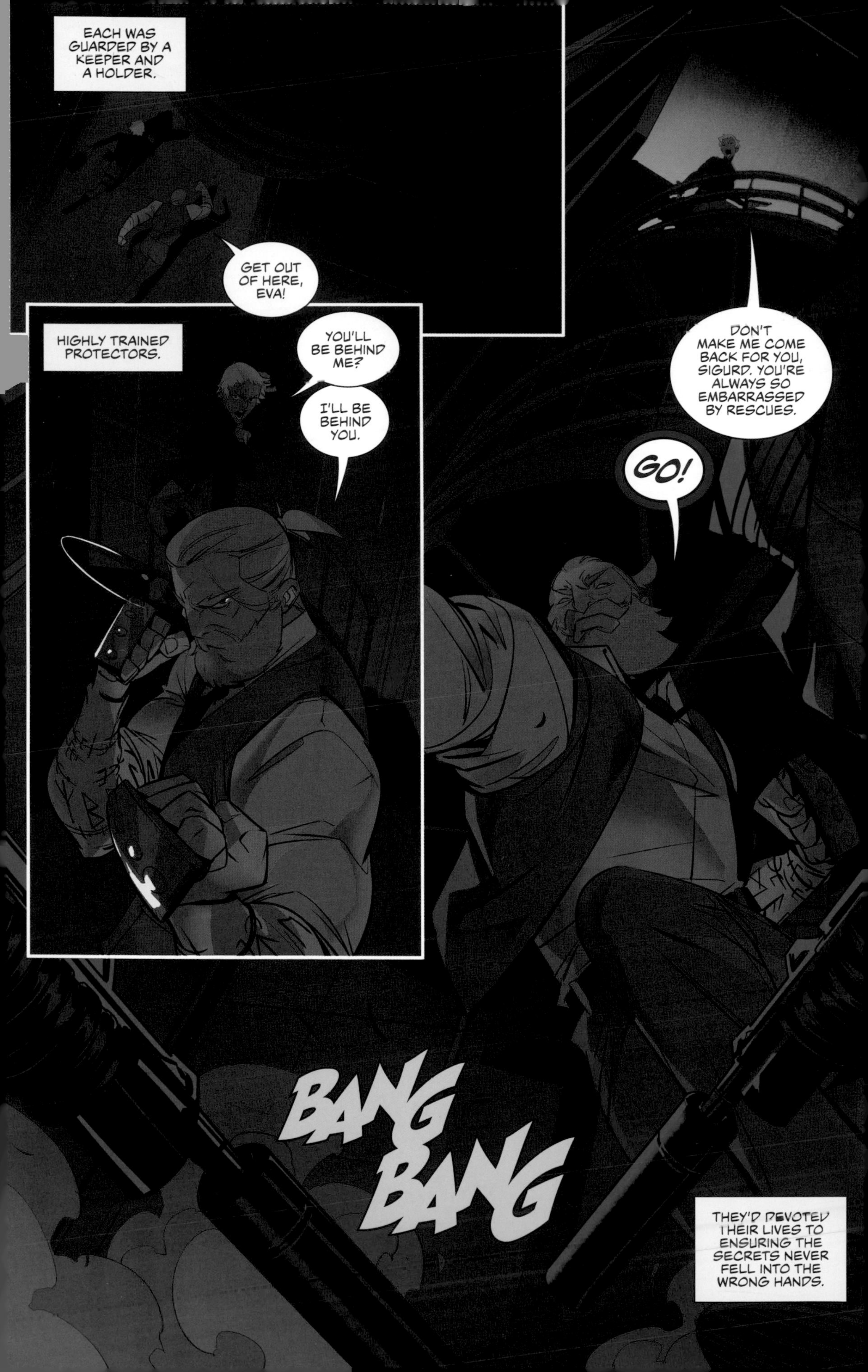
EACH WAS GUARDED BY A KEEPER AND A HOLDER.
GET OUT OF HERE, EVA!
HIGHLY TRAINED PROTECTORS.
YOU'LL BE BEHIND ME?
I'LL BE BEHIND YOU.
DON'T MAKE ME COME BACK FOR YOU, SIGURD. YOU'RE ALWAYS SO EMBARRASSED BY RESCUES.
GO!
BANG BANG
THEY'D DEVOTED THEIR LIVES TO ENSURING THE SECRETS NEVER FELL INTO THE WRONG HANDS.

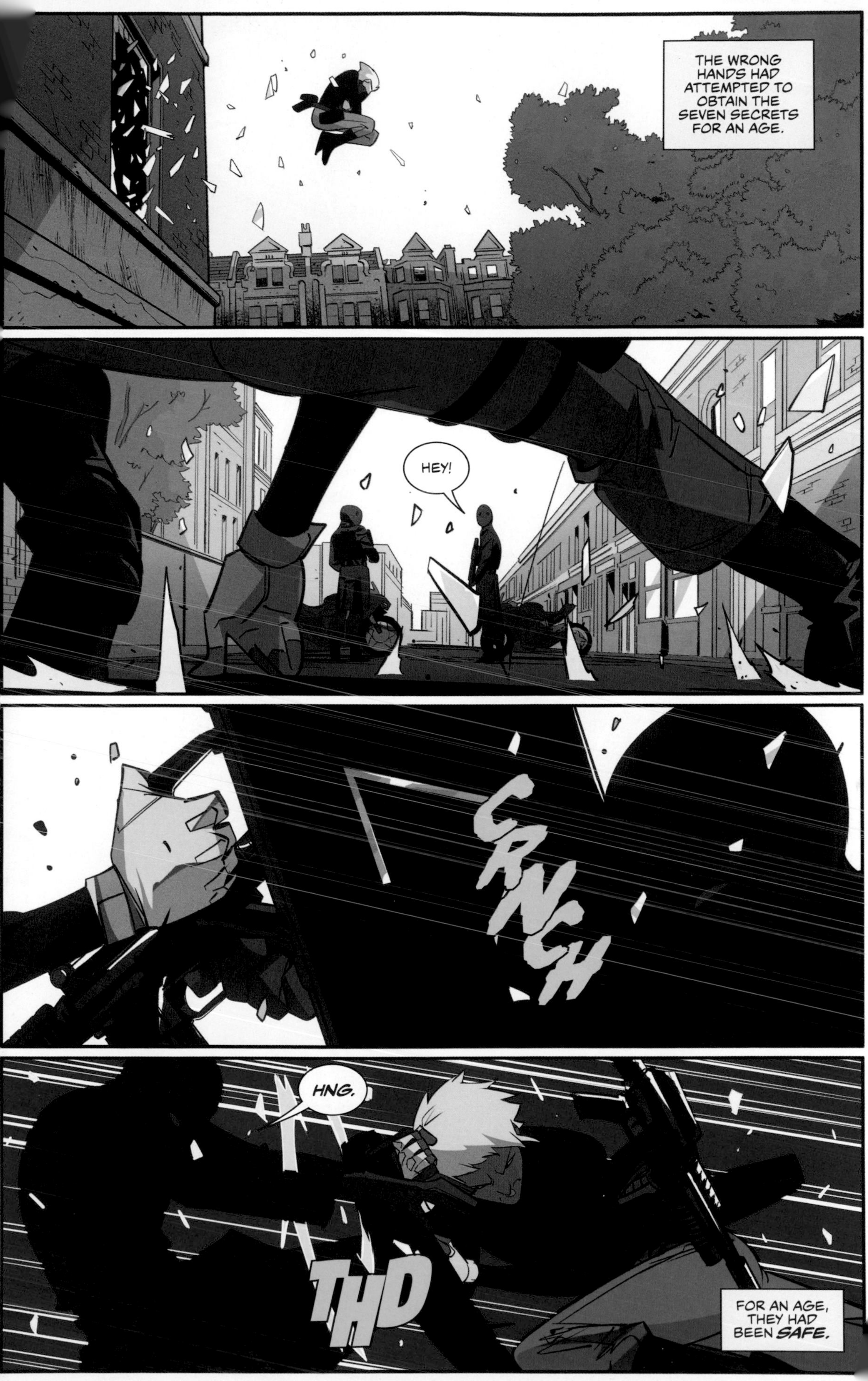
THE WRONG HANDS HAD ATTEMPTED TO OBTAIN THE SEVEN SECRETS FOR AN AGE.
HEY!
CRNCH
HNG.
THD
FOR AN AGE, THEY HAD BEEN *SAFE.*

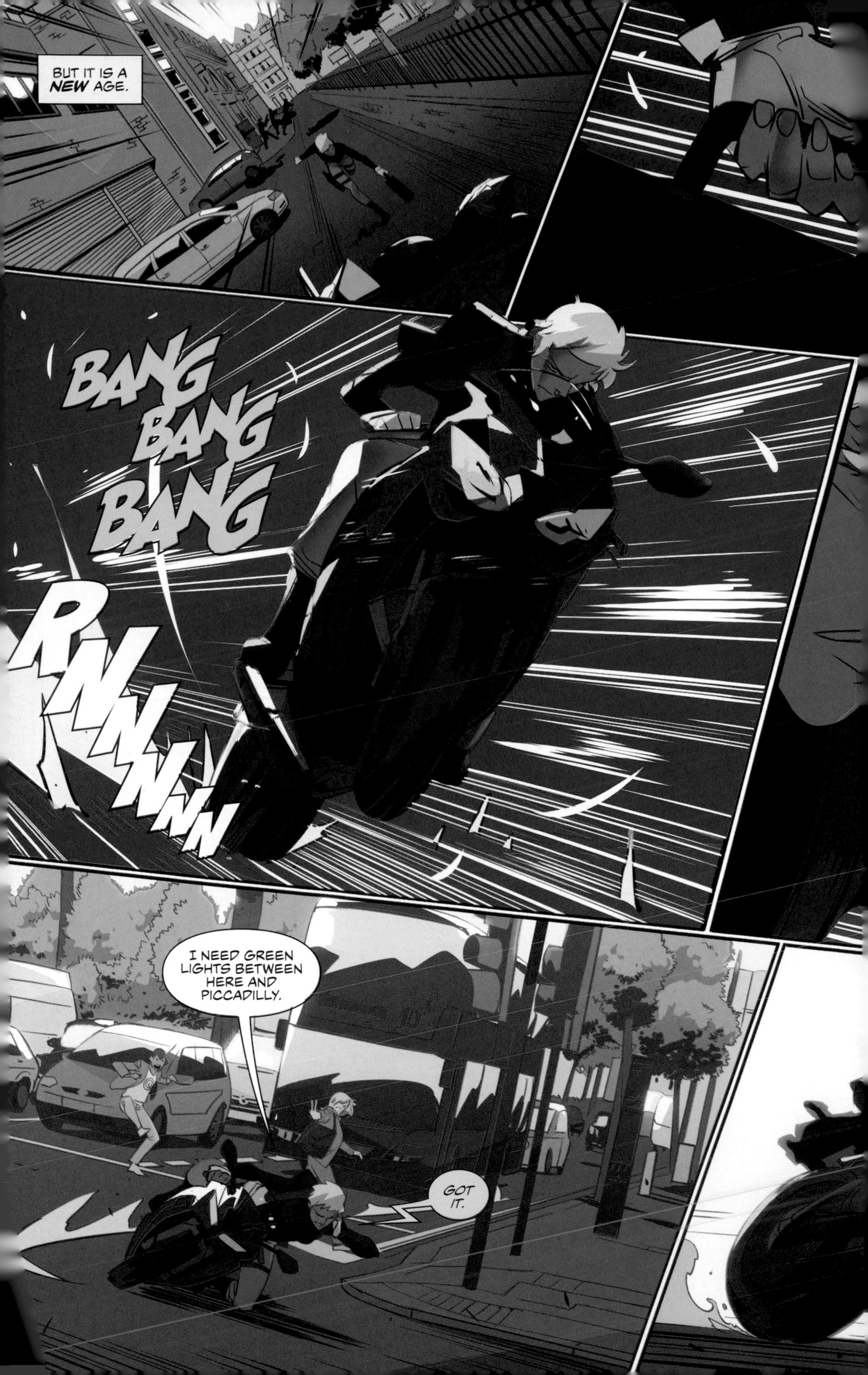
BUT IT IS A NEW AGE.
BANG BANG BANG
RNNNNNNN
I NEED GREEN LIGHTS BETWEEN HERE AND PICCADILLY.
GOT IT.

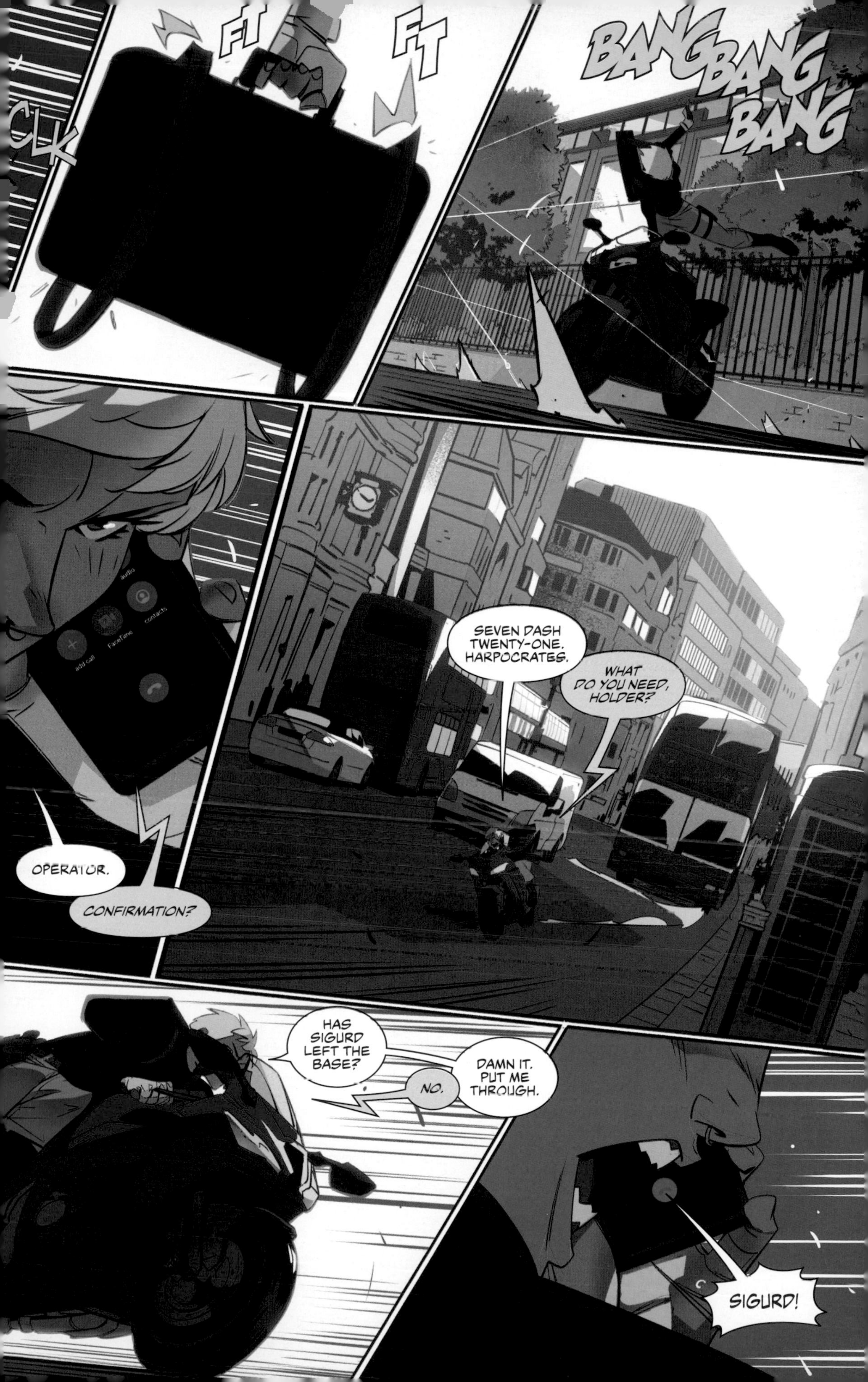
CLK
FT
FT
BANG BANG BANG
OPERATOR.
CONFIRMATION?
SEVEN DASH TWENTY-ONE. HARPOCRATES.
WHAT DO YOU NEED, HOLDER?
HAS SIGURD LEFT THE BASE?
NO.
DAMN IT. PUT ME THROUGH.
SIGURD!

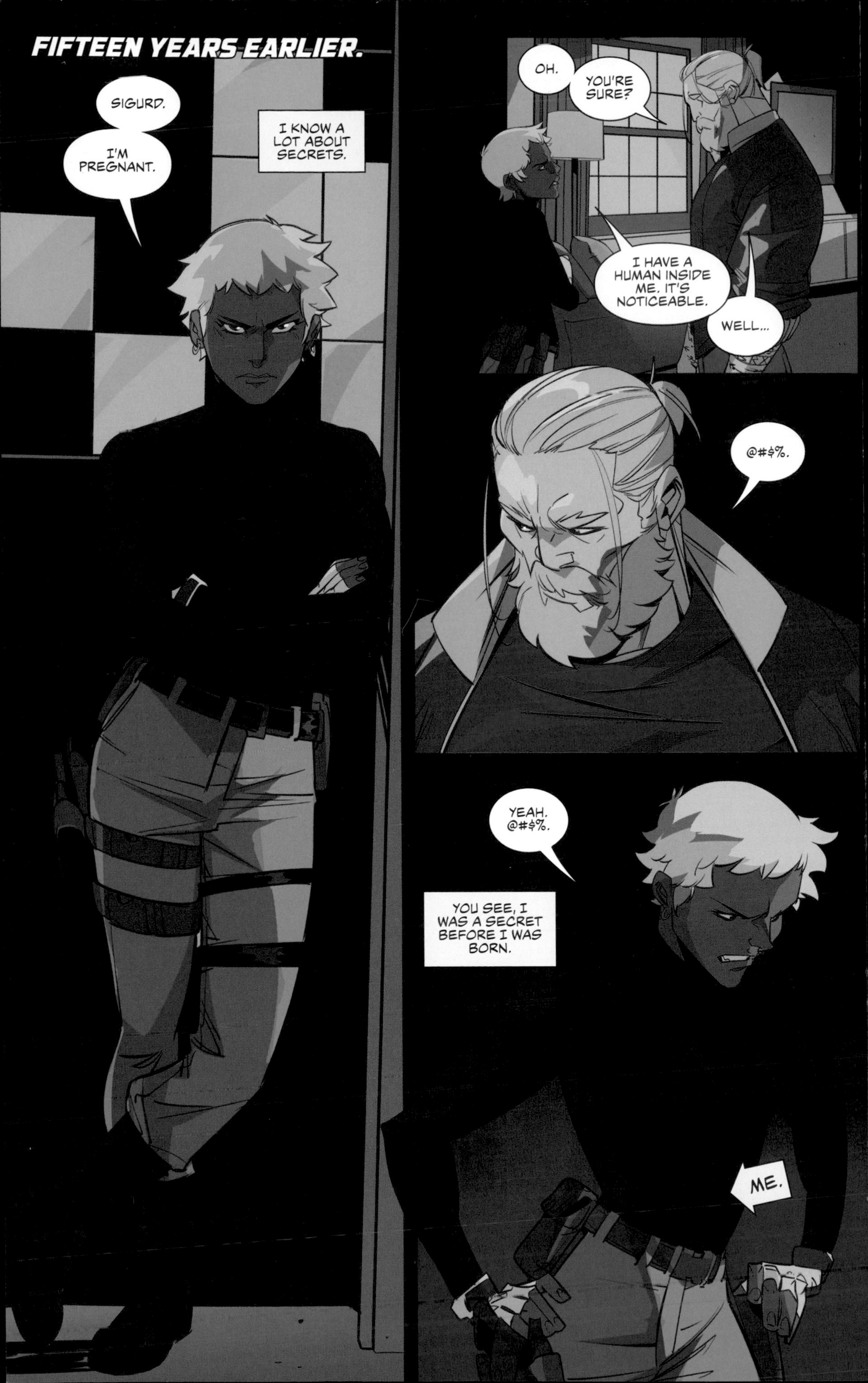
FIFTEEN YEARS EARLIER.
SIGURD.
I'M PREGNANT.
I KNOW A LOT ABOUT SECRETS.
OH.
YOU'RE SURE?
I HAVE A HUMAN INSIDE ME. IT'S NOTICEABLE.
WELL...
@#$%.
YEAH. @#$%.
YOU SEE, I WAS A SECRET BEFORE I WAS BORN.
ME.

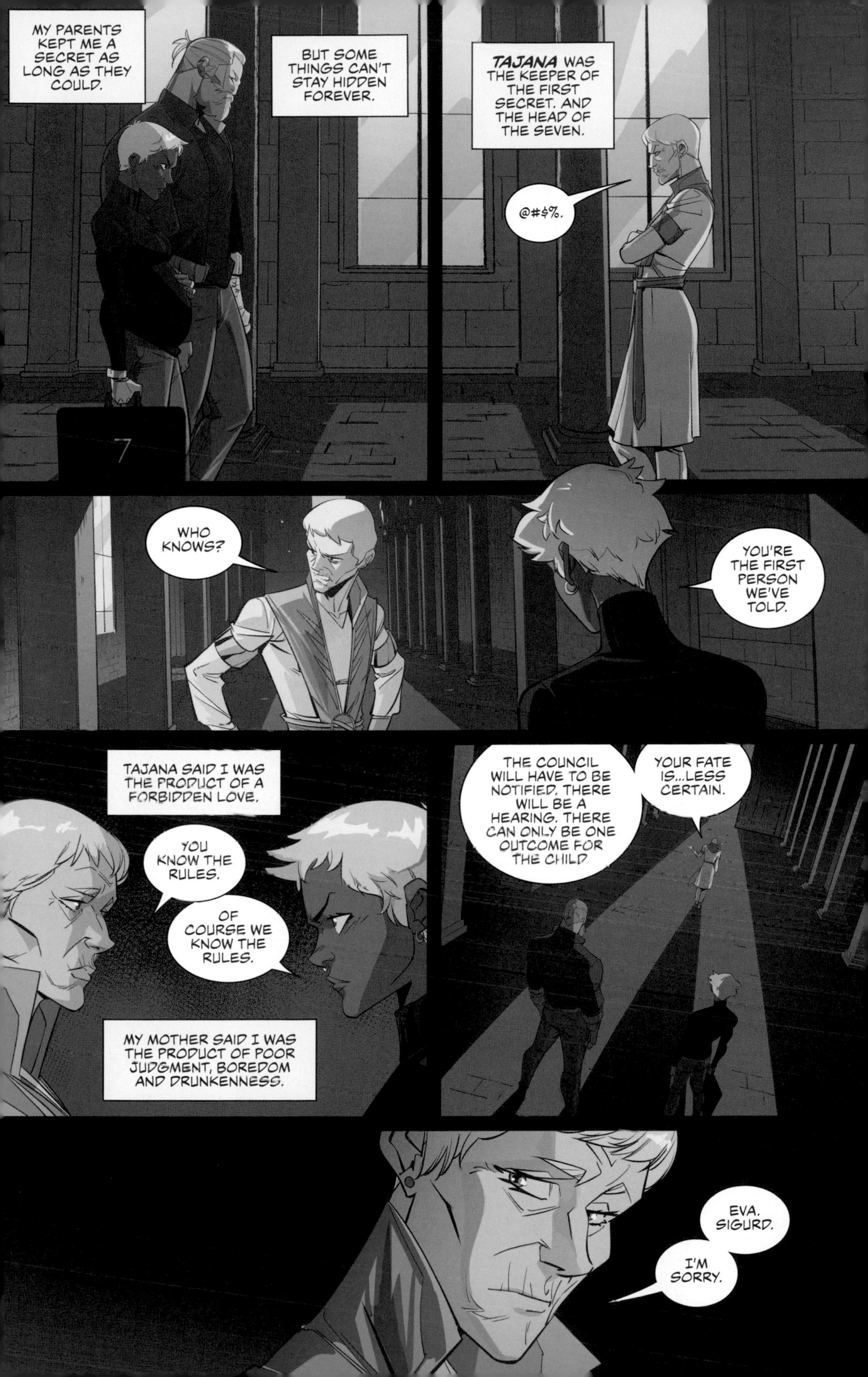
MY PARENTS KEPT ME A SECRET AS LONG AS THEY COULD.
BUT SOME THINGS CAN'T STAY HIDDEN FOREVER.
TAJANA WAS THE KEEPER OF THE FIRST SECRET. AND THE HEAD OF THE SEVEN.
@#$%.
WHO KNOWS?
YOU'RE THE FIRST PERSON WE'VE TOLD.
TAJANA SAID I WAS THE PRODUCT OF A FORBIDDEN LOVE.
YOU KNOW THE RULES.
OF COURSE WE KNOW THE RULES.
MY MOTHER SAID I WAS THE PRODUCT OF POOR JUDGMENT, BOREDOM AND DRUNKENNESS.
THE COUNCIL WILL HAVE TO BE NOTIFIED. THERE WILL BE A HEARING. THERE CAN ONLY BE ONE OUTCOME FOR THE CHILD.
YOUR FATE IS...LESS CERTAIN.
EVA. SIGURD.
I'M SORRY.

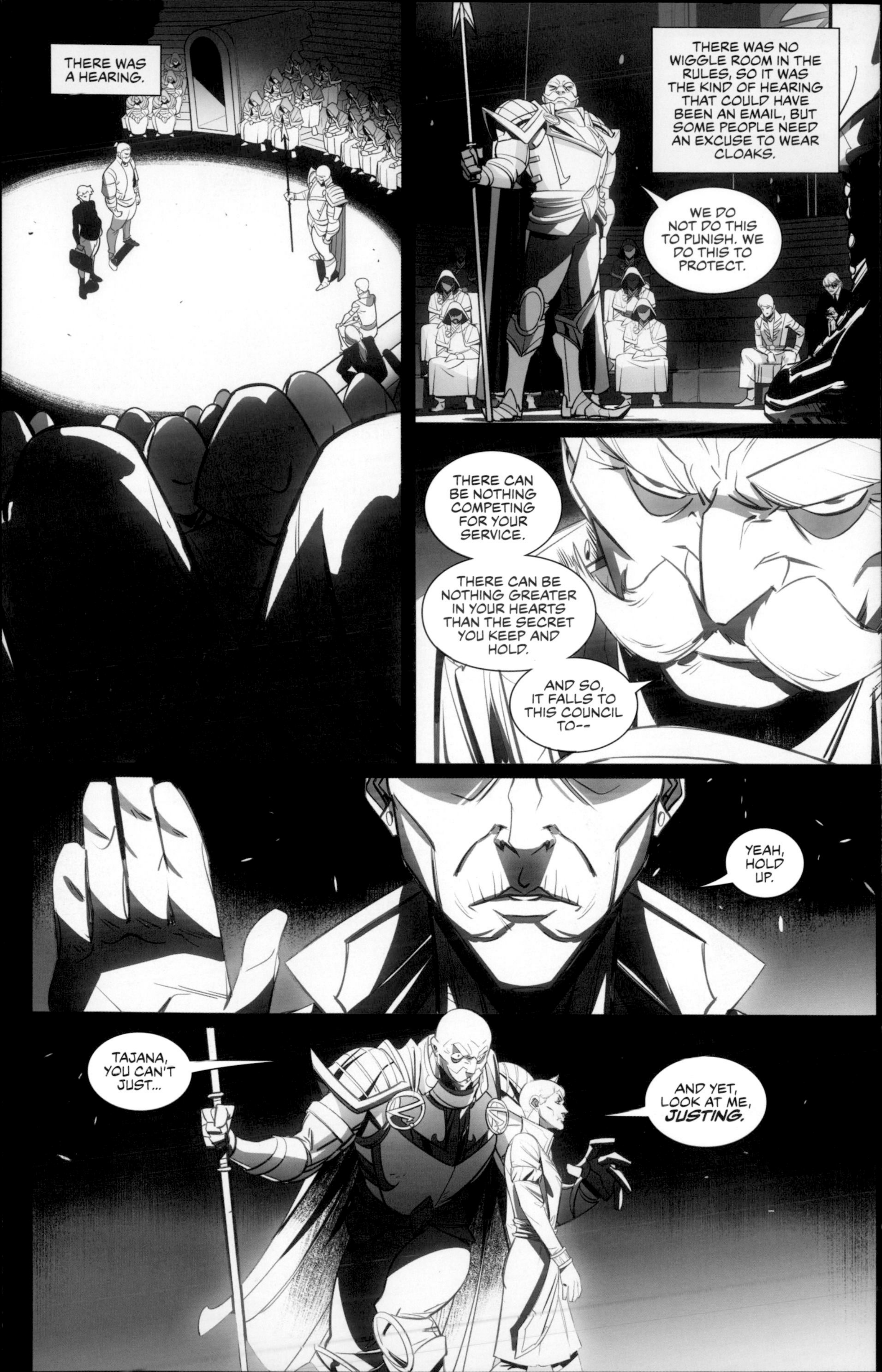
THERE WAS A HEARING.
THERE WAS NO WIGGLE ROOM IN THE RULES, SO IT WAS THE KIND OF HEARING THAT COULD HAVE BEEN AN EMAIL, BUT SOME PEOPLE NEED AN EXCUSE TO WEAR CLOAKS.
WE DO NOT DO THIS TO PUNISH. WE DO THIS TO PROTECT.
THERE CAN BE NOTHING COMPETING FOR YOUR SERVICE.
THERE CAN BE NOTHING GREATER IN YOUR HEARTS THAN THE SECRET YOU KEEP AND HOLD.
AND SO, IT FALLS TO THIS COUNCIL TO--
YEAH, HOLD UP.
TAJANA, YOU CAN'T JUST...
AND YET, LOOK AT ME, *JUSTING.*

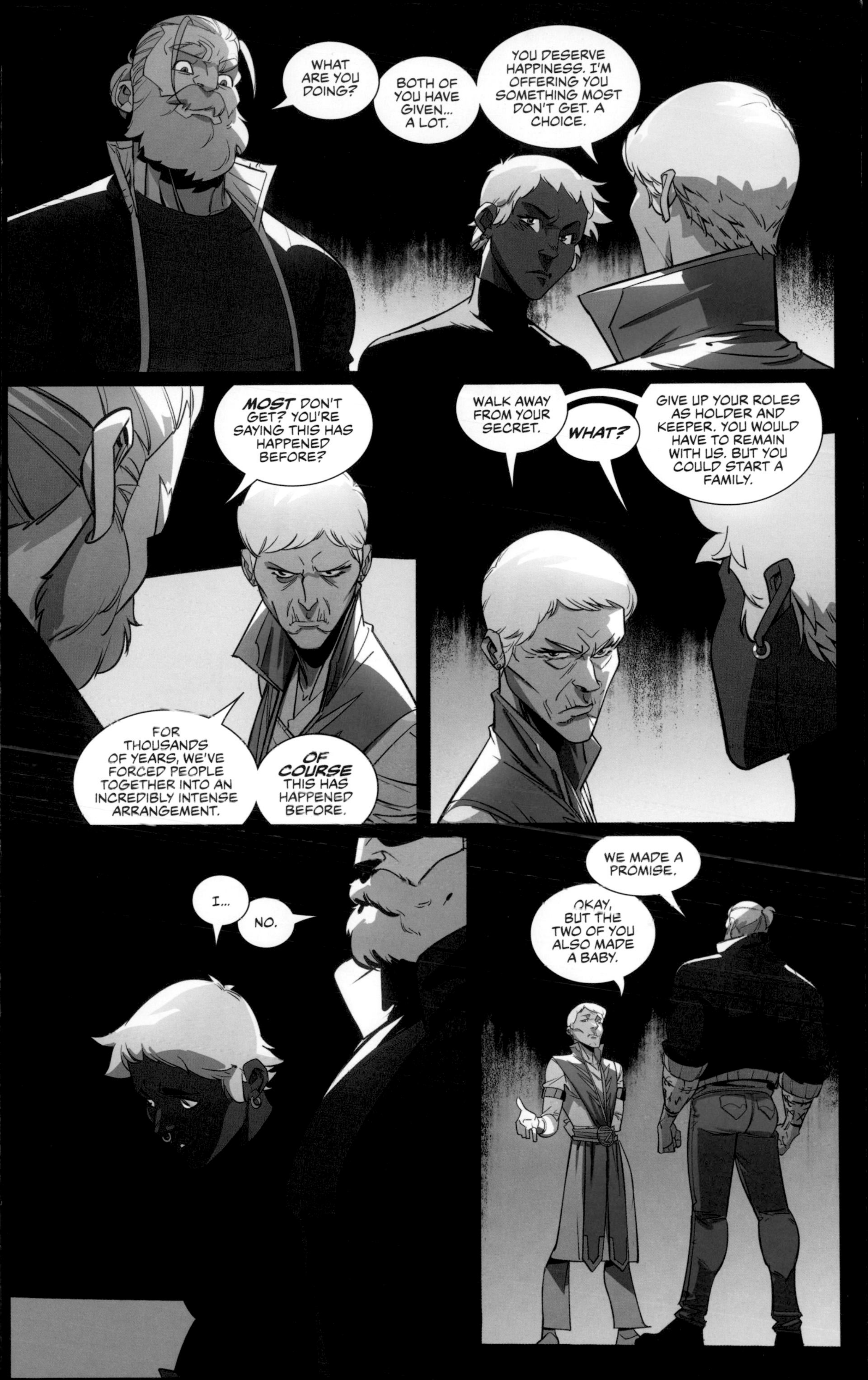
WHAT ARE YOU DOING?
BOTH OF YOU HAVE GIVEN... A LOT.
YOU DESERVE HAPPINESS. I'M OFFERING YOU SOMETHING MOST DON'T GET. A CHOICE.
MOST DON'T GET? YOU'RE SAYING THIS HAS HAPPENED BEFORE?
FOR THOUSANDS OF YEARS, WE'VE FORCED PEOPLE TOGETHER INTO AN INCREDIBLY INTENSE ARRANGEMENT.
OF COURSE THIS HAS HAPPENED BEFORE.
WALK AWAY FROM YOUR SECRET.
WHAT?
GIVE UP YOUR ROLES AS HOLDER AND KEEPER. YOU WOULD HAVE TO REMAIN WITH US. BUT YOU COULD START A FAMILY.
I...
NO.
WE MADE A PROMISE.
OKAY, BUT THE TWO OF YOU ALSO MADE A BABY.

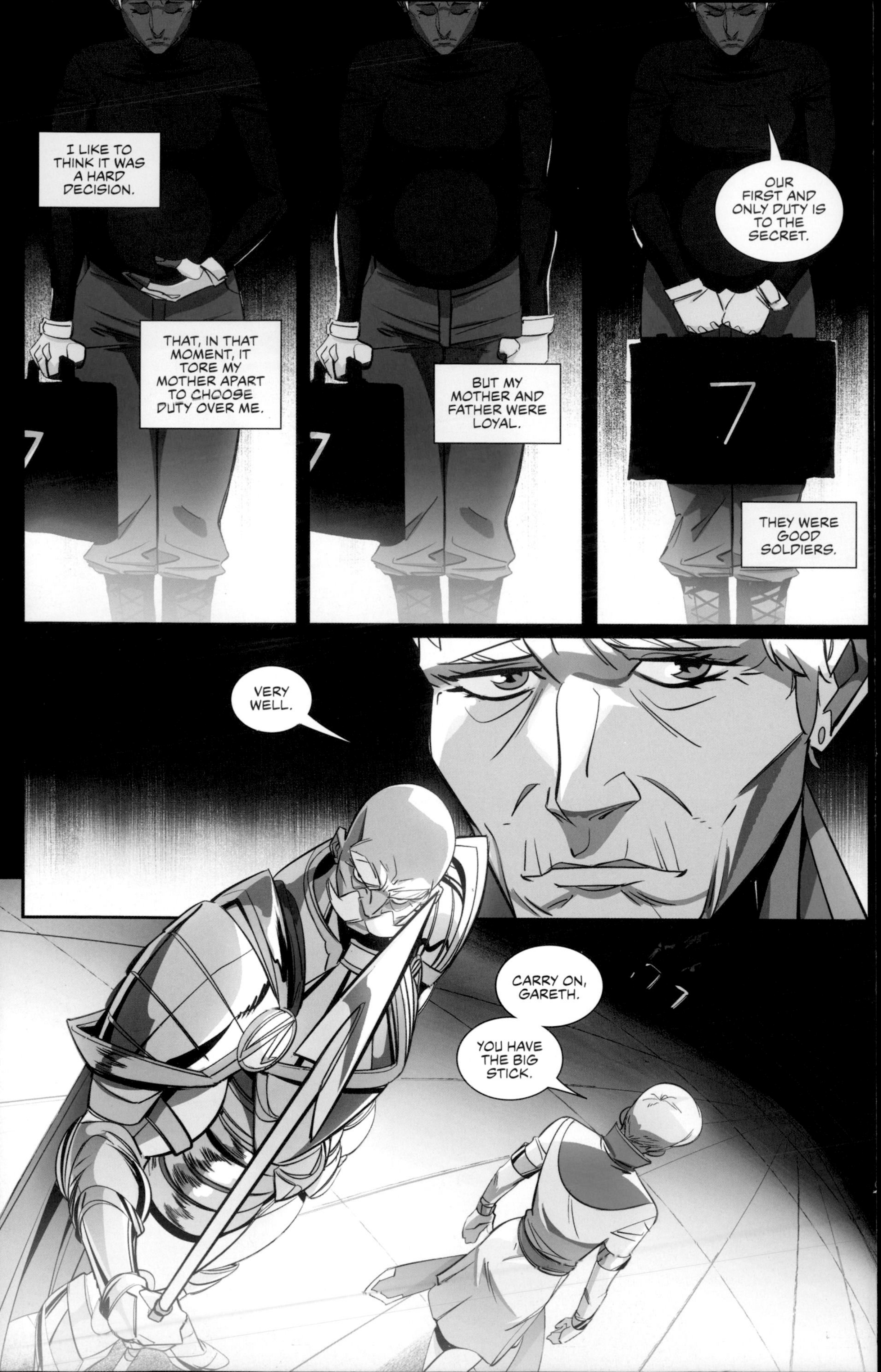
I LIKE TO THINK IT WAS A HARD DECISION.
THAT, IN THAT MOMENT, IT TORE MY MOTHER APART TO CHOOSE DUTY OVER ME.
BUT MY MOTHER AND FATHER WERE LOYAL.
OUR FIRST AND ONLY DUTY IS TO THE SECRET.
THEY WERE GOOD SOLDIERS.
VERY WELL.
CARRY ON, GARETH.
YOU HAVE THE BIG STICK.

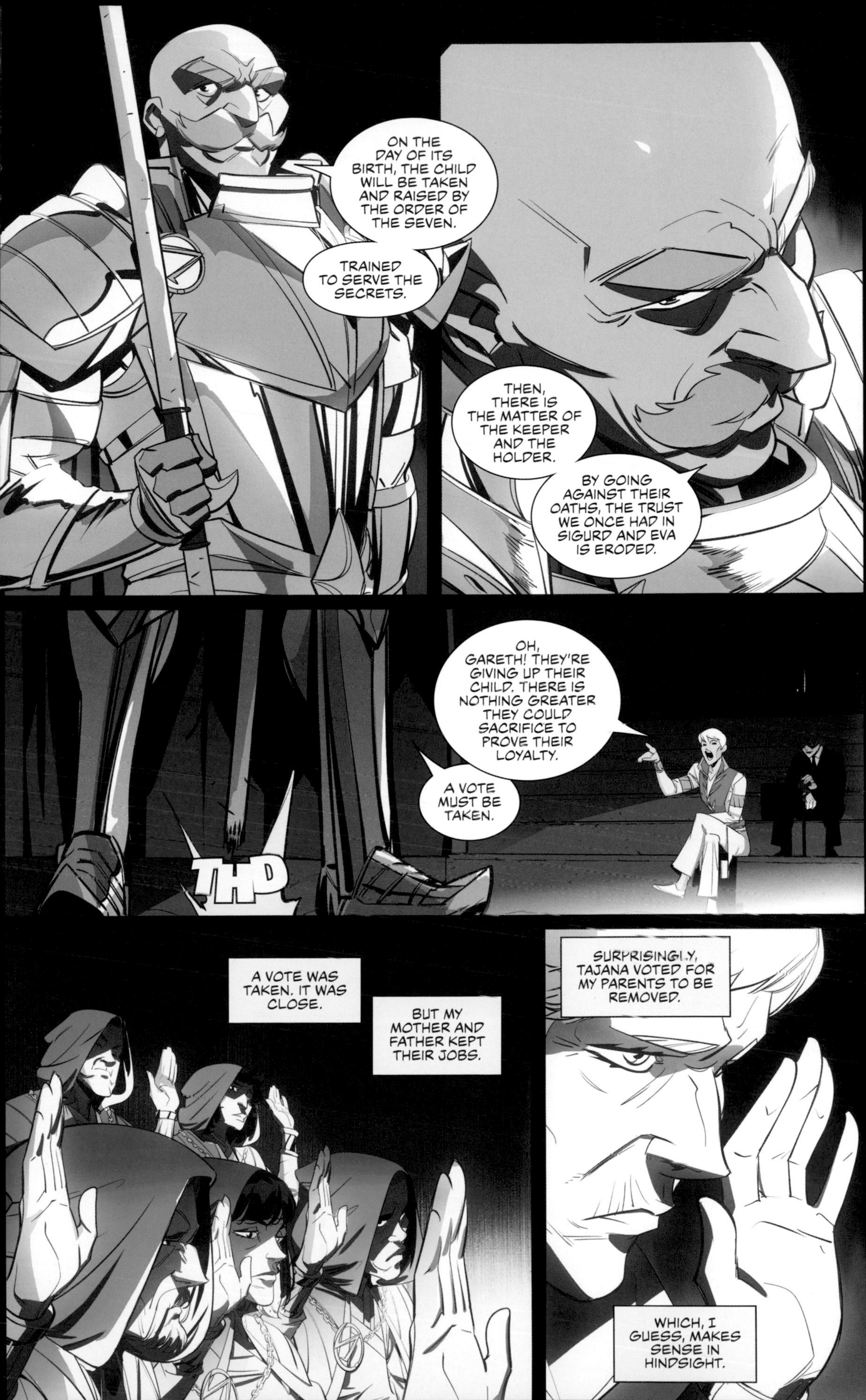
ON THE DAY OF ITS BIRTH, THE CHILD WILL BE TAKEN AND RAISED BY THE ORDER OF THE SEVEN.
TRAINED TO SERVE THE SECRETS.
THEN, THERE IS THE MATTER OF THE KEEPER AND THE HOLDER.
BY GOING AGAINST THEIR OATHS, THE TRUST WE ONCE HAD IN SIGURD AND EVA IS ERODED.
OH, GARETH! THEY'RE GIVING UP THEIR CHILD. THERE IS NOTHING GREATER THEY COULD SACRIFICE TO PROVE THEIR LOYALTY.
A VOTE MUST BE TAKEN.
THD
A VOTE WAS TAKEN. IT WAS CLOSE.
BUT MY MOTHER AND FATHER KEPT THEIR JOBS.
SURPRISINGLY, TAJANA VOTED FOR MY PARENTS TO BE REMOVED.
WHICH, I GUESS, MAKES SENSE IN HINDSIGHT.

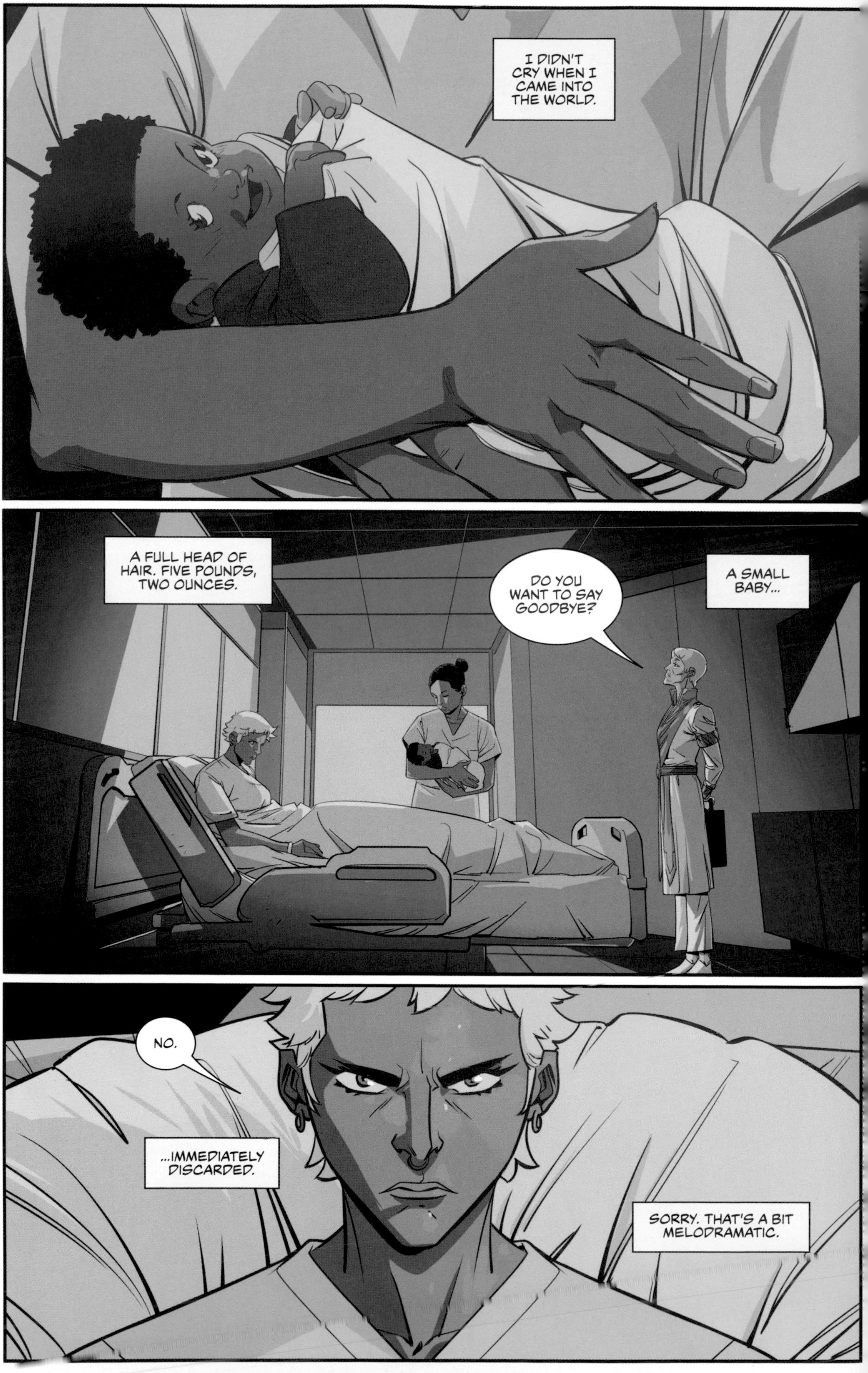
I DIDN'T CRY WHEN I CAME INTO THE WORLD.
A FULL HEAD OF HAIR. FIVE POUNDS, TWO OUNCES.
DO YOU WANT TO SAY GOODBYE?
A SMALL BABY...
NO.
...IMMEDIATELY DISCARDED.
SORRY. THAT'S A BIT MELODRAMATIC.

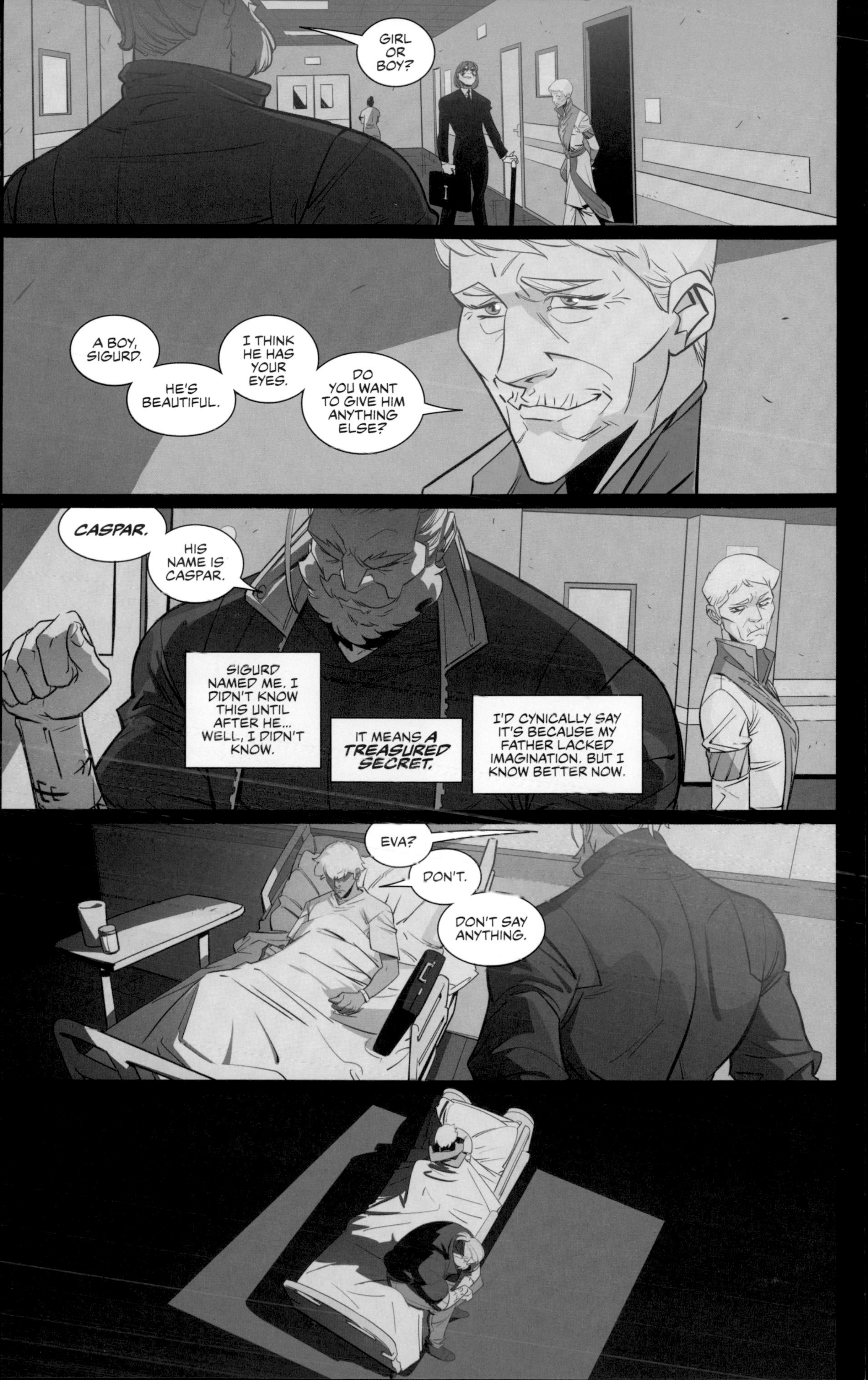

GIRL OR BOY?
A BOY, SIGURD.
HE'S BEAUTIFUL.
I THINK HE HAS YOUR EYES.
DO YOU WANT TO GIVE HIM ANYTHING ELSE?
CASPAR.
HIS NAME IS CASPAR.
SIGURD NAMED ME. I DIDN'T KNOW THIS UNTIL AFTER HE... WELL, I DIDN'T KNOW.
IT MEANS A TREASURED SECRET.
I'D CYNICALLY SAY IT'S BECAUSE MY FATHER LACKED IMAGINATION. BUT I KNOW BETTER NOW.
EVA?
DON'T.
DON'T SAY ANYTHING.

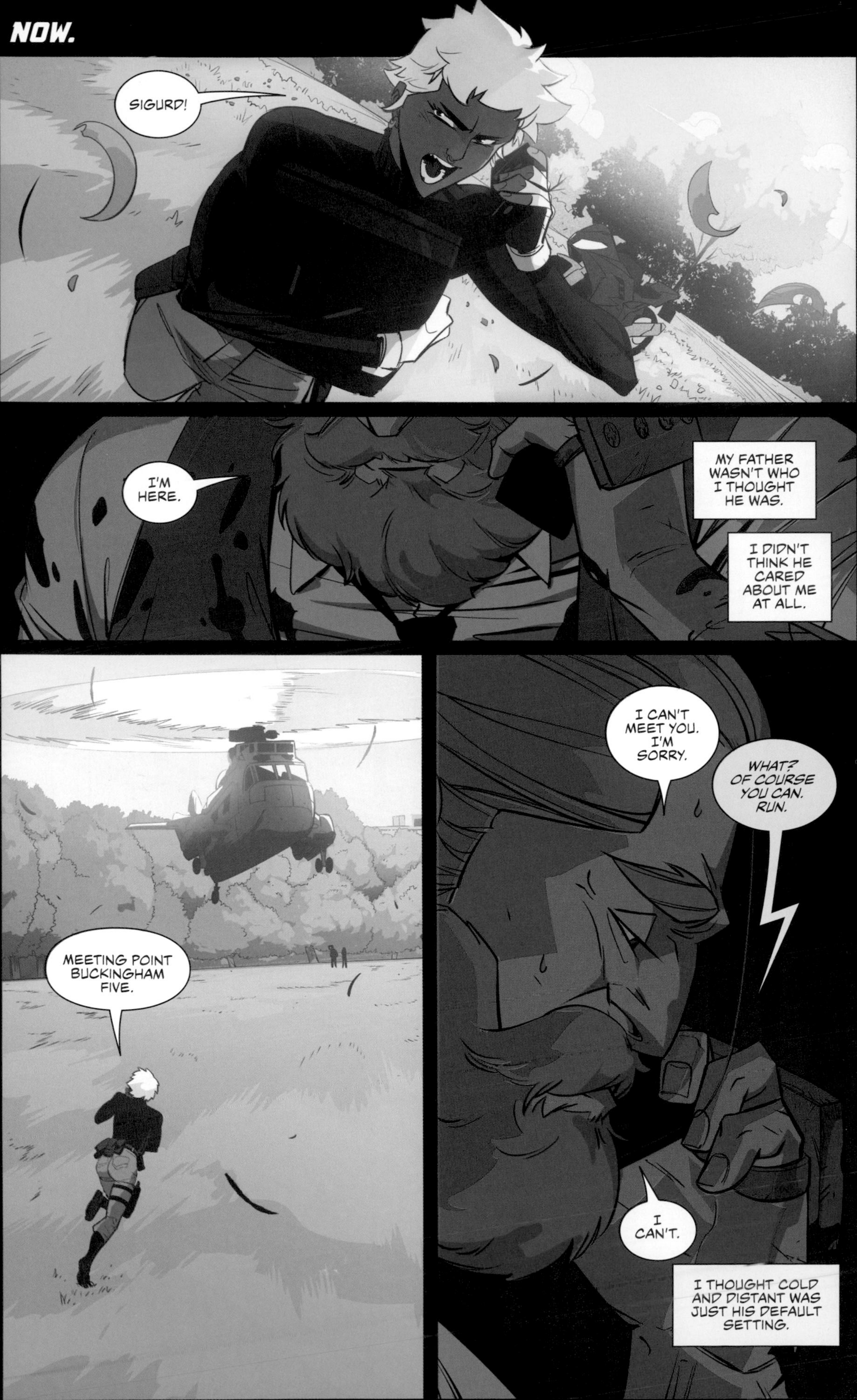
NOW.
SIGURD!
I'M HERE.
MY FATHER WASN'T WHO I THOUGHT HE WAS.
I DIDN'T THINK HE CARED ABOUT ME AT ALL.
MEETING POINT BUCKINGHAM FIVE.
I CAN'T MEET YOU. I'M SORRY.
WHAT? OF COURSE YOU CAN. RUN.
I CAN'T.
I THOUGHT COLD AND DISTANT WAS JUST HIS DEFAULT SETTING.

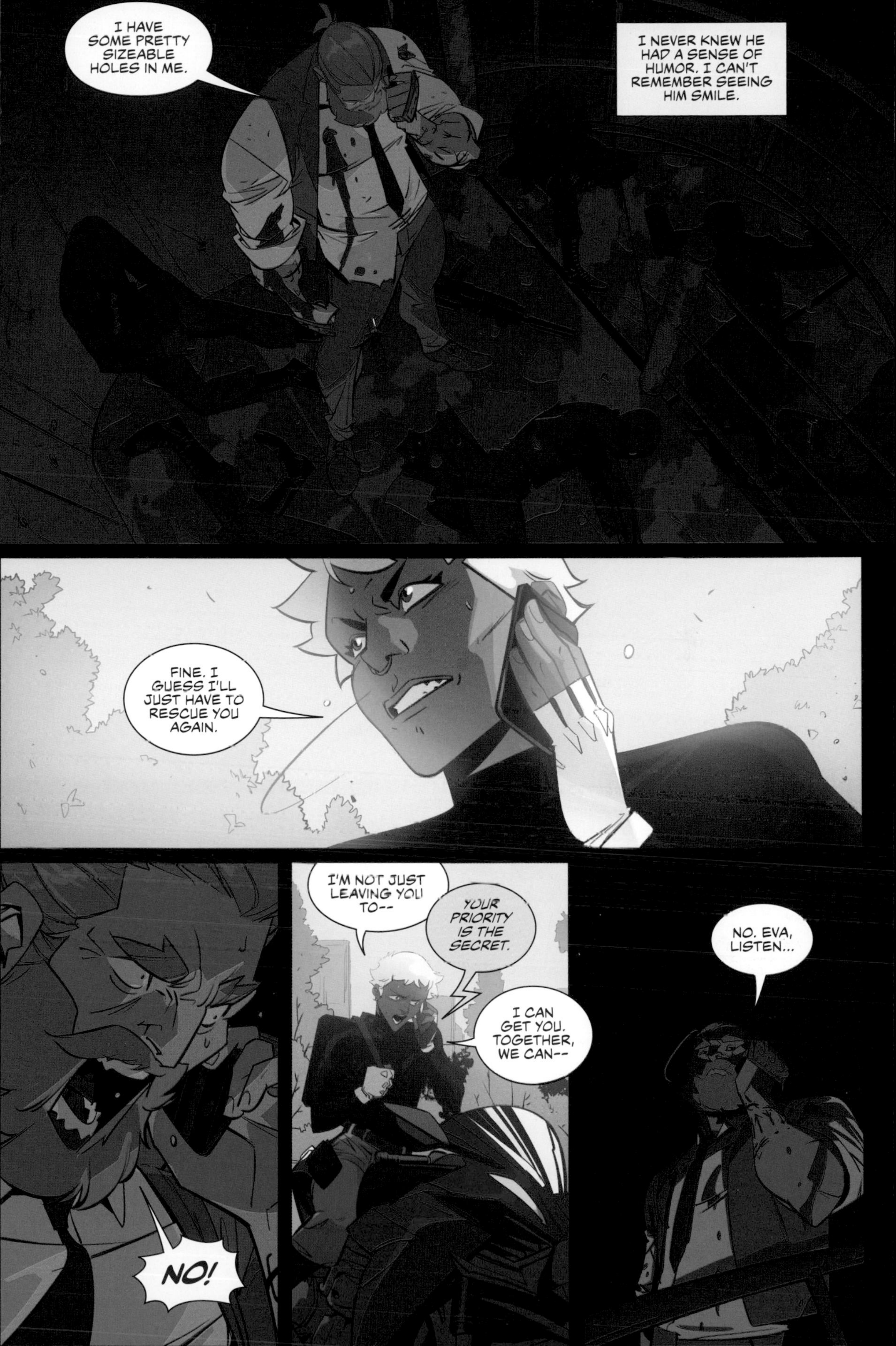

I HAVE SOME PRETTY SIZEABLE HOLES IN ME.
I NEVER KNEW HE HAD A SENSE OF HUMOR. I CAN'T REMEMBER SEEING HIM SMILE.
FINE. I GUESS I'LL JUST HAVE TO RESCUE YOU AGAIN.
NO!
I'M NOT JUST LEAVING YOU TO--
YOUR PRIORITY IS THE SECRET.
I CAN GET YOU. TOGETHER, WE CAN--
NO. EVA, LISTEN...

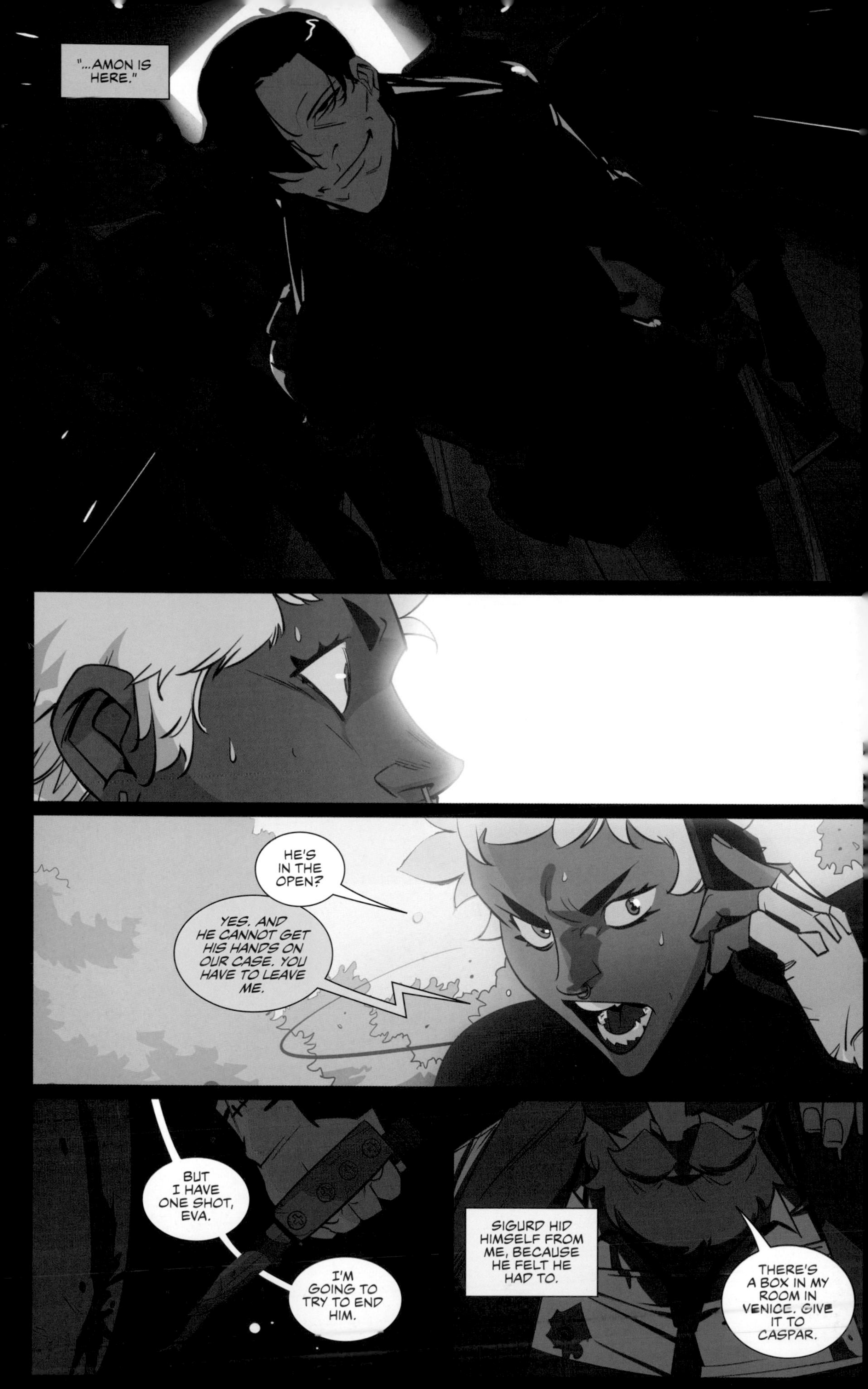
"...AMON IS HERE."
HE'S IN THE OPEN?
YES. AND HE CANNOT GET HIS HANDS ON OUR CASE. YOU HAVE TO LEAVE ME.
BUT I HAVE ONE SHOT, EVA.
I'M GOING TO TRY TO END HIM.
SIGURD HID HIMSELF FROM ME, BECAUSE HE FELT HE HAD TO.
THERE'S A BOX IN MY ROOM IN VENICE. GIVE IT TO CASPAR.

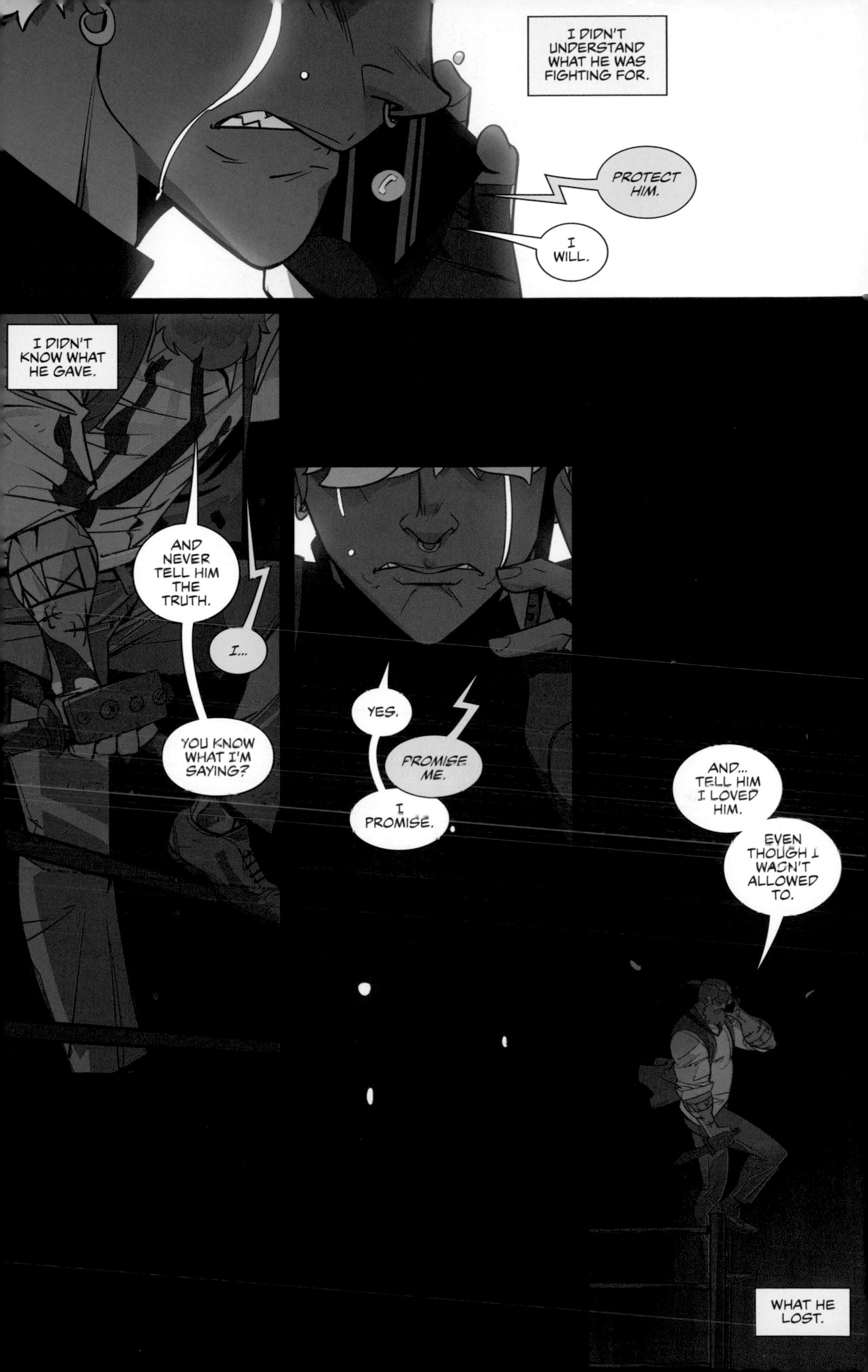
I DIDN'T UNDERSTAND WHAT HE WAS FIGHTING FOR.
PROTECT HIM.
I WILL.
I DIDN'T KNOW WHAT HE GAVE.
AND NEVER TELL HIM THE TRUTH.
I...
YOU KNOW WHAT I'M SAYING?
YES.
PROMISE ME.
I PROMISE.
AND... TELL HIM I LOVED HIM.
EVEN THOUGH I WASN'T ALLOWED TO.
WHAT HE LOST.

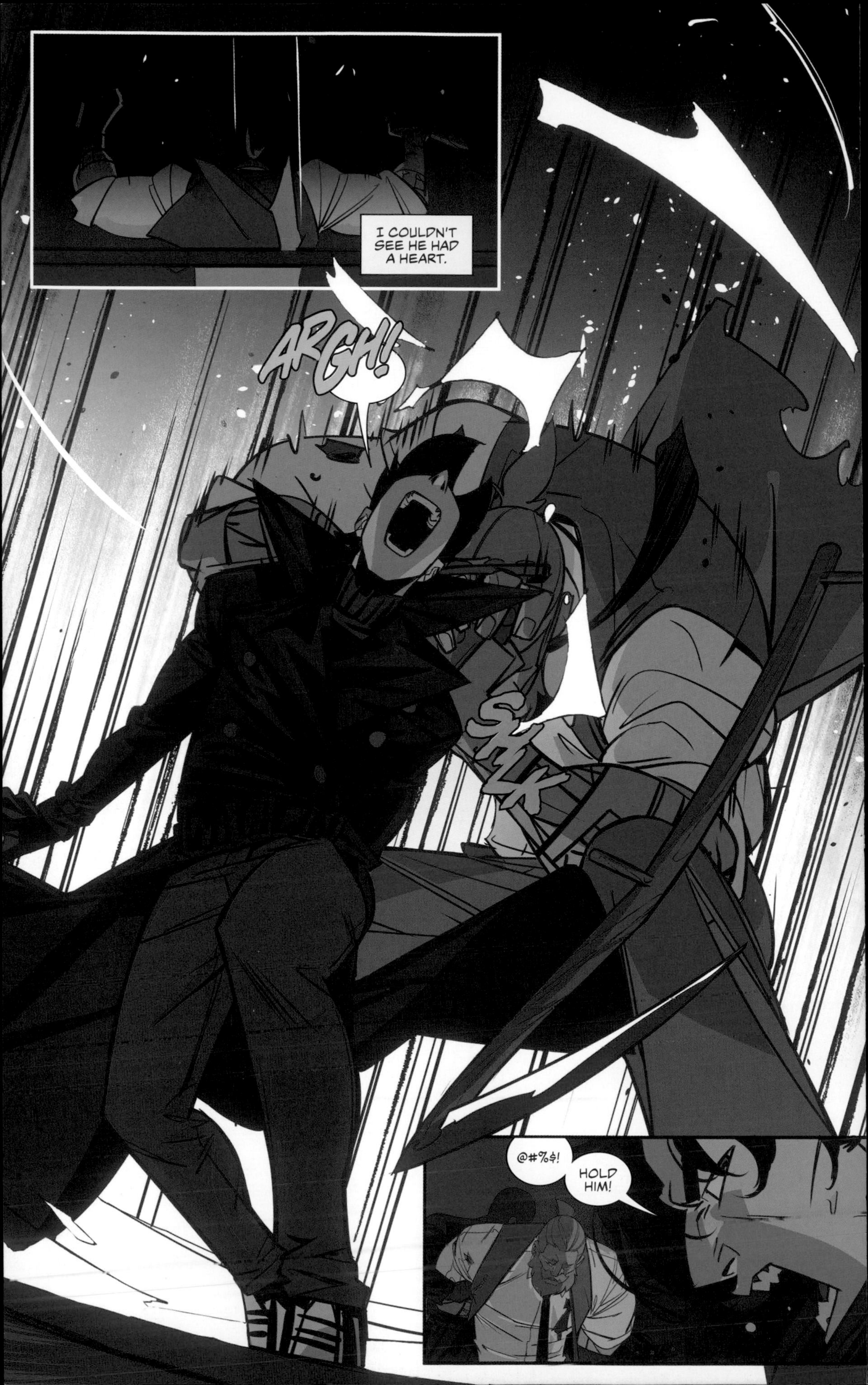
I COULDN'T SEE HE HAD A HEART.
ARGH!
SHLK
@#%$!
HOLD HIM!

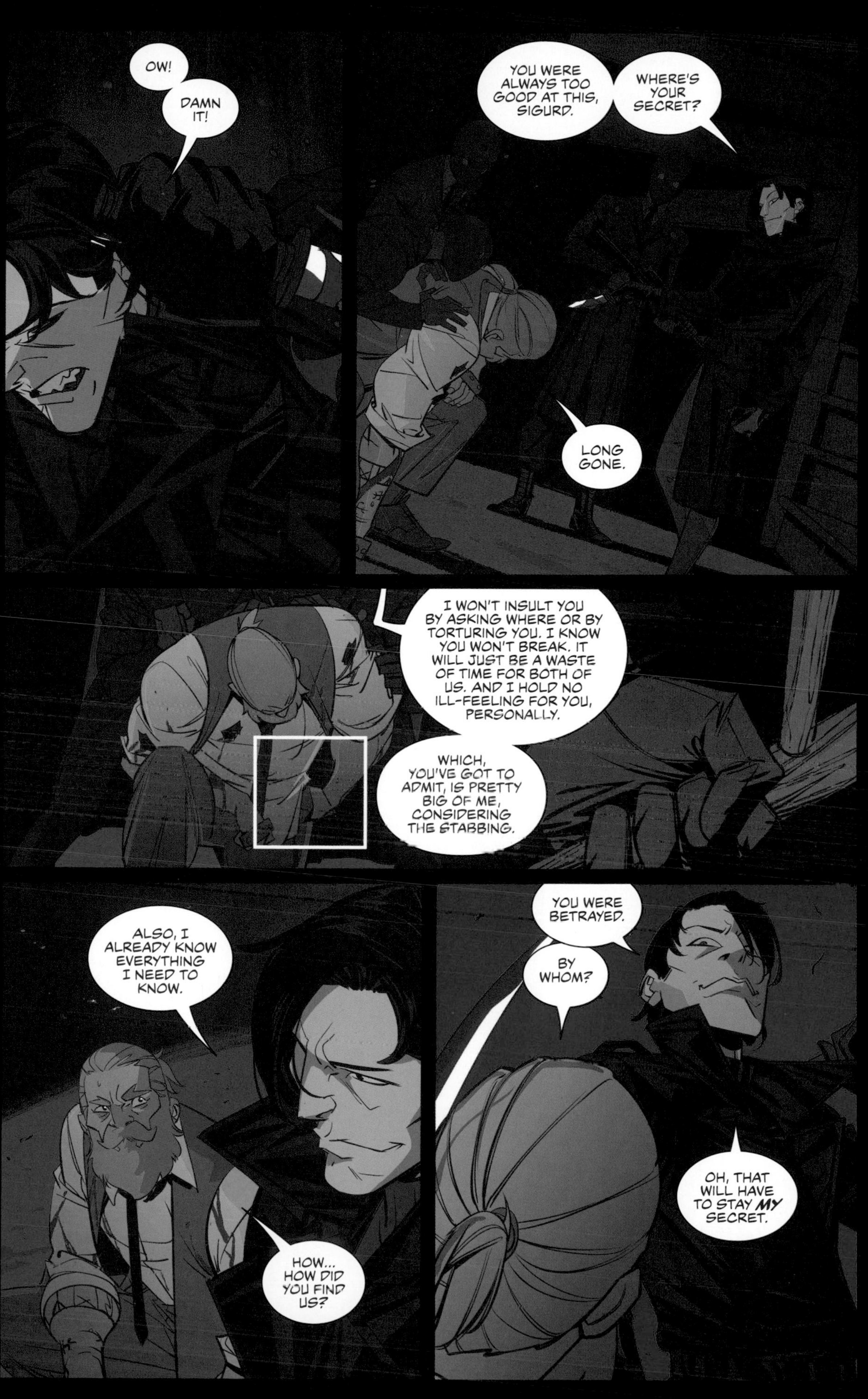
OW!
DAMN IT!
YOU WERE ALWAYS TOO GOOD AT THIS, SIGURD.
WHERE'S YOUR SECRET?
LONG GONE.
I WON'T INSULT YOU BY ASKING WHERE OR BY TORTURING YOU. I KNOW YOU WON'T BREAK. IT WILL JUST BE A WASTE OF TIME FOR BOTH OF US. AND I HOLD NO ILL-FEELING FOR YOU, PERSONALLY.
WHICH, YOU'VE GOT TO ADMIT, IS PRETTY BIG OF ME, CONSIDERING THE STABBING.
ALSO, I ALREADY KNOW EVERYTHING I NEED TO KNOW.
HOW... HOW DID YOU FIND US?
YOU WERE BETRAYED.
BY WHOM?
OH, THAT WILL HAVE TO STAY MY SECRET.

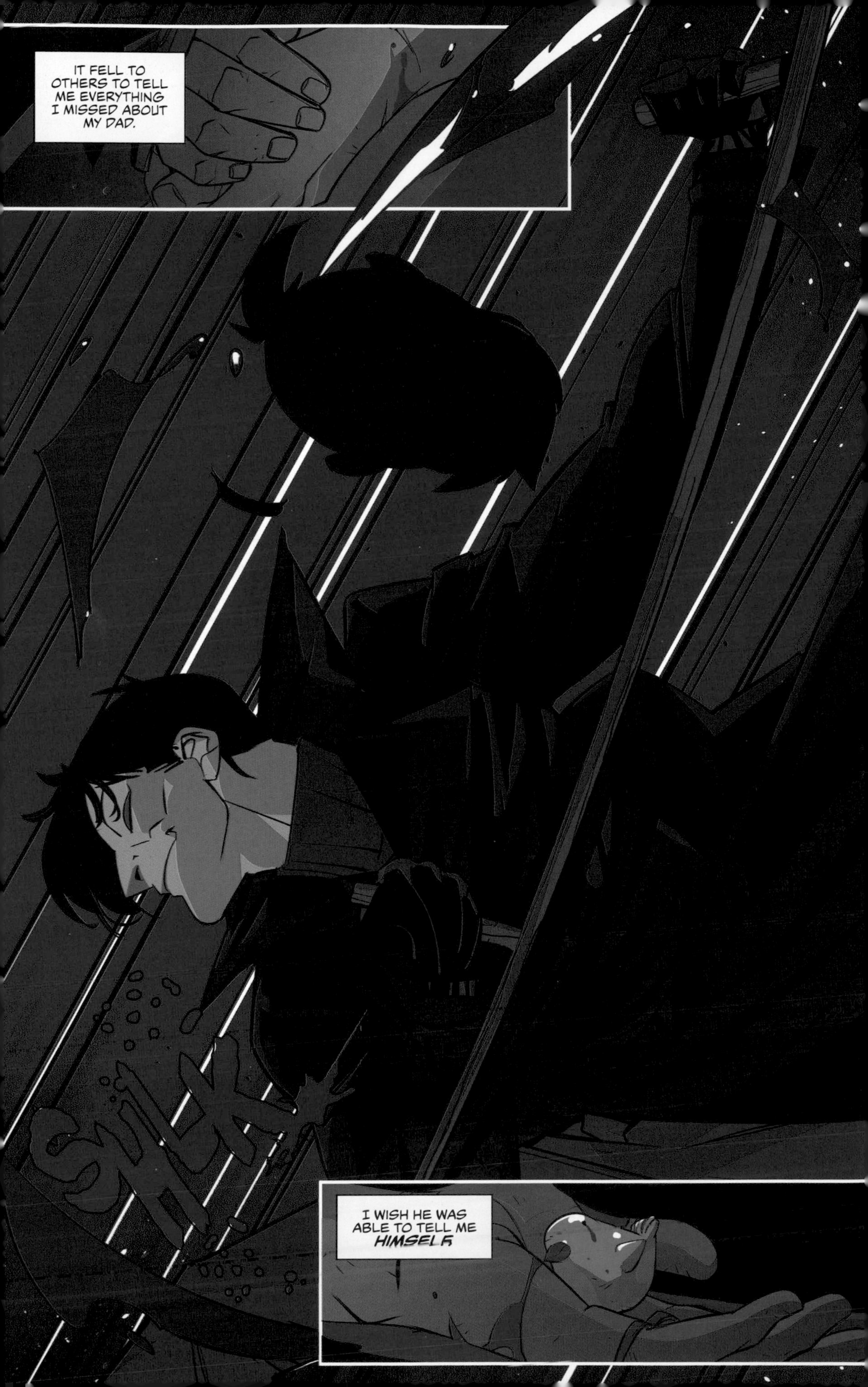
IT FELL TO OTHERS TO TELL ME EVERYTHING I MISSED ABOUT MY DAD.
I WISH HE WAS ABLE TO TELL ME *HIMSELF*.

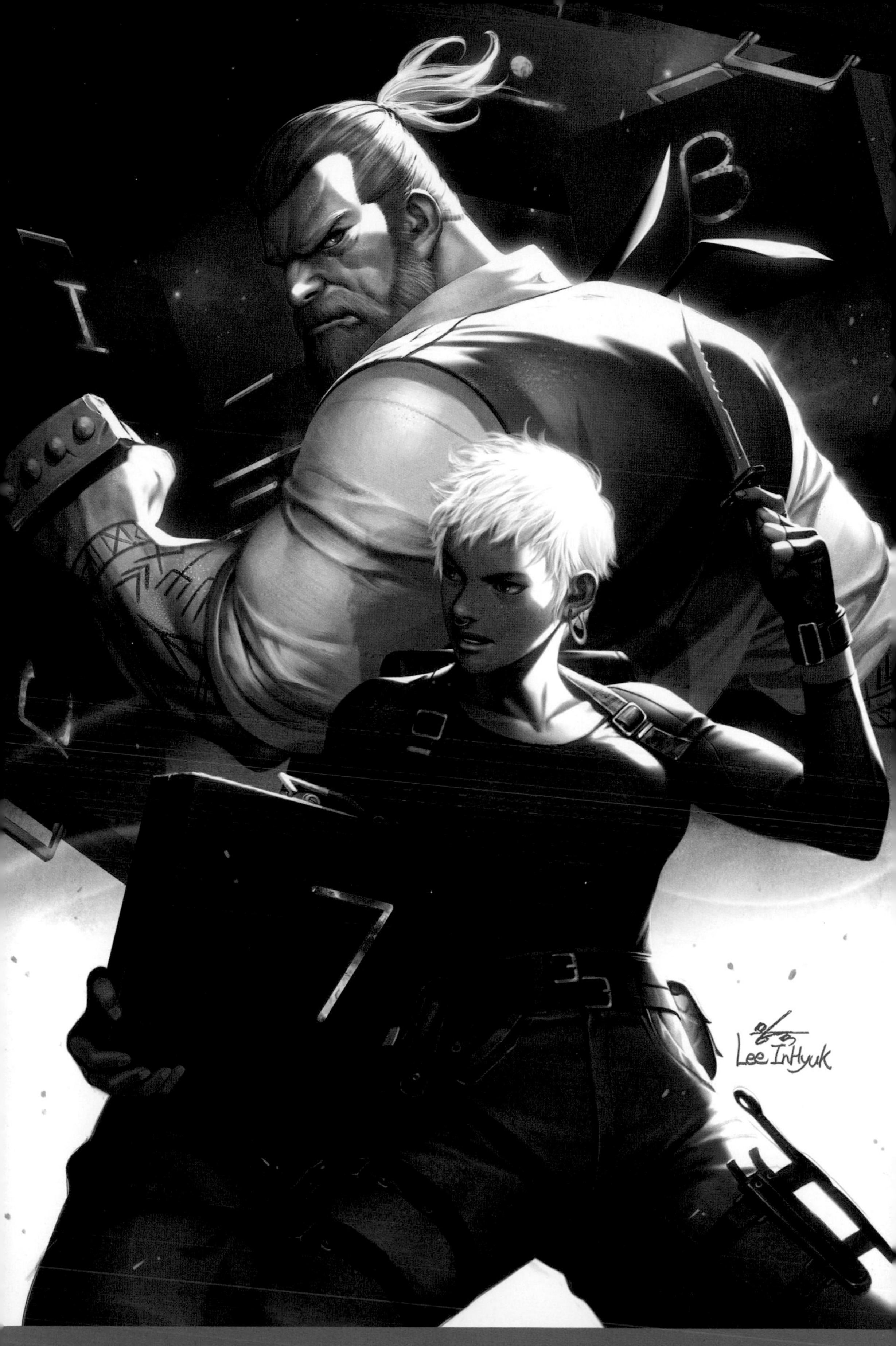
7
Lee InHyuk

INHYUK LEE ISSUE ONE VARIANT COVER

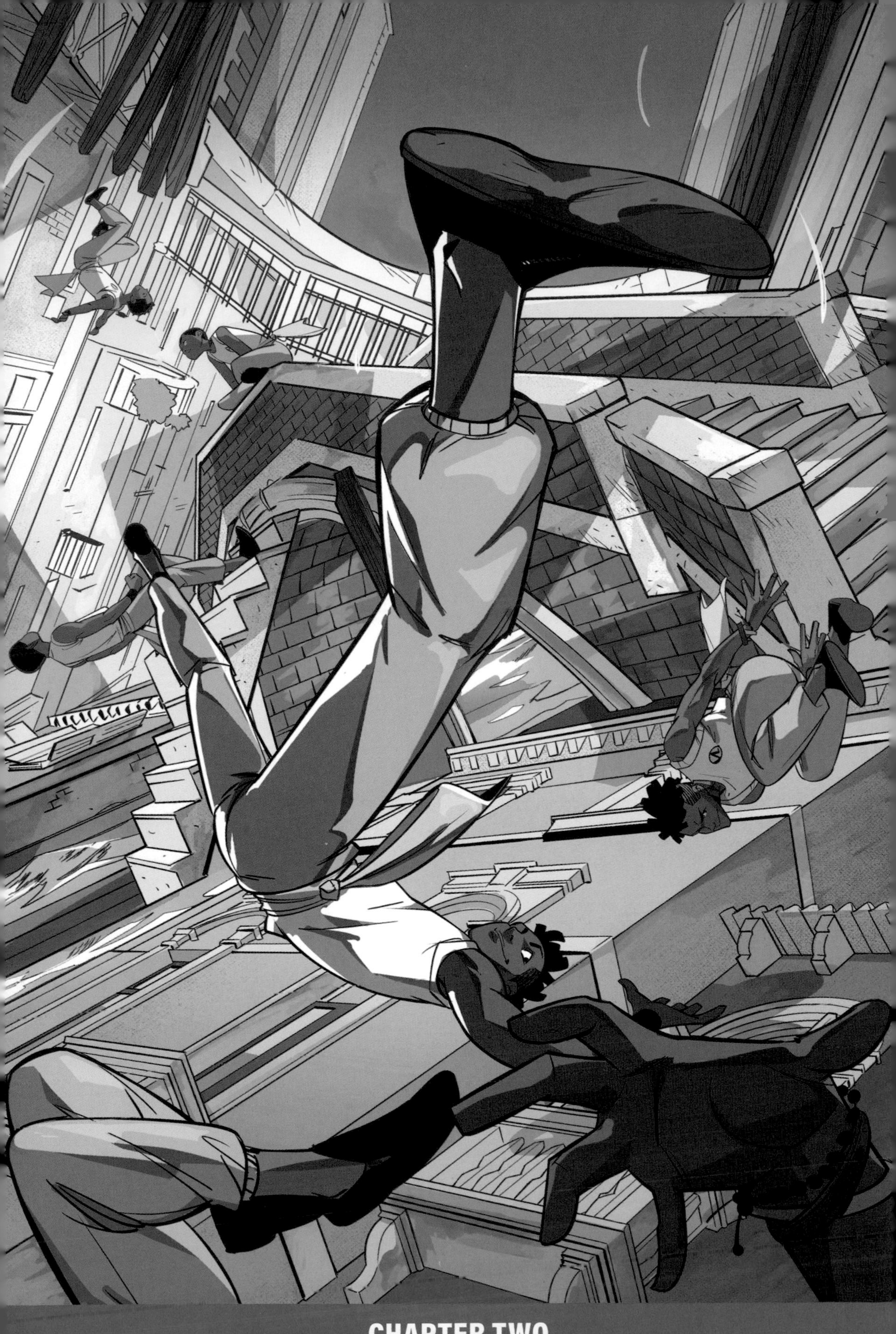

CHAPTER TWO

DANIELE DI NICUOLO WITH COLORS BY **WALTER BAIAMONTE** ISSUE TWO COVER

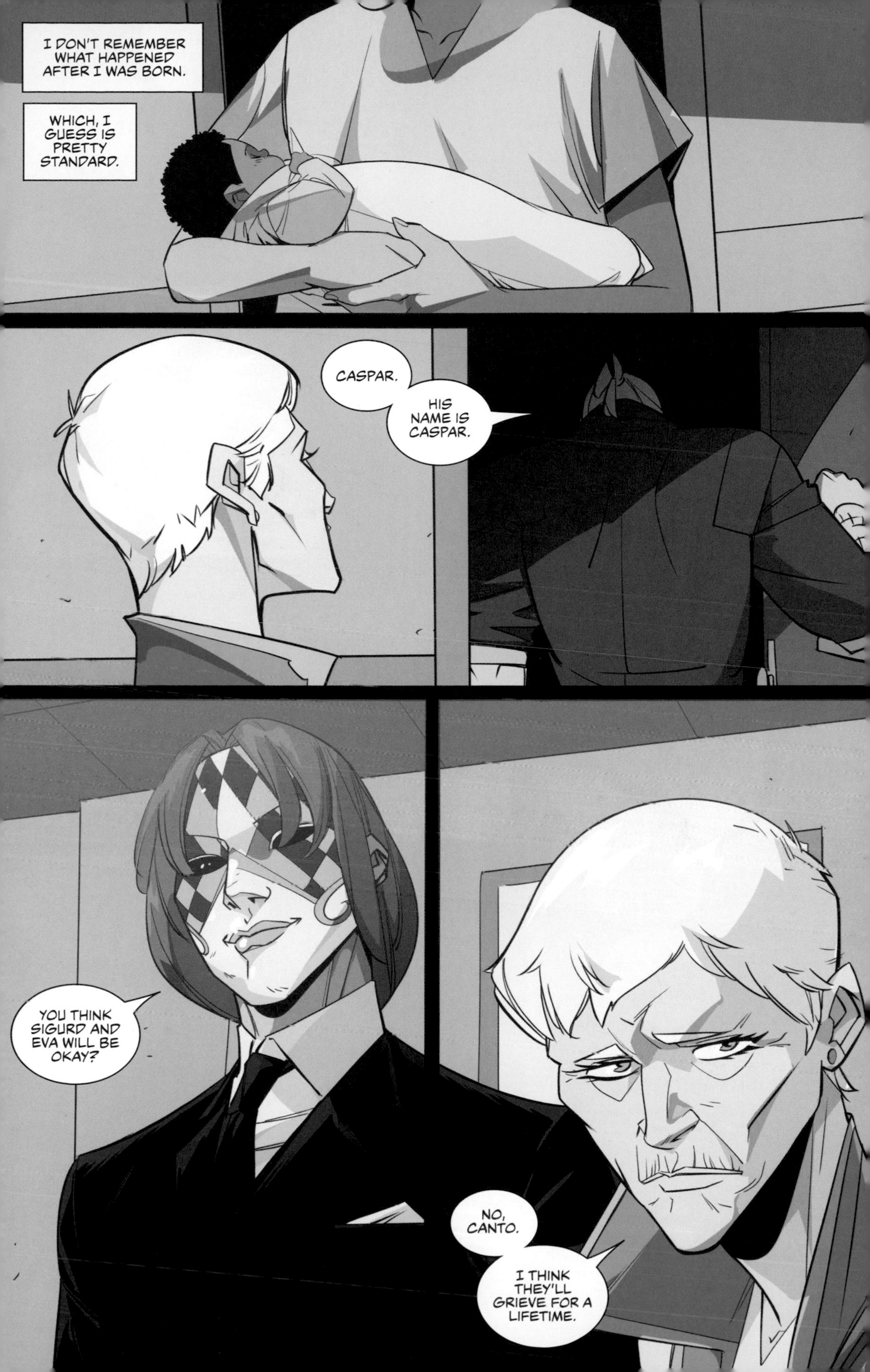
I DON'T REMEMBER WHAT HAPPENED AFTER I WAS BORN.
WHICH, I GUESS IS PRETTY STANDARD.
CASPAR.
HIS NAME IS CASPAR.
YOU THINK SIGURD AND EVA WILL BE OKAY?
NO, CANTO.
I THINK THEY'LL GRIEVE FOR A LIFETIME.

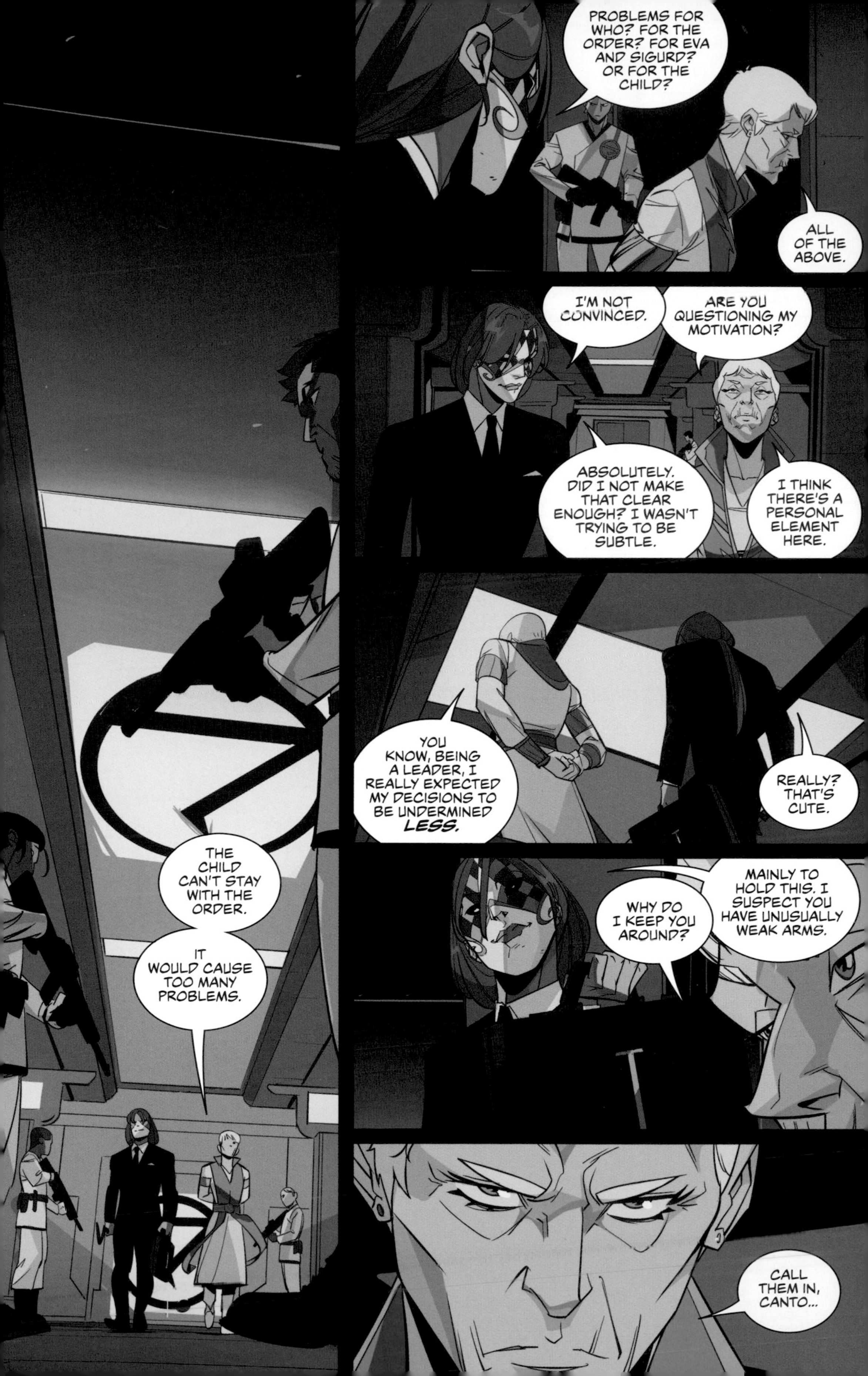
THE CHILD CAN'T STAY WITH THE ORDER.
IT WOULD CAUSE TOO MANY PROBLEMS.
PROBLEMS FOR WHO? FOR THE ORDER? FOR EVA AND SIGURD? OR FOR THE CHILD?
ALL OF THE ABOVE.
I'M NOT CONVINCED.
ARE YOU QUESTIONING MY MOTIVATION?
ABSOLUTELY. DID I NOT MAKE THAT CLEAR ENOUGH? I WASN'T TRYING TO BE SUBTLE.
I THINK THERE'S A PERSONAL ELEMENT HERE.
YOU KNOW, BEING A LEADER, I REALLY EXPECTED MY DECISIONS TO BE UNDERMINED LESS.
REALLY? THAT'S CUTE.
WHY DO I KEEP YOU AROUND?
MAINLY TO HOLD THIS. I SUSPECT YOU HAVE UNUSUALLY WEAK ARMS.
CALL THEM IN, CANTO...

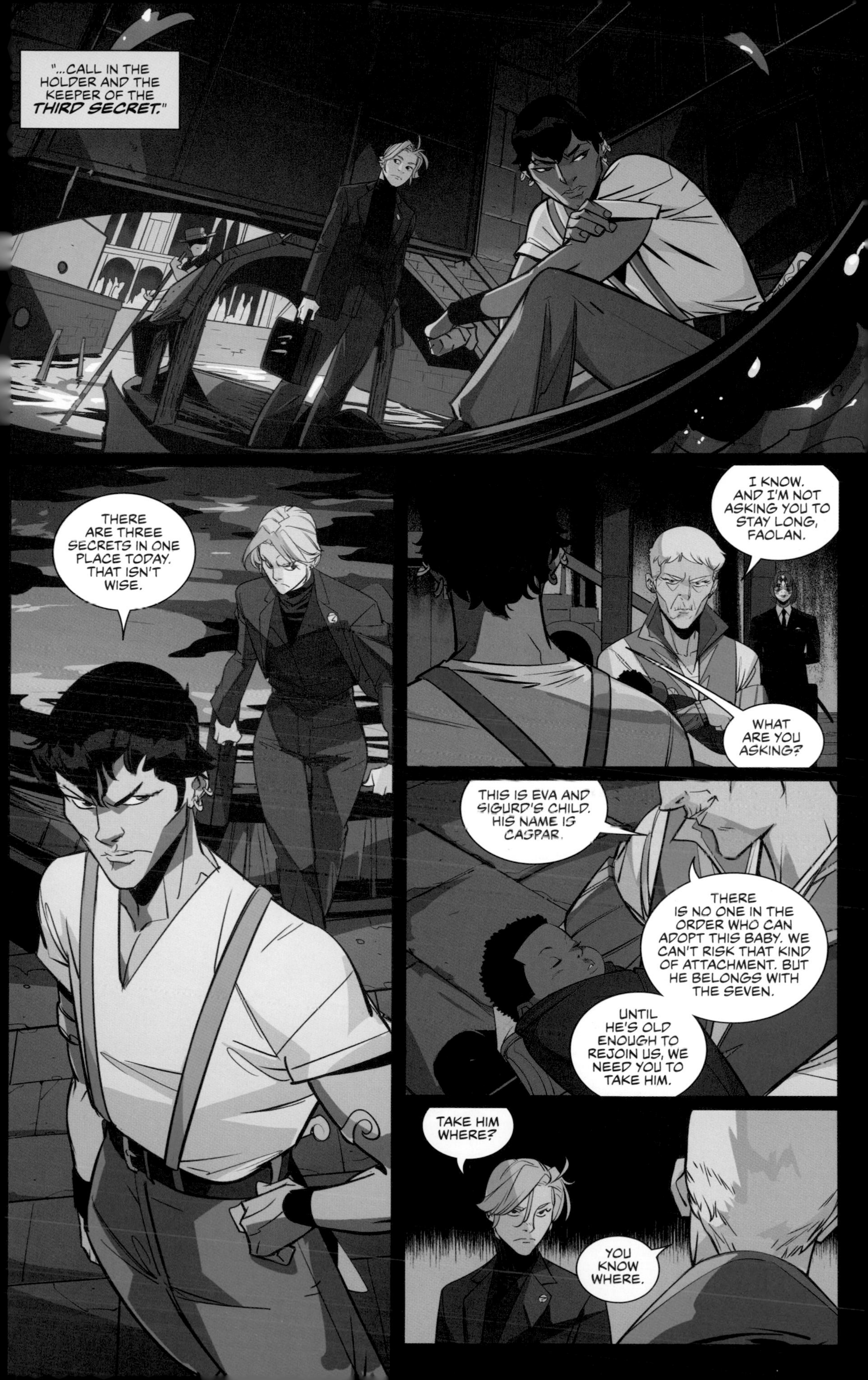
"...CALL IN THE HOLDER AND THE KEEPER OF THE THIRD SECRET."
THERE ARE THREE SECRETS IN ONE PLACE TODAY. THAT ISN'T WISE.
I KNOW. AND I'M NOT ASKING YOU TO STAY LONG, FAOLAN.
WHAT ARE YOU ASKING?
THIS IS EVA AND SIGURD'S CHILD. HIS NAME IS CASPAR.
THERE IS NO ONE IN THE ORDER WHO CAN ADOPT THIS BABY. WE CAN'T RISK THAT KIND OF ATTACHMENT. BUT HE BELONGS WITH THE SEVEN.
UNTIL HE'S OLD ENOUGH TO REJOIN US, WE NEED YOU TO TAKE HIM.
TAKE HIM WHERE?
YOU KNOW WHERE.

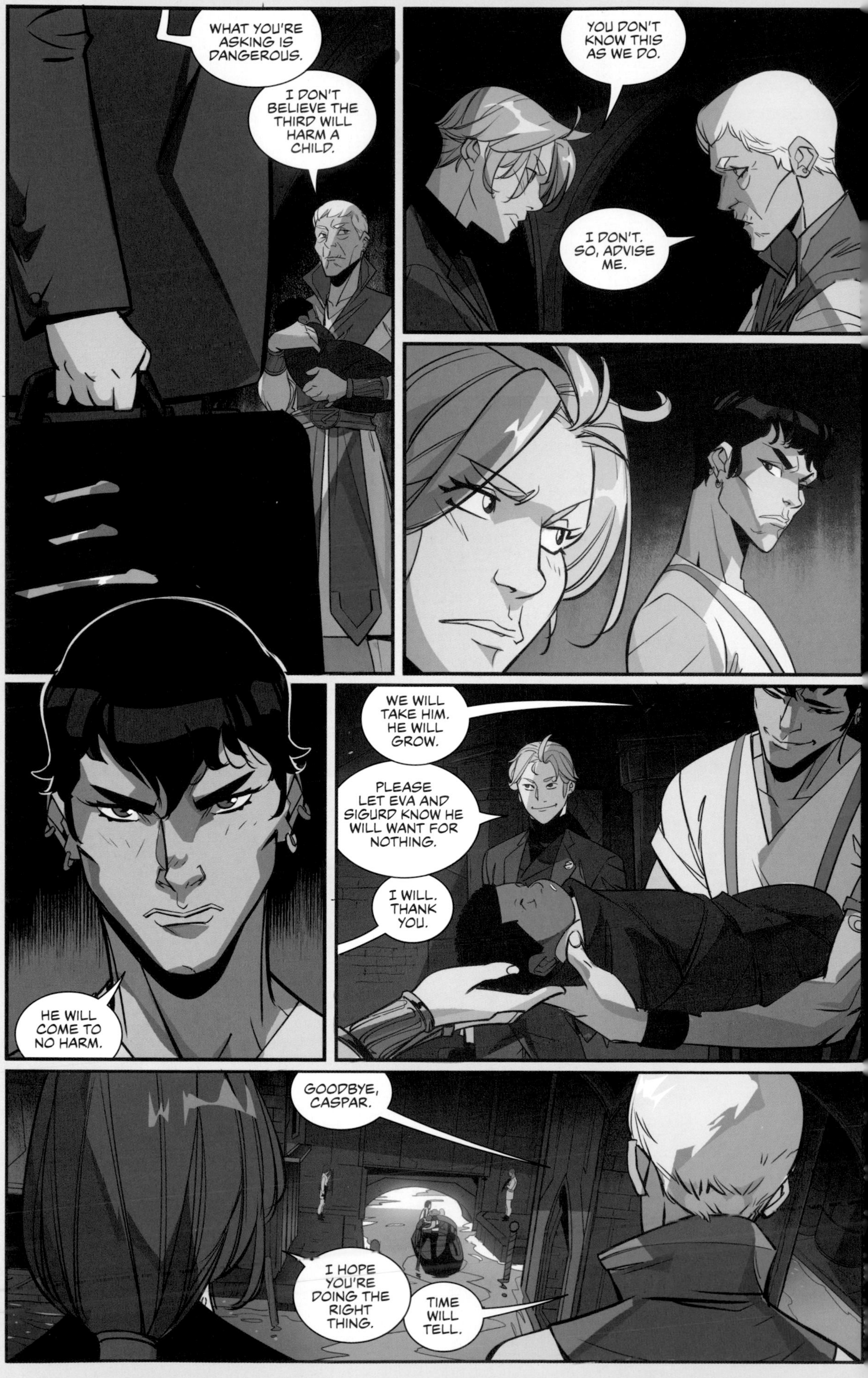
WHAT YOU'RE ASKING IS DANGEROUS.
I DON'T BELIEVE THE THIRD WILL HARM A CHILD.
YOU DON'T KNOW THIS AS WE DO.
I DON'T. SO, ADVISE ME.
HE WILL COME TO NO HARM.
WE WILL TAKE HIM. HE WILL GROW.
PLEASE LET EVA AND SIGURD KNOW HE WILL WANT FOR NOTHING.
I WILL. THANK YOU.
GOODBYE, CASPAR.
I HOPE YOU'RE DOING THE RIGHT THING.
TIME WILL TELL.

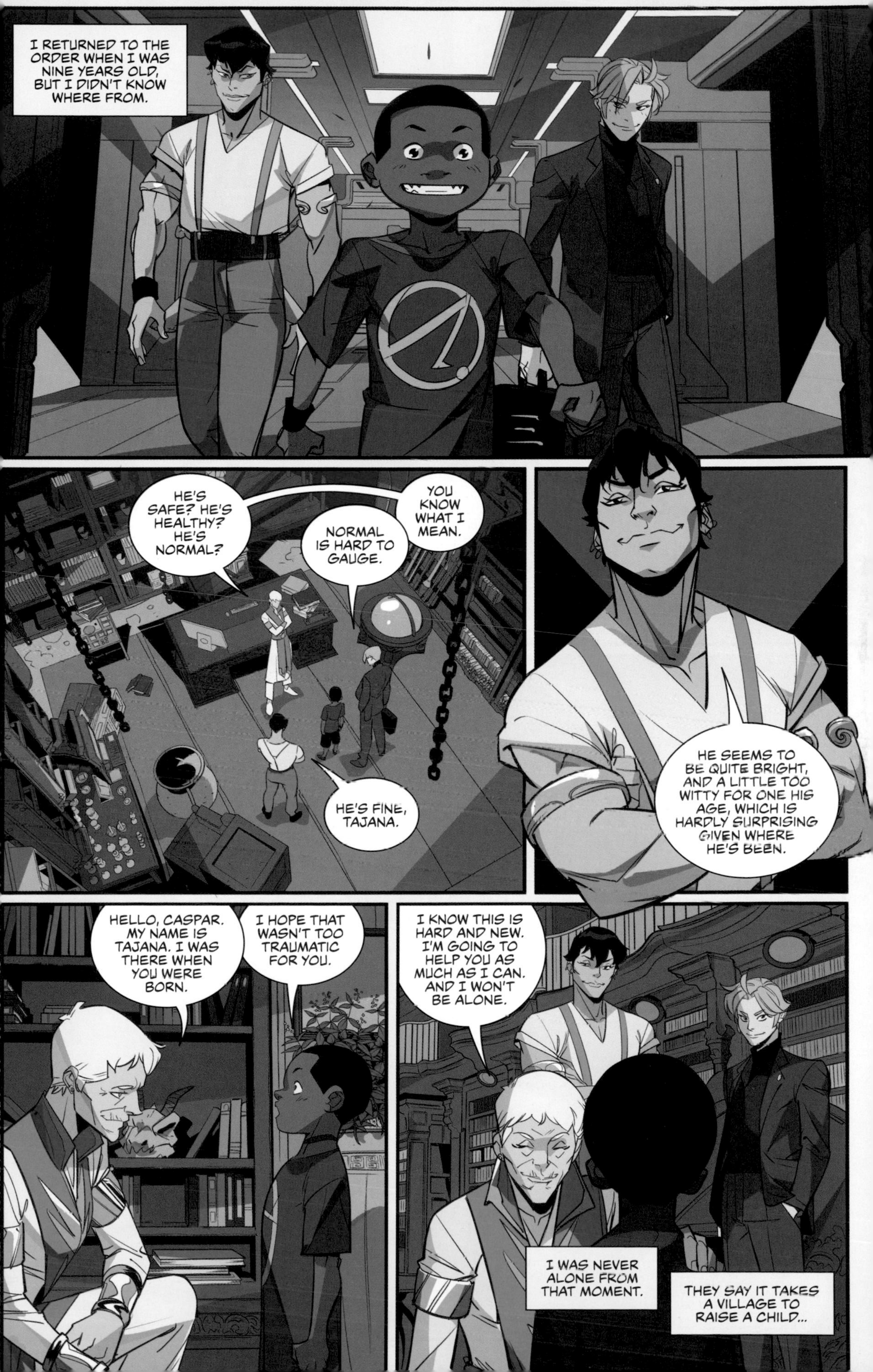
I RETURNED TO THE ORDER WHEN I WAS NINE YEARS OLD, BUT I DIDN'T KNOW WHERE FROM.
HE'S SAFE? HE'S HEALTHY? HE'S NORMAL?
NORMAL IS HARD TO GAUGE.
YOU KNOW WHAT I MEAN.
HE'S FINE, TAJANA.
HE SEEMS TO BE QUITE BRIGHT, AND A LITTLE TOO WITTY FOR ONE HIS AGE, WHICH IS HARDLY SURPRISING GIVEN WHERE HE'S BEEN.
HELLO, CASPAR. MY NAME IS TAJANA. I WAS THERE WHEN YOU WERE BORN.
I HOPE THAT WASN'T TOO TRAUMATIC FOR YOU.
I KNOW THIS IS HARD AND NEW. I'M GOING TO HELP YOU AS MUCH AS I CAN. AND I WON'T BE ALONE.
I WAS NEVER ALONE FROM THAT MOMENT.
THEY SAY IT TAKES A VILLAGE TO RAISE A CHILD...

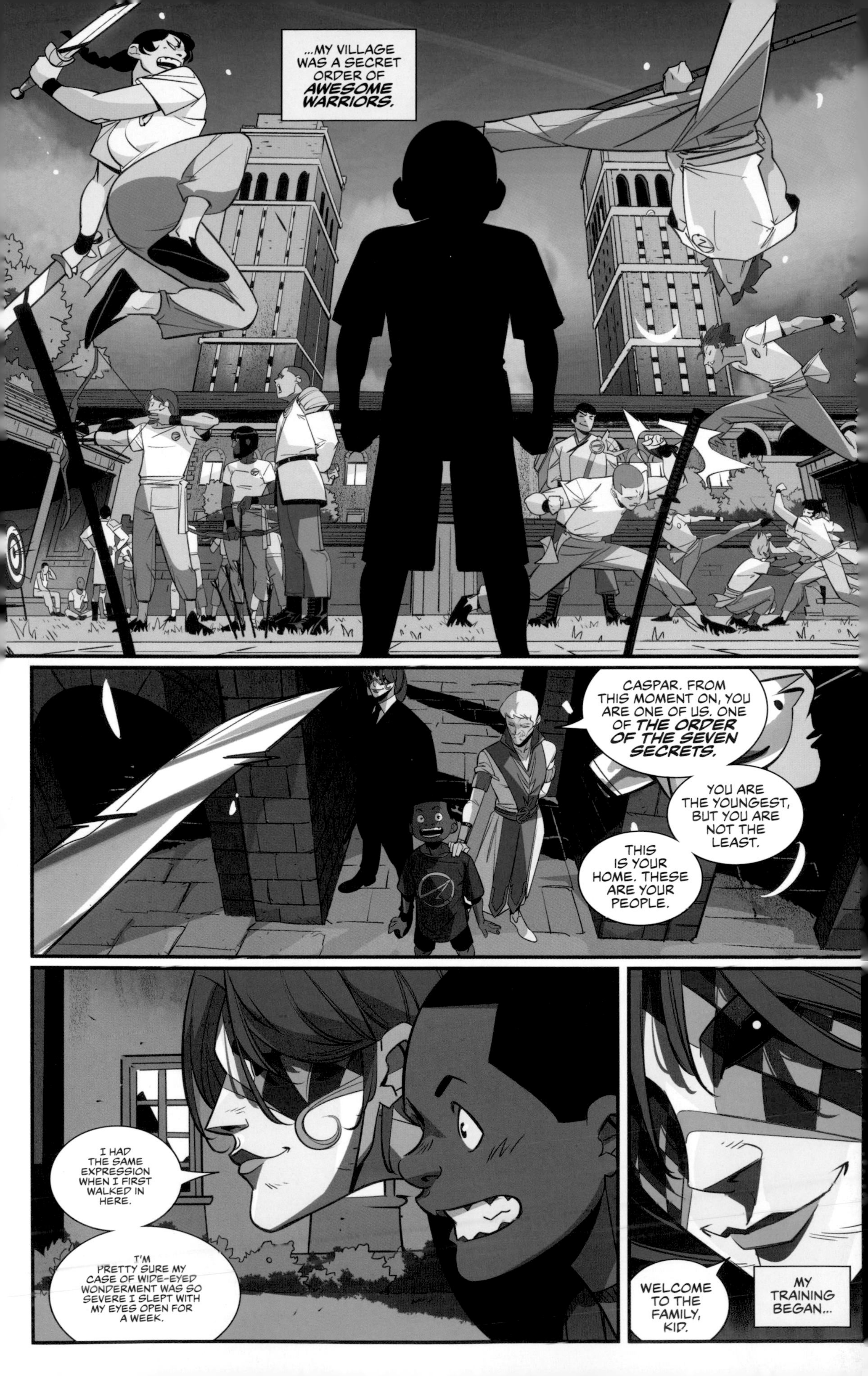
...MY VILLAGE WAS A SECRET ORDER OF ***AWESOME WARRIORS.***
CASPAR. FROM THIS MOMENT ON, YOU ARE ONE OF US. ONE OF ***THE ORDER OF THE SEVEN SECRETS.***
YOU ARE THE YOUNGEST, BUT YOU ARE NOT THE LEAST.
THIS IS YOUR HOME. THESE ARE YOUR PEOPLE.
I HAD THE SAME EXPRESSION WHEN I FIRST WALKED IN HERE.
I'M PRETTY SURE MY CASE OF WIDE-EYED WONDERMENT WAS SO SEVERE I SLEPT WITH MY EYES OPEN FOR A WEEK.
WELCOME TO THE FAMILY, KID.
MY TRAINING BEGAN...

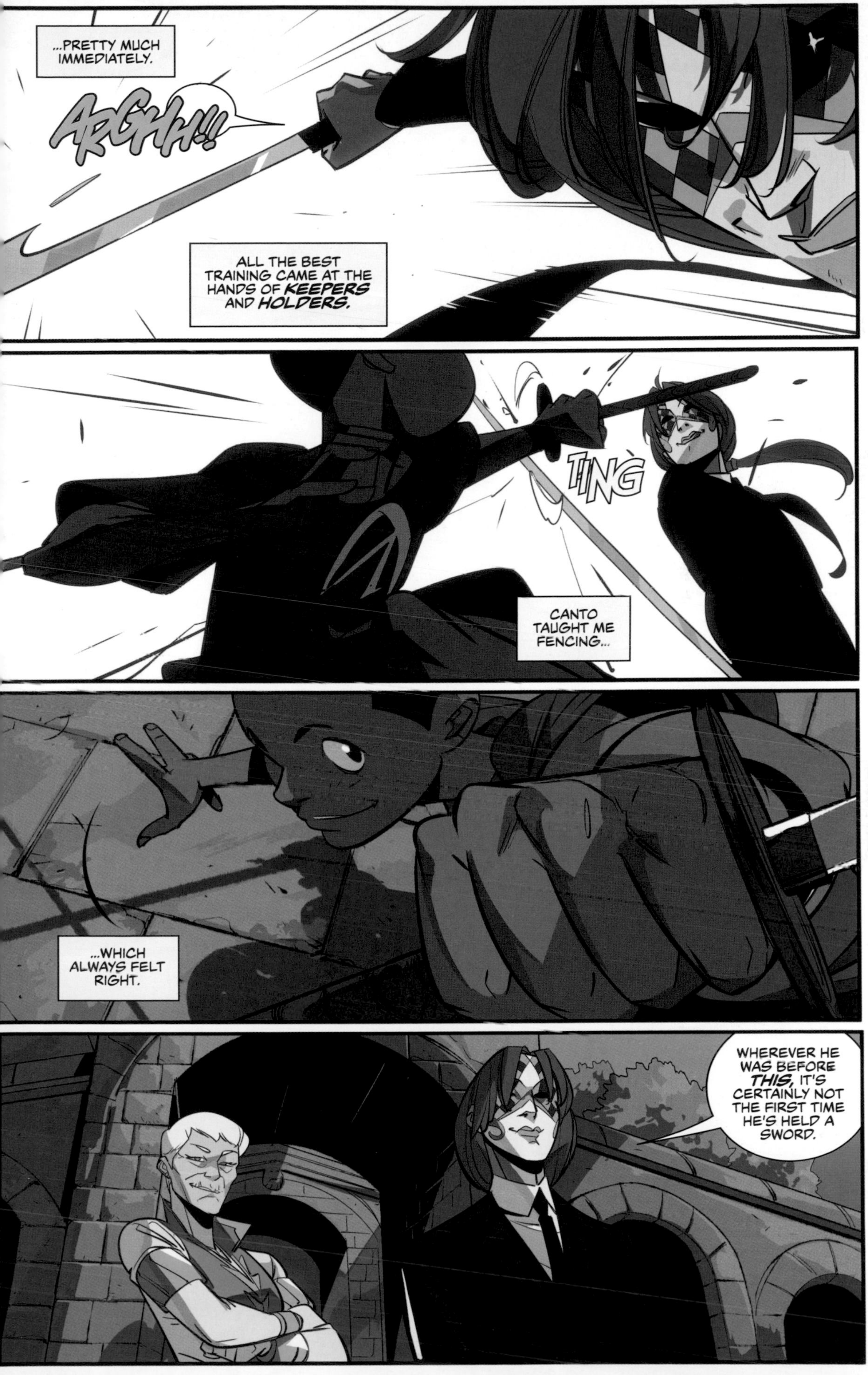
...PRETTY MUCH IMMEDIATELY.
ARGHH!!
ALL THE BEST TRAINING CAME AT THE HANDS OF KEEPERS AND HOLDERS.
TING
CANTO TAUGHT ME FENCING...
...WHICH ALWAYS FELT RIGHT.
WHEREVER HE WAS BEFORE THIS, IT'S CERTAINLY NOT THE FIRST TIME HE'S HELD A SWORD.

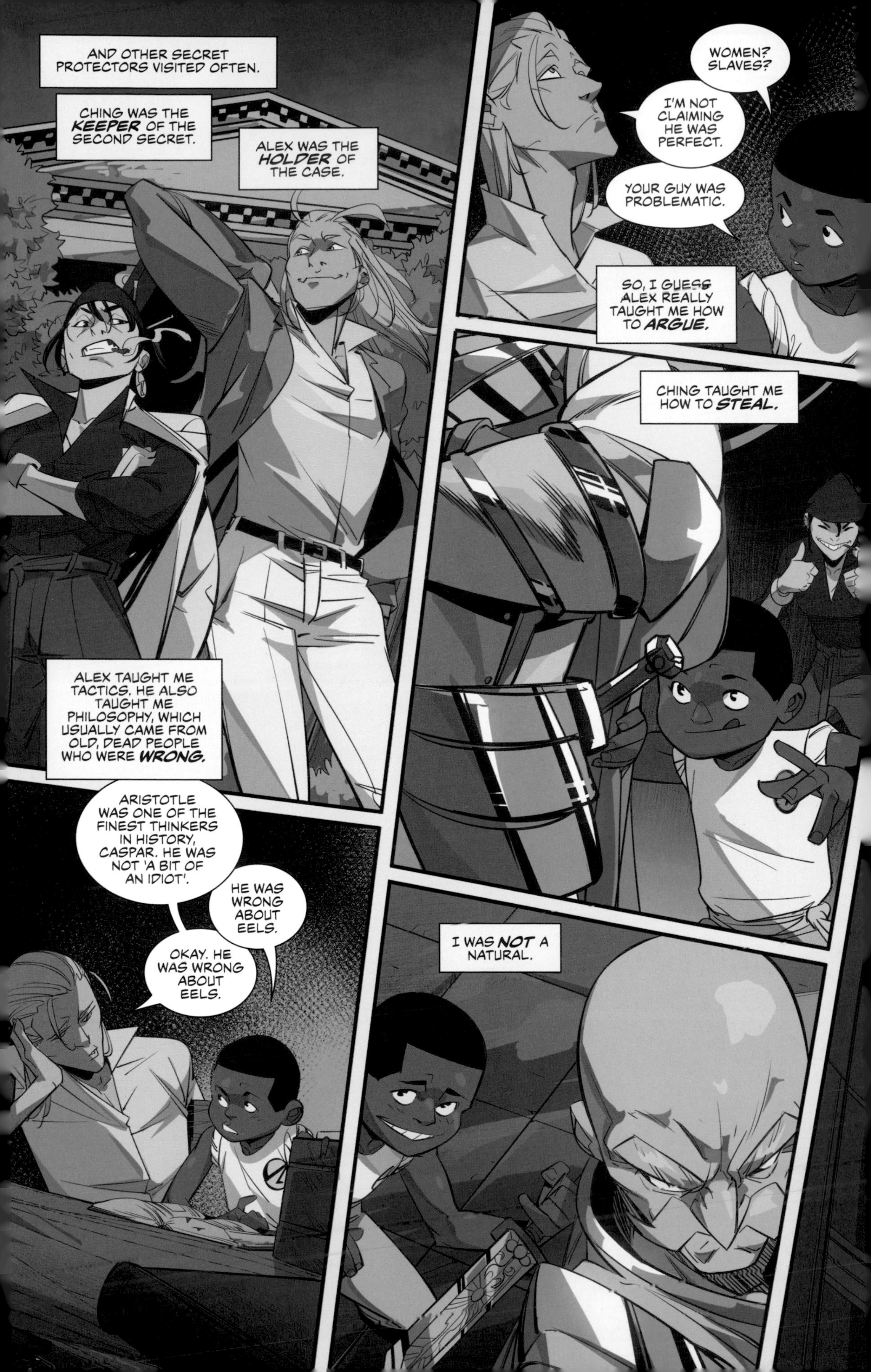

AND OTHER SECRET PROTECTORS VISITED OFTEN.
CHING WAS THE KEEPER OF THE SECOND SECRET.
ALEX WAS THE HOLDER OF THE CASE.
WOMEN? SLAVES?
I'M NOT CLAIMING HE WAS PERFECT.
YOUR GUY WAS PROBLEMATIC.
SO, I GUESS ALEX REALLY TAUGHT ME HOW TO ARGUE.
CHING TAUGHT ME HOW TO STEAL.
ALEX TAUGHT ME TACTICS. HE ALSO TAUGHT ME PHILOSOPHY, WHICH USUALLY CAME FROM OLD, DEAD PEOPLE WHO WERE WRONG.
ARISTOTLE WAS ONE OF THE FINEST THINKERS IN HISTORY, CASPAR. HE WAS NOT 'A BIT OF AN IDIOT'.
HE WAS WRONG ABOUT EELS.
OKAY. HE WAS WRONG ABOUT EELS.
I WAS NOT A NATURAL.

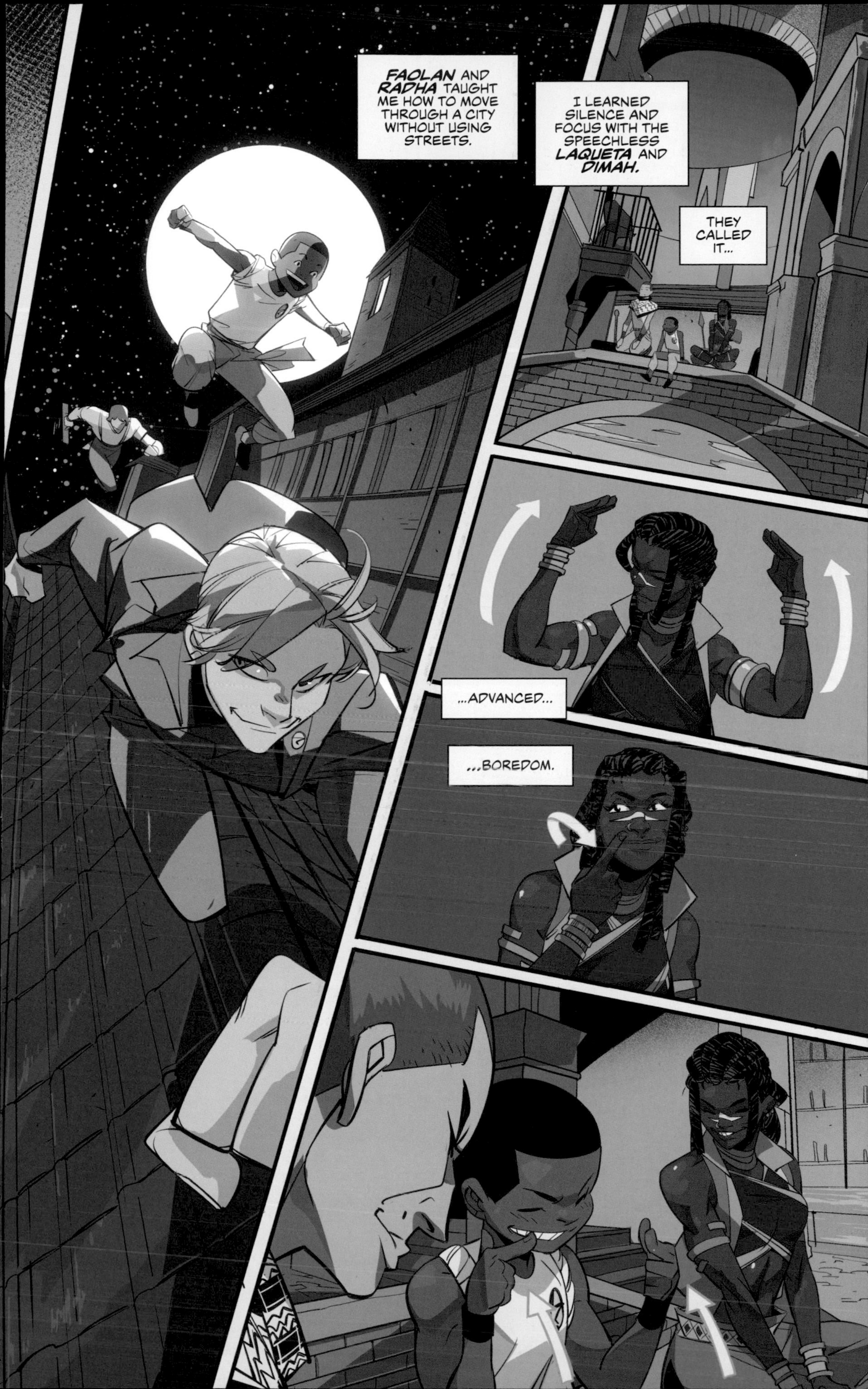
FAOLAN AND RADHA TAUGHT ME HOW TO MOVE THROUGH A CITY WITHOUT USING STREETS.
I LEARNED SILENCE AND FOCUS WITH THE SPEECHLESS LAQUETA AND DIMAH.
THEY CALLED IT...
...ADVANCED...
...BOREDOM.

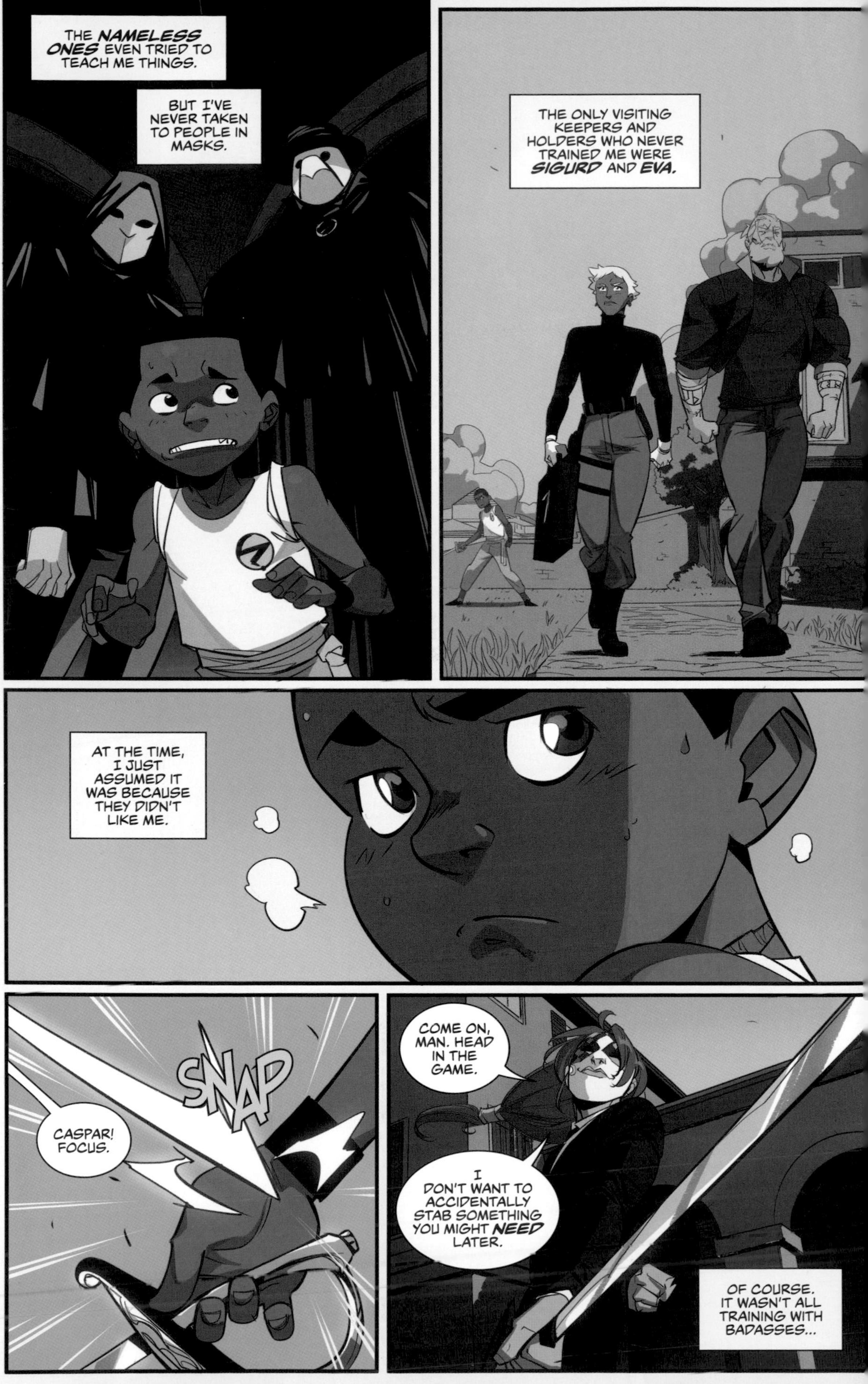
THE NAMELESS ONES EVEN TRIED TO TEACH ME THINGS.
BUT I'VE NEVER TAKEN TO PEOPLE IN MASKS.
THE ONLY VISITING KEEPERS AND HOLDERS WHO NEVER TRAINED ME WERE SIGURD AND EVA.
AT THE TIME, I JUST ASSUMED IT WAS BECAUSE THEY DIDN'T LIKE ME.
SNAP
CASPAR! FOCUS.
COME ON, MAN. HEAD IN THE GAME.
I DON'T WANT TO ACCIDENTALLY STAB SOMETHING YOU MIGHT NEED LATER.
OF COURSE. IT WASN'T ALL TRAINING WITH BADASSES...

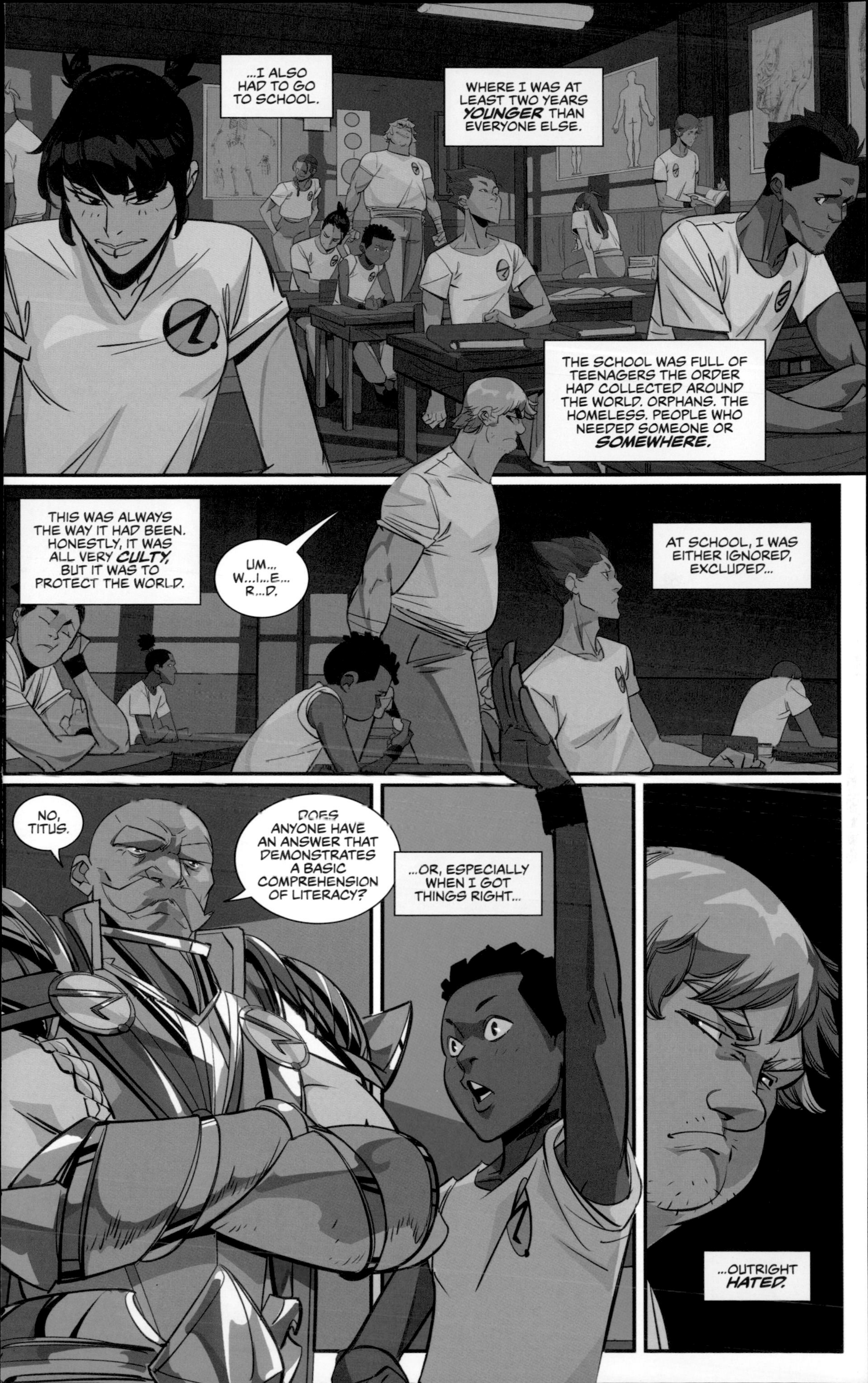
...I ALSO HAD TO GO TO SCHOOL.
WHERE I WAS AT LEAST TWO YEARS YOUNGER THAN EVERYONE ELSE.
THE SCHOOL WAS FULL OF TEENAGERS THE ORDER HAD COLLECTED AROUND THE WORLD. ORPHANS. THE HOMELESS. PEOPLE WHO NEEDED SOMEONE OR SOMEWHERE.
THIS WAS ALWAYS THE WAY IT HAD BEEN. HONESTLY, IT WAS ALL VERY CULTY, BUT IT WAS TO PROTECT THE WORLD.
UM... W...I...E... R...D.
AT SCHOOL, I WAS EITHER IGNORED, EXCLUDED...
NO, TITUS.
DOES ANYONE HAVE AN ANSWER THAT DEMONSTRATES A BASIC COMPREHENSION OF LITERACY?
...OR, ESPECIALLY WHEN I GOT THINGS RIGHT...
...OUTRIGHT HATED.

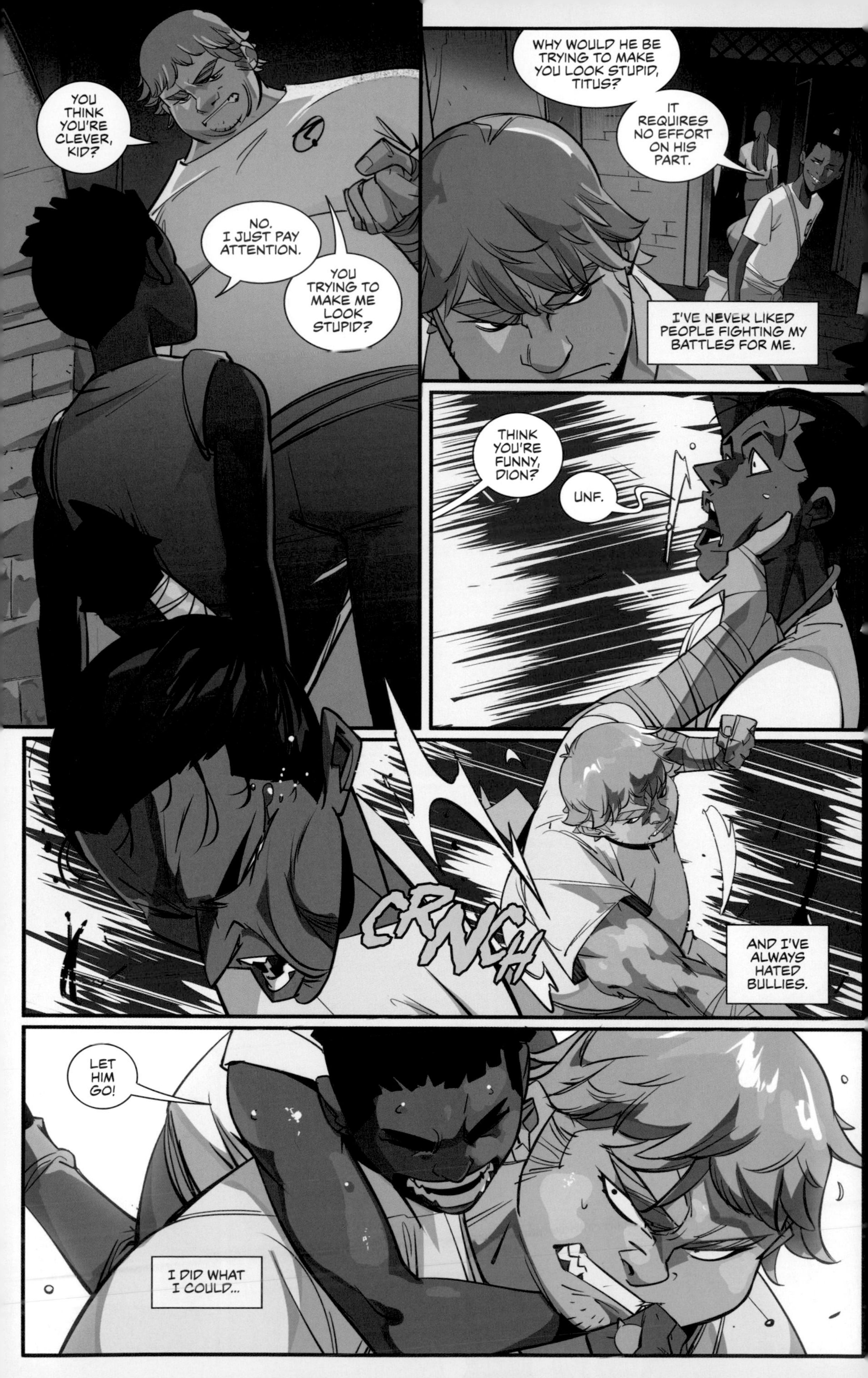
YOU THINK YOU'RE CLEVER, KID?
NO. I JUST PAY ATTENTION.
YOU TRYING TO MAKE ME LOOK STUPID?
WHY WOULD HE BE TRYING TO MAKE YOU LOOK STUPID, TITUS?
IT REQUIRES NO EFFORT ON HIS PART.
I'VE NEVER LIKED PEOPLE FIGHTING MY BATTLES FOR ME.
THINK YOU'RE FUNNY, DION?
UNF.
CRNCH
AND I'VE ALWAYS HATED BULLIES.
LET HIM GO!
I DID WHAT I COULD...

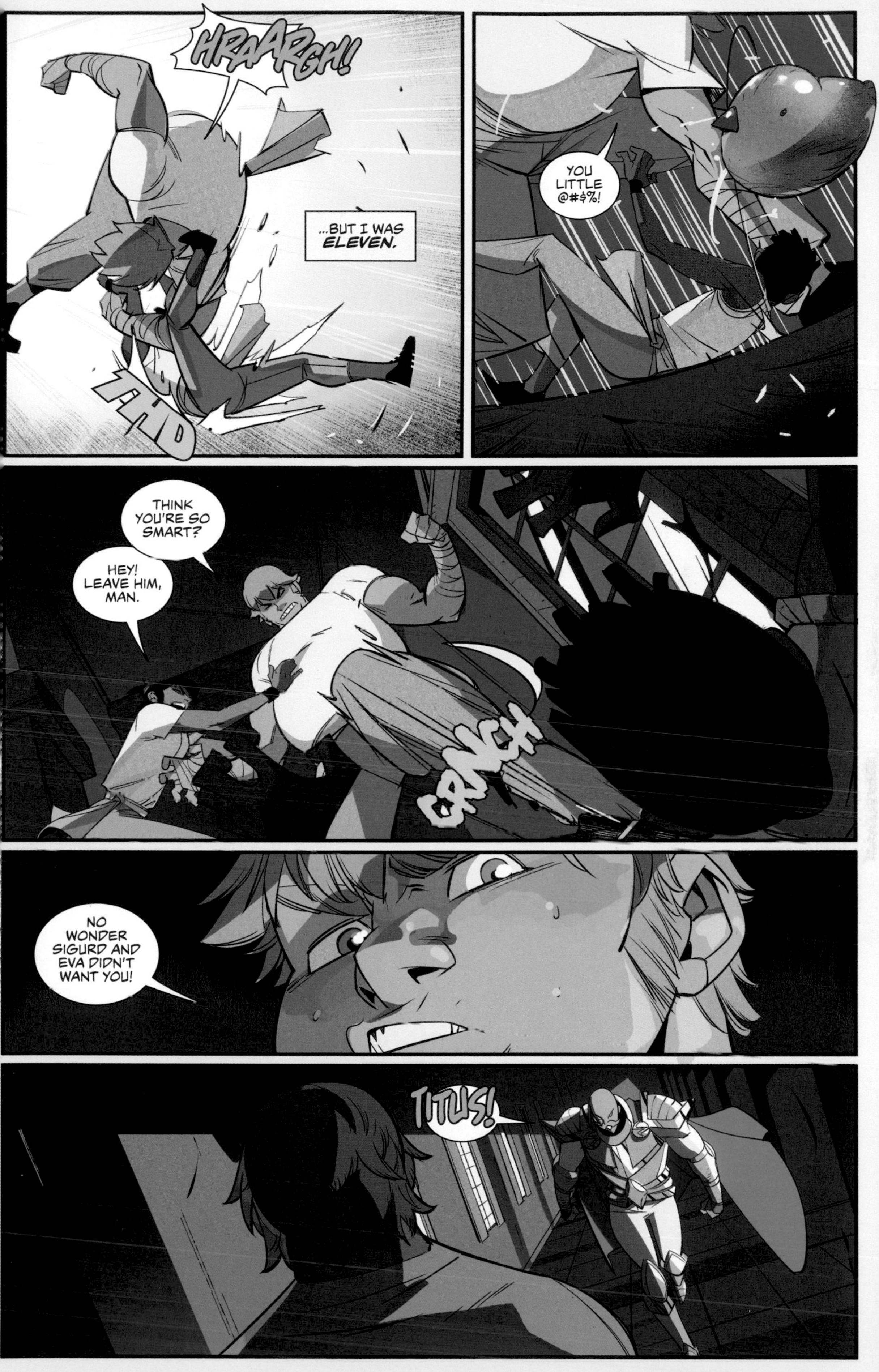
HRAARGH!
...BUT I WAS ELEVEN.
THD
YOU LITTLE @#$%!
THINK YOU'RE SO SMART?
HEY! LEAVE HIM, MAN.
CRNCH
NO WONDER SIGURD AND EVA DIDN'T WANT YOU!
TITUS!

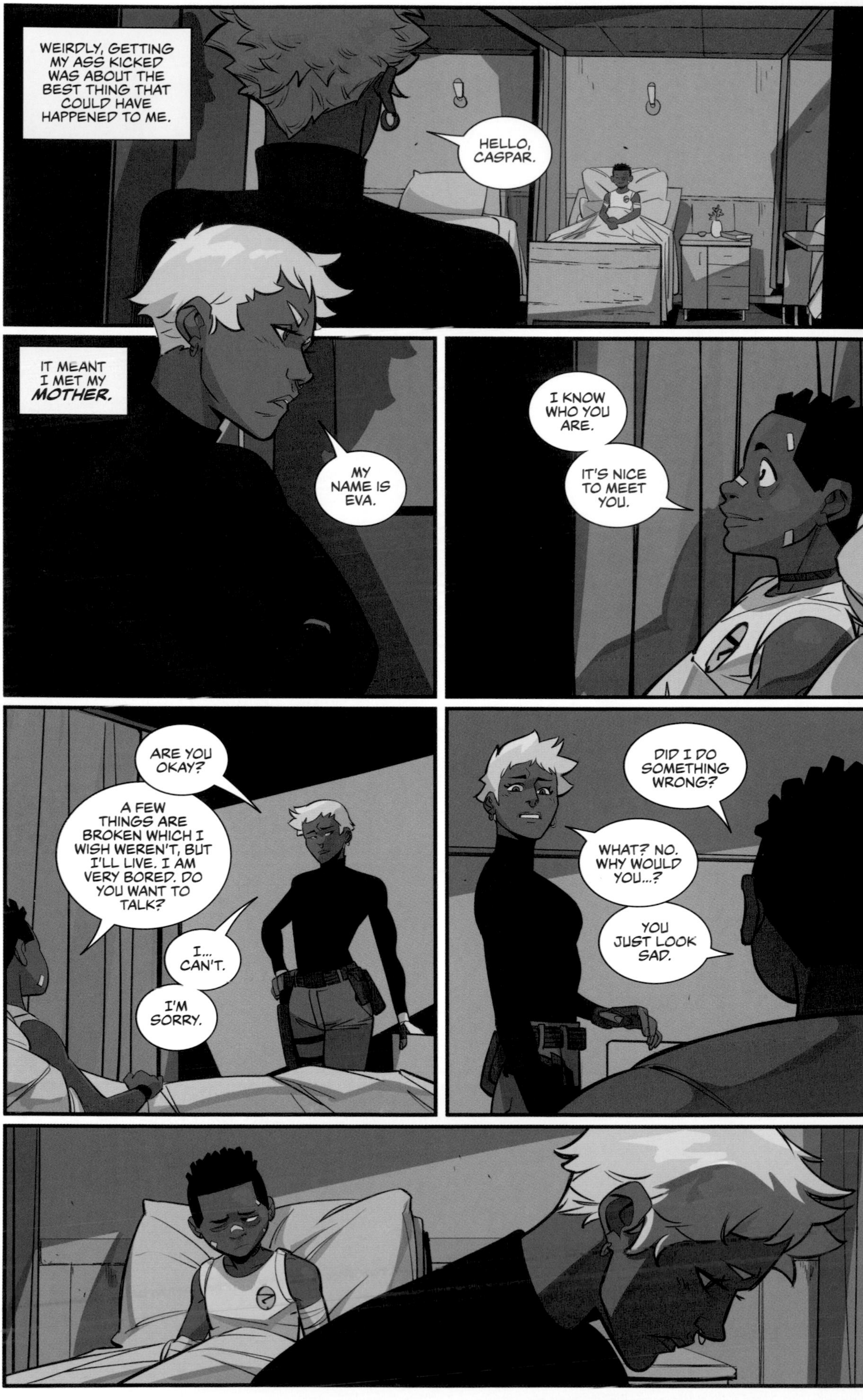
WEIRDLY, GETTING MY ASS KICKED WAS ABOUT THE BEST THING THAT COULD HAVE HAPPENED TO ME.
HELLO, CASPAR.
IT MEANT I MET MY *MOTHER.*
MY NAME IS EVA.
I KNOW WHO YOU ARE.
IT'S NICE TO MEET YOU.
ARE YOU OKAY?
A FEW THINGS ARE BROKEN WHICH I WISH WEREN'T, BUT I'LL LIVE. I AM VERY BORED. DO YOU WANT TO TALK?
I... CAN'T.
I'M SORRY.
DID I DO SOMETHING WRONG?
WHAT? NO. WHY WOULD YOU...?
YOU JUST LOOK SAD.

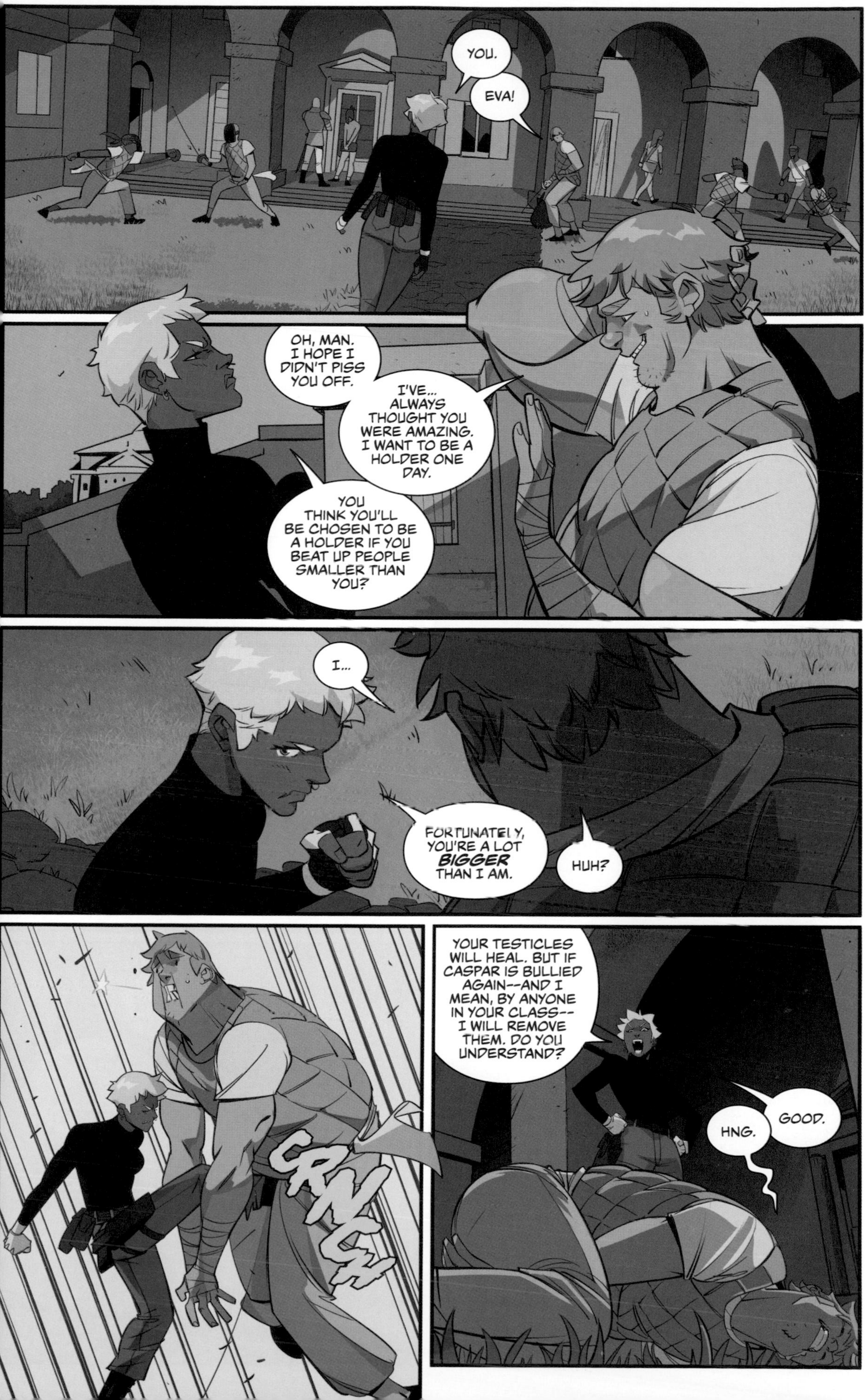
YOU.
EVA!
OH, MAN. I HOPE I DIDN'T PISS YOU OFF.
I'VE... ALWAYS THOUGHT YOU WERE AMAZING. I WANT TO BE A HOLDER ONE DAY.
YOU THINK YOU'LL BE CHOSEN TO BE A HOLDER IF YOU BEAT UP PEOPLE SMALLER THAN YOU?
I...
FORTUNATELY, YOU'RE A LOT ***BIGGER*** THAN I AM.
HUH?
CRNCH
YOUR TESTICLES WILL HEAL. BUT IF CASPAR IS BULLIED AGAIN--AND I MEAN, BY ANYONE IN YOUR CLASS--I WILL REMOVE THEM. DO YOU UNDERSTAND?
HNG.
GOOD.

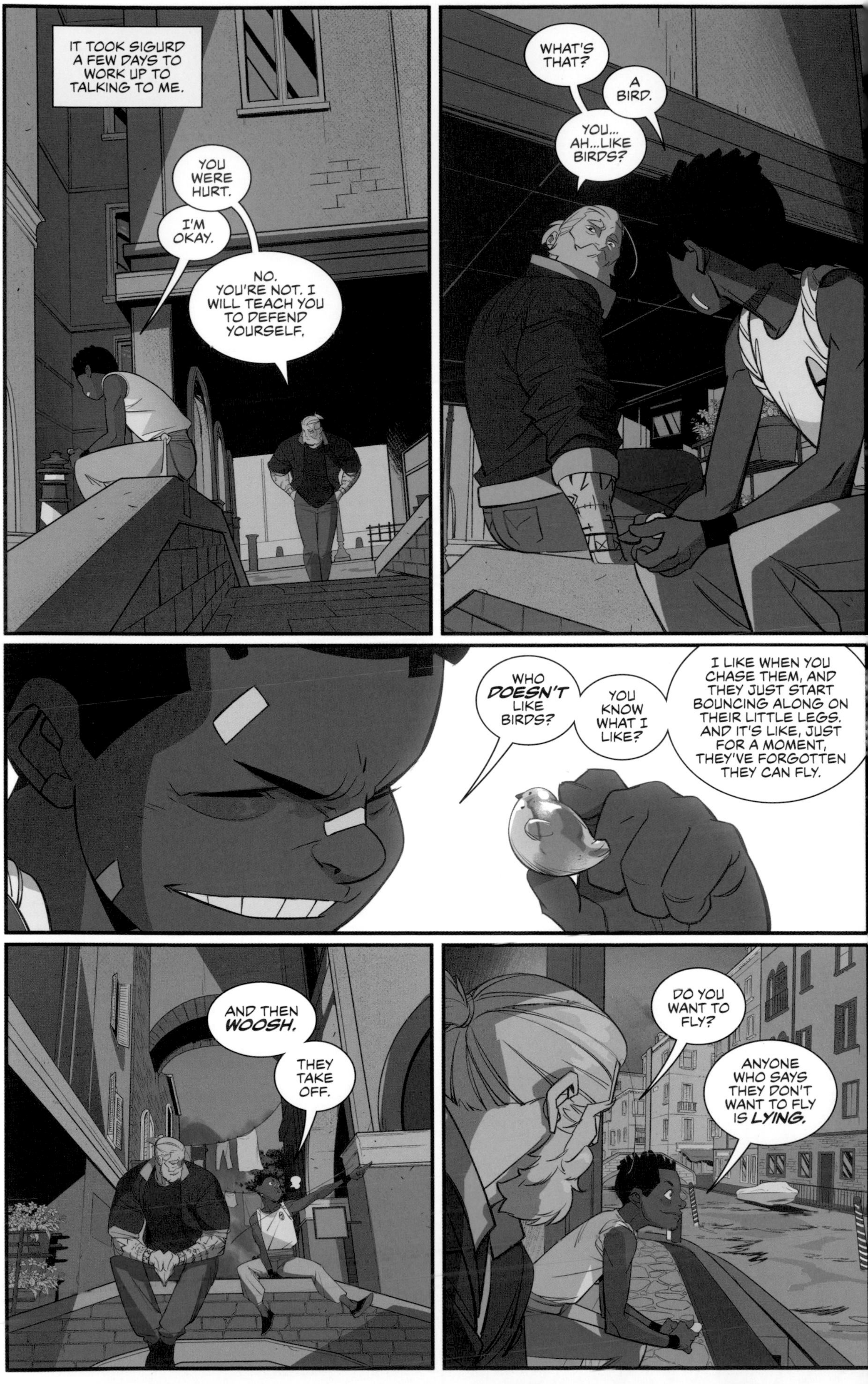
IT TOOK SIGURD A FEW DAYS TO WORK UP TO TALKING TO ME.
YOU WERE HURT.
I'M OKAY.
NO. YOU'RE NOT. I WILL TEACH YOU TO DEFEND YOURSELF.
WHAT'S THAT?
A BIRD.
YOU... AH...LIKE BIRDS?
WHO *DOESN'T* LIKE BIRDS?
YOU KNOW WHAT I LIKE?
I LIKE WHEN YOU CHASE THEM, AND THEY JUST START BOUNCING ALONG ON THEIR LITTLE LEGS. AND IT'S LIKE, JUST FOR A MOMENT, THEY'VE FORGOTTEN THEY CAN FLY.
AND THEN *WOOSH.*
THEY TAKE OFF.
DO YOU WANT TO FLY?
ANYONE WHO SAYS THEY DON'T WANT TO FLY IS *LYING.*

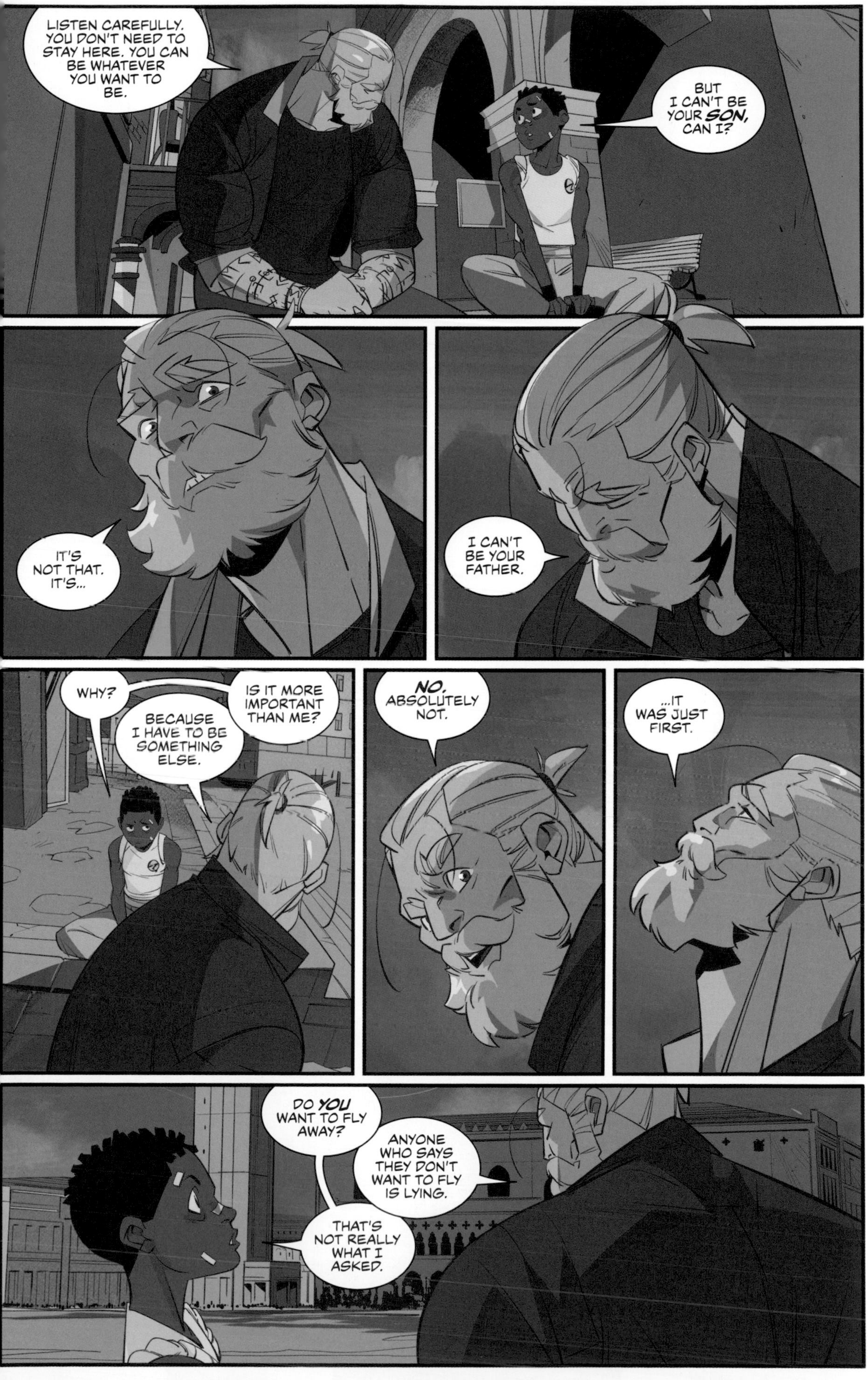
LISTEN CAREFULLY. YOU DON'T NEED TO STAY HERE. YOU CAN BE WHATEVER YOU WANT TO BE.
BUT I CAN'T BE YOUR *SON,* CAN I?
IT'S NOT THAT. IT'S...
I CAN'T BE YOUR FATHER.
WHY?
IS IT MORE IMPORTANT THAN ME?
BECAUSE I HAVE TO BE SOMETHING ELSE.
NO. ABSOLUTELY NOT.
...IT WAS JUST FIRST.
DO *YOU* WANT TO FLY AWAY?
ANYONE WHO SAYS THEY DON'T WANT TO FLY IS LYING.
THAT'S NOT REALLY WHAT I ASKED.

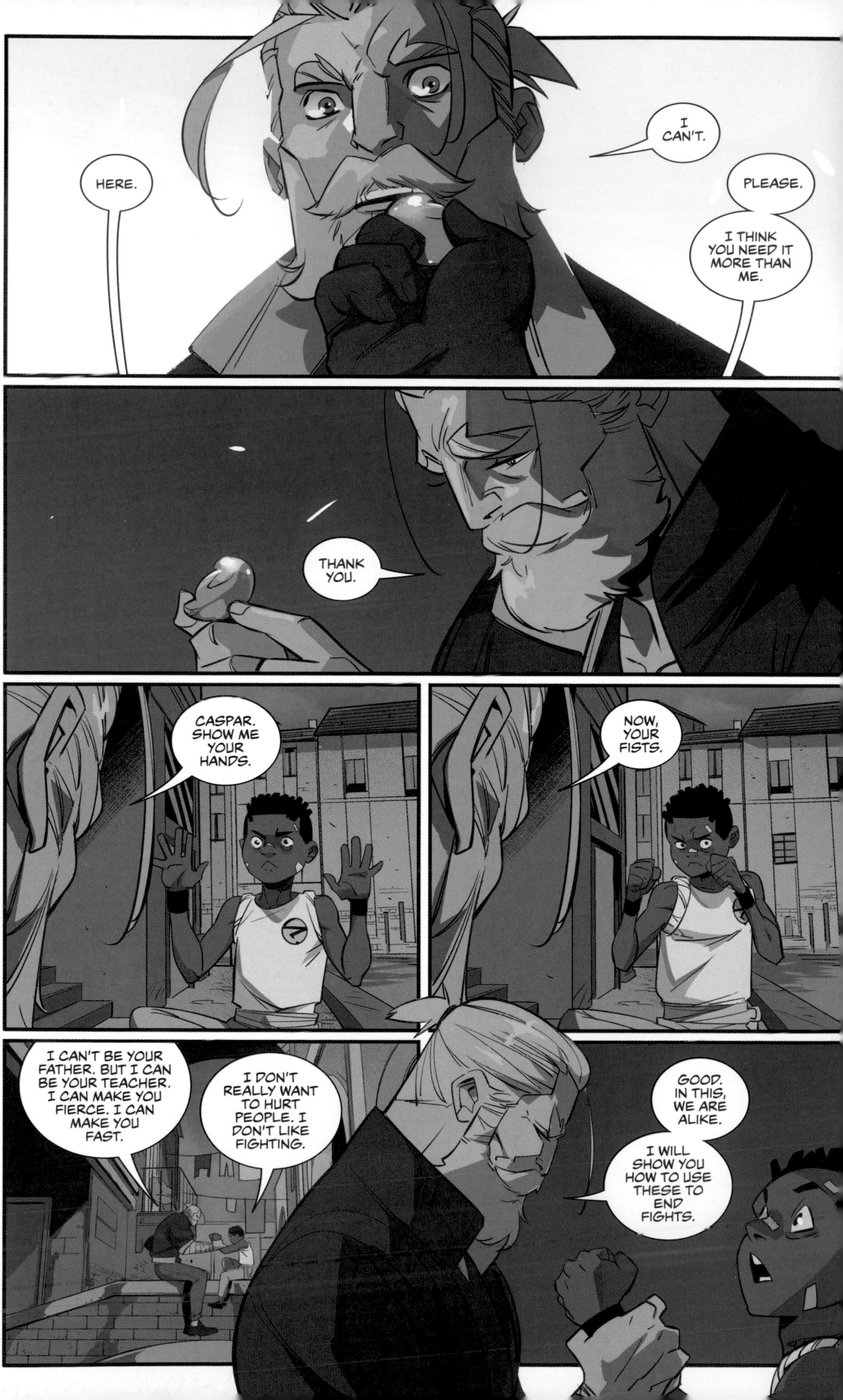
HERE.
I CAN'T.
PLEASE.
I THINK YOU NEED IT MORE THAN ME.
THANK YOU.
CASPAR. SHOW ME YOUR HANDS.
NOW, YOUR FISTS.
I CAN'T BE YOUR FATHER. BUT I CAN BE YOUR TEACHER. I CAN MAKE YOU FIERCE. I CAN MAKE YOU FAST.
I DON'T REALLY WANT TO HURT PEOPLE. I DON'T LIKE FIGHTING.
GOOD. IN THIS, WE ARE ALIKE.
I WILL SHOW YOU HOW TO USE THESE TO END FIGHTS.

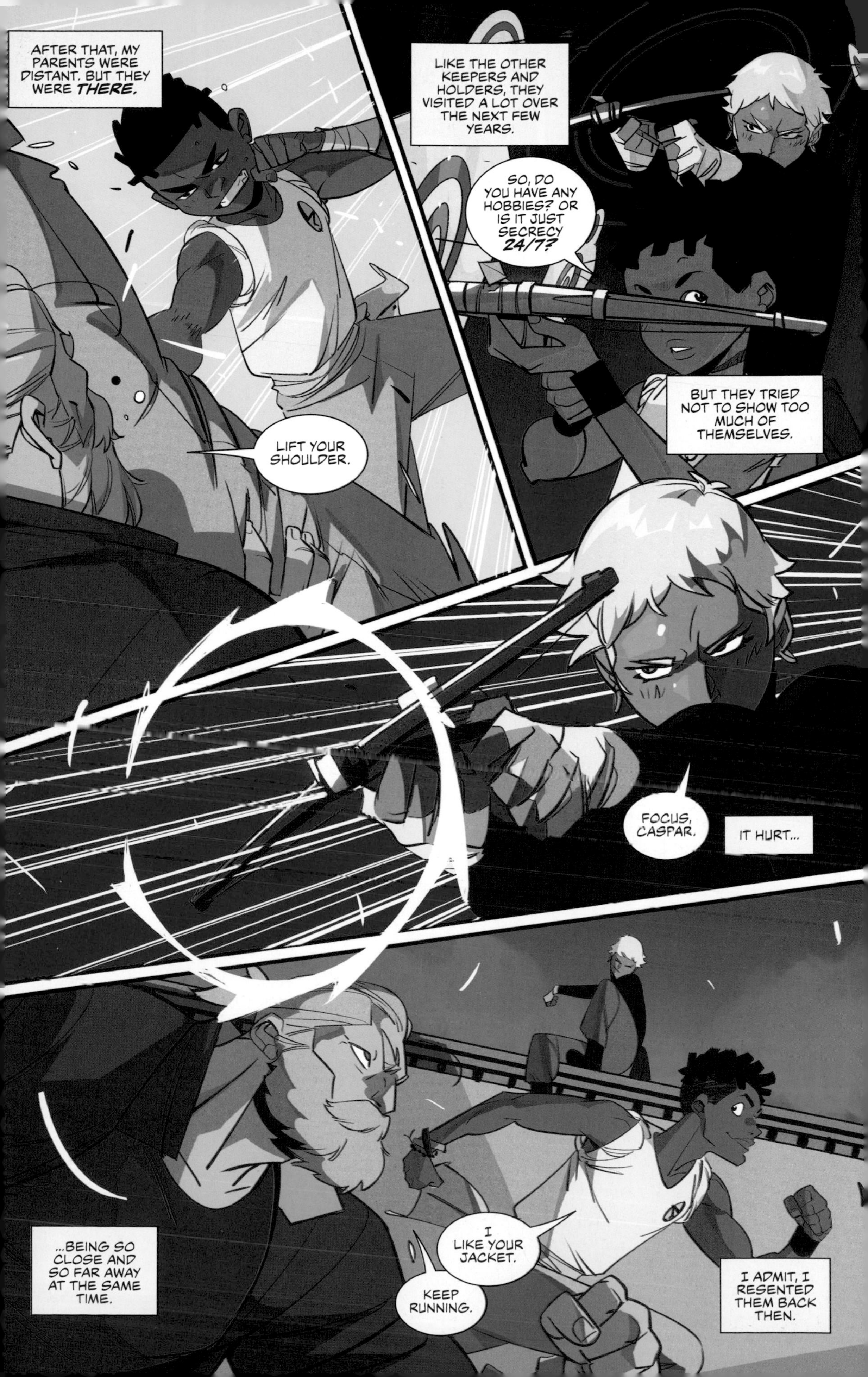
AFTER THAT, MY PARENTS WERE DISTANT. BUT THEY WERE THERE.
LIFT YOUR SHOULDER.
LIKE THE OTHER KEEPERS AND HOLDERS, THEY VISITED A LOT OVER THE NEXT FEW YEARS.
SO, DO YOU HAVE ANY HOBBIES? OR IS IT JUST SECRECY 24/7?
BUT THEY TRIED NOT TO SHOW TOO MUCH OF THEMSELVES.
FOCUS, CASPAR.
IT HURT...
...BEING SO CLOSE AND SO FAR AWAY AT THE SAME TIME.
I LIKE YOUR JACKET.
KEEP RUNNING.
I ADMIT, I RESENTED THEM BACK THEN.

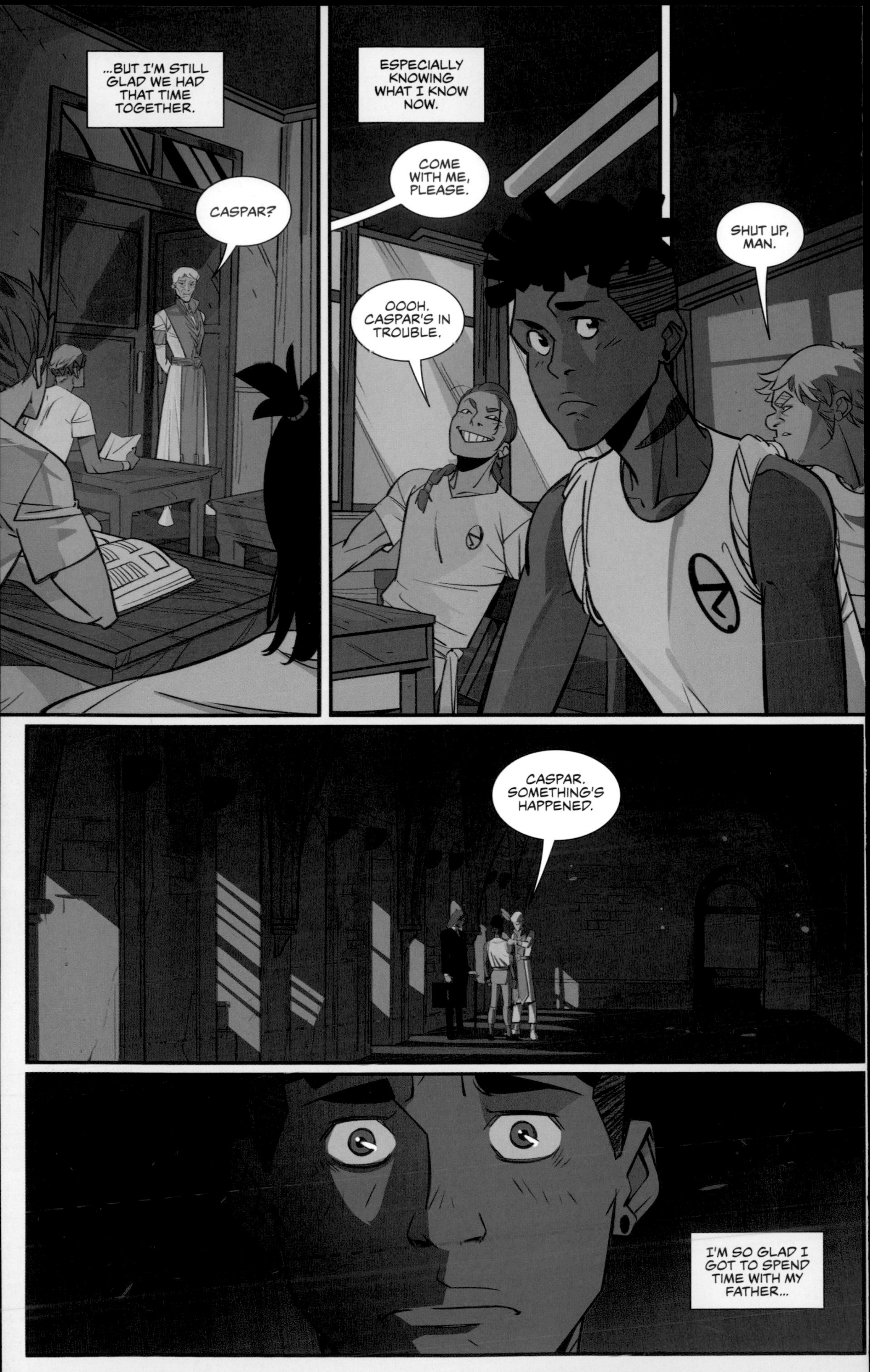
...BUT I'M STILL GLAD WE HAD THAT TIME TOGETHER.
CASPAR?
ESPECIALLY KNOWING WHAT I KNOW NOW.
COME WITH ME, PLEASE.
OOOH. CASPAR'S IN TROUBLE.
SHUT UP, MAN.
CASPAR. SOMETHING'S HAPPENED.
I'M SO GLAD I GOT TO SPEND TIME WITH MY FATHER...

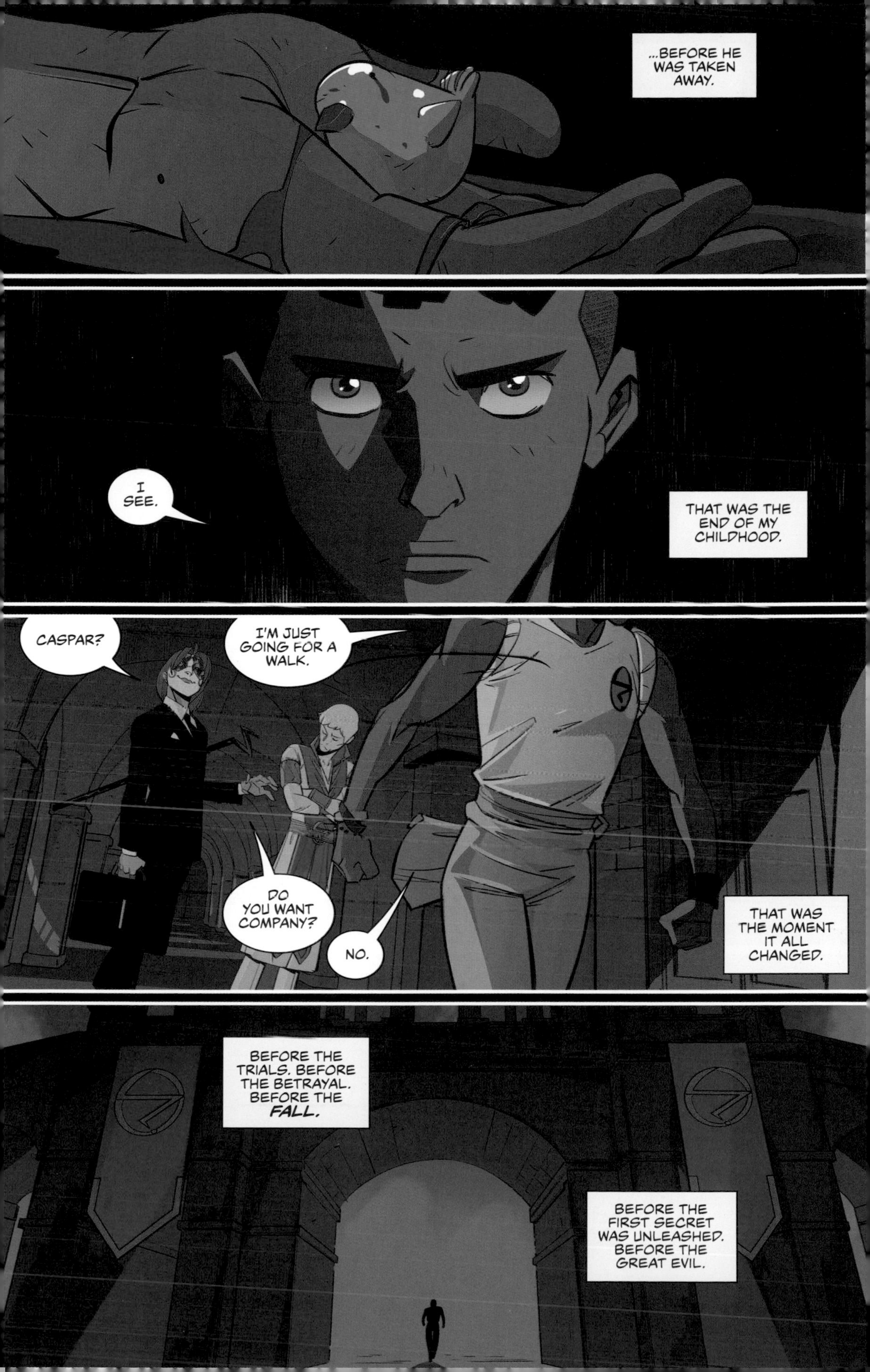
...BEFORE HE WAS TAKEN AWAY.
I SEE.
THAT WAS THE END OF MY CHILDHOOD.
CASPAR?
I'M JUST GOING FOR A WALK.
DO YOU WANT COMPANY?
NO.
THAT WAS THE MOMENT IT ALL CHANGED.
BEFORE THE TRIALS. BEFORE THE BETRAYAL. BEFORE THE FALL.
BEFORE THE FIRST SECRET WAS UNLEASHED. BEFORE THE GREAT EVIL.

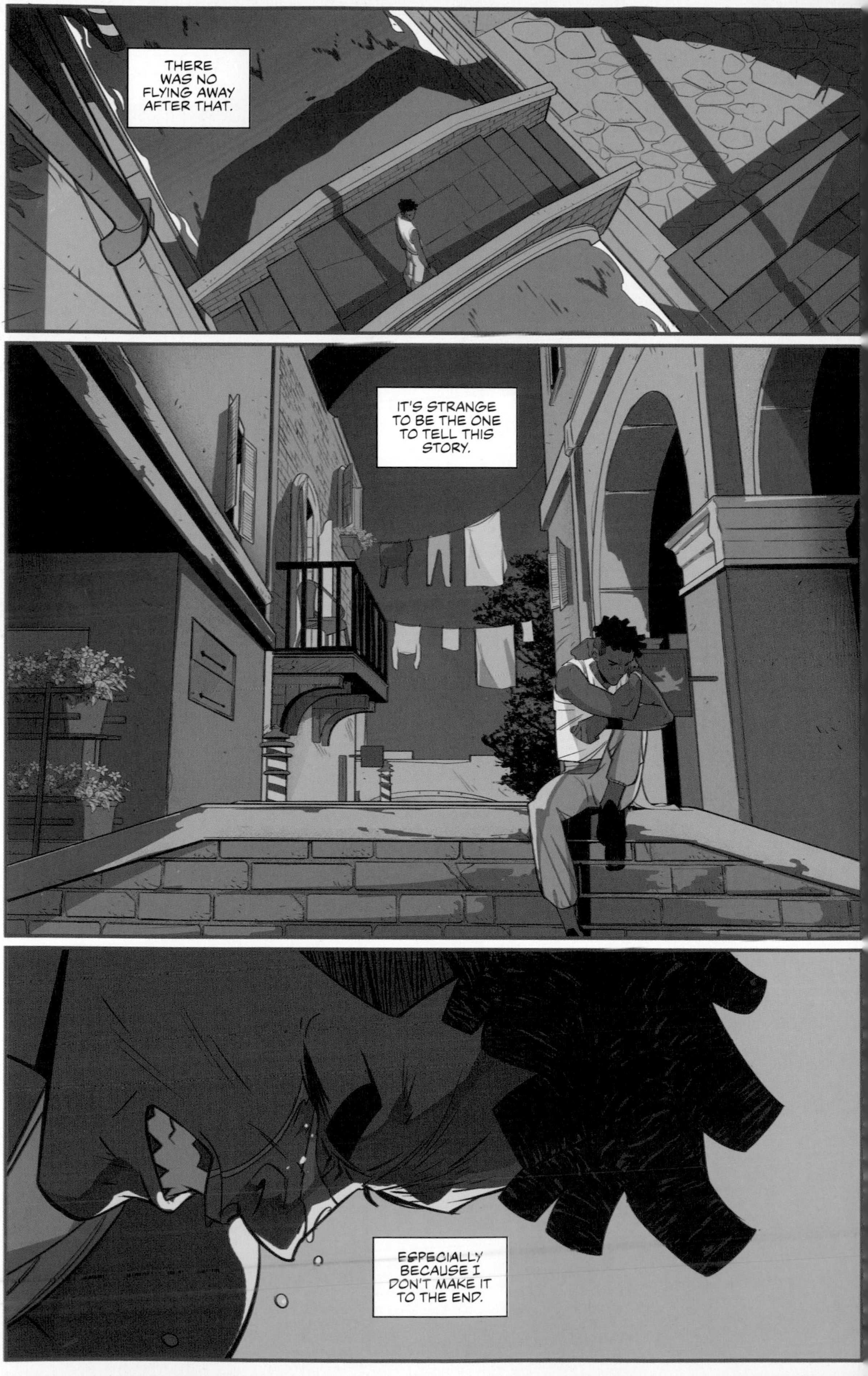
THERE WAS NO FLYING AWAY AFTER THAT.
IT'S STRANGE TO BE THE ONE TO TELL THIS STORY.
ESPECIALLY BECAUSE I DON'T MAKE IT TO THE END.

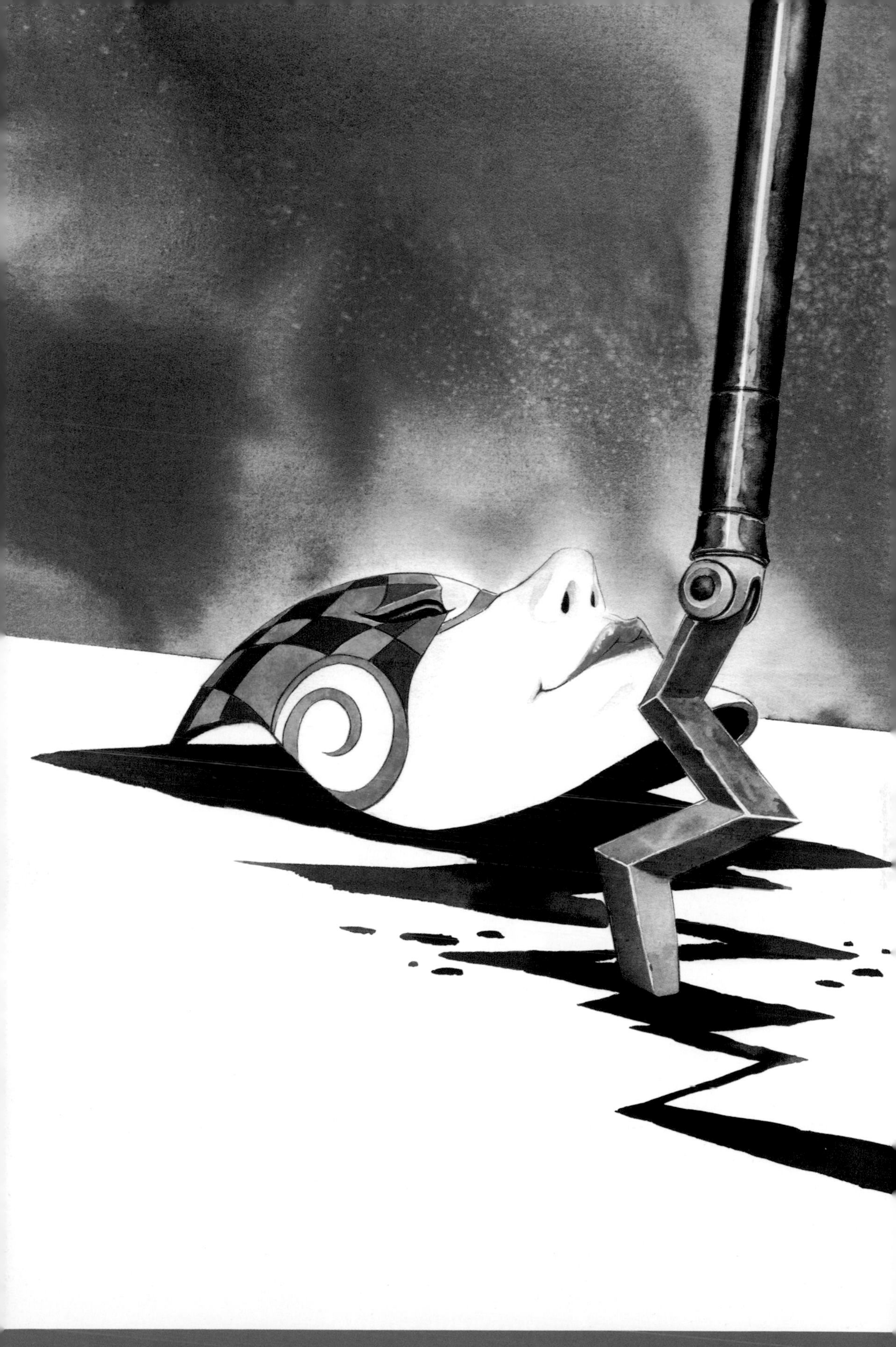

DUSTIN NGYUEN ISSUE TWO VARIANT COVER

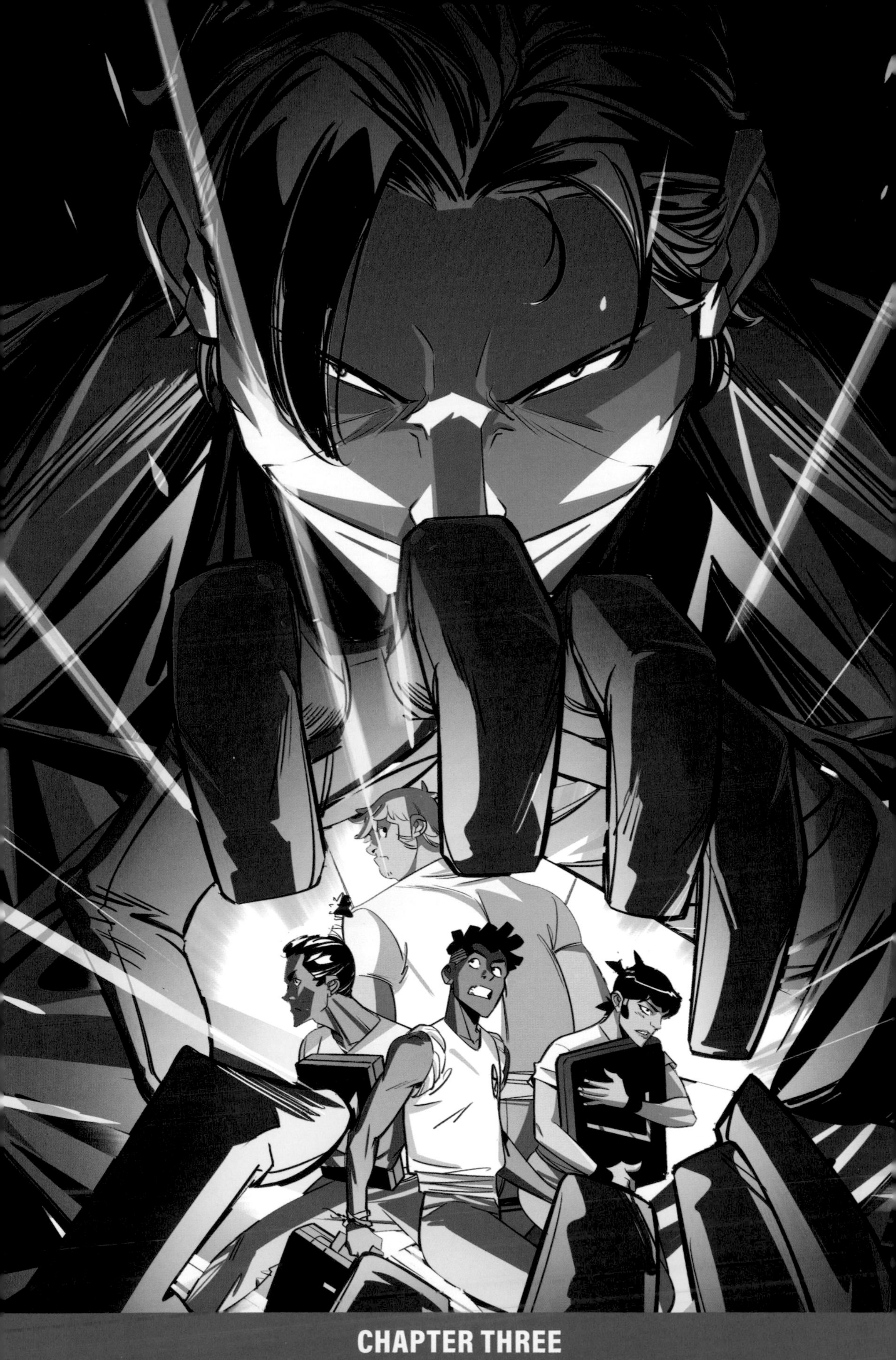

CHAPTER THREE

DANIELE DI NICUOLO ISSUE THREE COVER

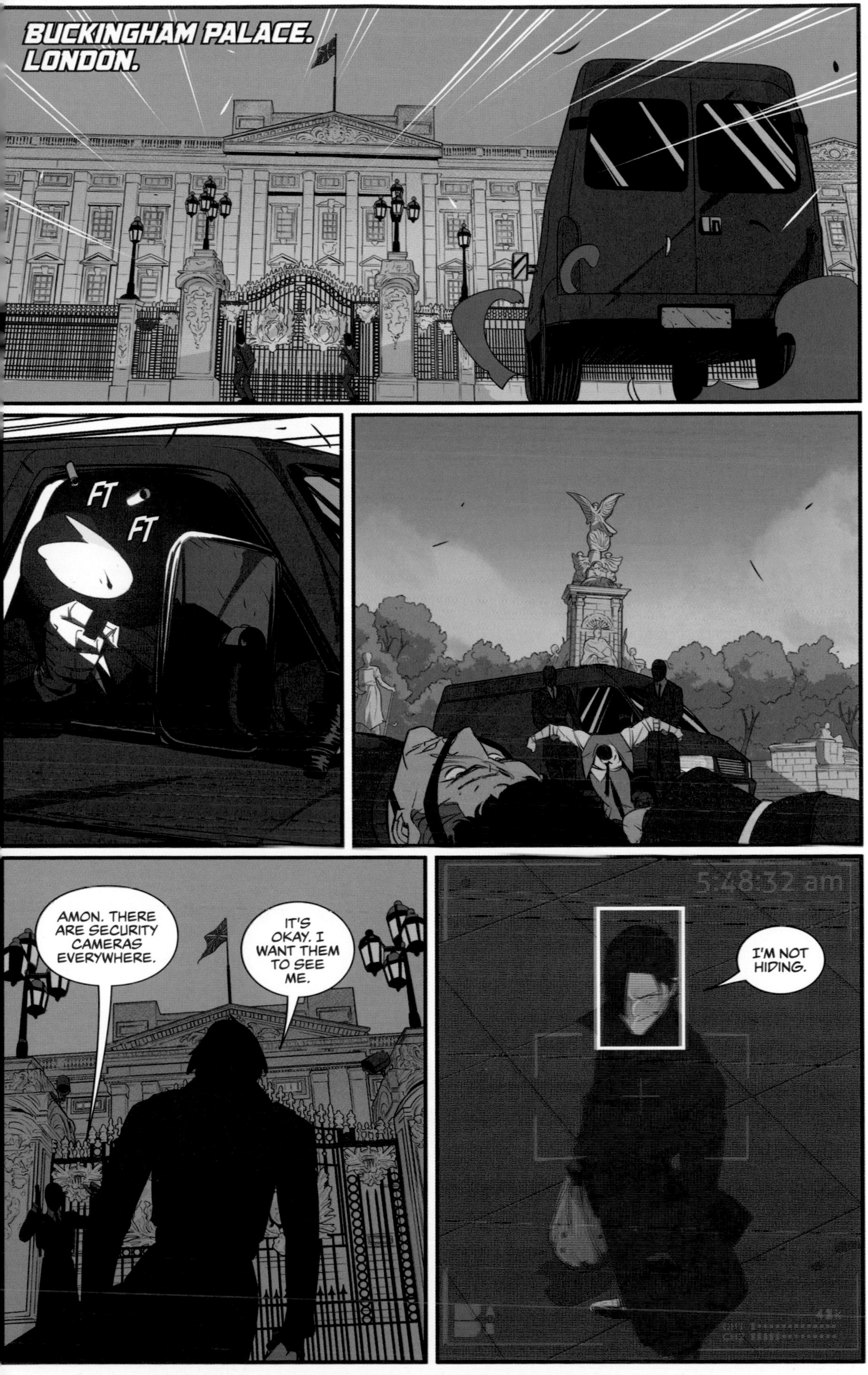
BUCKINGHAM PALACE. LONDON.
FT
FT
AMON. THERE ARE SECURITY CAMERAS EVERYWHERE.
IT'S OKAY. I WANT THEM TO SEE ME.
5:48:32 am
I'M NOT HIDING.

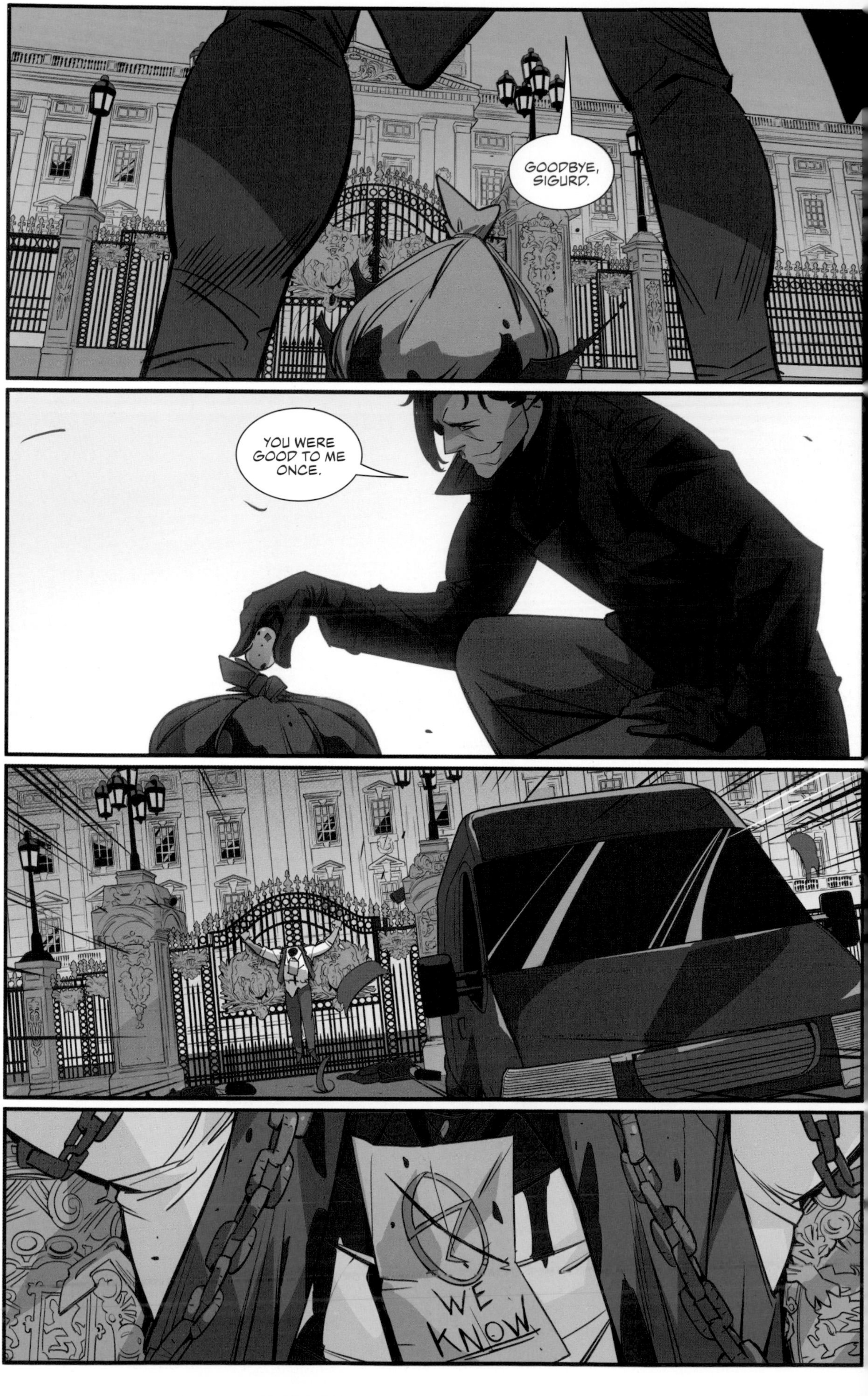
GOODBYE, SIGURD.
YOU WERE GOOD TO ME ONCE.
WE KNOW

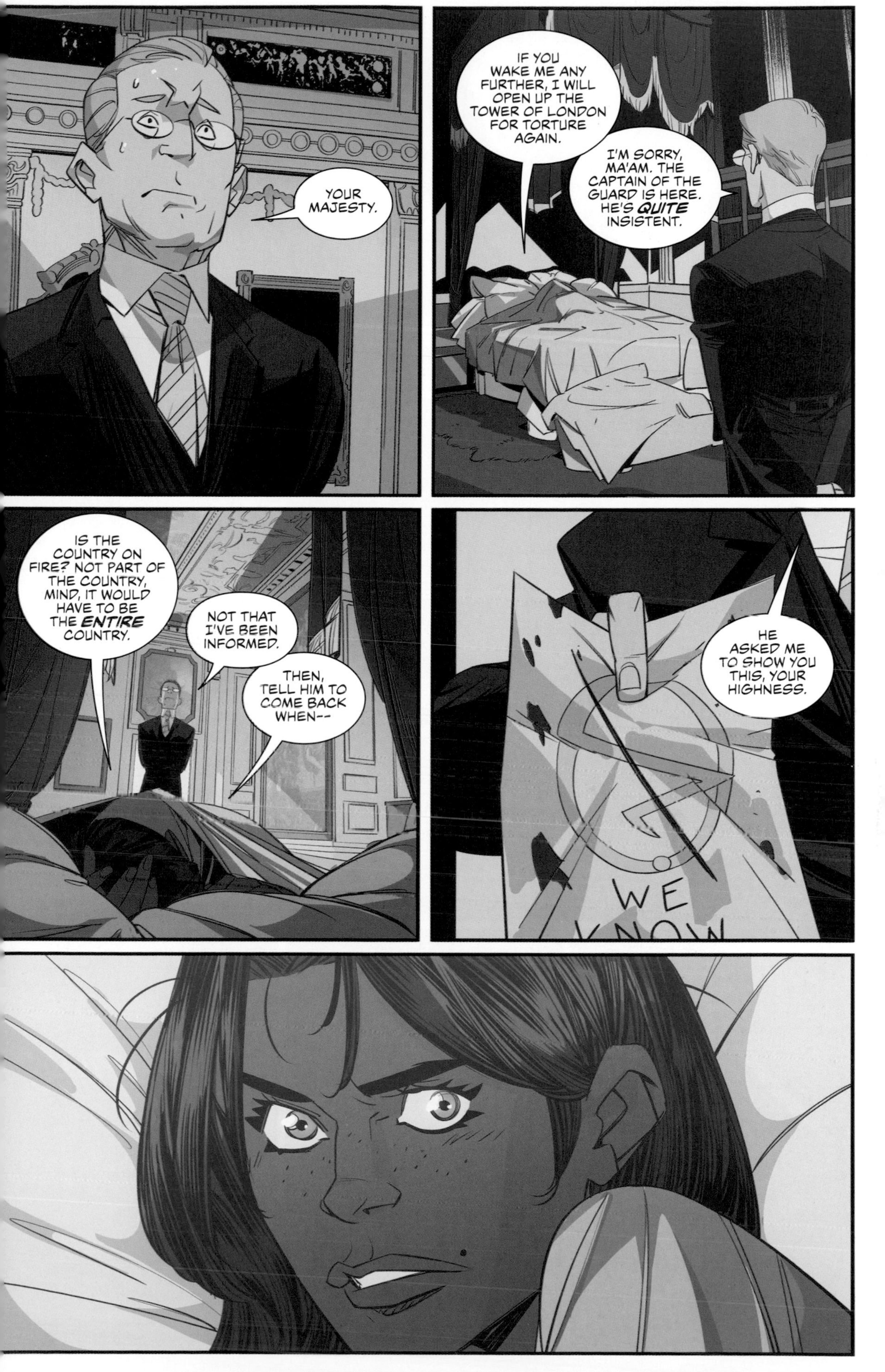
YOUR MAJESTY.
IF YOU WAKE ME ANY FURTHER, I WILL OPEN UP THE TOWER OF LONDON FOR TORTURE AGAIN.
I'M SORRY, MA'AM. THE CAPTAIN OF THE GUARD IS HERE. HE'S *QUITE* INSISTENT.
IS THE COUNTRY ON FIRE? NOT PART OF THE COUNTRY, MIND, IT WOULD HAVE TO BE THE *ENTIRE* COUNTRY.
NOT THAT I'VE BEEN INFORMED.
THEN, TELL HIM TO COME BACK WHEN--
HE ASKED ME TO SHOW YOU THIS, YOUR HIGHNESS.
WE

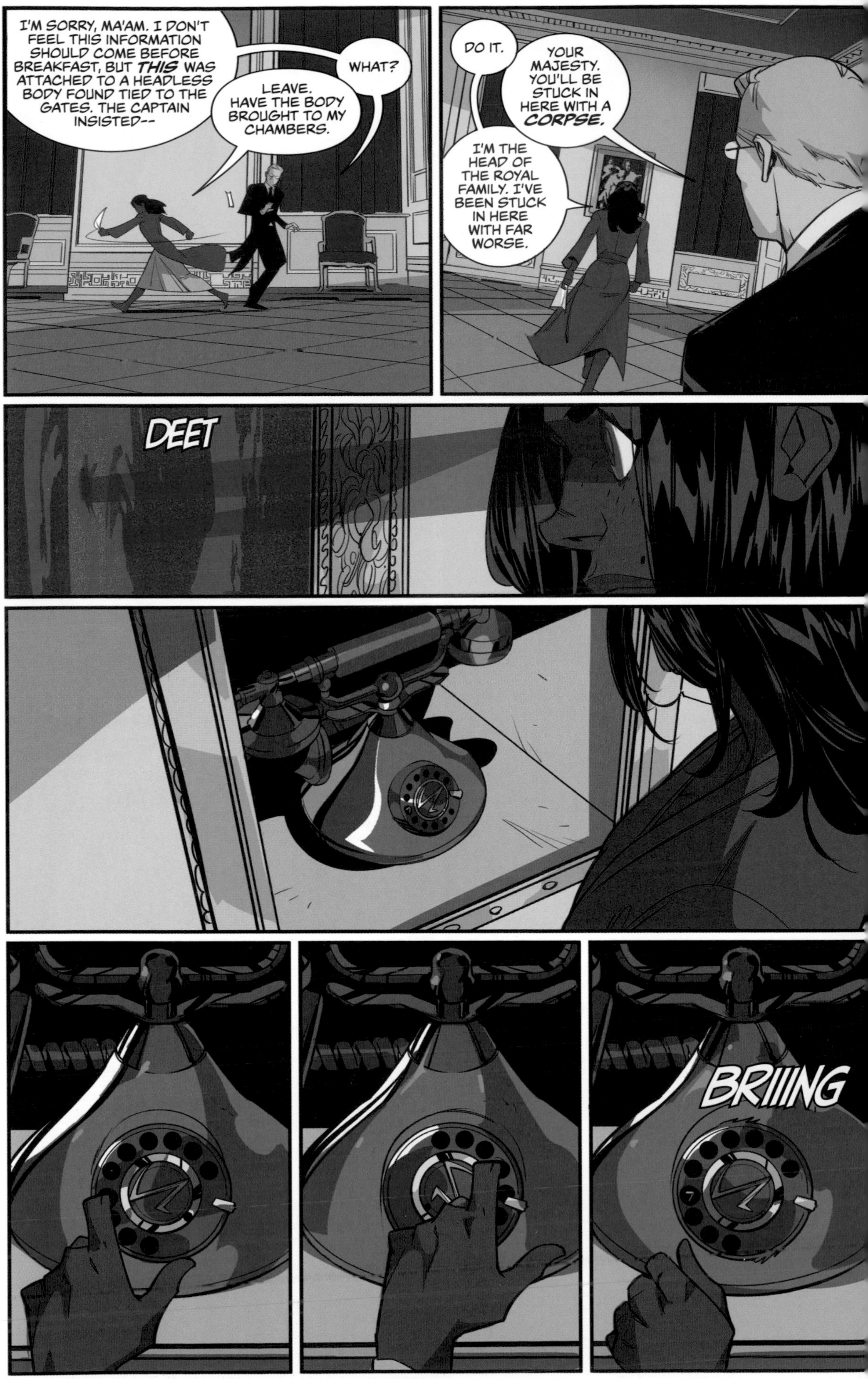
I'M SORRY, MA'AM. I DON'T FEEL THIS INFORMATION SHOULD COME BEFORE BREAKFAST, BUT THIS WAS ATTACHED TO A HEADLESS BODY FOUND TIED TO THE GATES. THE CAPTAIN INSISTED--
WHAT?
LEAVE. HAVE THE BODY BROUGHT TO MY CHAMBERS.
YOUR MAJESTY. YOU'LL BE STUCK IN HERE WITH A CORPSE.
DO IT.
I'M THE HEAD OF THE ROYAL FAMILY. I'VE BEEN STUCK IN HERE WITH FAR WORSE.
DEET
BRIIING

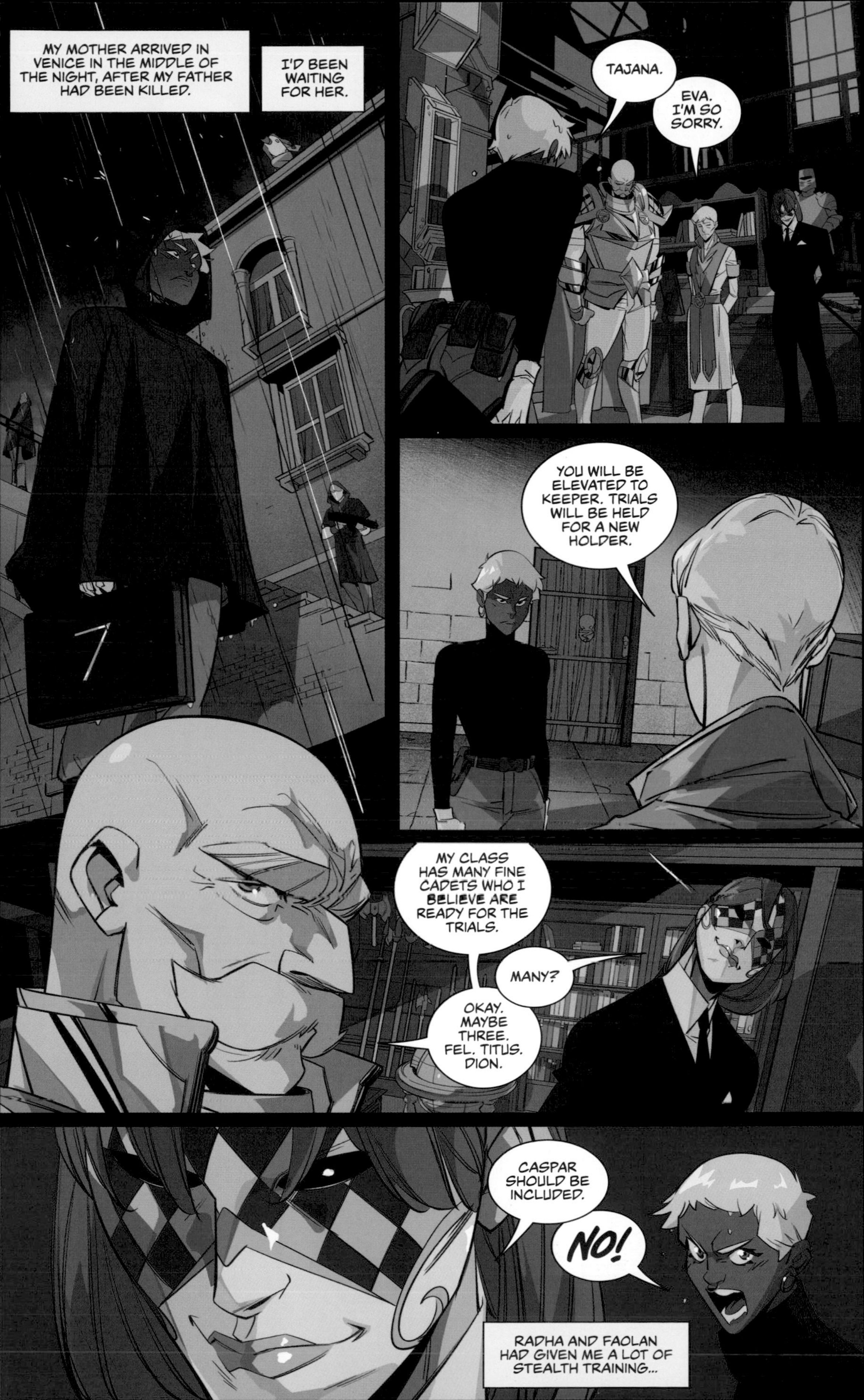
MY MOTHER ARRIVED IN VENICE IN THE MIDDLE OF THE NIGHT, AFTER MY FATHER HAD BEEN KILLED.
I'D BEEN WAITING FOR HER.
TAJANA.
EVA. I'M SO SORRY.
YOU WILL BE ELEVATED TO KEEPER. TRIALS WILL BE HELD FOR A NEW HOLDER.
MY CLASS HAS MANY FINE CADETS WHO I BELIEVE ARE READY FOR THE TRIALS.
MANY?
OKAY. MAYBE THREE. FEL. TITUS. DION.
CASPAR SHOULD BE INCLUDED.
NO!
RADHA AND FAOLAN HAD GIVEN ME A LOT OF STEALTH TRAINING...

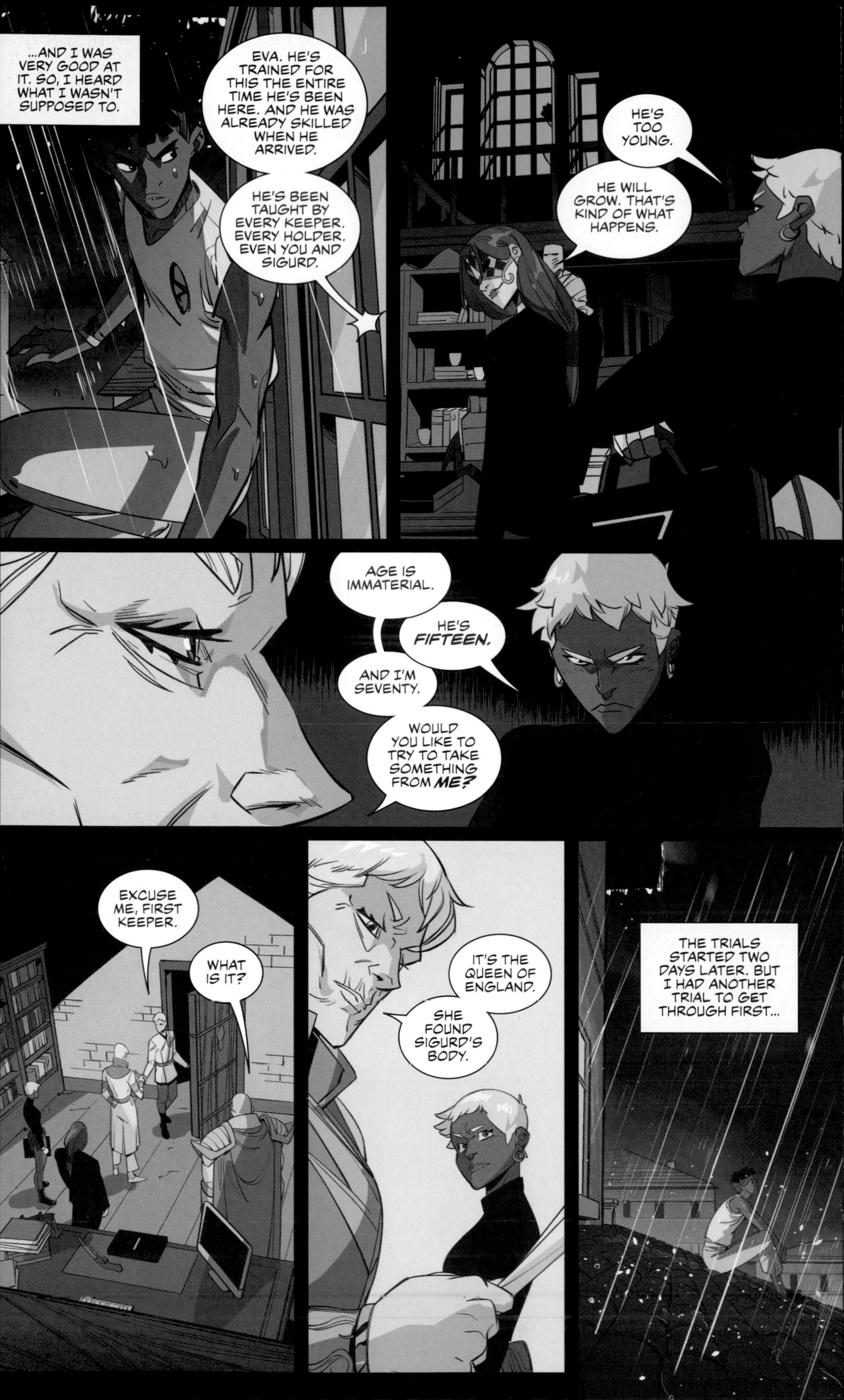
...AND I WAS VERY GOOD AT IT. SO, I HEARD WHAT I WASN'T SUPPOSED TO.
EVA. HE'S TRAINED FOR THIS THE ENTIRE TIME HE'S BEEN HERE. AND HE WAS ALREADY SKILLED WHEN HE ARRIVED.
HE'S BEEN TAUGHT BY EVERY KEEPER. EVERY HOLDER. EVEN YOU AND SIGURD.
HE'S TOO YOUNG.
HE WILL GROW. THAT'S KIND OF WHAT HAPPENS.
AGE IS IMMATERIAL.
HE'S *FIFTEEN.*
AND I'M SEVENTY.
WOULD YOU LIKE TO TRY TO TAKE SOMETHING FROM *ME?*
EXCUSE ME, FIRST KEEPER.
WHAT IS IT?
IT'S THE QUEEN OF ENGLAND.
SHE FOUND SIGURD'S BODY.
THE TRIALS STARTED TWO DAYS LATER. BUT I HAD ANOTHER TRIAL TO GET THROUGH FIRST...

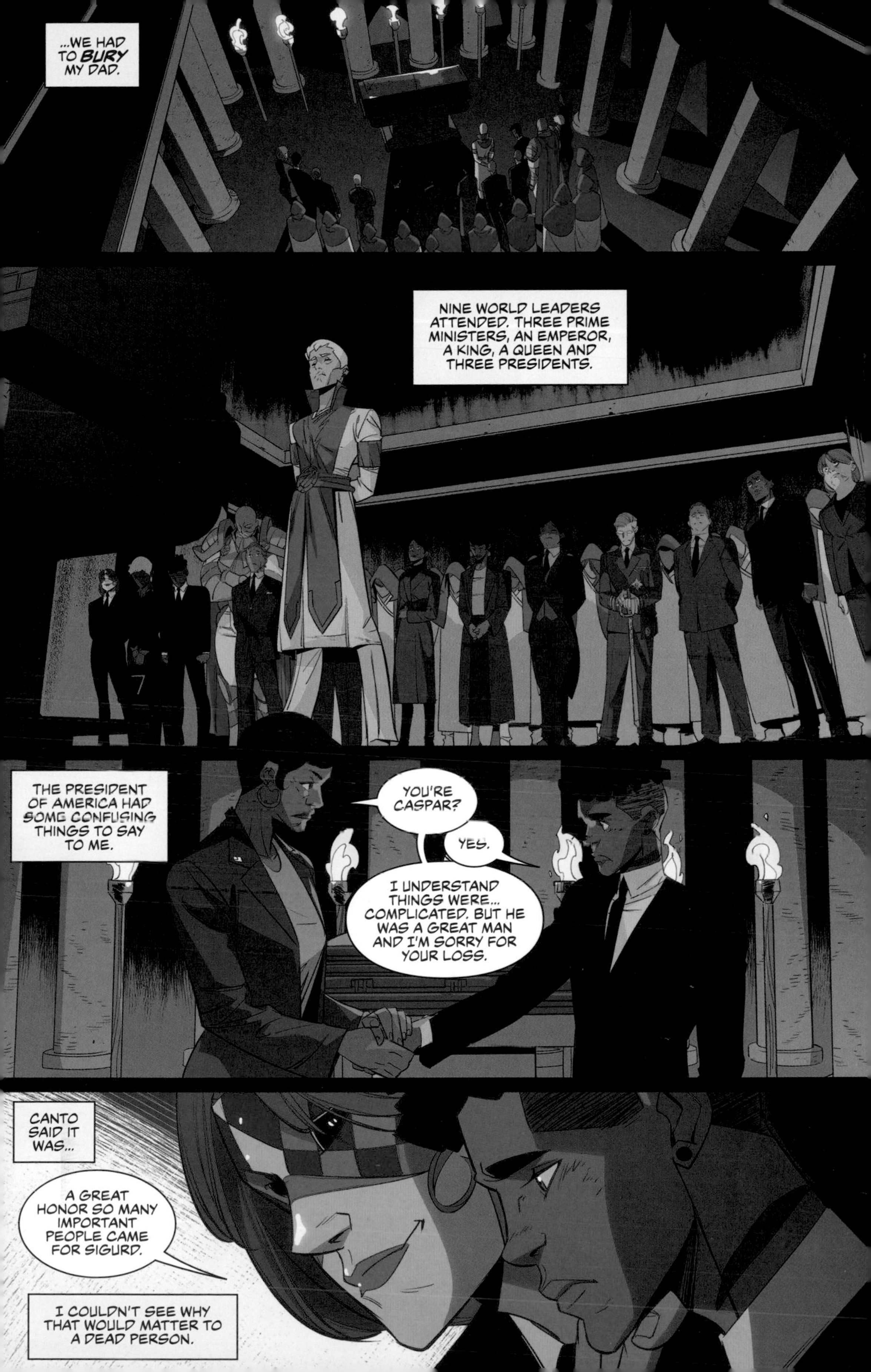
...WE HAD TO BURY MY DAD.
NINE WORLD LEADERS ATTENDED. THREE PRIME MINISTERS, AN EMPEROR, A KING, A QUEEN AND THREE PRESIDENTS.
THE PRESIDENT OF AMERICA HAD SOME CONFUSING THINGS TO SAY TO ME.
YOU'RE CASPAR?
YES.
I UNDERSTAND THINGS WERE... COMPLICATED. BUT HE WAS A GREAT MAN AND I'M SORRY FOR YOUR LOSS.
CANTO SAID IT WAS...
A GREAT HONOR SO MANY IMPORTANT PEOPLE CAME FOR SIGURD.
I COULDN'T SEE WHY THAT WOULD MATTER TO A DEAD PERSON.

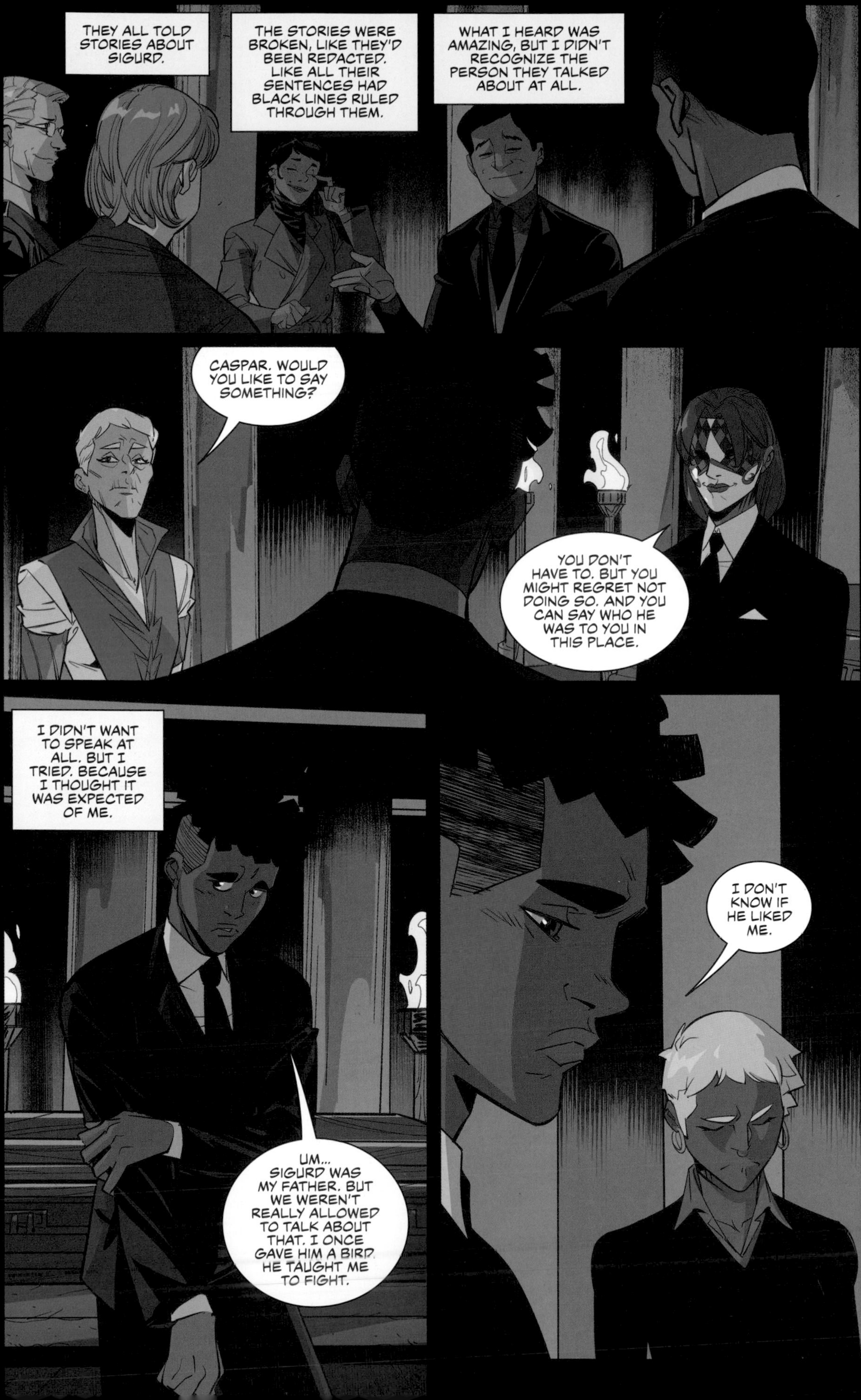
THEY ALL TOLD STORIES ABOUT SIGURD.
THE STORIES WERE BROKEN, LIKE THEY'D BEEN REDACTED. LIKE ALL THEIR SENTENCES HAD BLACK LINES RULED THROUGH THEM.
WHAT I HEARD WAS AMAZING, BUT I DIDN'T RECOGNIZE THE PERSON THEY TALKED ABOUT AT ALL.
CASPAR. WOULD YOU LIKE TO SAY SOMETHING?
YOU DON'T HAVE TO. BUT YOU MIGHT REGRET NOT DOING SO. AND YOU CAN SAY WHO HE WAS TO YOU IN THIS PLACE.
I DIDN'T WANT TO SPEAK AT ALL. BUT I TRIED. BECAUSE I THOUGHT IT WAS EXPECTED OF ME.
UM... SIGURD WAS MY FATHER. BUT WE WEREN'T REALLY ALLOWED TO TALK ABOUT THAT. I ONCE GAVE HIM A BIRD. HE TAUGHT ME TO FIGHT.
I DON'T KNOW IF HE LIKED ME.

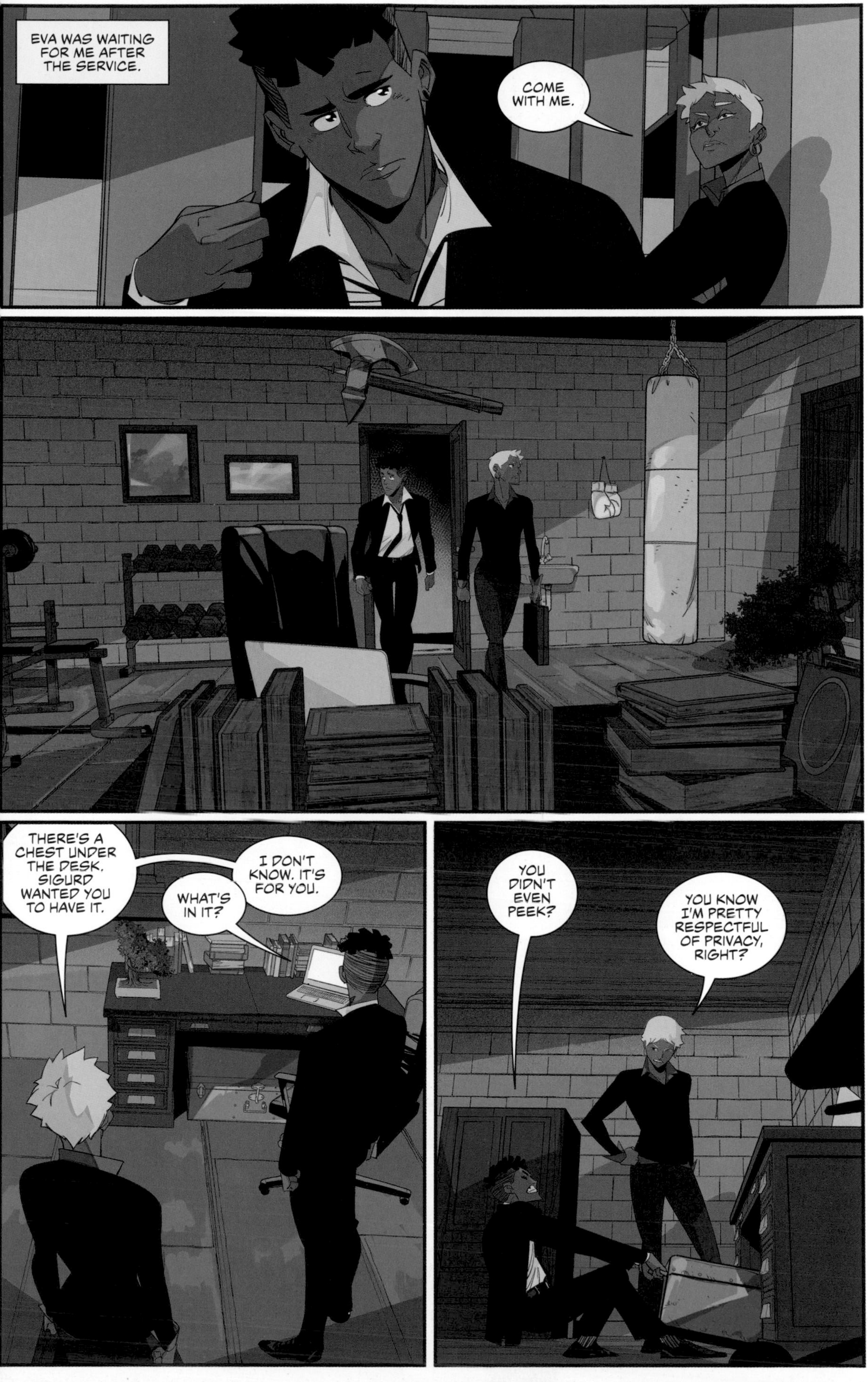
EVA WAS WAITING FOR ME AFTER THE SERVICE.
COME WITH ME.
THERE'S A CHEST UNDER THE DESK. SIGURD WANTED YOU TO HAVE IT.
WHAT'S IN IT?
I DON'T KNOW. IT'S FOR YOU.
YOU DIDN'T EVEN PEEK?
YOU KNOW I'M PRETTY RESPECTFUL OF PRIVACY, RIGHT?

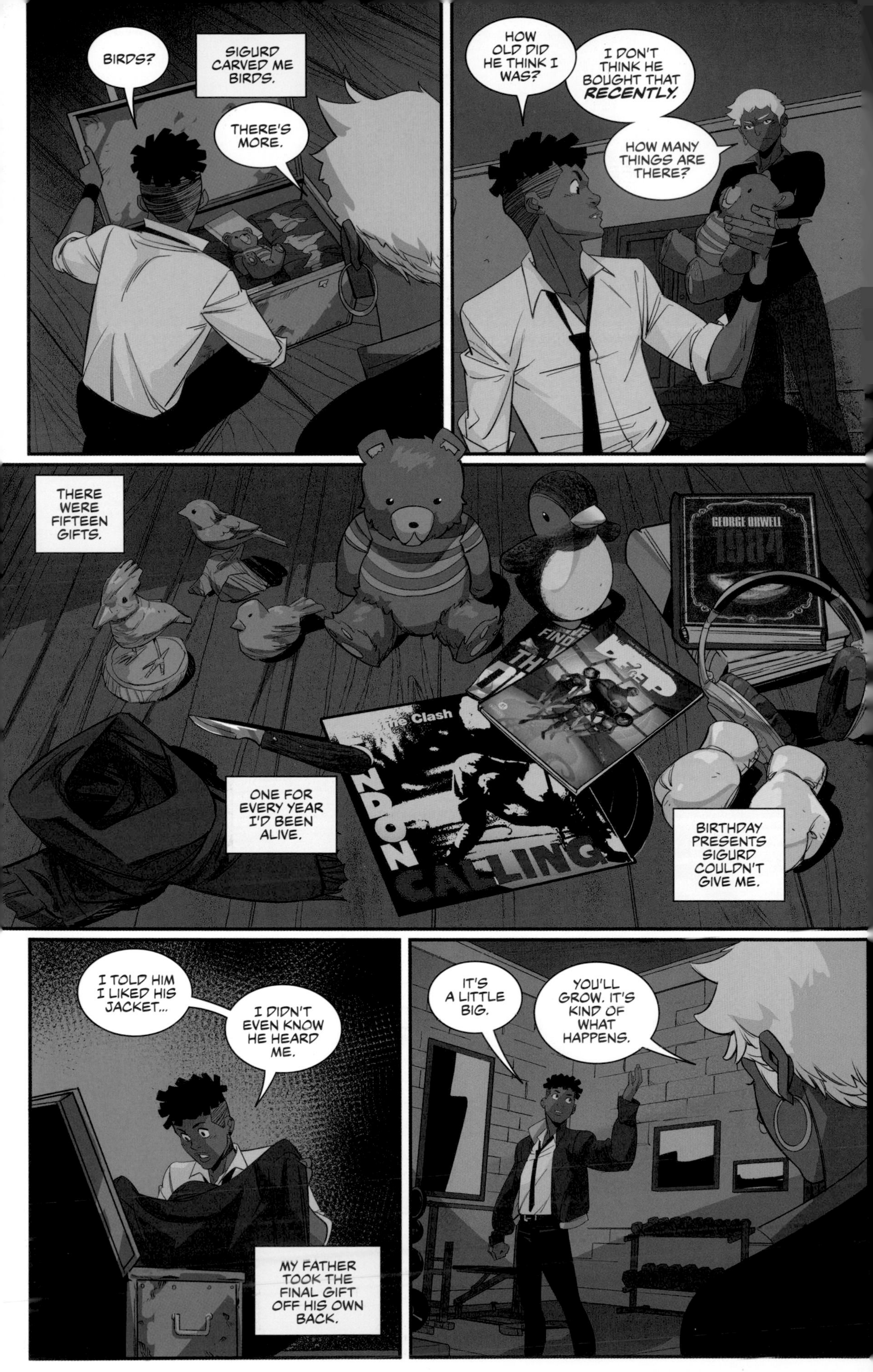
SIGURD CARVED ME BIRDS.
BIRDS?
THERE'S MORE.
HOW OLD DID HE THINK I WAS?
I DON'T THINK HE BOUGHT THAT RECENTLY.
HOW MANY THINGS ARE THERE?
THERE WERE FIFTEEN GIFTS.
GEORGE ORWELL
1984
The Clash
LONDON CALLING
ONE FOR EVERY YEAR I'D BEEN ALIVE.
BIRTHDAY PRESENTS SIGURD COULDN'T GIVE ME.
I TOLD HIM I LIKED HIS JACKET...
I DIDN'T EVEN KNOW HE HEARD ME.
MY FATHER TOOK THE FINAL GIFT OFF HIS OWN BACK.
IT'S A LITTLE BIG.
YOU'LL GROW. IT'S KIND OF WHAT HAPPENS.

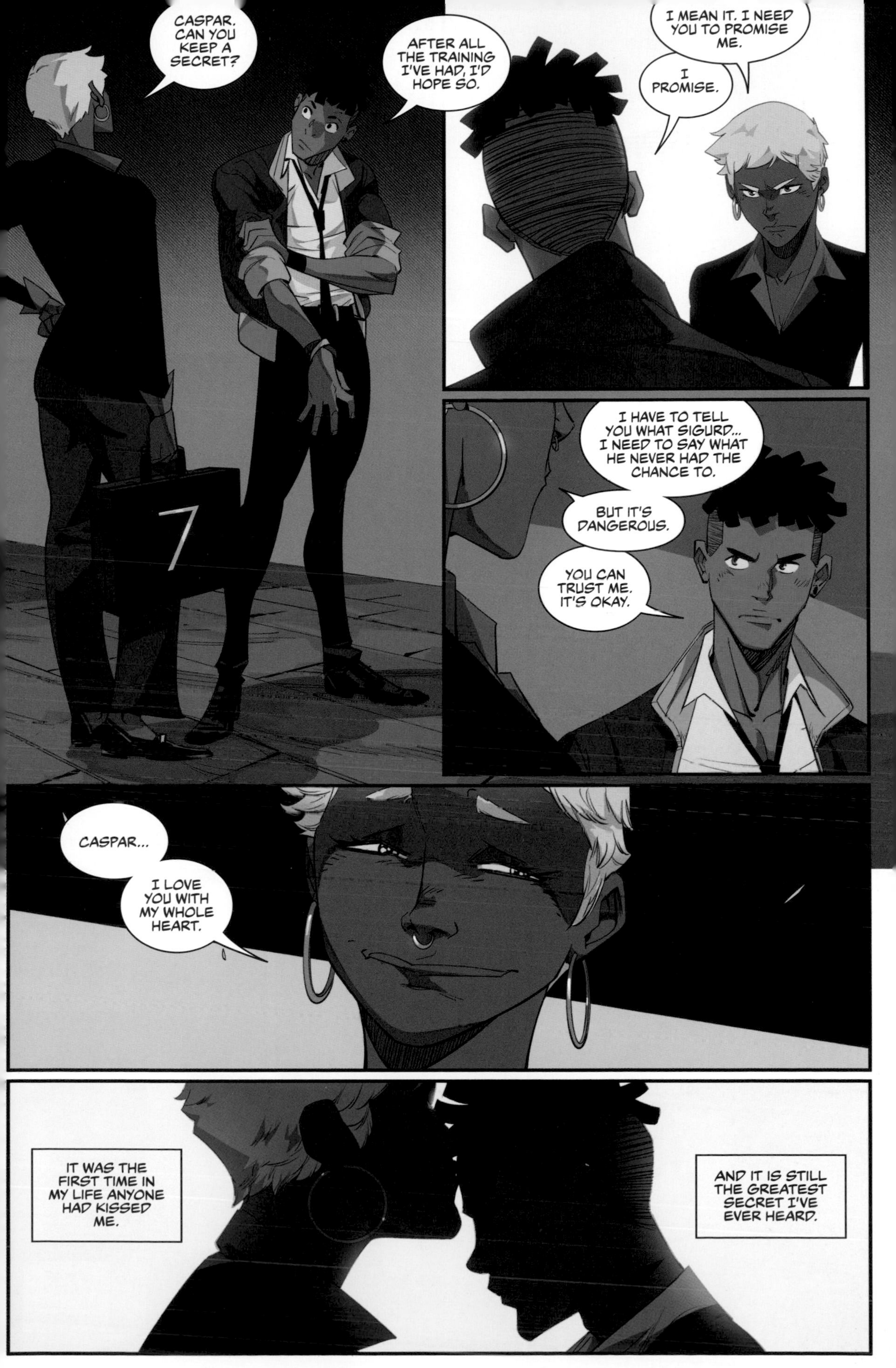
CASPAR. CAN YOU KEEP A SECRET?
AFTER ALL THE TRAINING I'VE HAD, I'D HOPE SO.
I MEAN IT. I NEED YOU TO PROMISE ME.
I PROMISE.
I HAVE TO TELL YOU WHAT SIGURD... I NEED TO SAY WHAT HE NEVER HAD THE CHANCE TO.
BUT IT'S DANGEROUS.
YOU CAN TRUST ME. IT'S OKAY.
CASPAR...
I LOVE YOU WITH MY WHOLE HEART.
IT WAS THE FIRST TIME IN MY LIFE ANYONE HAD KISSED ME.
AND IT IS STILL THE GREATEST SECRET I'VE EVER HEARD.

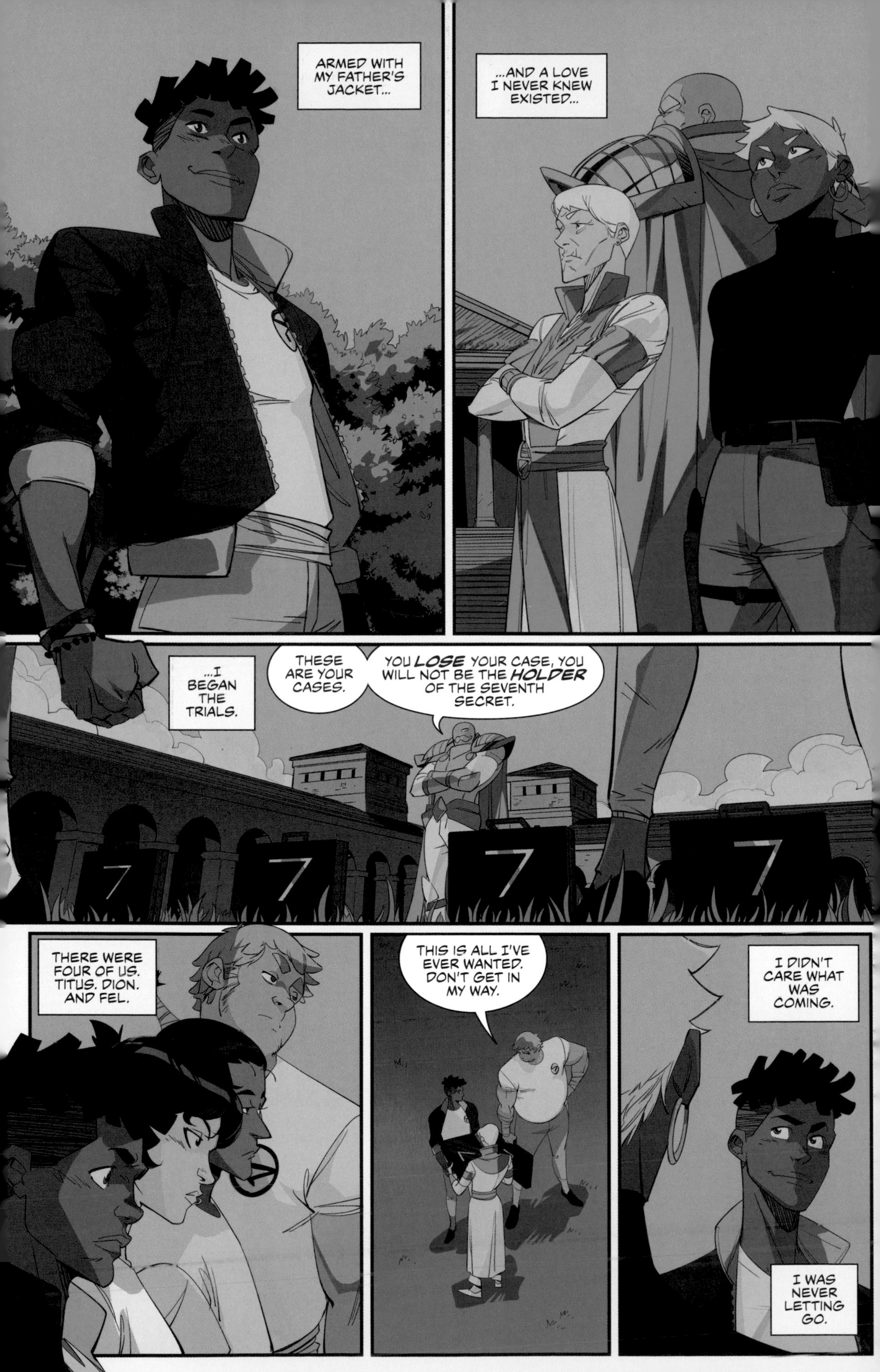
ARMED WITH MY FATHER'S JACKET...
...AND A LOVE I NEVER KNEW EXISTED...
...I BEGAN THE TRIALS.
THESE ARE YOUR CASES.
YOU LOSE YOUR CASE, YOU WILL NOT BE THE HOLDER OF THE SEVENTH SECRET.
7
7
7
7
THERE WERE FOUR OF US. TITUS. DION. AND FEL.
THIS IS ALL I'VE EVER WANTED. DON'T GET IN MY WAY.
I DIDN'T CARE WHAT WAS COMING.
I WAS NEVER LETTING GO.

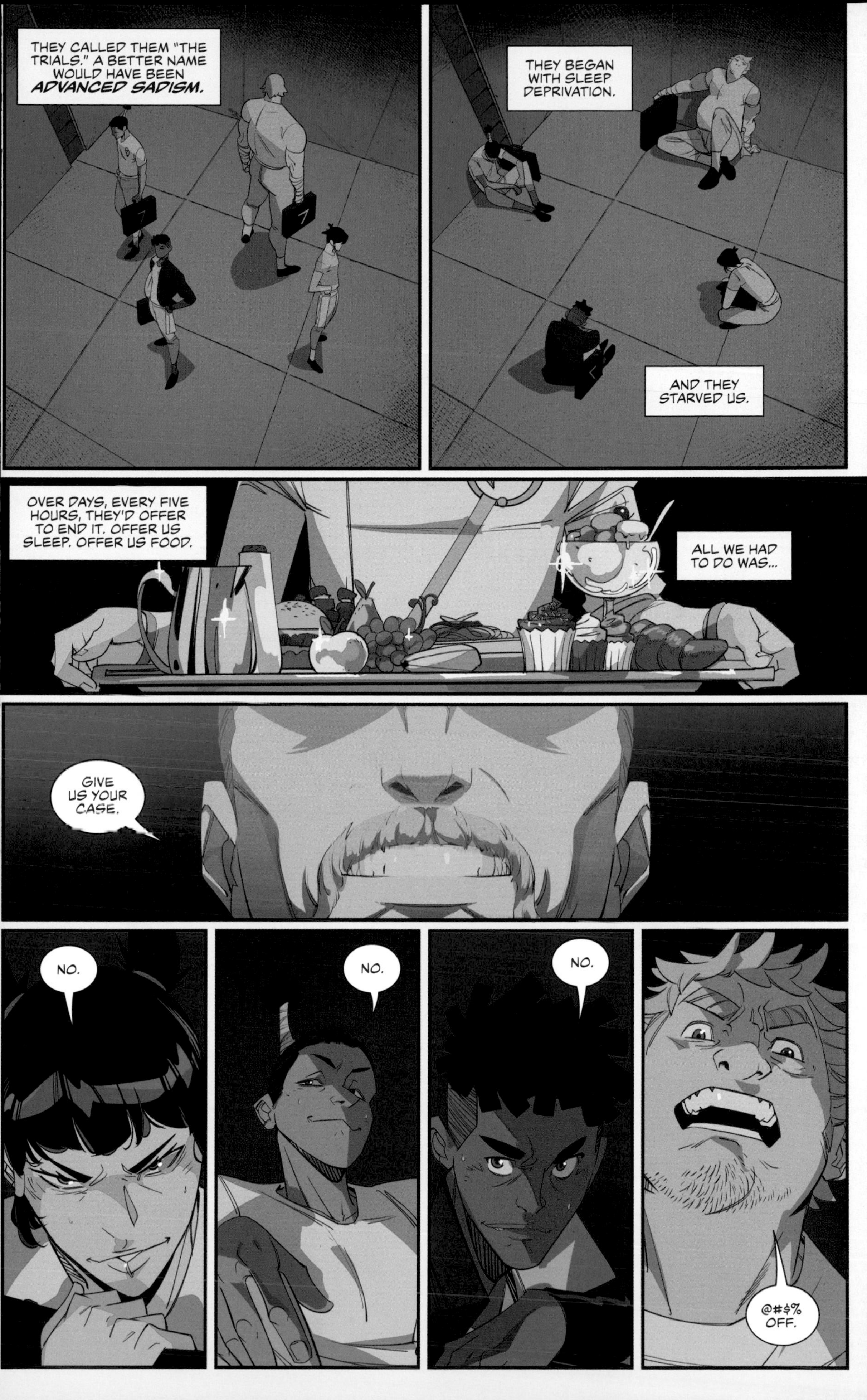
THEY CALLED THEM "THE TRIALS." A BETTER NAME WOULD HAVE BEEN ADVANCED SADISM.
THEY BEGAN WITH SLEEP DEPRIVATION.
AND THEY STARVED US.
OVER DAYS, EVERY FIVE HOURS, THEY'D OFFER TO END IT. OFFER US SLEEP. OFFER US FOOD.
ALL WE HAD TO DO WAS...
GIVE US YOUR CASE.
NO.
NO.
NO.
@#$% OFF.

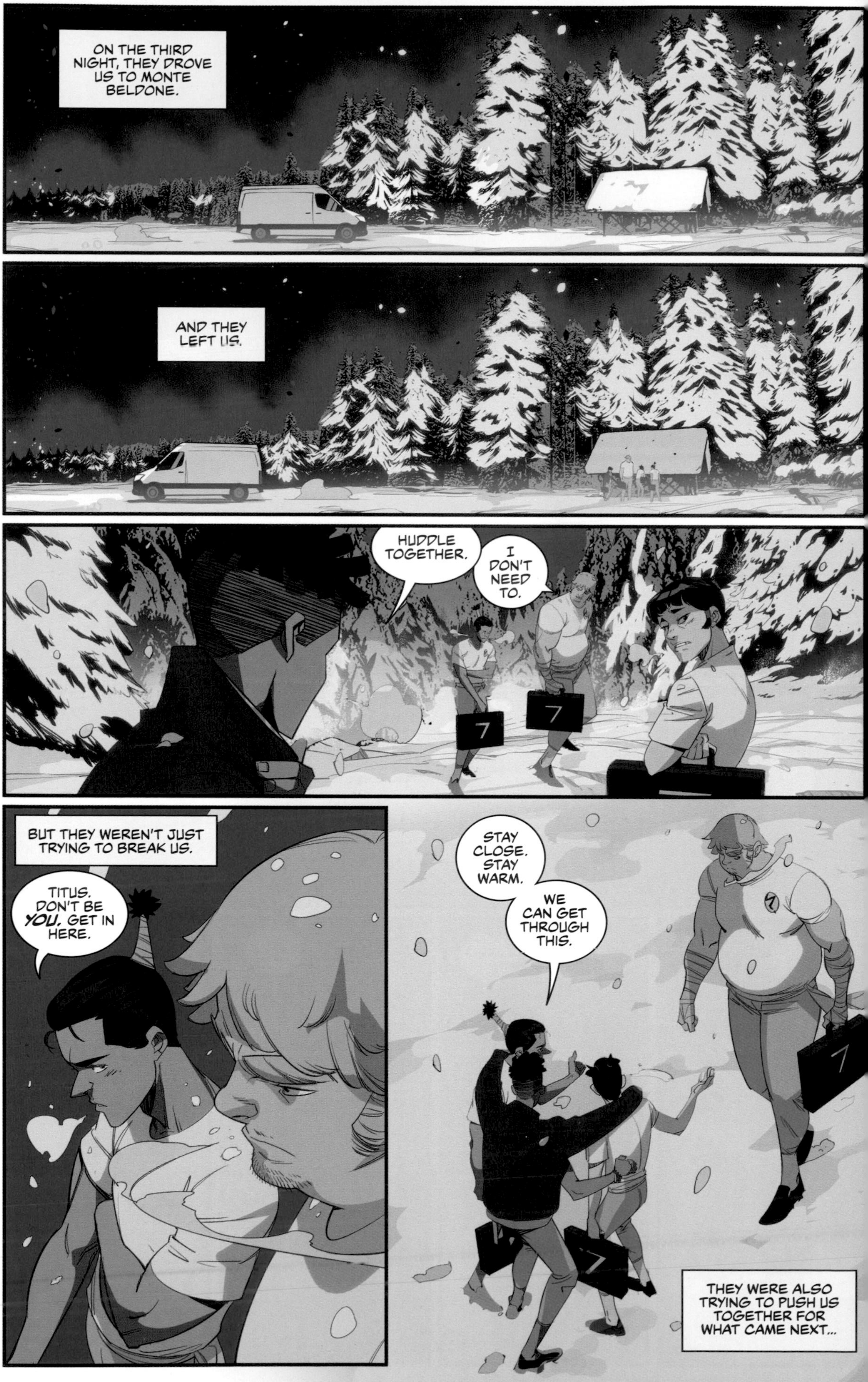
ON THE THIRD NIGHT, THEY DROVE US TO MONTE BELDONE.
AND THEY LEFT US.
HUDDLE TOGETHER.
I DON'T NEED TO.
BUT THEY WEREN'T JUST TRYING TO BREAK US.
TITUS. DON'T BE *YOU.* GET IN HERE.
STAY CLOSE. STAY WARM.
WE CAN GET THROUGH THIS.
THEY WERE ALSO TRYING TO PUSH US TOGETHER FOR WHAT CAME NEXT...

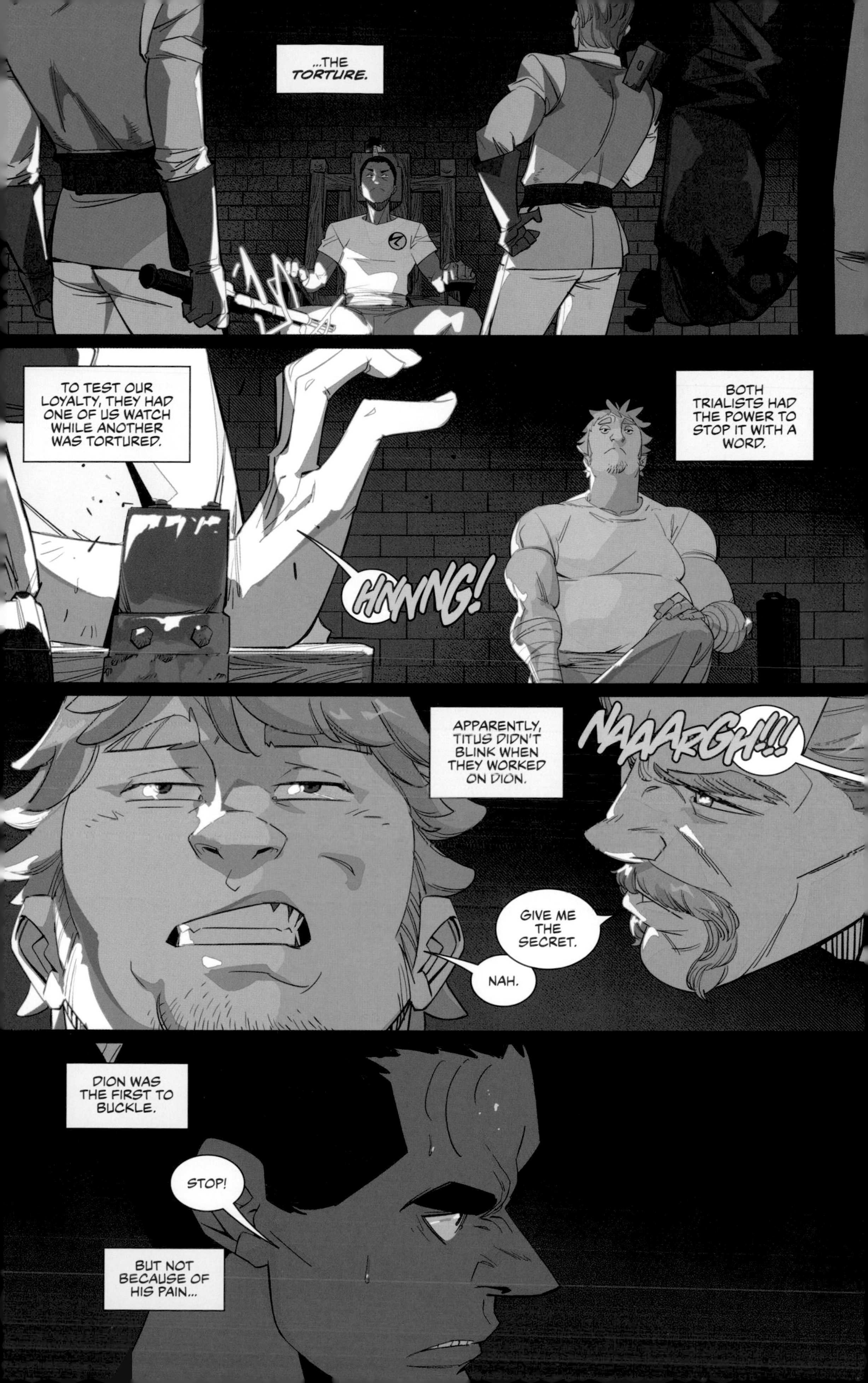

...THE TORTURE.
TO TEST OUR LOYALTY, THEY HAD ONE OF US WATCH WHILE ANOTHER WAS TORTURED.
HNNNG!
BOTH TRIALISTS HAD THE POWER TO STOP IT WITH A WORD.
APPARENTLY, TITUS DIDN'T BLINK WHEN THEY WORKED ON DION.
NAAARGH!!!
GIVE ME THE SECRET.
NAH.
DION WAS THE FIRST TO BUCKLE.
STOP!
BUT NOT BECAUSE OF HIS PAIN...

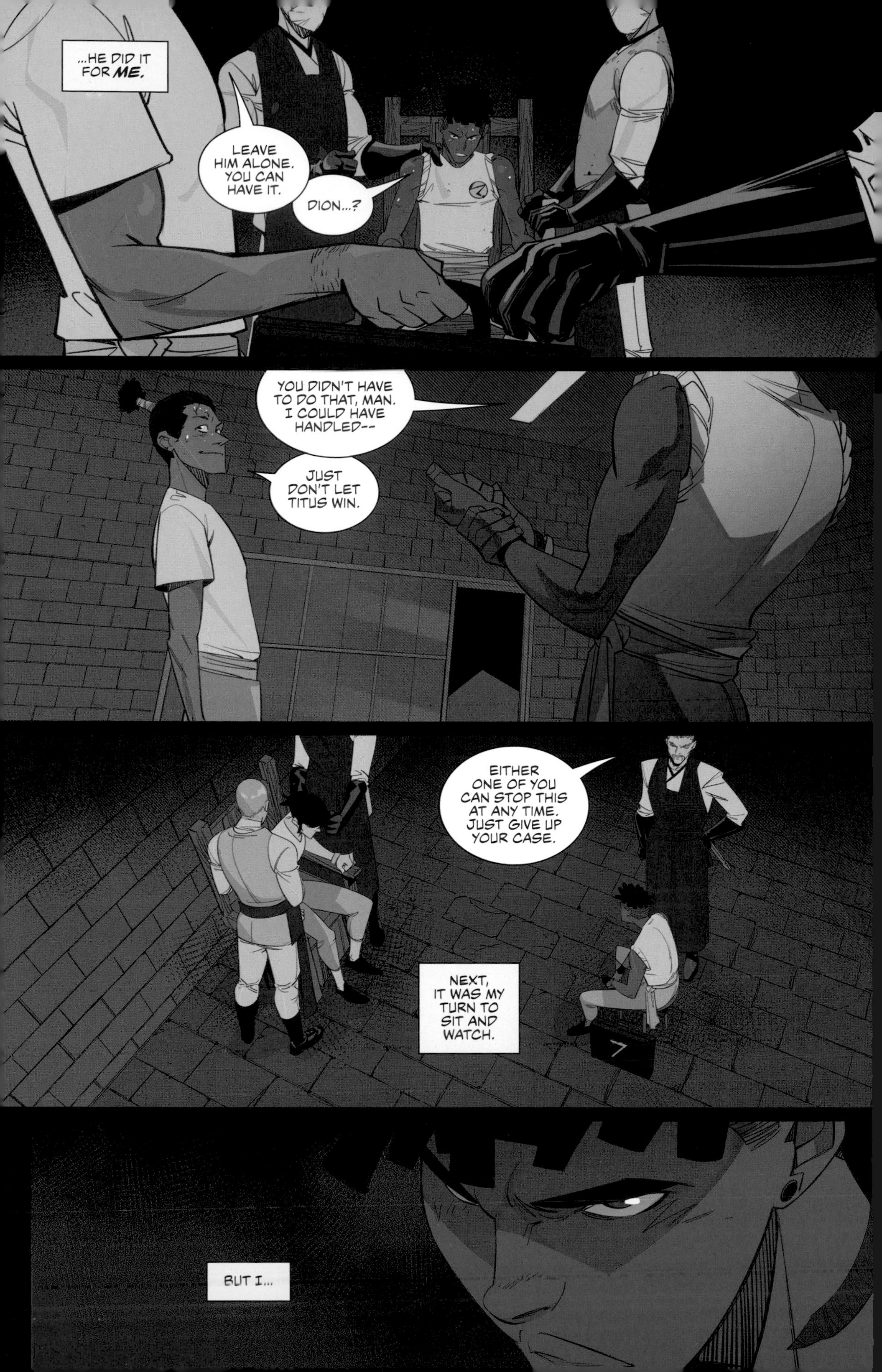

...HE DID IT FOR *ME.*
LEAVE HIM ALONE. YOU CAN HAVE IT.
DION...?
YOU DIDN'T HAVE TO DO THAT, MAN. I COULD HAVE HANDLED--
JUST DON'T LET TITUS WIN.
EITHER ONE OF YOU CAN STOP THIS AT ANY TIME. JUST GIVE UP YOUR CASE.
NEXT, IT WAS MY TURN TO SIT AND WATCH.
BUT I...

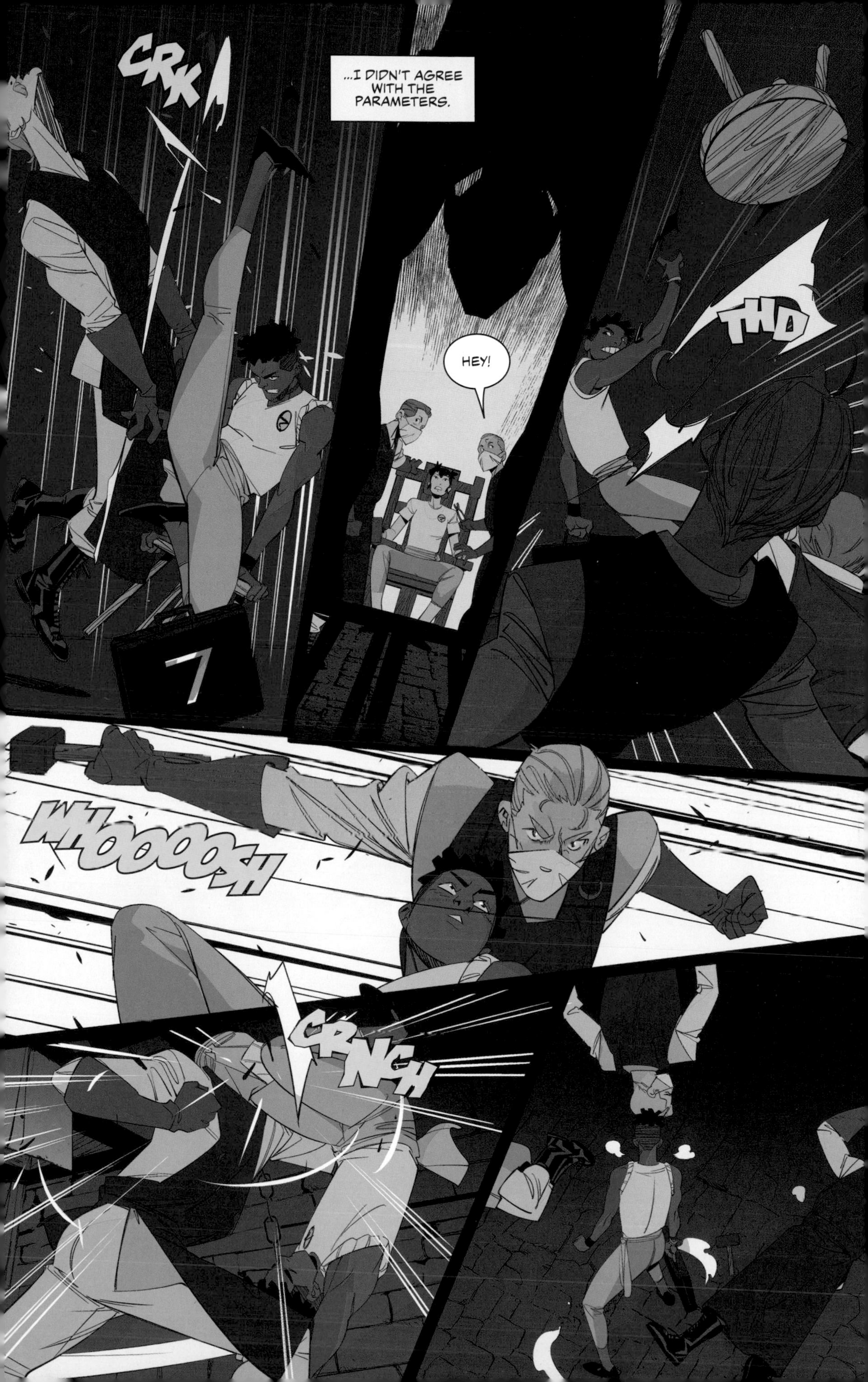
CRK
...I DIDN'T AGREE WITH THE PARAMETERS.
HEY!
THD
WHOOOOSH
CRNCH

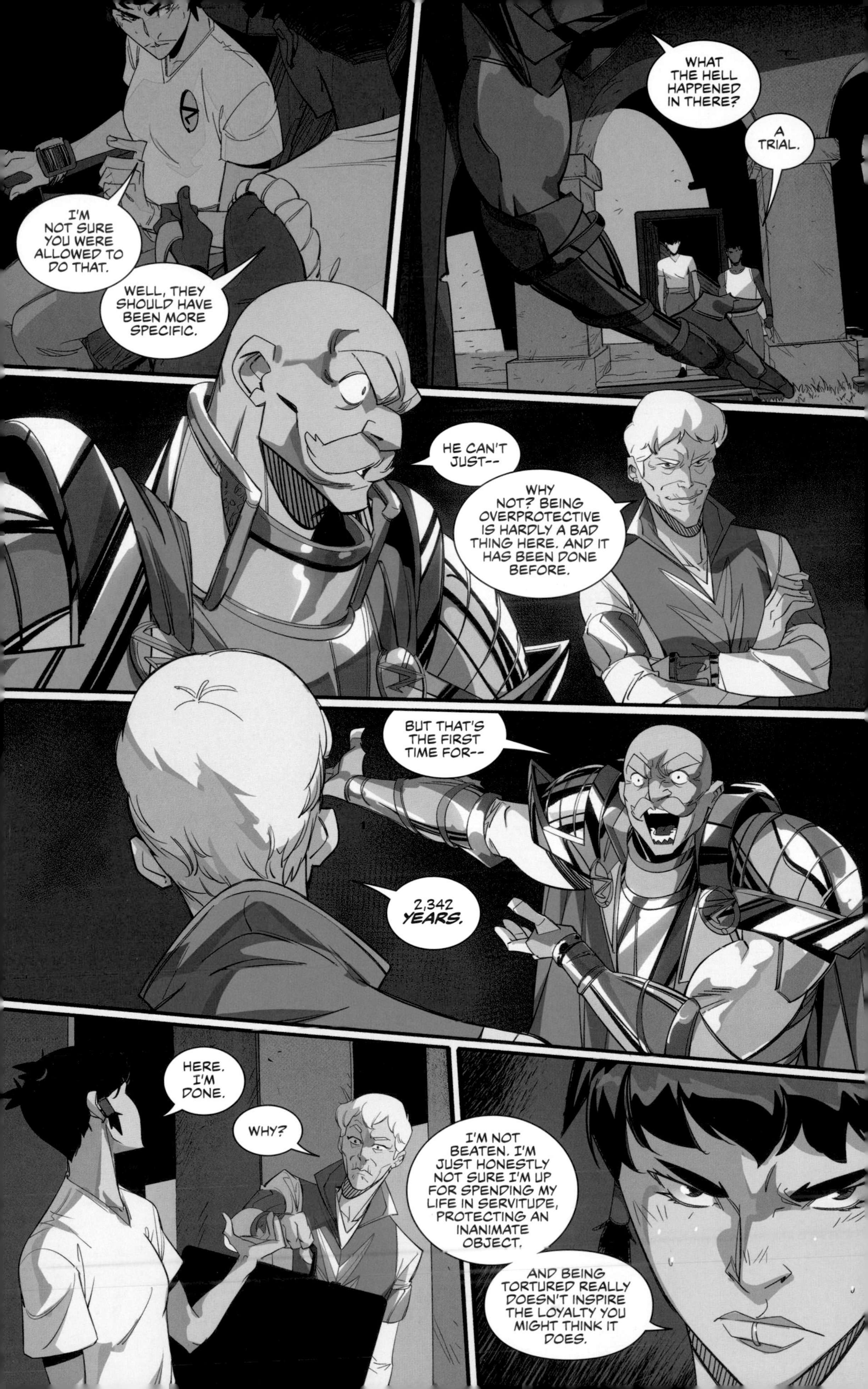

I'M NOT SURE YOU WERE ALLOWED TO DO THAT.
WELL, THEY SHOULD HAVE BEEN MORE SPECIFIC.
WHAT THE HELL HAPPENED IN THERE?
A TRIAL.
HE CAN'T JUST--
WHY NOT? BEING OVERPROTECTIVE IS HARDLY A BAD THING HERE. AND IT HAS BEEN DONE BEFORE.
BUT THAT'S THE FIRST TIME FOR--
2,342 YEARS.
HERE. I'M DONE.
WHY?
I'M NOT BEATEN. I'M JUST HONESTLY NOT SURE I'M UP FOR SPENDING MY LIFE IN SERVITUDE, PROTECTING AN INANIMATE OBJECT.
AND BEING TORTURED REALLY DOESN'T INSPIRE THE LOYALTY YOU MIGHT THINK IT DOES.

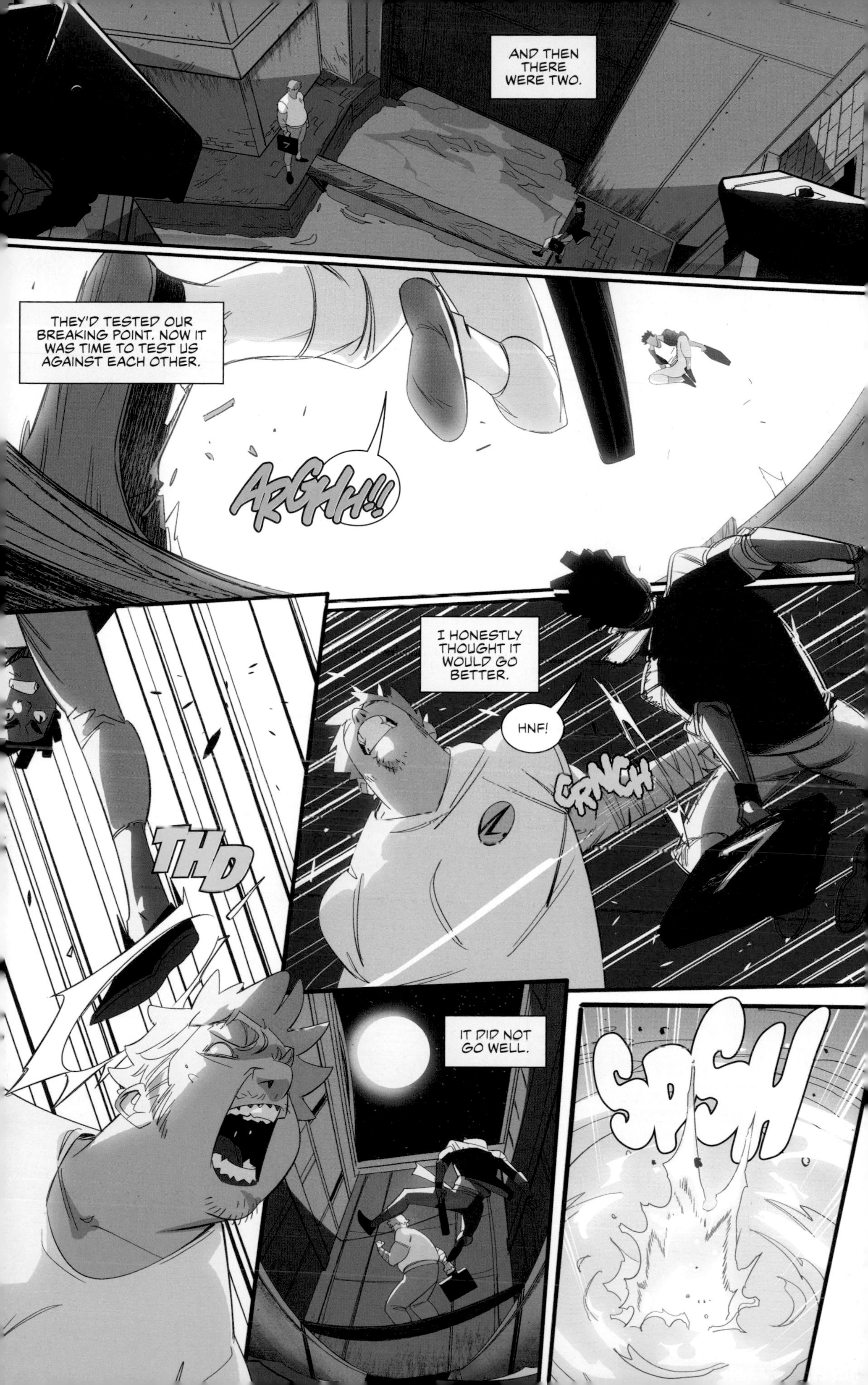
AND THEN THERE WERE TWO.
THEY'D TESTED OUR BREAKING POINT. NOW IT WAS TIME TO TEST US AGAINST EACH OTHER.
ARGHH!!
I HONESTLY THOUGHT IT WOULD GO BETTER.
HNF!
CRNCH
THD
IT DID NOT GO WELL.
SPSCH

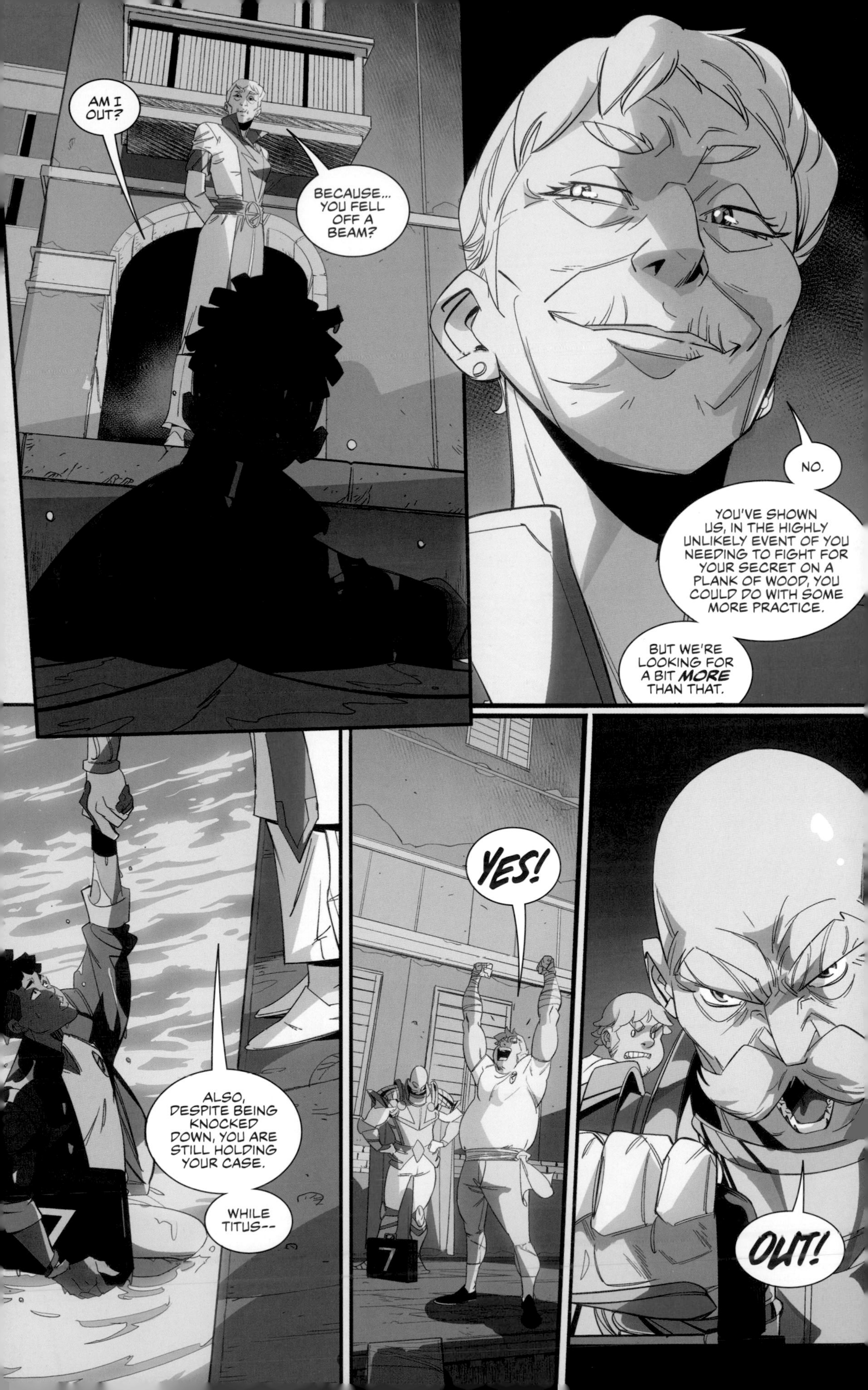
AM I OUT?
BECAUSE... YOU FELL OFF A BEAM?
NO.
YOU'VE SHOWN US, IN THE HIGHLY UNLIKELY EVENT OF YOU NEEDING TO FIGHT FOR YOUR SECRET ON A PLANK OF WOOD, YOU COULD DO WITH SOME MORE PRACTICE.
BUT WE'RE LOOKING FOR A BIT MORE THAN THAT.
ALSO, DESPITE BEING KNOCKED DOWN, YOU ARE STILL HOLDING YOUR CASE.
WHILE TITUS--
YES!
OUT!

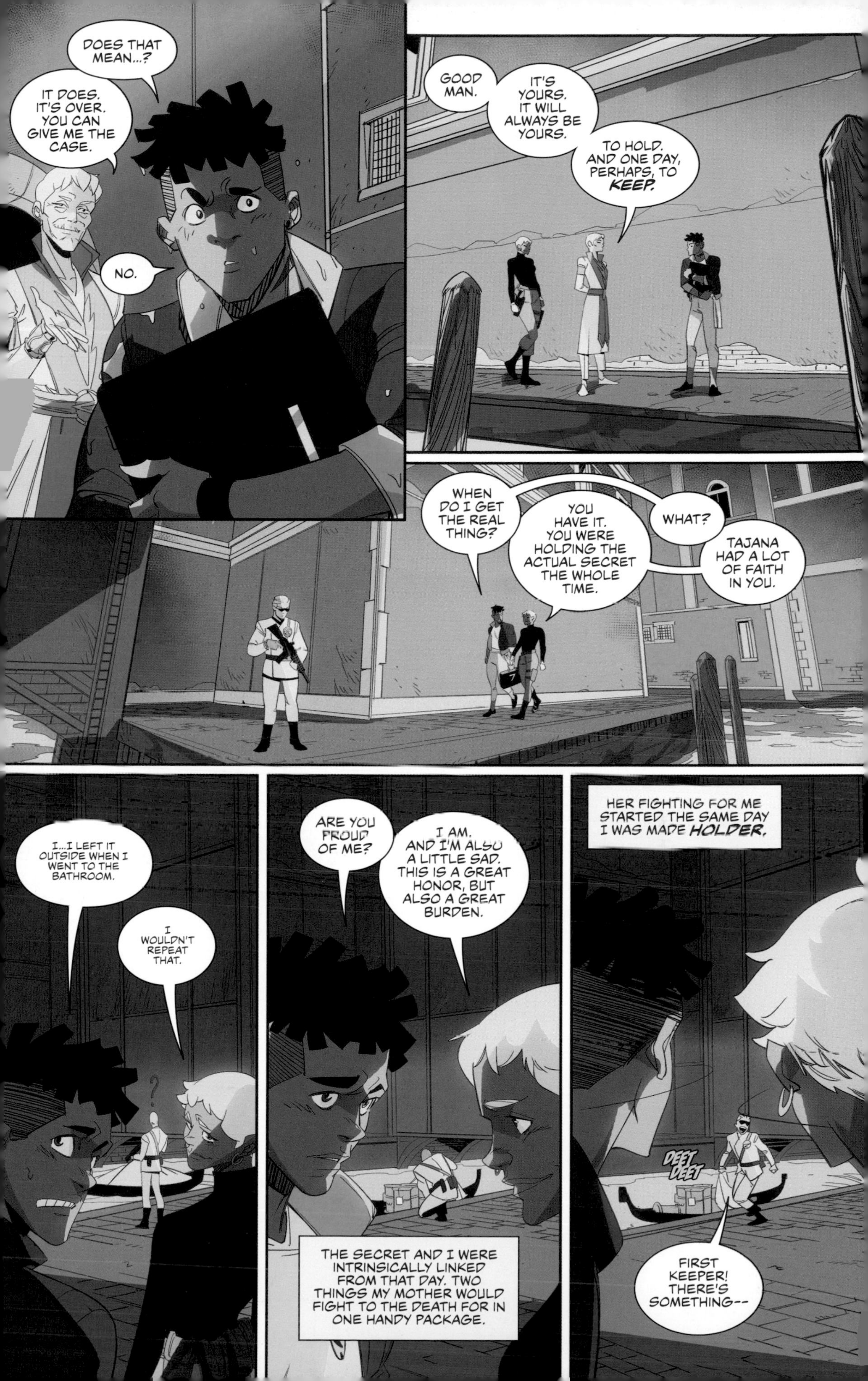
DOES THAT MEAN...?
IT DOES. IT'S OVER. YOU CAN GIVE ME THE CASE.
NO.
GOOD MAN.
IT'S YOURS. IT WILL ALWAYS BE YOURS.
TO HOLD. AND ONE DAY, PERHAPS, TO KEEP.
WHEN DO I GET THE REAL THING?
YOU HAVE IT. YOU WERE HOLDING THE ACTUAL SECRET THE WHOLE TIME.
WHAT?
TAJANA HAD A LOT OF FAITH IN YOU.
I...I LEFT IT OUTSIDE WHEN I WENT TO THE BATHROOM.
I WOULDN'T REPEAT THAT.
?
ARE YOU PROUD OF ME?
I AM. AND I'M ALSO A LITTLE SAD. THIS IS A GREAT HONOR, BUT ALSO A GREAT BURDEN.
THE SECRET AND I WERE INTRINSICALLY LINKED FROM THAT DAY. TWO THINGS MY MOTHER WOULD FIGHT TO THE DEATH FOR IN ONE HANDY PACKAGE.
HER FIGHTING FOR ME STARTED THE SAME DAY I WAS MADE HOLDER.
DEET DEET
FIRST KEEPER! THERE'S SOMETHING--

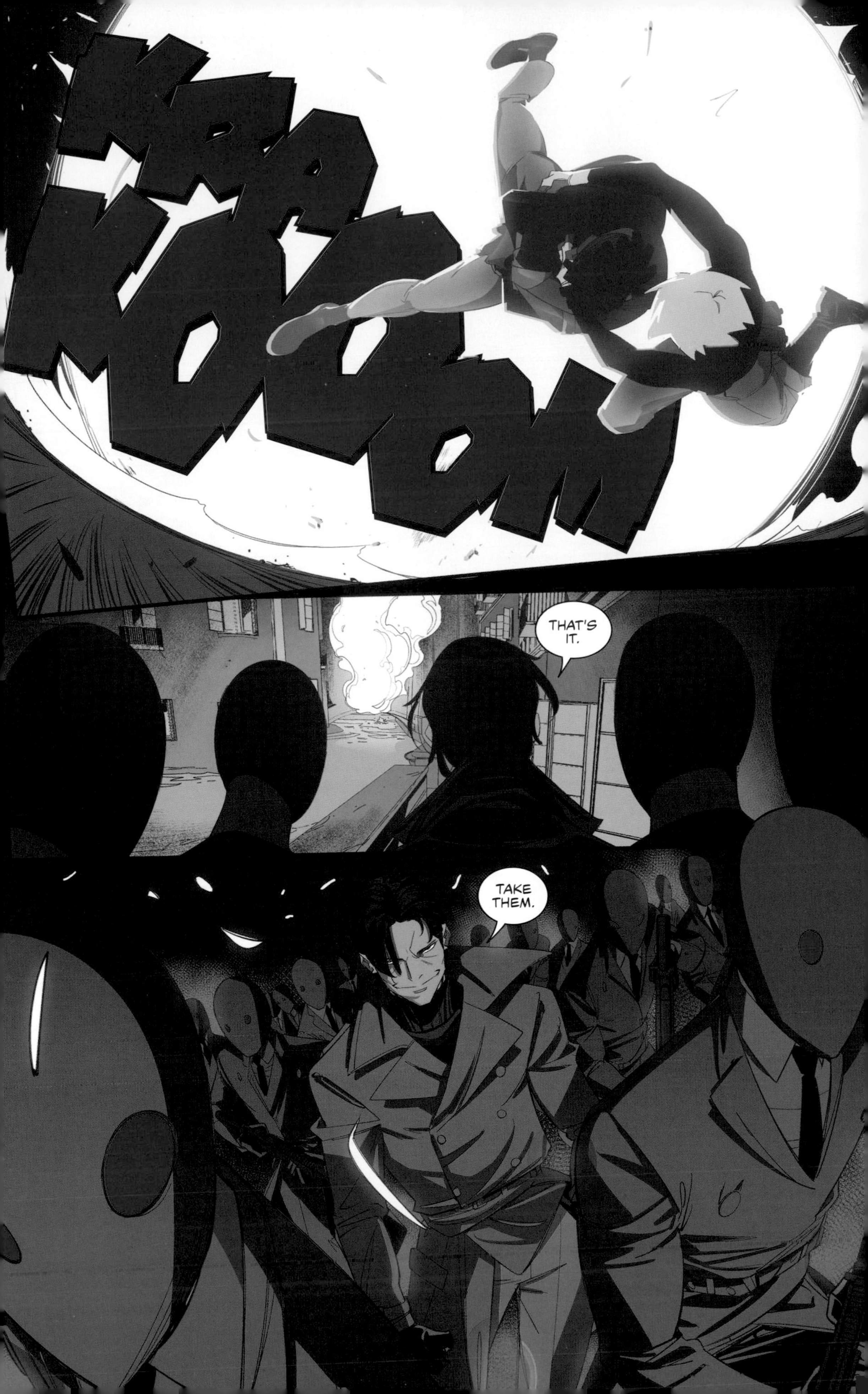
KRA
KOOOM
THAT'S IT.
TAKE THEM.

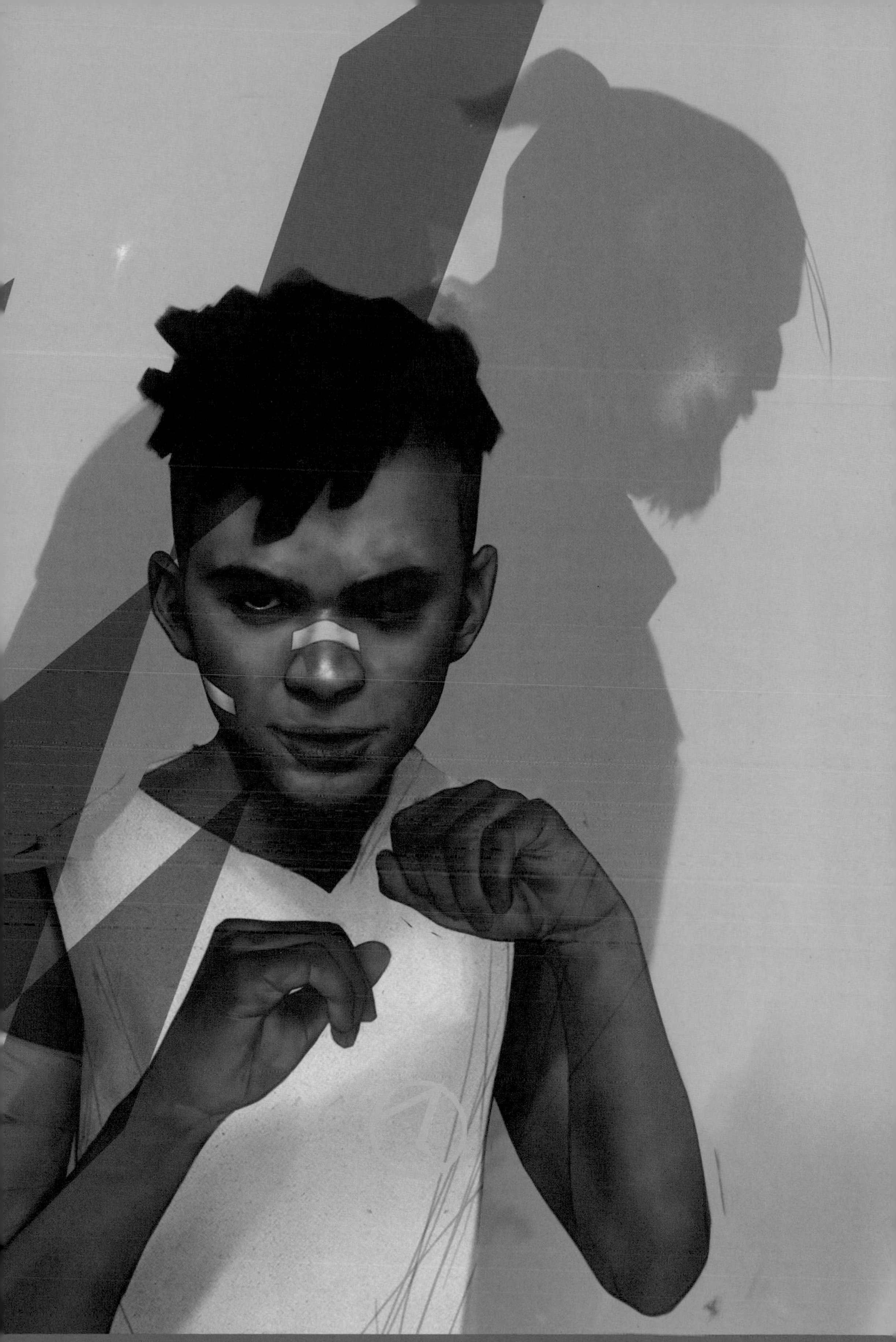

BEN OLIVER ISSUE THREE VARIANT COVER

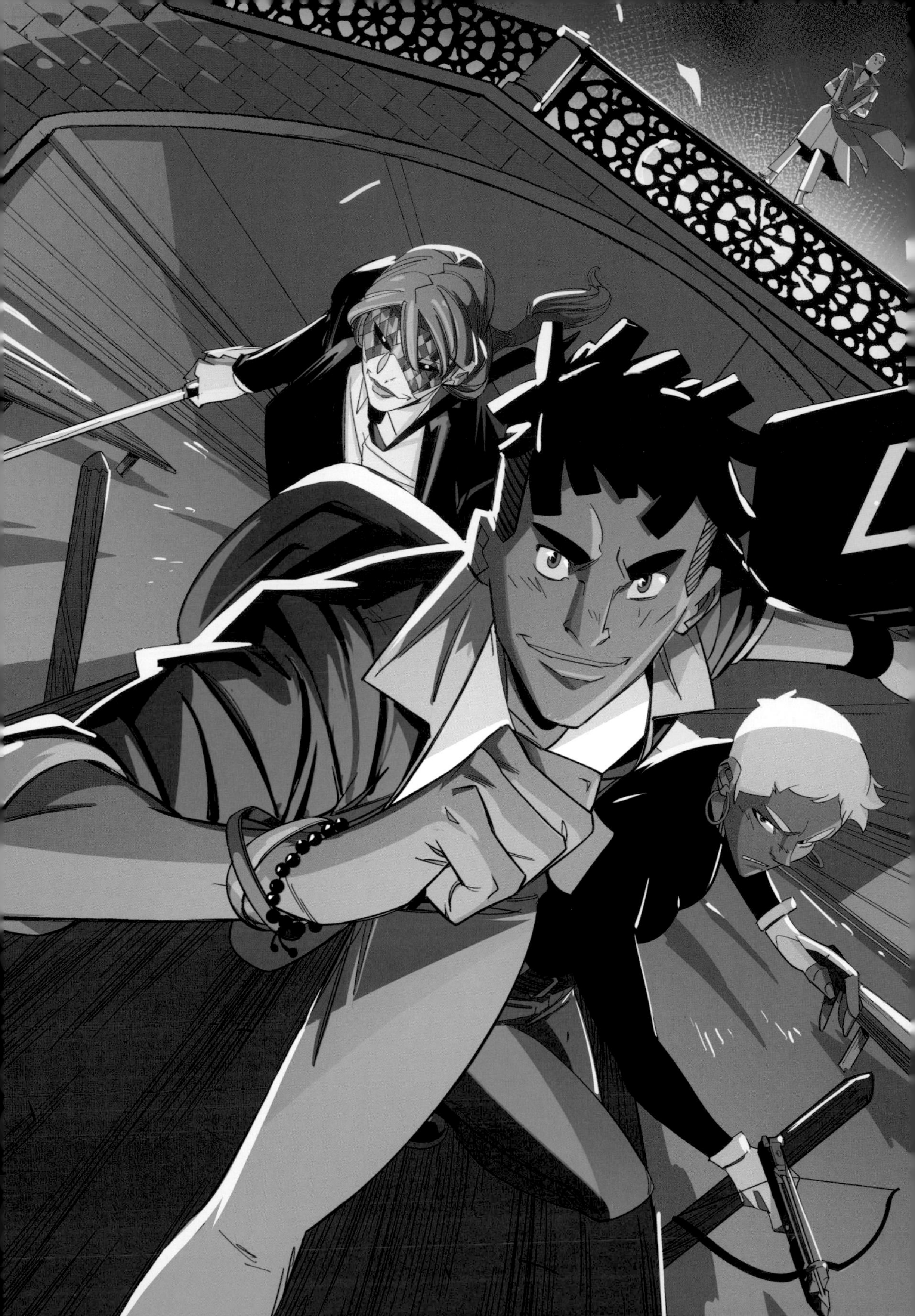

CHAPTER FOUR

DANIELE DI NICUOLO ISSUE FOUR COVER

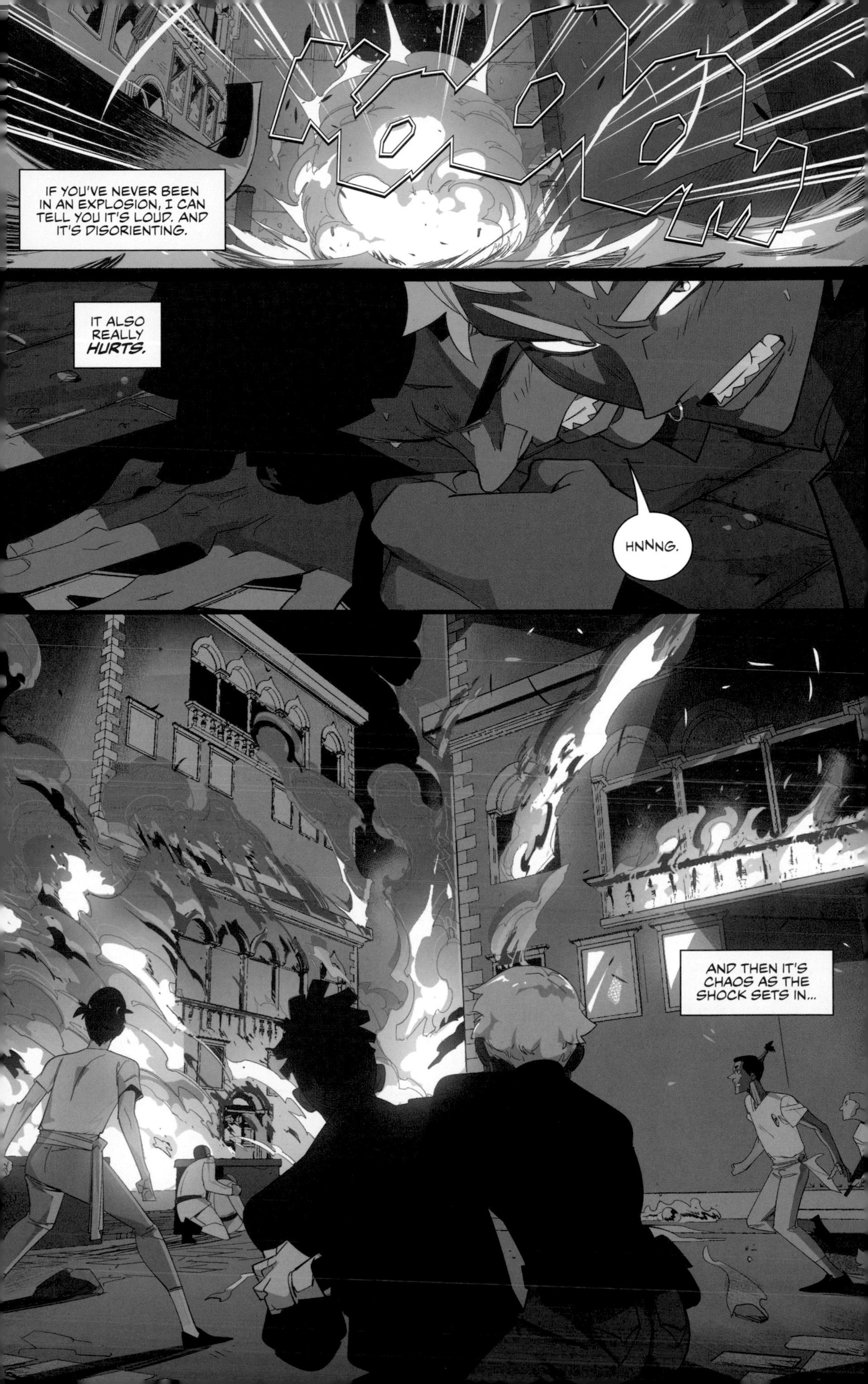
BOOOOM
IF YOU'VE NEVER BEEN IN AN EXPLOSION, I CAN TELL YOU IT'S LOUD. AND IT'S DISORIENTING.
IT ALSO REALLY HURTS.
HNNNG.
AND THEN IT'S CHAOS AS THE SHOCK SETS IN...

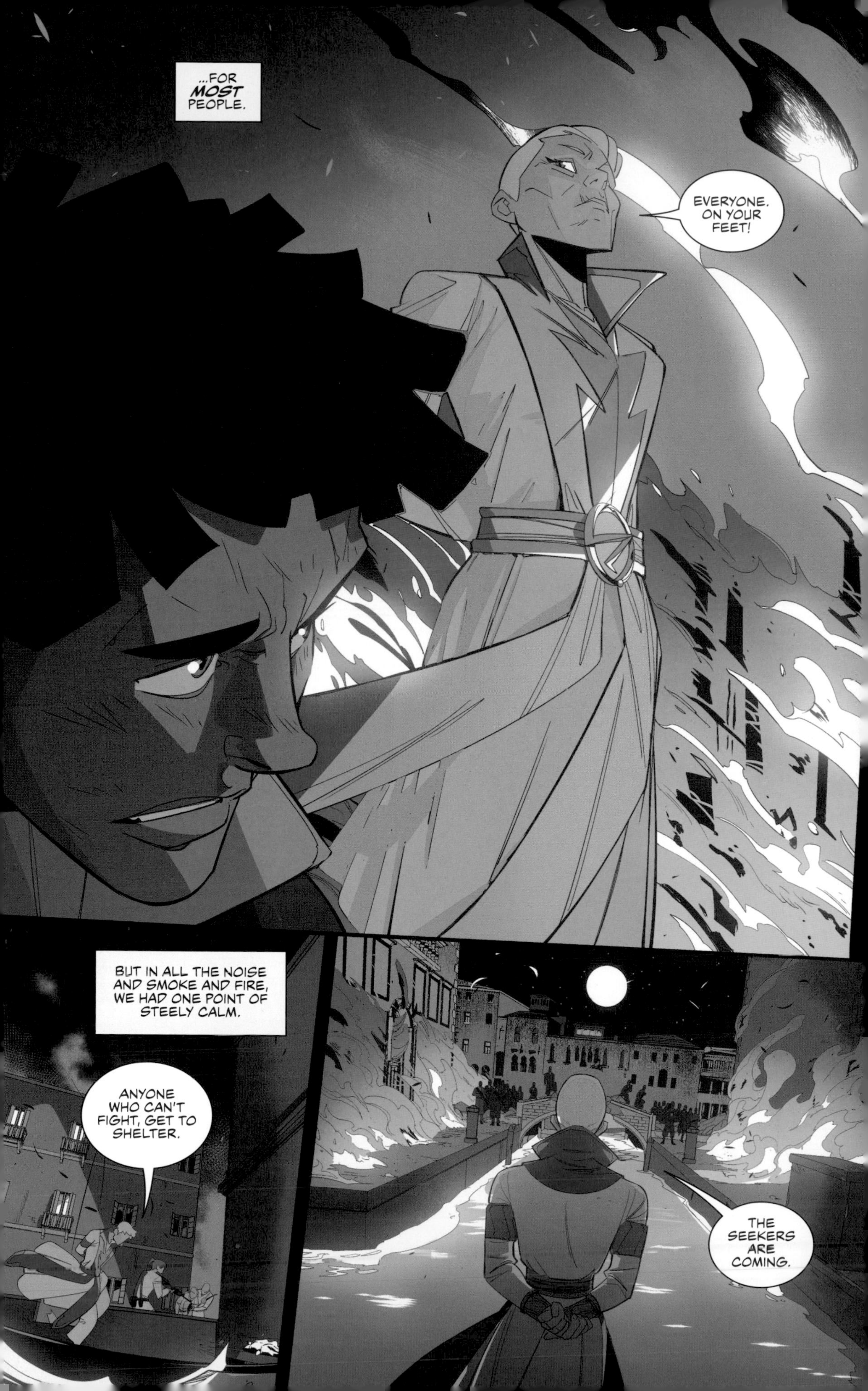
...FOR MOST PEOPLE.
EVERYONE. ON YOUR FEET!
BUT IN ALL THE NOISE AND SMOKE AND FIRE, WE HAD ONE POINT OF STEELY CALM.
ANYONE WHO CAN'T FIGHT, GET TO SHELTER.
THE SEEKERS ARE COMING.

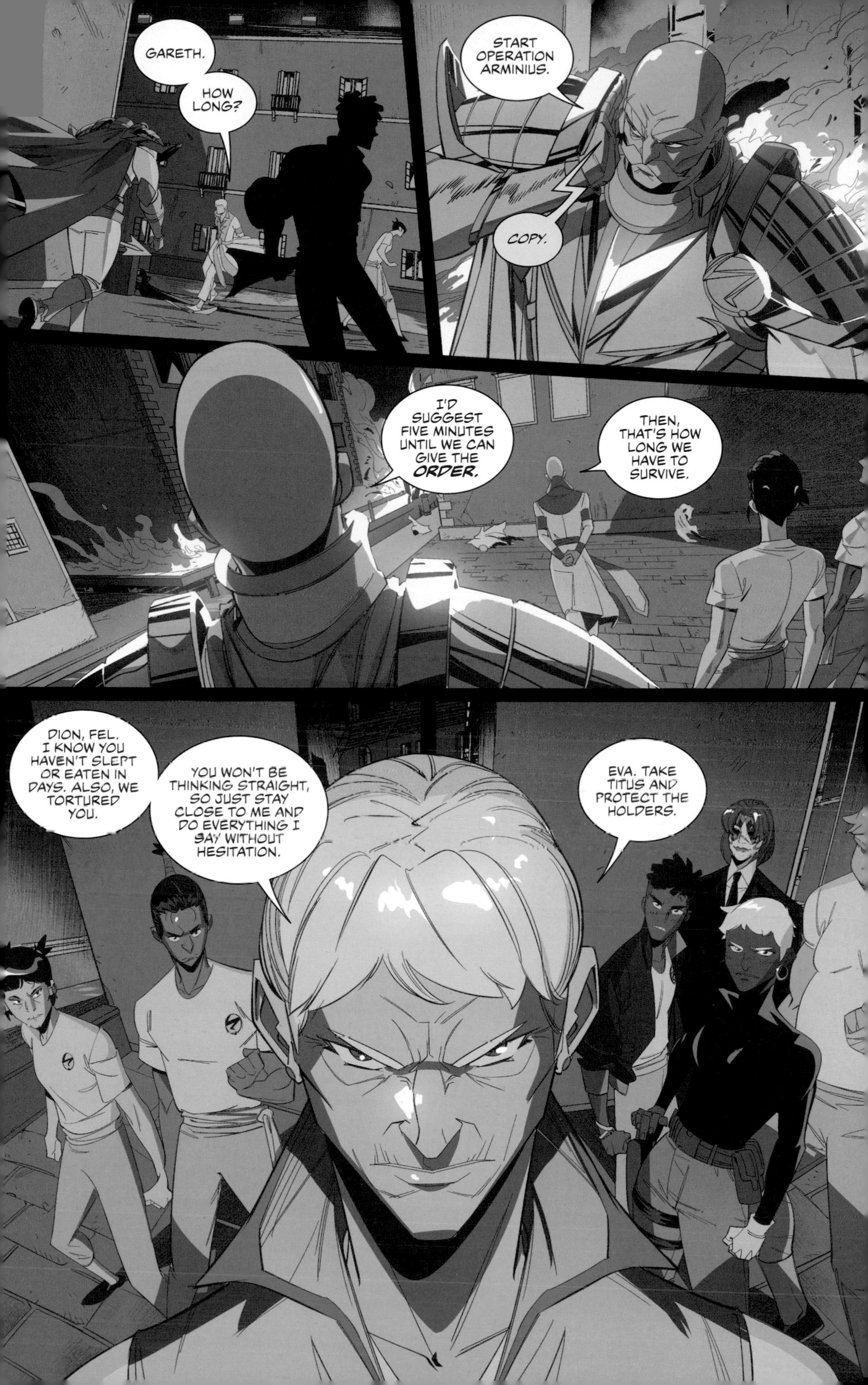
GARETH.
HOW LONG?
START OPERATION ARMINIUS.
COPY.
I'D SUGGEST FIVE MINUTES UNTIL WE CAN GIVE THE ORDER.
THEN, THAT'S HOW LONG WE HAVE TO SURVIVE.
DION, FEL. I KNOW YOU HAVEN'T SLEPT OR EATEN IN DAYS. ALSO, WE TORTURED YOU.
YOU WON'T BE THINKING STRAIGHT, SO JUST STAY CLOSE TO ME AND DO EVERYTHING I SAY WITHOUT HESITATION.
EVA. TAKE TITUS AND PROTECT THE HOLDERS.

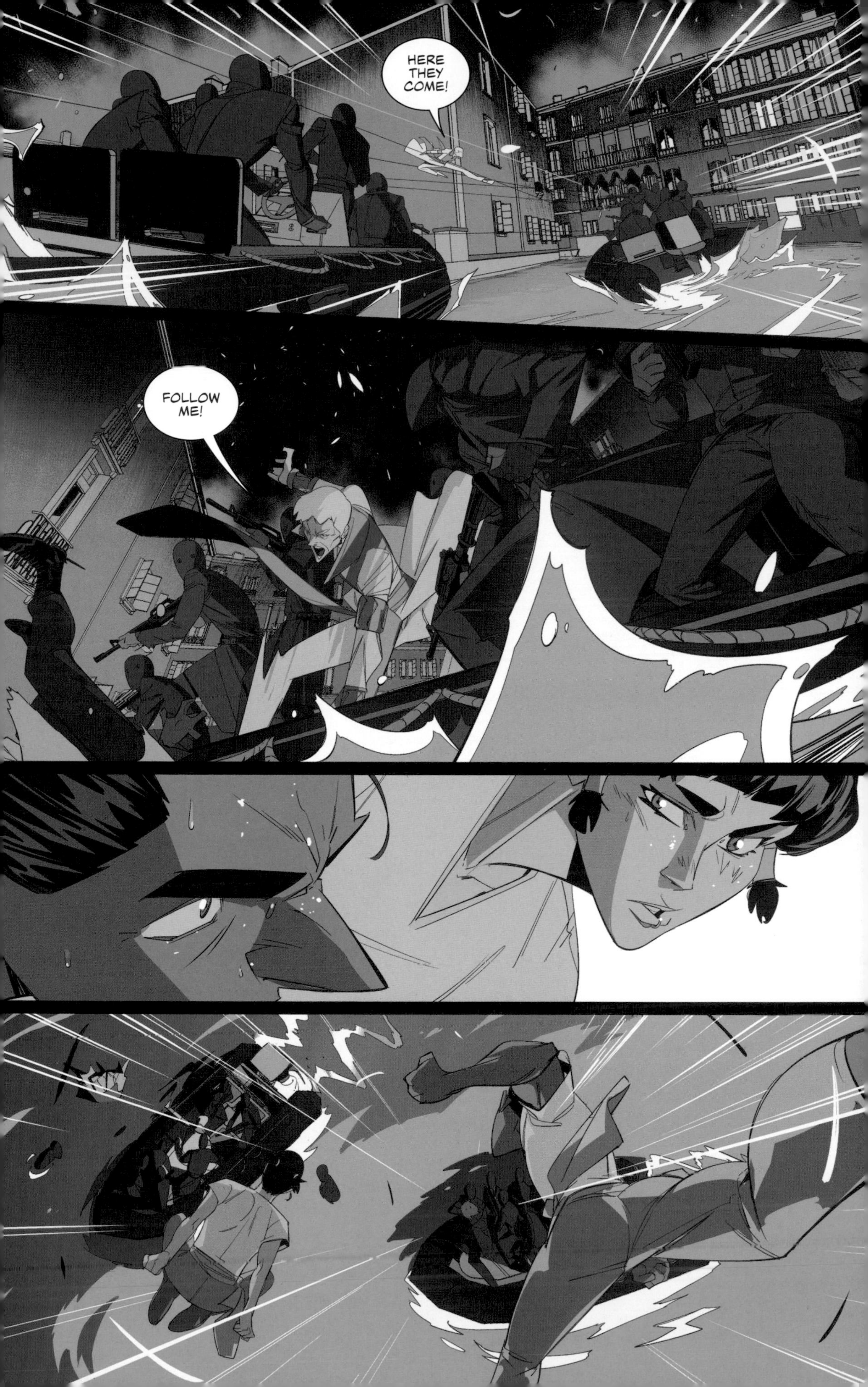
HERE THEY COME!
FOLLOW ME!

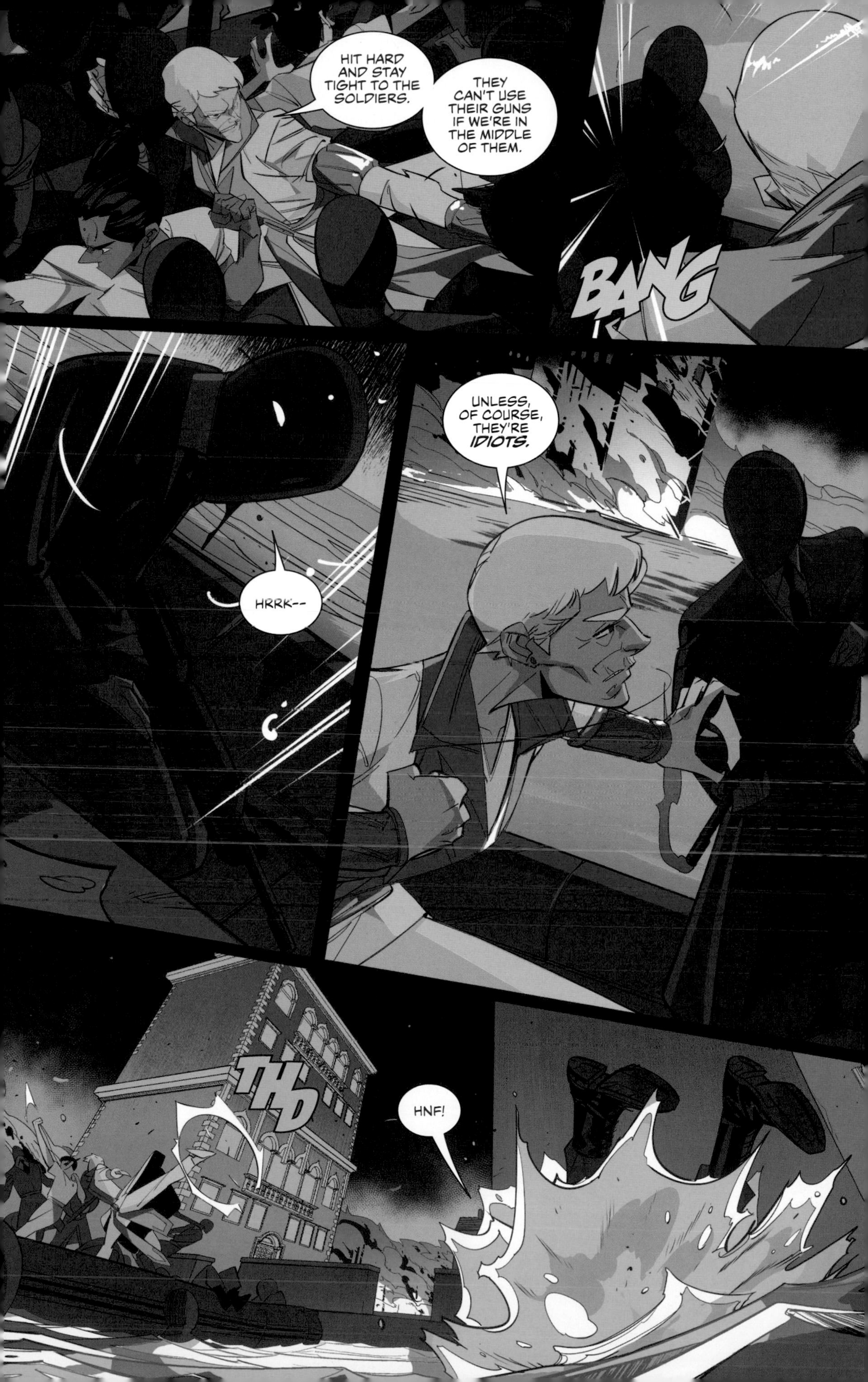
HIT HARD AND STAY TIGHT TO THE SOLDIERS.
THEY CAN'T USE THEIR GUNS IF WE'RE IN THE MIDDLE OF THEM.
BANG
UNLESS, OF COURSE, THEY'RE *IDIOTS.*
HRRK--
THD
HNF!

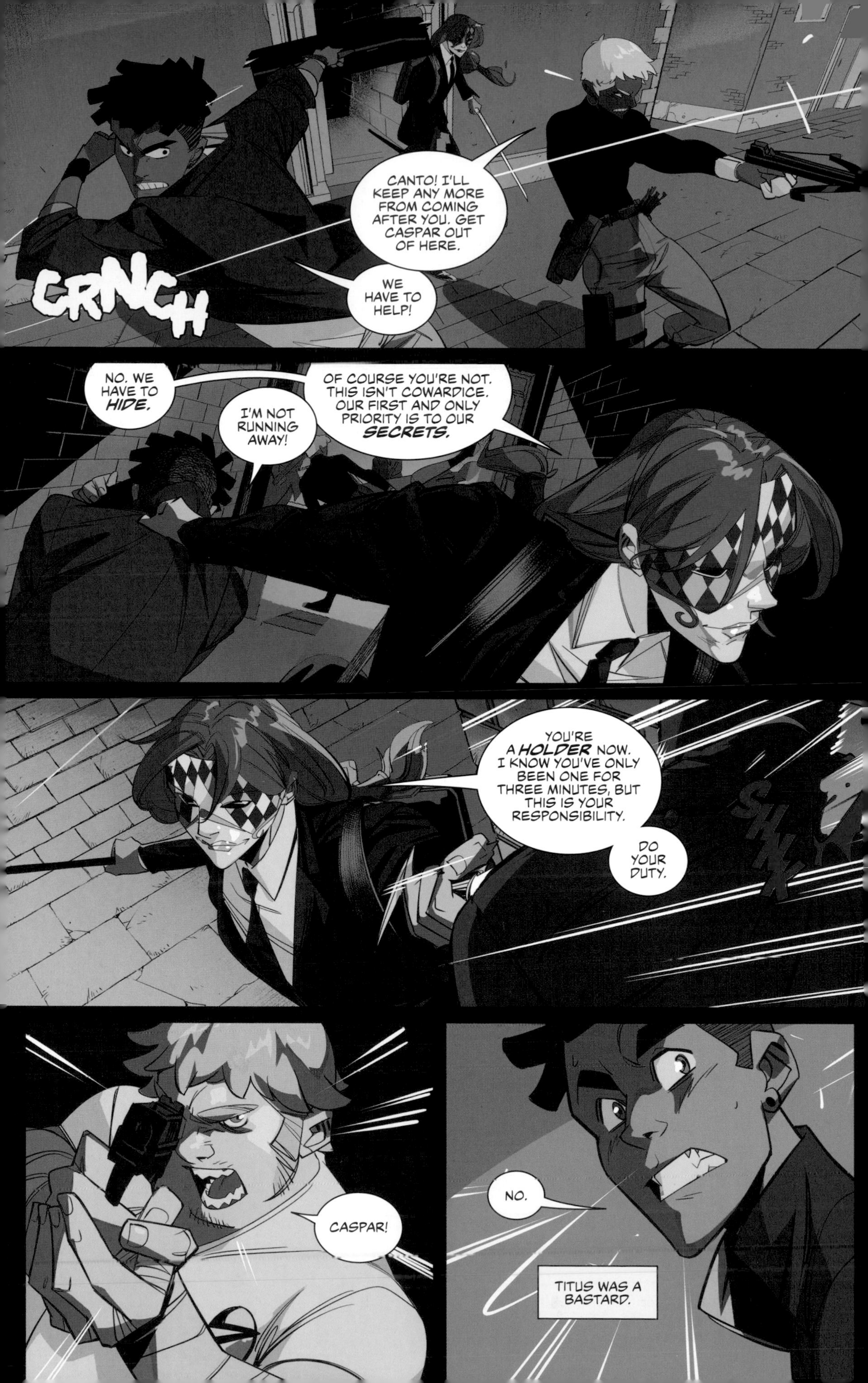
CANTO! I'LL KEEP ANY MORE FROM COMING AFTER YOU. GET CASPAR OUT OF HERE.
GRNCH
WE HAVE TO HELP!
NO. WE HAVE TO *HIDE.*
I'M NOT RUNNING AWAY!
OF COURSE YOU'RE NOT. THIS ISN'T COWARDICE. OUR FIRST AND ONLY PRIORITY IS TO OUR *SECRETS.*
YOU'RE A *HOLDER* NOW. I KNOW YOU'VE ONLY BEEN ONE FOR THREE MINUTES, BUT THIS IS YOUR RESPONSIBILITY.
DO YOUR DUTY.
SHNK
CASPAR!
NO.
TITUS WAS A BASTARD.

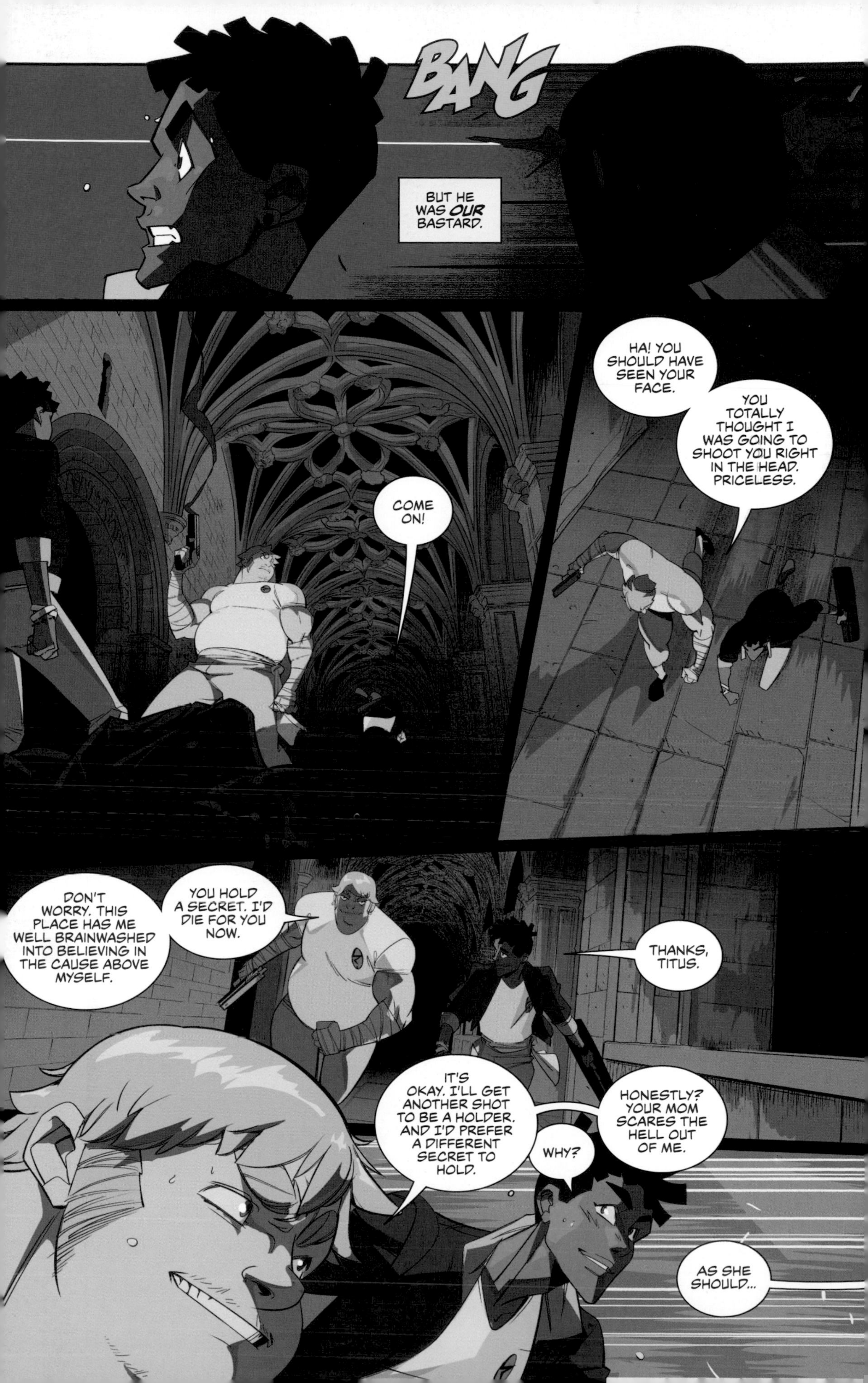
BANG
BUT HE WAS OUR BASTARD.
COME ON!
HA! YOU SHOULD HAVE SEEN YOUR FACE.
YOU TOTALLY THOUGHT I WAS GOING TO SHOOT YOU RIGHT IN THE HEAD. PRICELESS.
YOU HOLD A SECRET. I'D DIE FOR YOU NOW.
DON'T WORRY. THIS PLACE HAS ME WELL BRAINWASHED INTO BELIEVING IN THE CAUSE ABOVE MYSELF.
THANKS, TITUS.
IT'S OKAY. I'LL GET ANOTHER SHOT TO BE A HOLDER. AND I'D PREFER A DIFFERENT SECRET TO HOLD.
HONESTLY? YOUR MOM SCARES THE HELL OUT OF ME.
WHY?
AS SHE SHOULD...

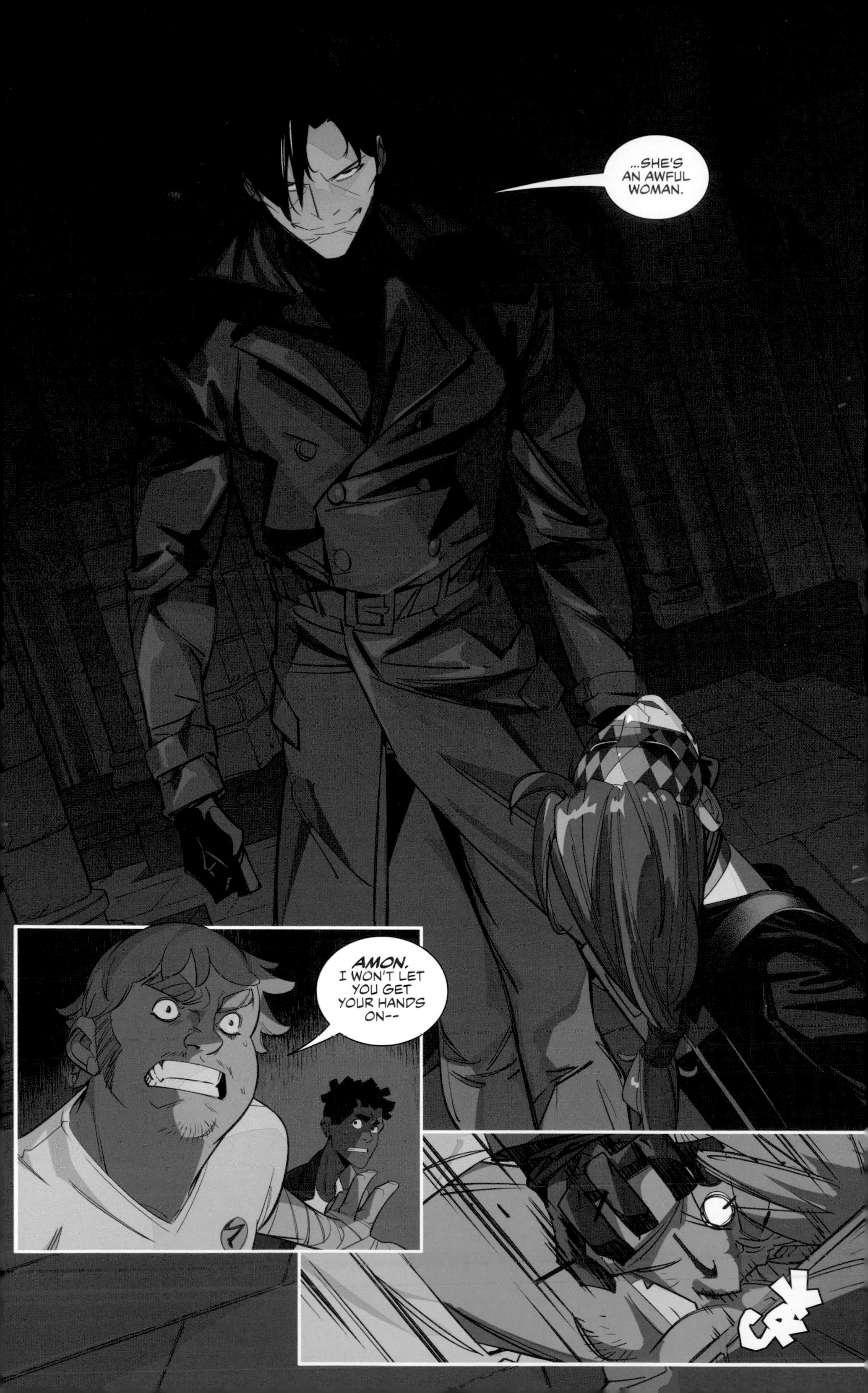
...SHE'S AN AWFUL WOMAN.
AMON. I WON'T LET YOU GET YOUR HANDS ON--
CRK

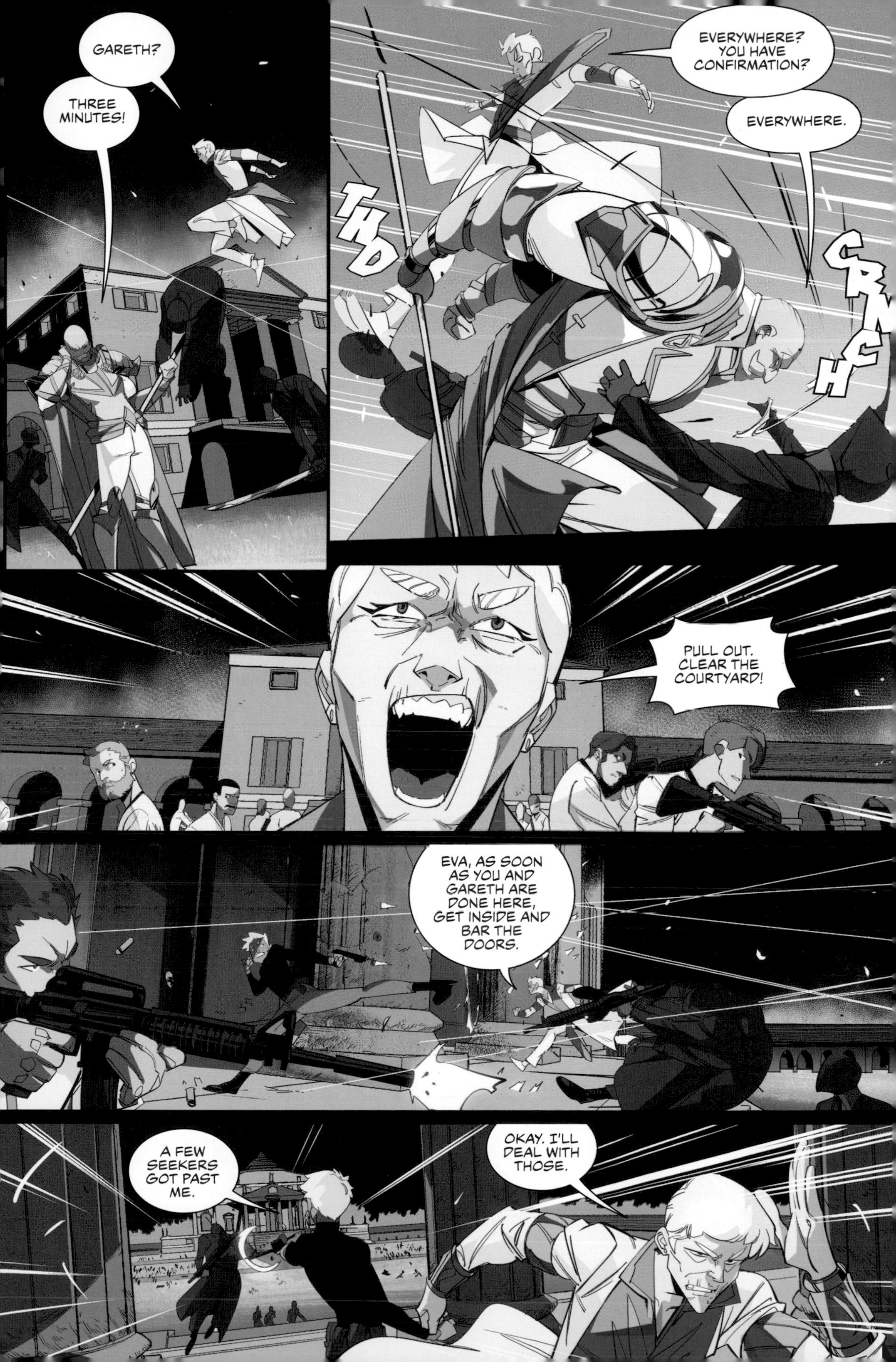
GARETH?
THREE MINUTES!
EVERYWHERE? YOU HAVE CONFIRMATION?
EVERYWHERE.
THD
CRNCH
PULL OUT. CLEAR THE COURTYARD!
EVA, AS SOON AS YOU AND GARETH ARE DONE HERE, GET INSIDE AND BAR THE DOORS.
A FEW SEEKERS GOT PAST ME.
OKAY. I'LL DEAL WITH THOSE.

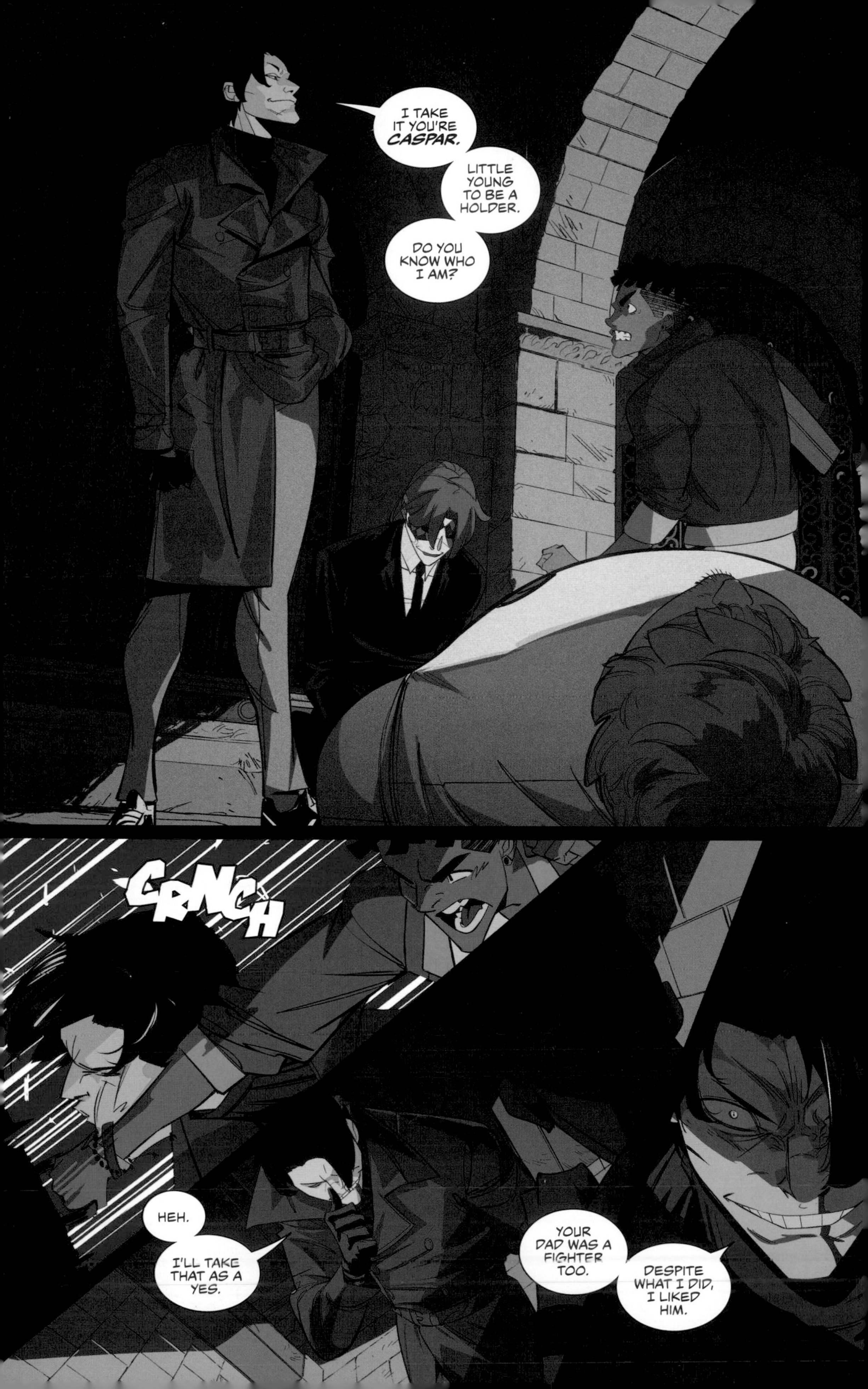

I TAKE IT YOU'RE *CASPAR.*
LITTLE YOUNG TO BE A HOLDER.
DO YOU KNOW WHO I AM?
CRNCH
HEH.
I'LL TAKE THAT AS A YES.
YOUR DAD WAS A FIGHTER TOO.
DESPITE WHAT I DID, I LIKED HIM.

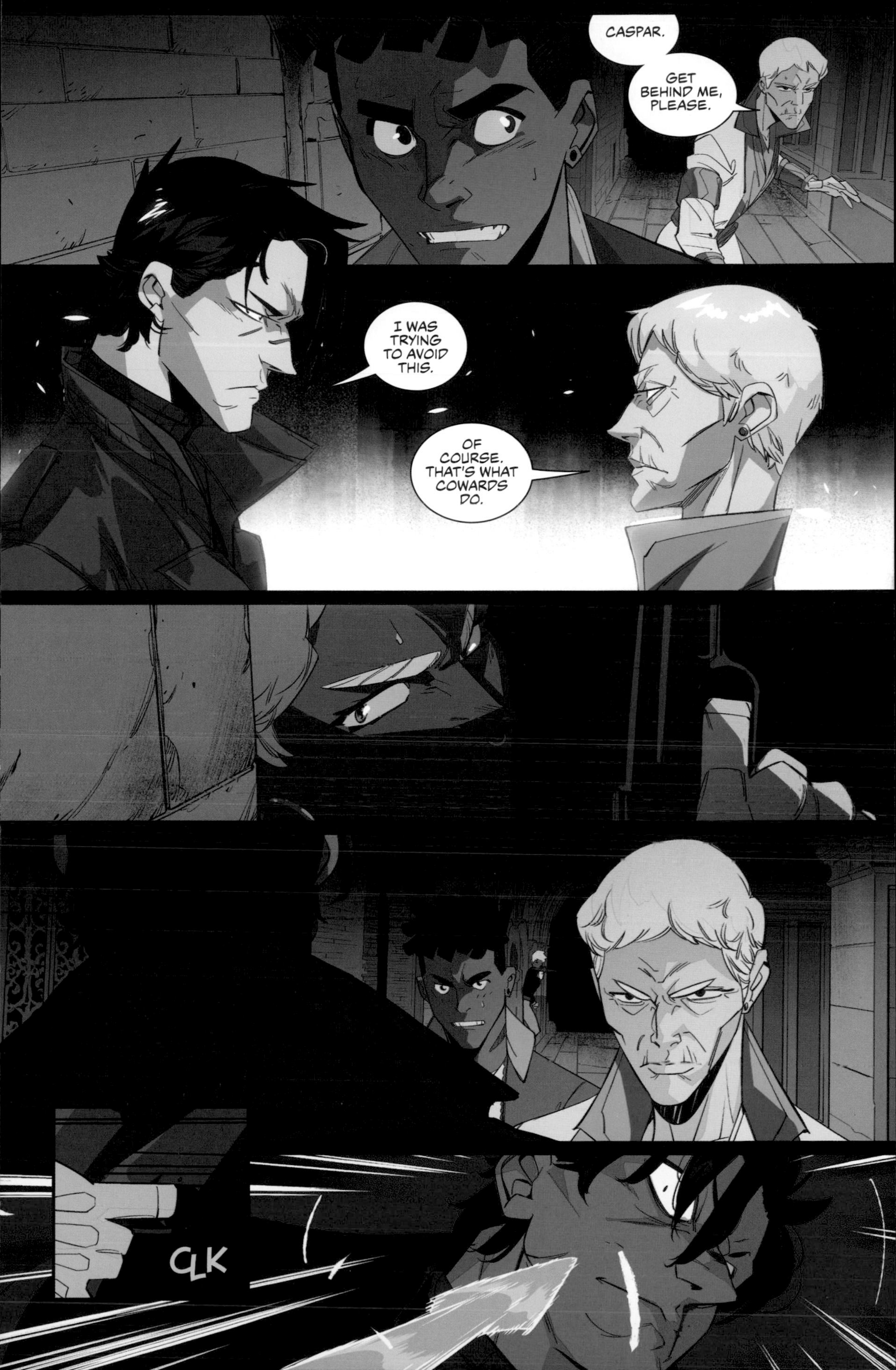
CASPAR.
GET BEHIND ME, PLEASE.
I WAS TRYING TO AVOID THIS.
OF COURSE. THAT'S WHAT COWARDS DO.
CLK

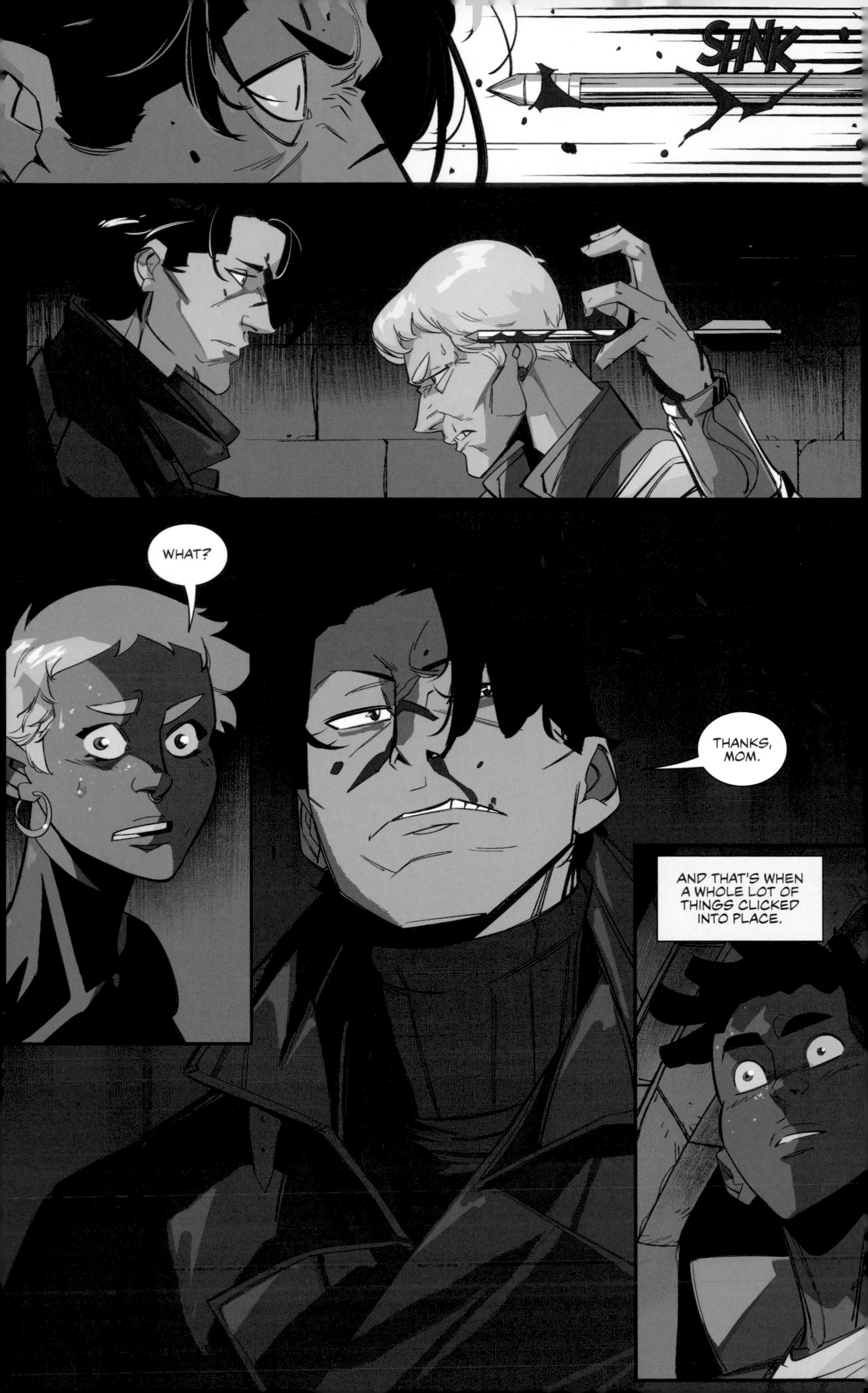
SHNK
WHAT?
THANKS, MOM.
AND THAT'S WHEN A WHOLE LOT OF THINGS CLICKED INTO PLACE.

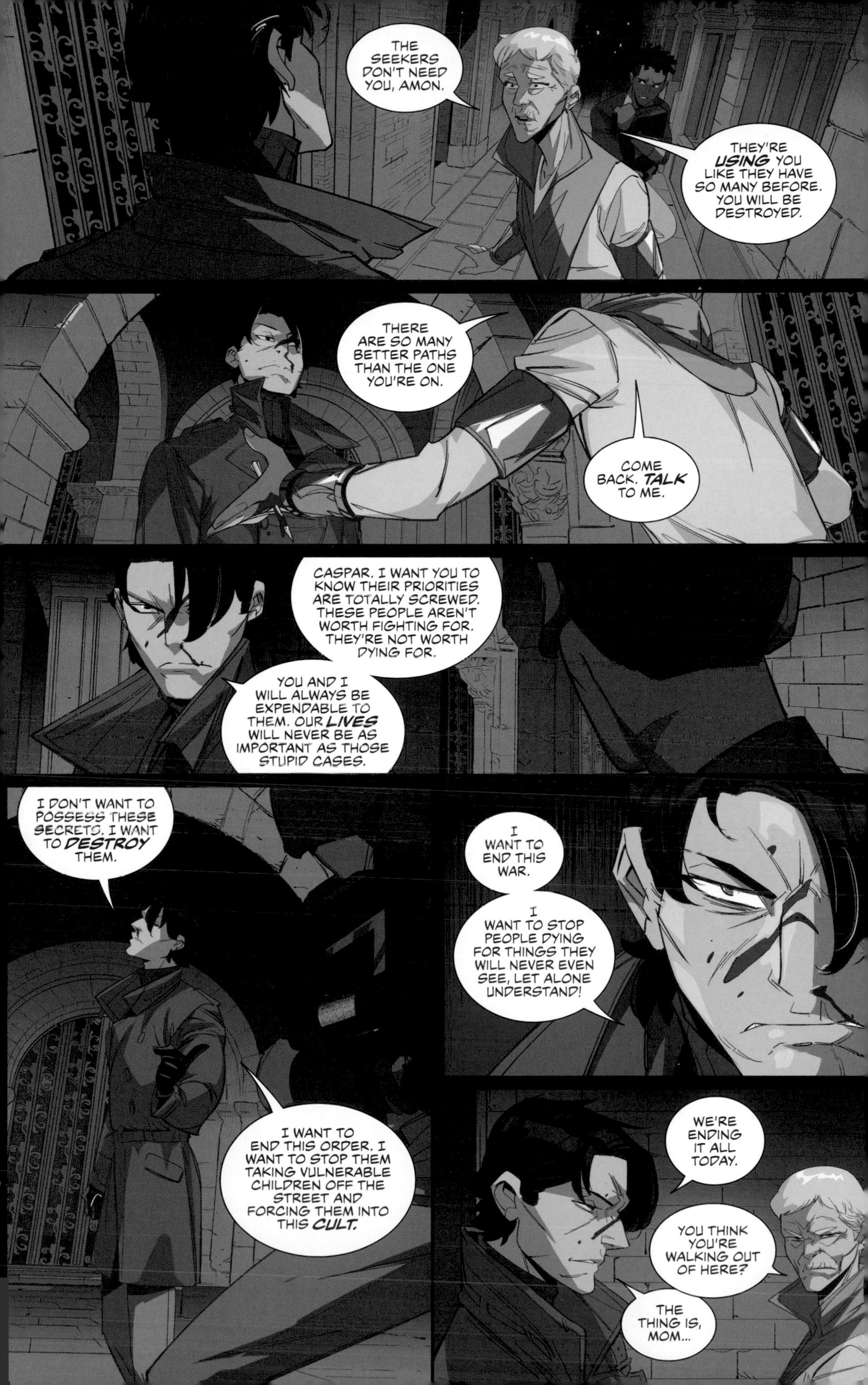
THE SEEKERS DON'T NEED YOU, AMON.
THEY'RE *USING* YOU LIKE THEY HAVE SO MANY BEFORE. YOU WILL BE DESTROYED.
THERE ARE SO MANY BETTER PATHS THAN THE ONE YOU'RE ON.
COME BACK. *TALK* TO ME.
CASPAR. I WANT YOU TO KNOW THEIR PRIORITIES ARE TOTALLY SCREWED. THESE PEOPLE AREN'T WORTH FIGHTING FOR. THEY'RE NOT WORTH DYING FOR.
YOU AND I WILL ALWAYS BE EXPENDABLE TO THEM. OUR *LIVES* WILL NEVER BE AS IMPORTANT AS THOSE STUPID CASES.
I DON'T WANT TO POSSESS THESE SECRETS. I WANT TO *DESTROY* THEM.
I WANT TO END THIS ORDER. I WANT TO STOP THEM TAKING VULNERABLE CHILDREN OFF THE STREET AND FORCING THEM INTO THIS *CULT.*
I WANT TO END THIS WAR.
I WANT TO STOP PEOPLE DYING FOR THINGS THEY WILL NEVER EVEN SEE, LET ALONE UNDERSTAND!
WE'RE ENDING IT ALL TODAY.
YOU THINK YOU'RE WALKING OUT OF HERE?
THE THING IS, MOM...

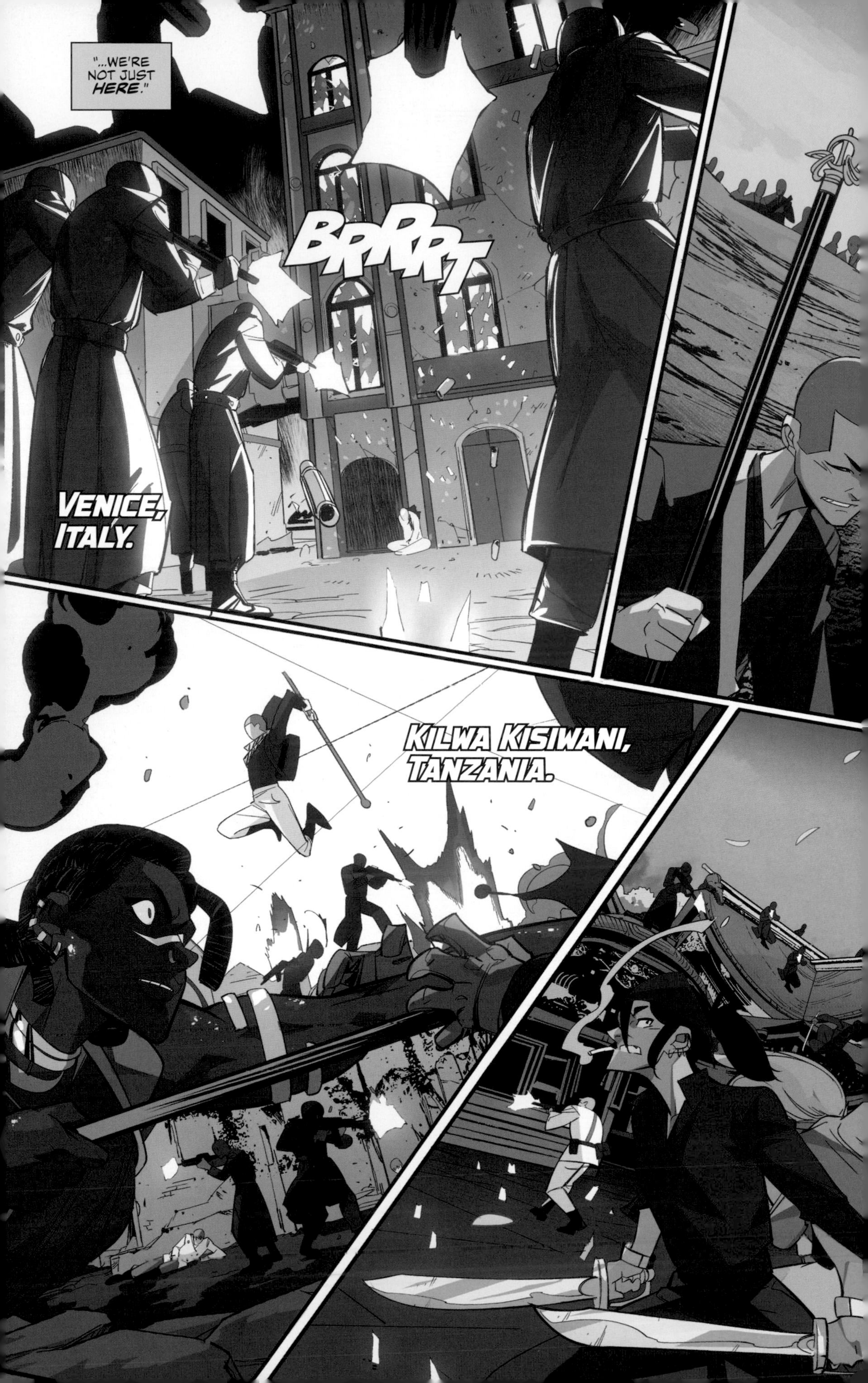
"...WE'RE NOT JUST HERE."
BRRRT
VENICE, ITALY.
KILWA KISIWANI, TANZANIA.

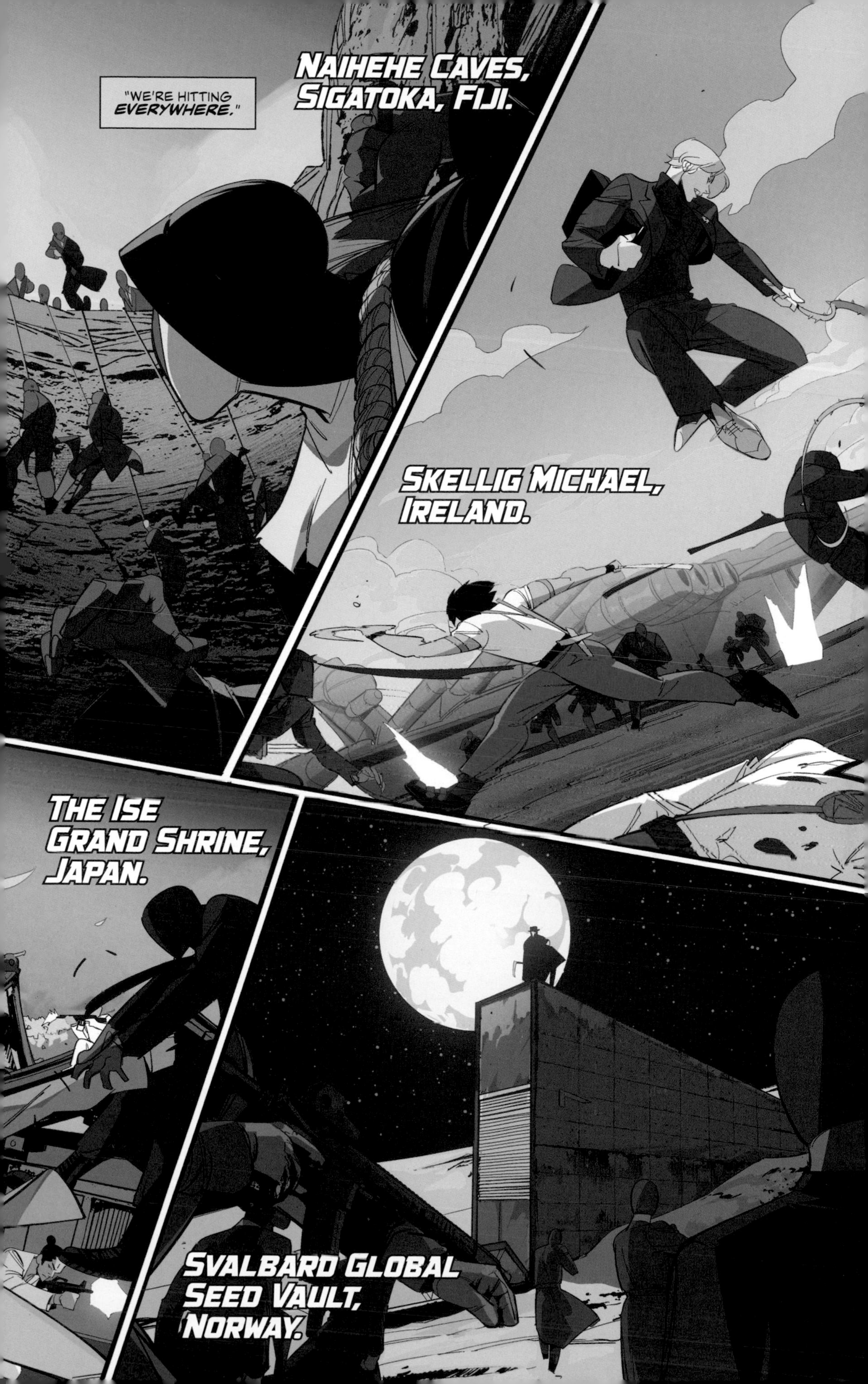
"WE'RE HITTING EVERYWHERE."
NAIHEHE CAVES, SIGATOKA, FIJI.
SKELLIG MICHAEL, IRELAND.
THE ISE GRAND SHRINE, JAPAN.
SVALBARD GLOBAL SEED VAULT, NORWAY.

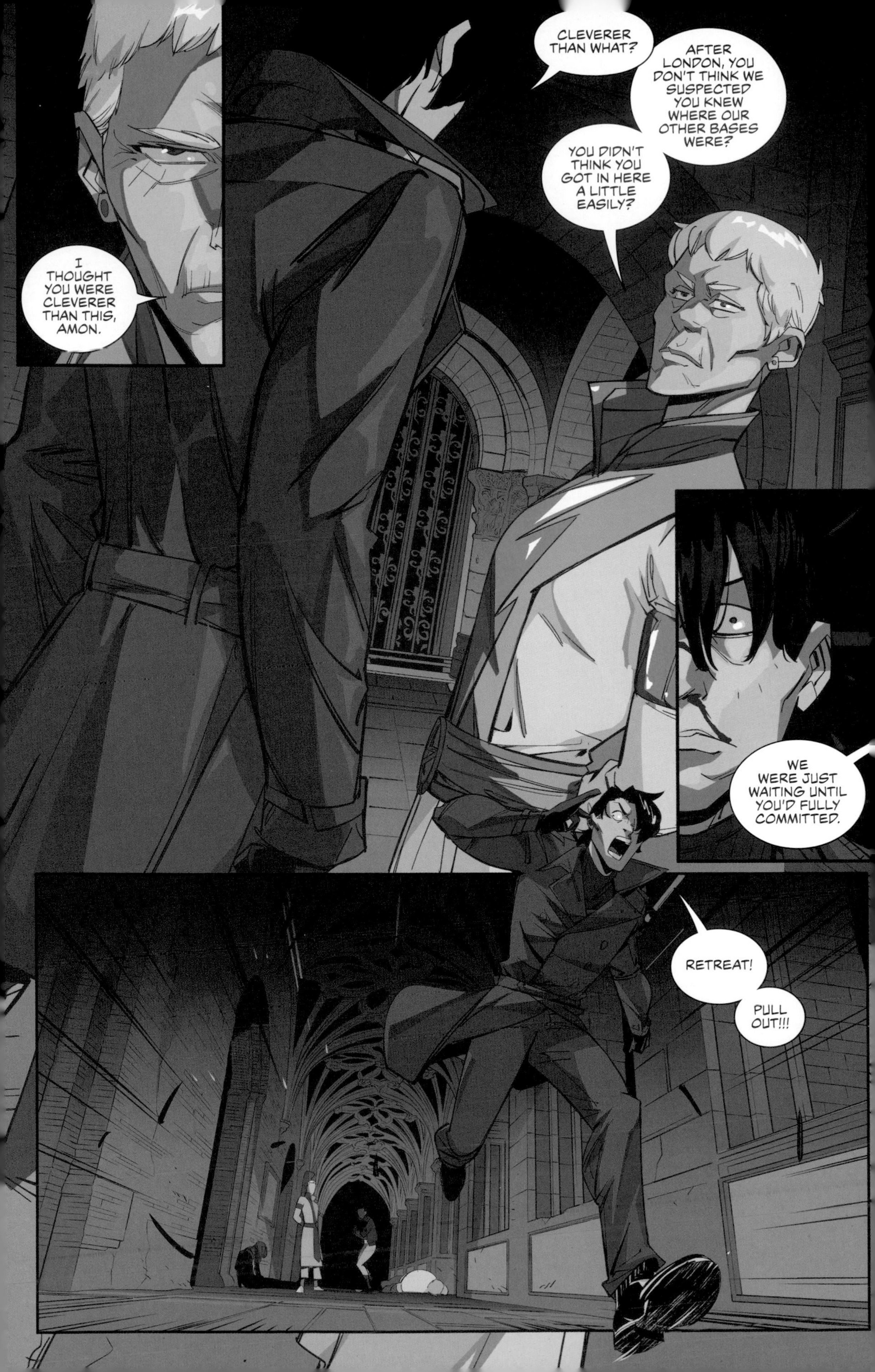
I THOUGHT YOU WERE CLEVERER THAN THIS, AMON.
CLEVERER THAN WHAT?
AFTER LONDON, YOU DON'T THINK WE SUSPECTED YOU KNEW WHERE OUR OTHER BASES WERE?
YOU DIDN'T THINK YOU GOT IN HERE A LITTLE EASILY?
WE WERE JUST WAITING UNTIL YOU'D FULLY COMMITTED.
RETREAT!
PULL OUT!!!

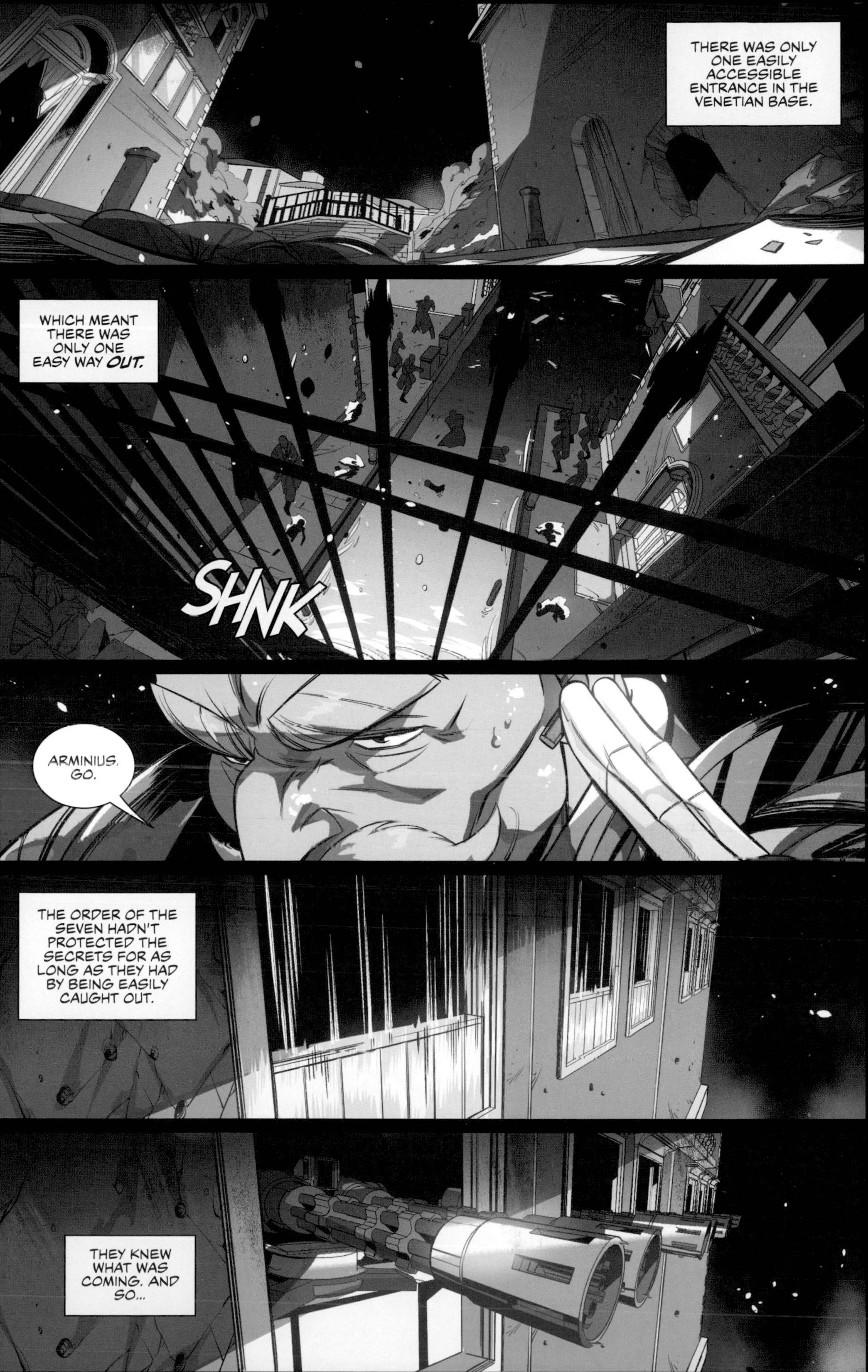
THERE WAS ONLY ONE EASILY ACCESSIBLE ENTRANCE IN THE VENETIAN BASE.
WHICH MEANT THERE WAS ONLY ONE EASY WAY OUT.
SHNK
ARMINIUS, GO.
THE ORDER OF THE SEVEN HADN'T PROTECTED THE SECRETS FOR AS LONG AS THEY HAD BY BEING EASILY CAUGHT OUT.
THEY KNEW WHAT WAS COMING. AND SO...

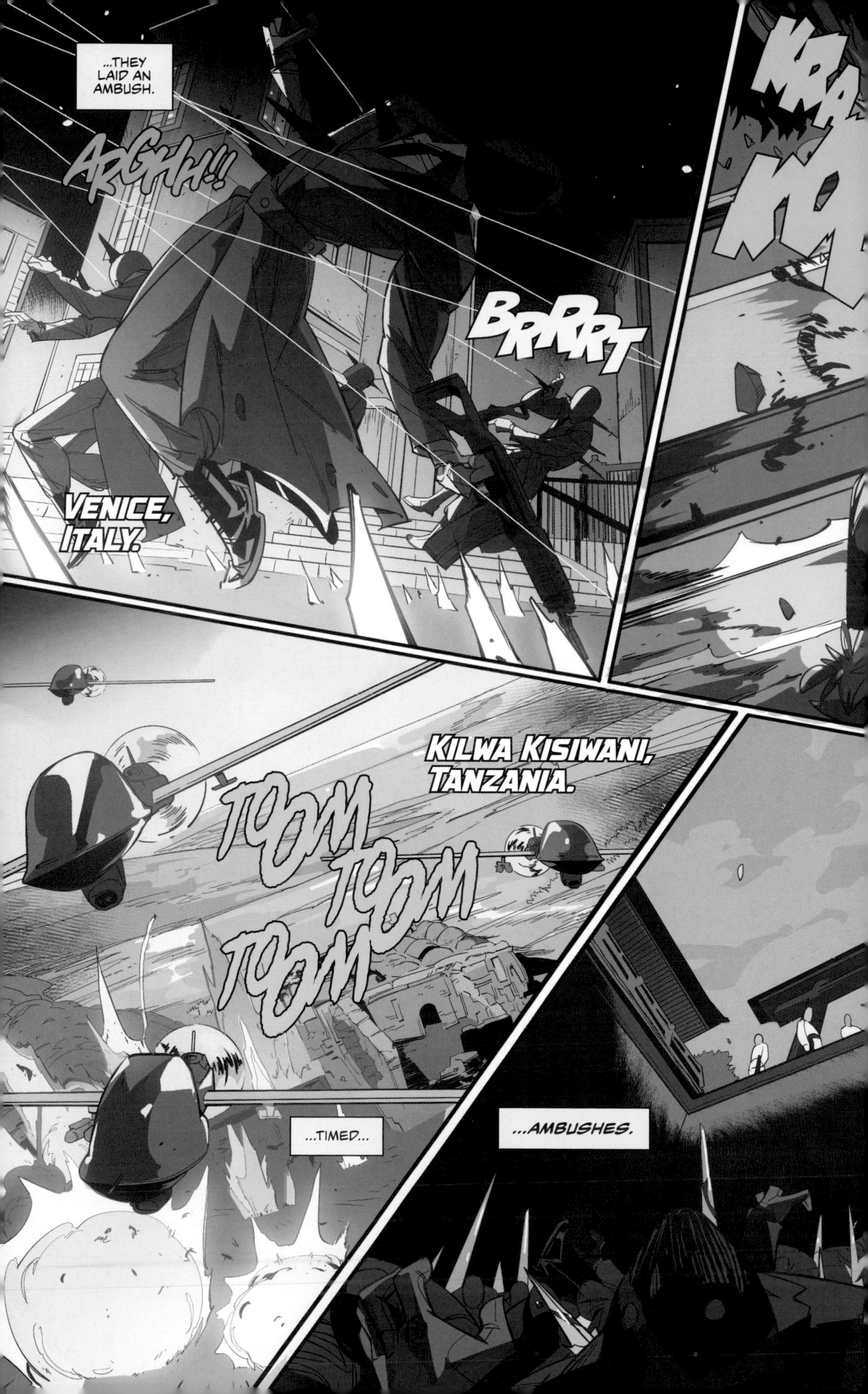
...THEY LAID AN AMBUSH.
ARGHH!!
BRRRRT
VENICE, ITALY.
KILWA KISIWANI, TANZANIA.
TOOM TOOM TOOM
...TIMED...
...AMBUSHES.

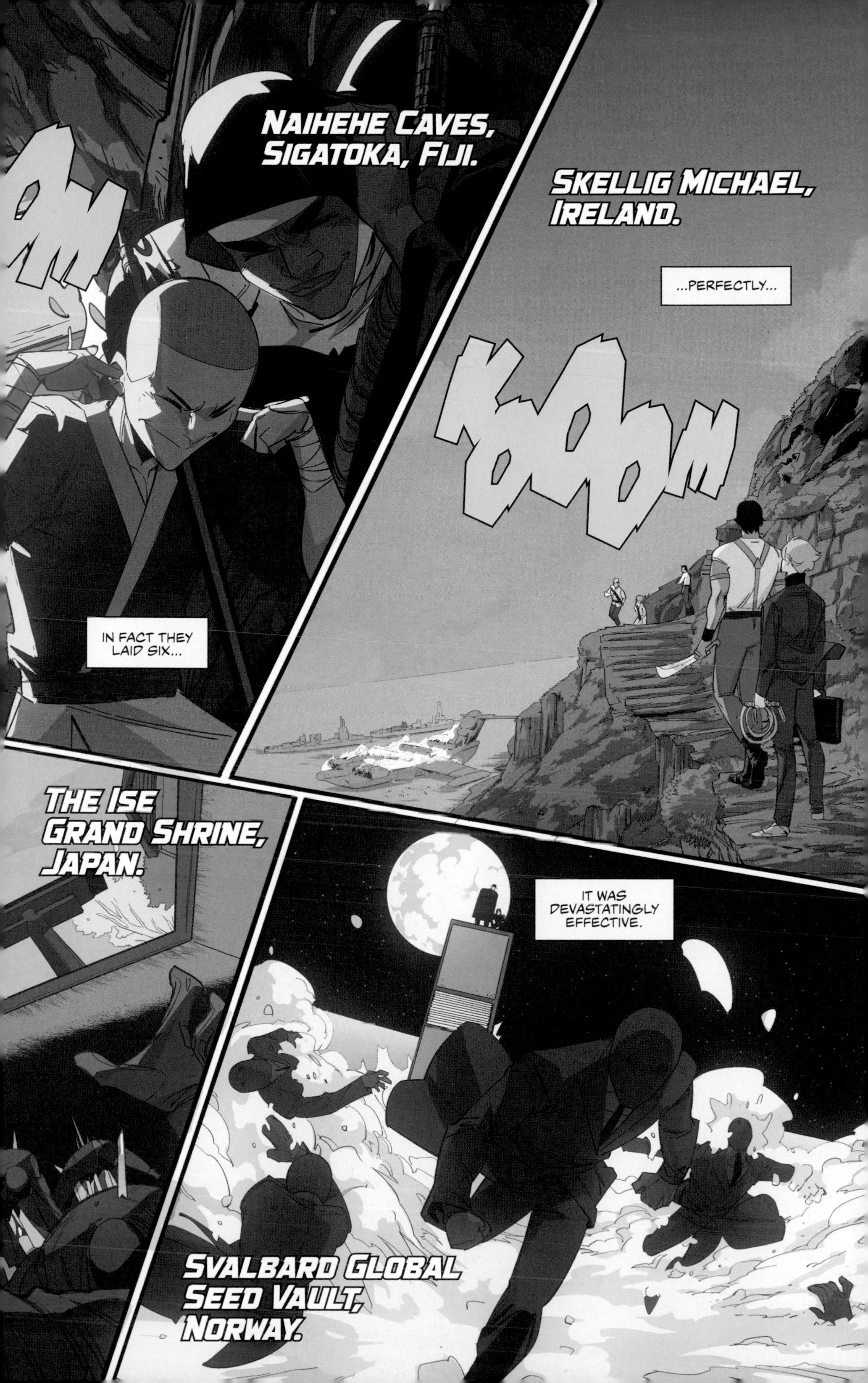

Naihehe Caves, Sigatoka, Fiji.
In fact they laid six...
Skellig Michael, Ireland.
...perfectly...
KOOOM
The Ise Grand Shrine, Japan.
It was devastatingly effective.
Svalbard Global Seed Vault, Norway.

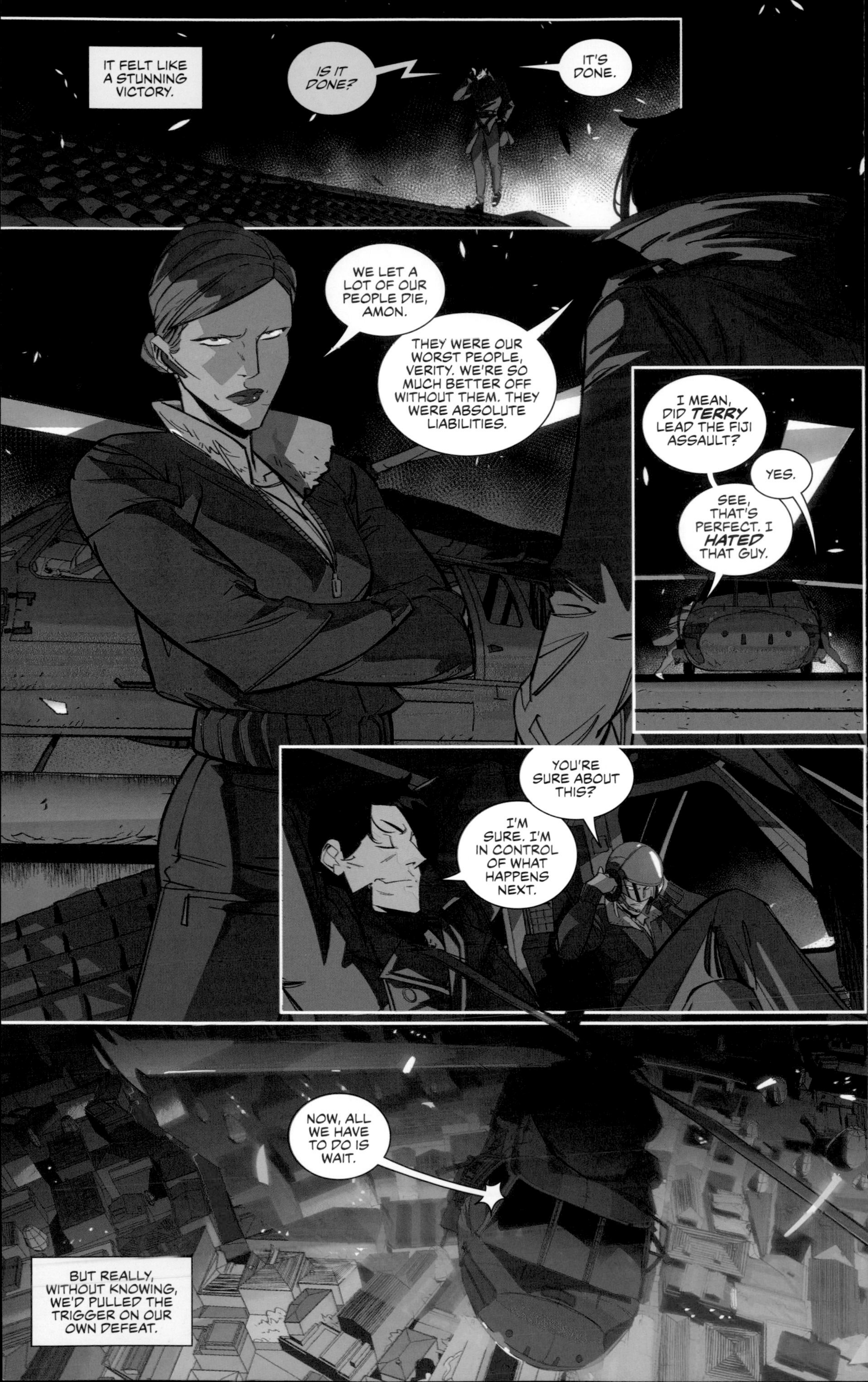

IT FELT LIKE A STUNNING VICTORY.
IS IT DONE?
IT'S DONE.
WE LET A LOT OF OUR PEOPLE DIE, AMON.
THEY WERE OUR WORST PEOPLE, VERITY. WE'RE SO MUCH BETTER OFF WITHOUT THEM. THEY WERE ABSOLUTE LIABILITIES.
I MEAN, DID TERRY LEAD THE FIJI ASSAULT?
YES.
SEE, THAT'S PERFECT. I HATED THAT GUY.
YOU'RE SURE ABOUT THIS?
I'M SURE. I'M IN CONTROL OF WHAT HAPPENS NEXT.
NOW, ALL WE HAVE TO DO IS WAIT.
BUT REALLY, WITHOUT KNOWING, WE'D PULLED THE TRIGGER ON OUR OWN DEFEAT.

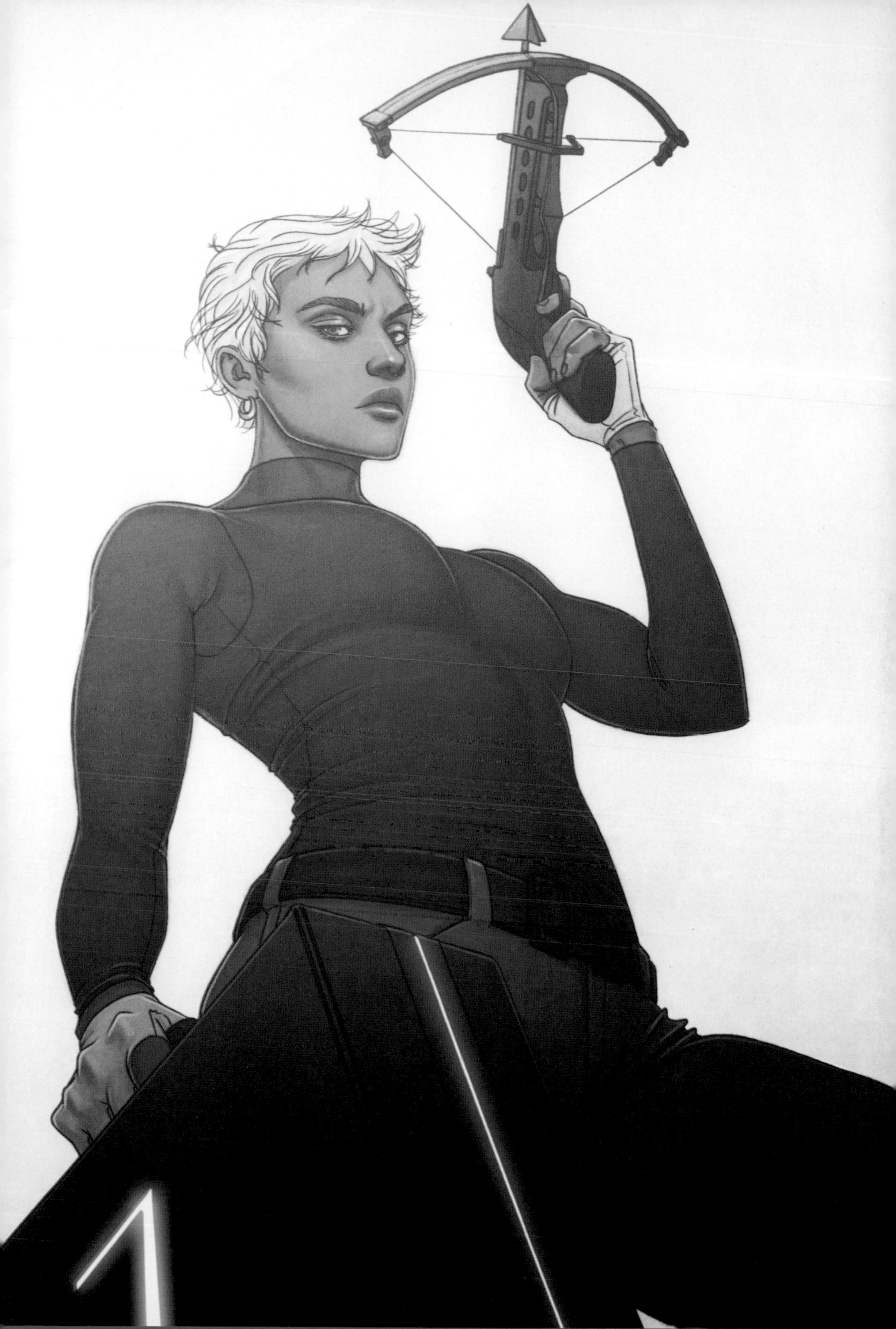

JENNY FRISON ISSUE FOUR VARIANT COVER

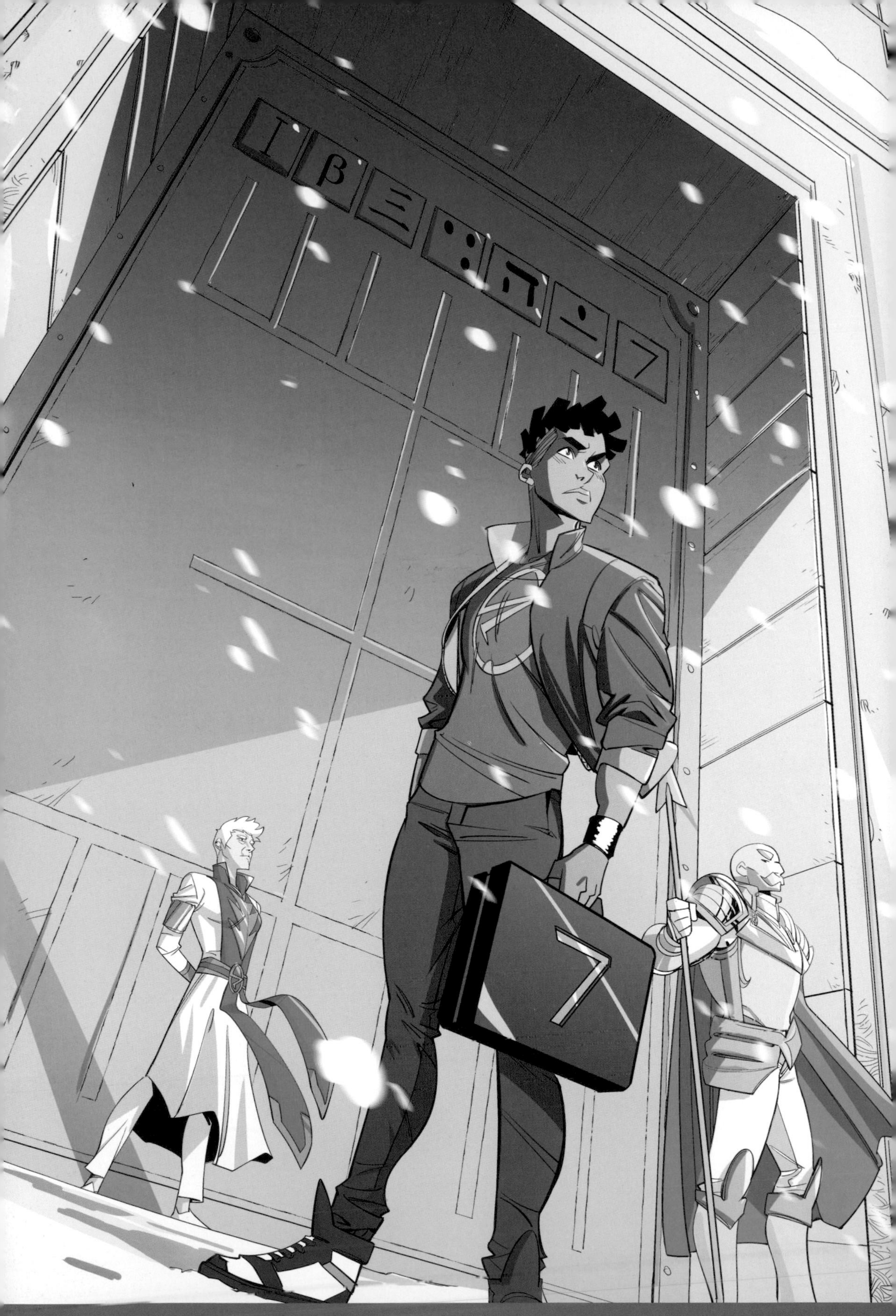

CHAPTER FIVE

DANIELE DI NICUOLO ISSUE FIVE COVER

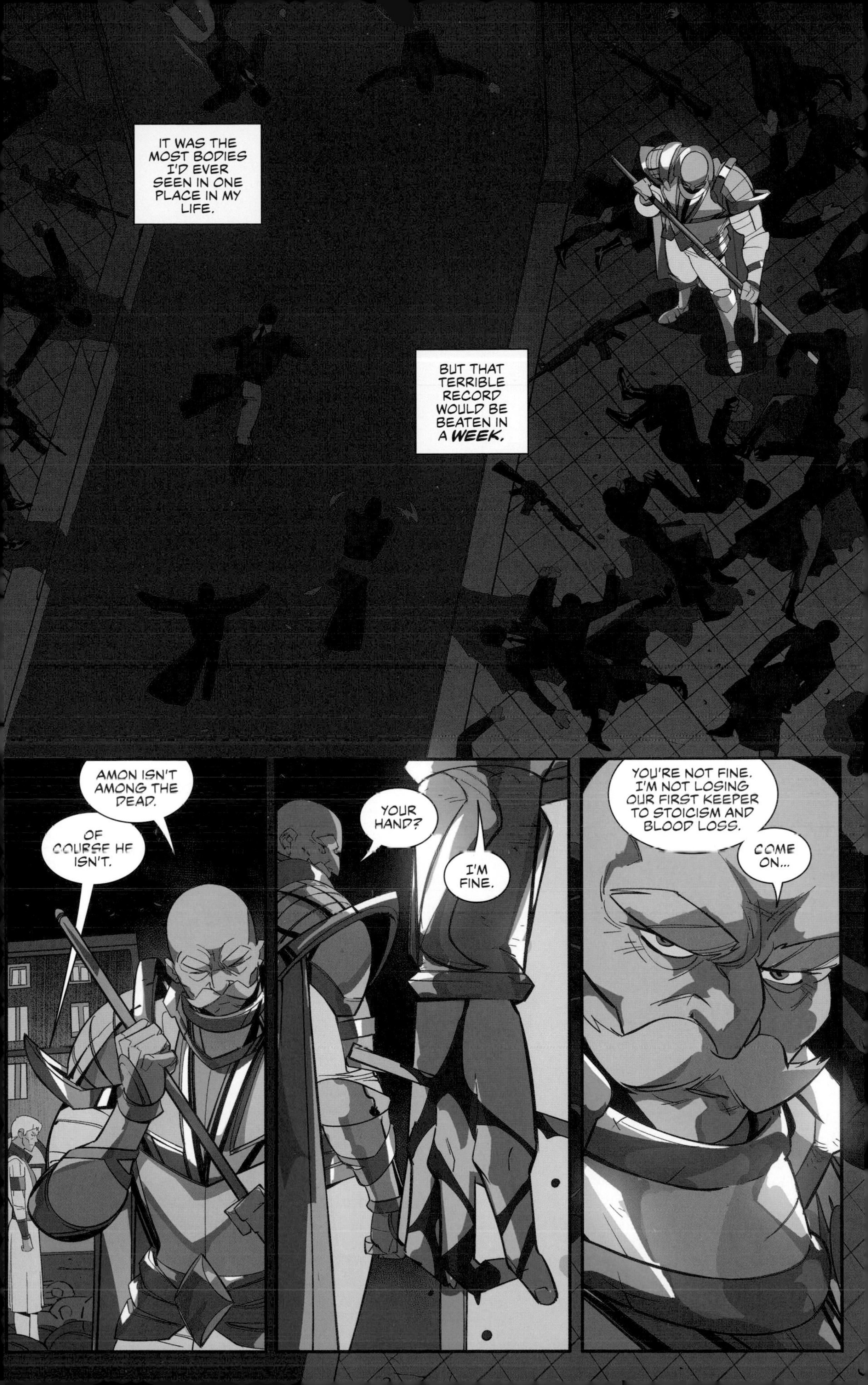
IT WAS THE MOST BODIES I'D EVER SEEN IN ONE PLACE IN MY LIFE.
BUT THAT TERRIBLE RECORD WOULD BE BEATEN IN A ***WEEK.***
AMON ISN'T AMONG THE DEAD.
OF COURSE HE ISN'T.
YOUR HAND?
I'M FINE.
YOU'RE NOT FINE. I'M NOT LOSING OUR FIRST KEEPER TO STOICISM AND BLOOD LOSS.
COME ON...

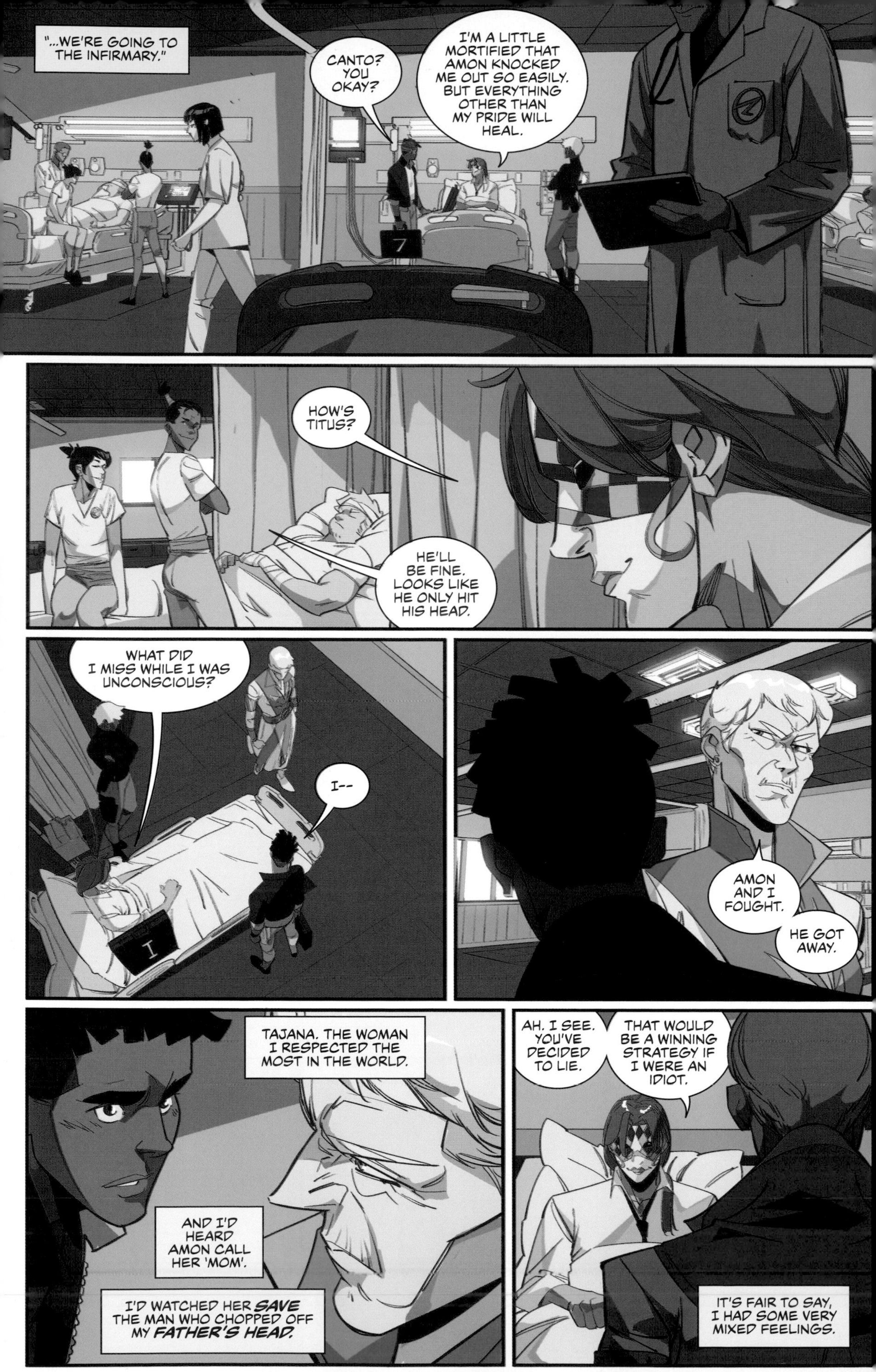
"...WE'RE GOING TO THE INFIRMARY."
CANTO? YOU OKAY?
I'M A LITTLE MORTIFIED THAT AMON KNOCKED ME OUT SO EASILY. BUT EVERYTHING OTHER THAN MY PRIDE WILL HEAL.
7
HOW'S TITUS?
HE'LL BE FINE. LOOKS LIKE HE ONLY HIT HIS HEAD.
WHAT DID I MISS WHILE I WAS UNCONSCIOUS?
I--
I
AMON AND I FOUGHT.
HE GOT AWAY.
TAJANA. THE WOMAN I RESPECTED THE MOST IN THE WORLD.
AND I'D HEARD AMON CALL HER 'MOM'.
I'D WATCHED HER SAVE THE MAN WHO CHOPPED OFF MY FATHER'S HEAD.
AH. I SEE. YOU'VE DECIDED TO LIE.
THAT WOULD BE A WINNING STRATEGY IF I WERE AN IDIOT.
IT'S FAIR TO SAY, I HAD SOME VERY MIXED FEELINGS.

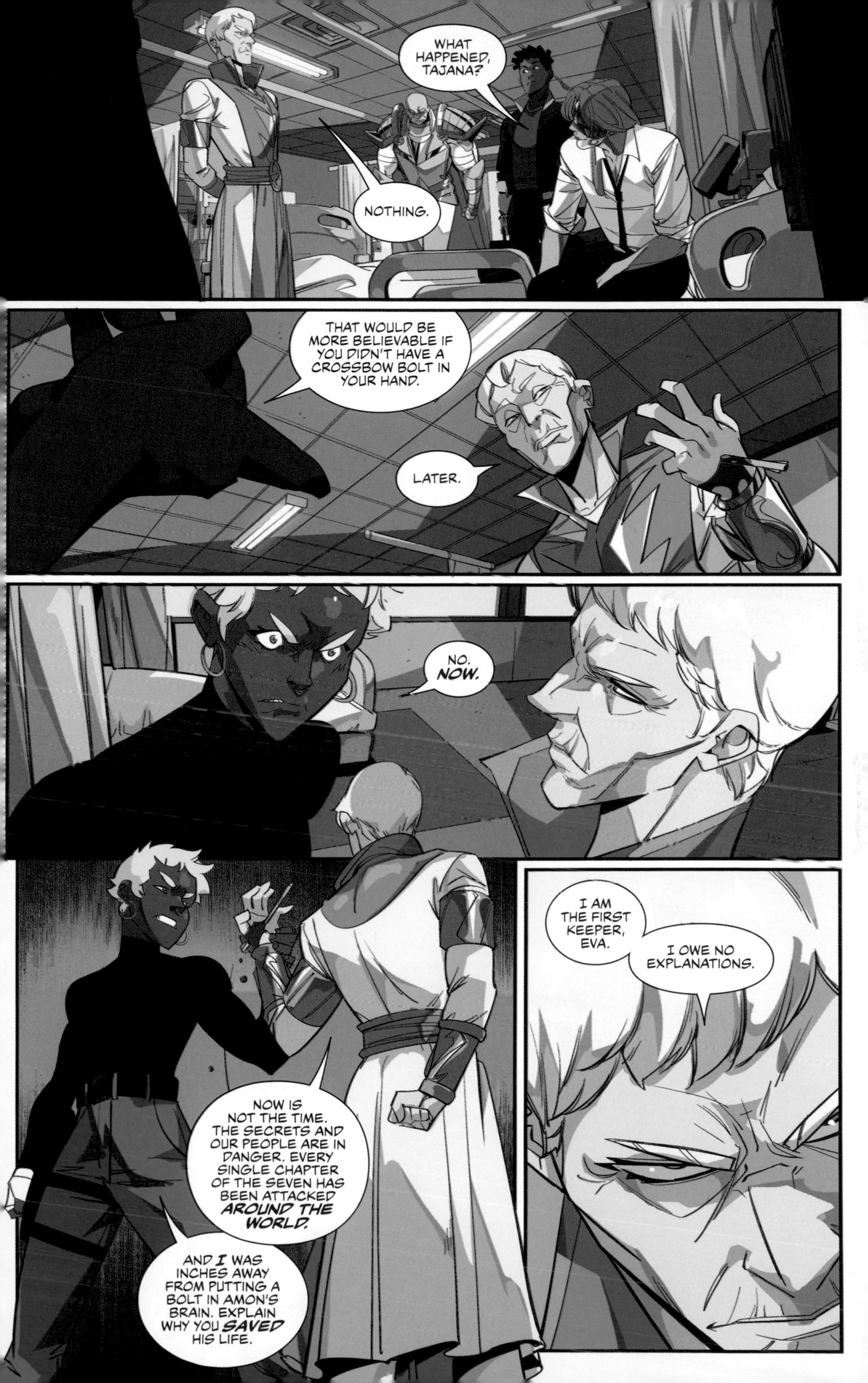
WHAT HAPPENED, TAJANA?
NOTHING.
THAT WOULD BE MORE BELIEVABLE IF YOU DIDN'T HAVE A CROSSBOW BOLT IN YOUR HAND.
LATER.
NO. *NOW.*
NOW IS NOT THE TIME. THE SECRETS AND OUR PEOPLE ARE IN DANGER. EVERY SINGLE CHAPTER OF THE SEVEN HAS BEEN ATTACKED *AROUND THE WORLD.*
AND *I* WAS INCHES AWAY FROM PUTTING A BOLT IN AMON'S BRAIN. EXPLAIN WHY YOU *SAVED* HIS LIFE.
I AM THE FIRST KEEPER, EVA.
I OWE NO EXPLANATIONS.

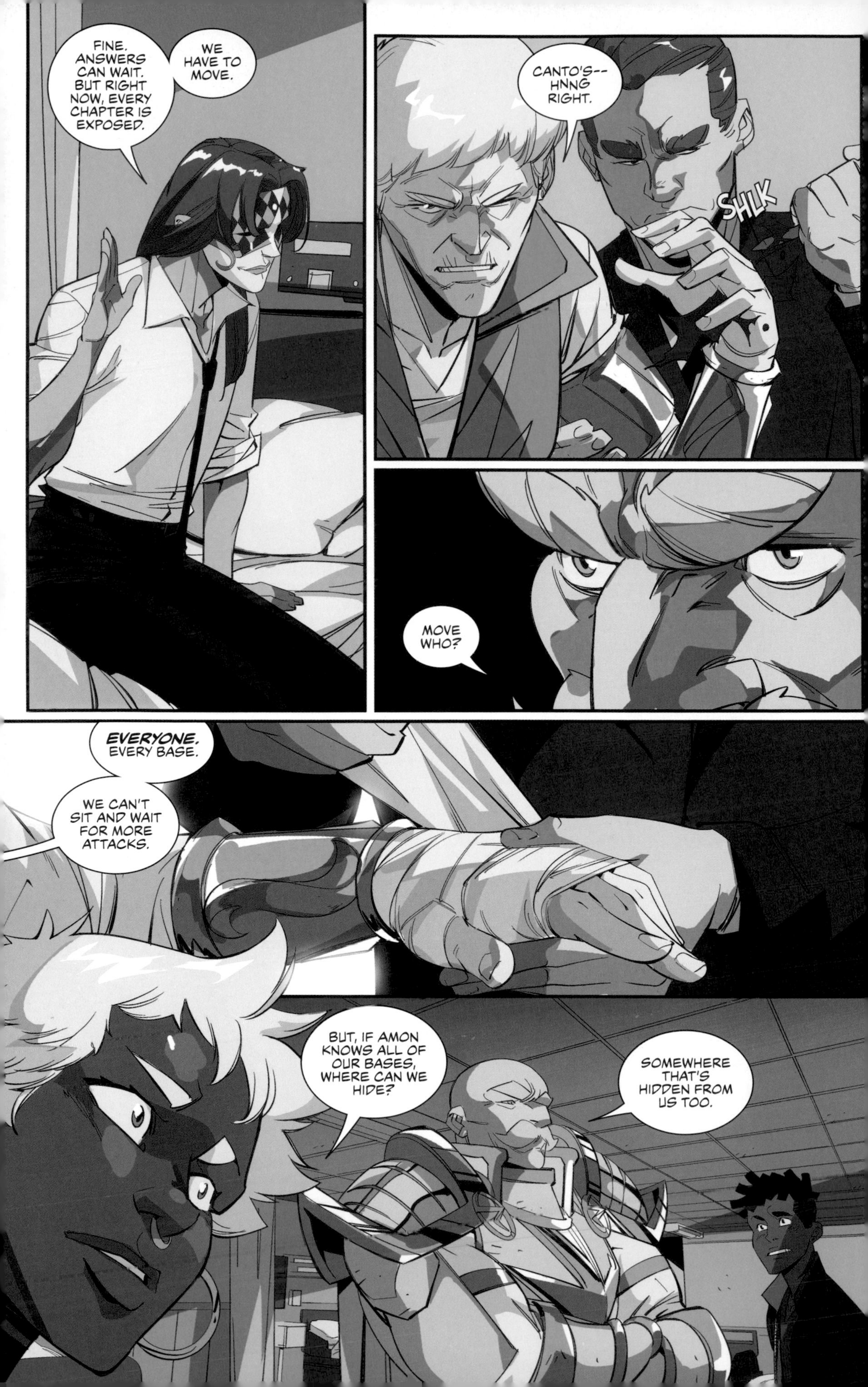
FINE. ANSWERS CAN WAIT. BUT RIGHT NOW, EVERY CHAPTER IS EXPOSED.
WE HAVE TO MOVE.
CANTO'S-- HNNG RIGHT.
SHLK
MOVE WHO?
EVERYONE. EVERY BASE.
WE CAN'T SIT AND WAIT FOR MORE ATTACKS.
BUT, IF AMON KNOWS ALL OF OUR BASES, WHERE CAN WE HIDE?
SOMEWHERE THAT'S HIDDEN FROM US TOO.

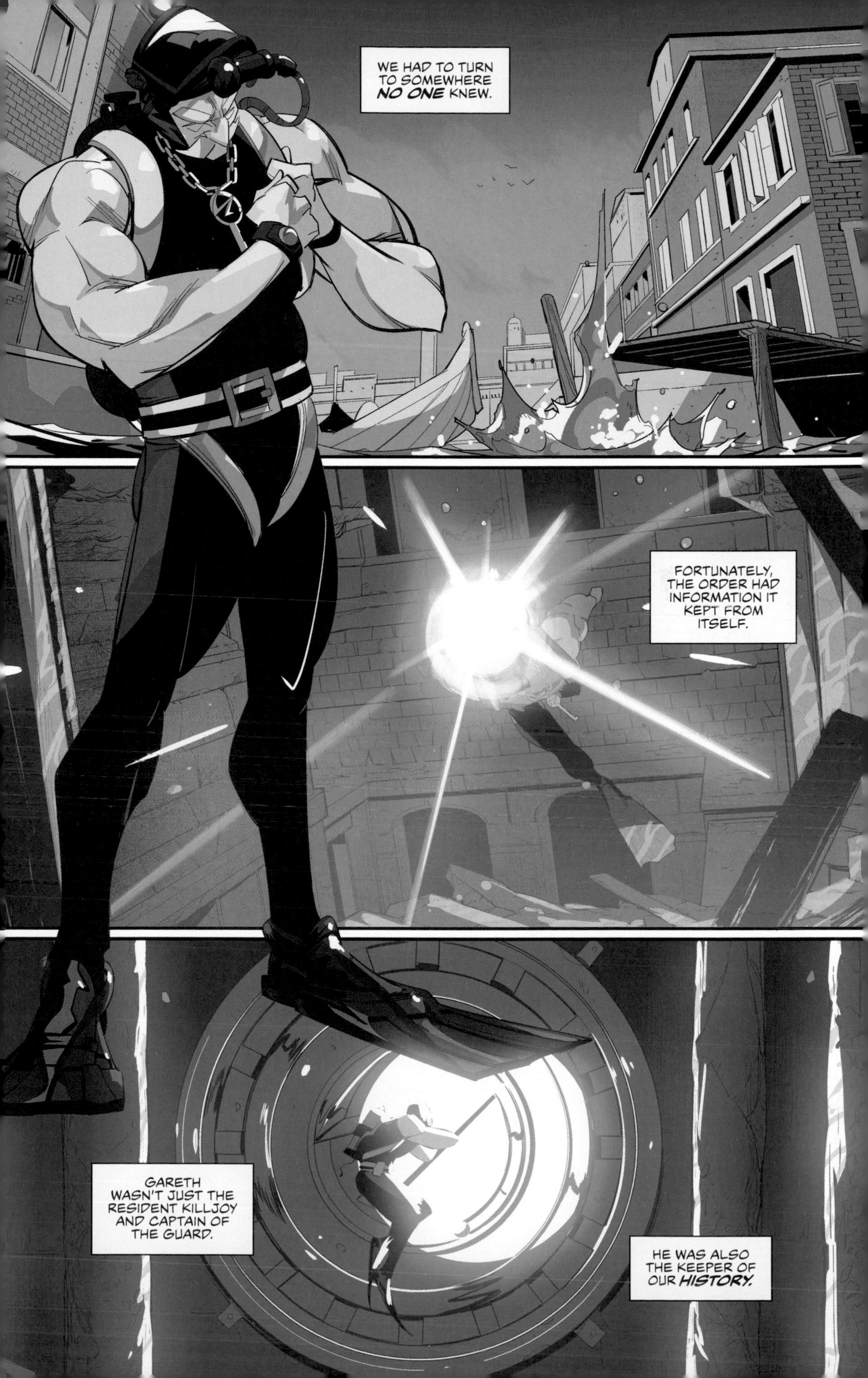
WE HAD TO TURN TO SOMEWHERE NO ONE KNEW.
FORTUNATELY, THE ORDER HAD INFORMATION IT KEPT FROM ITSELF.
GARETH WASN'T JUST THE RESIDENT KILLJOY AND CAPTAIN OF THE GUARD.
HE WAS ALSO THE KEEPER OF OUR HISTORY.

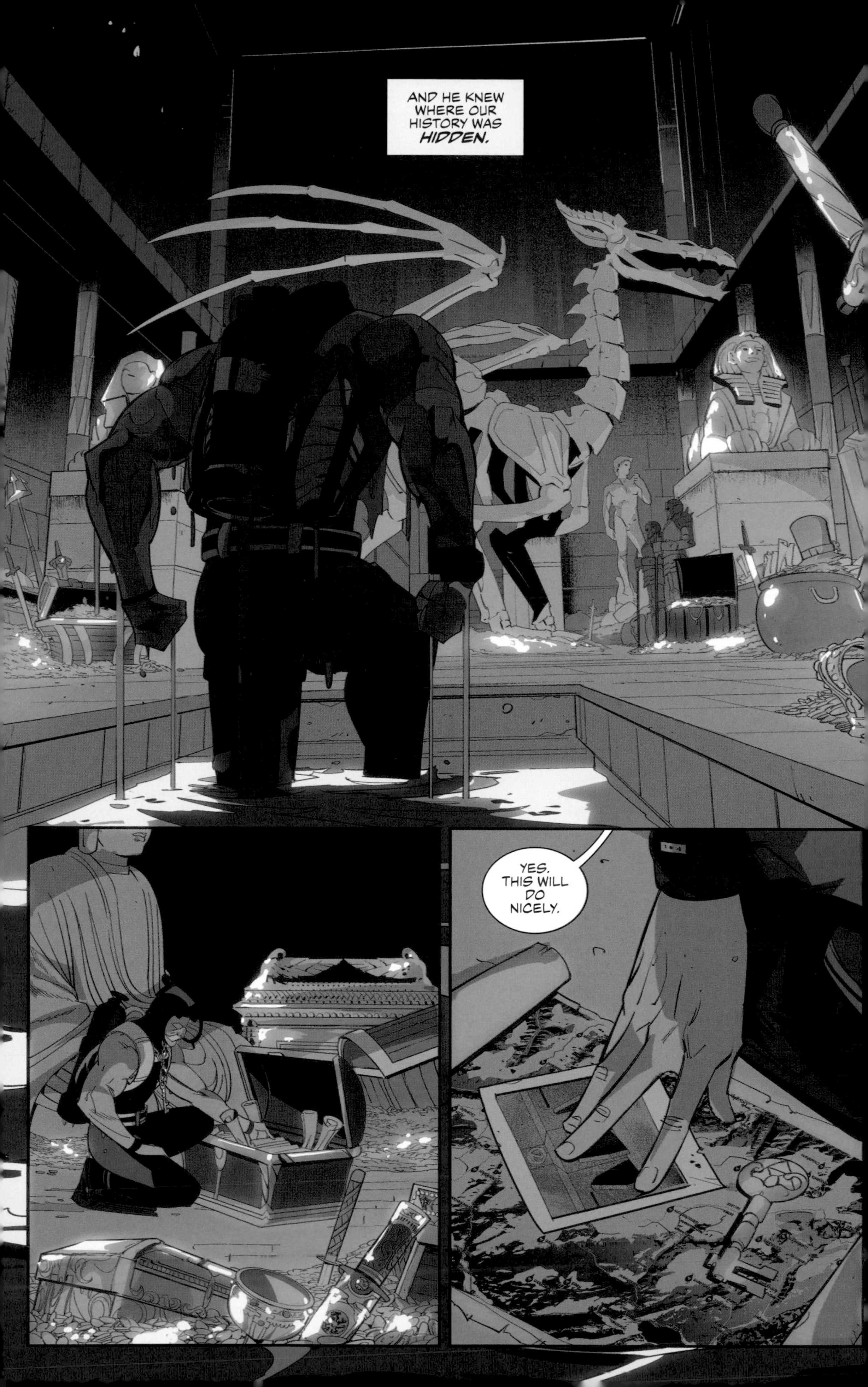
AND HE KNEW WHERE OUR HISTORY WAS HIDDEN.
YES. THIS WILL DO NICELY.

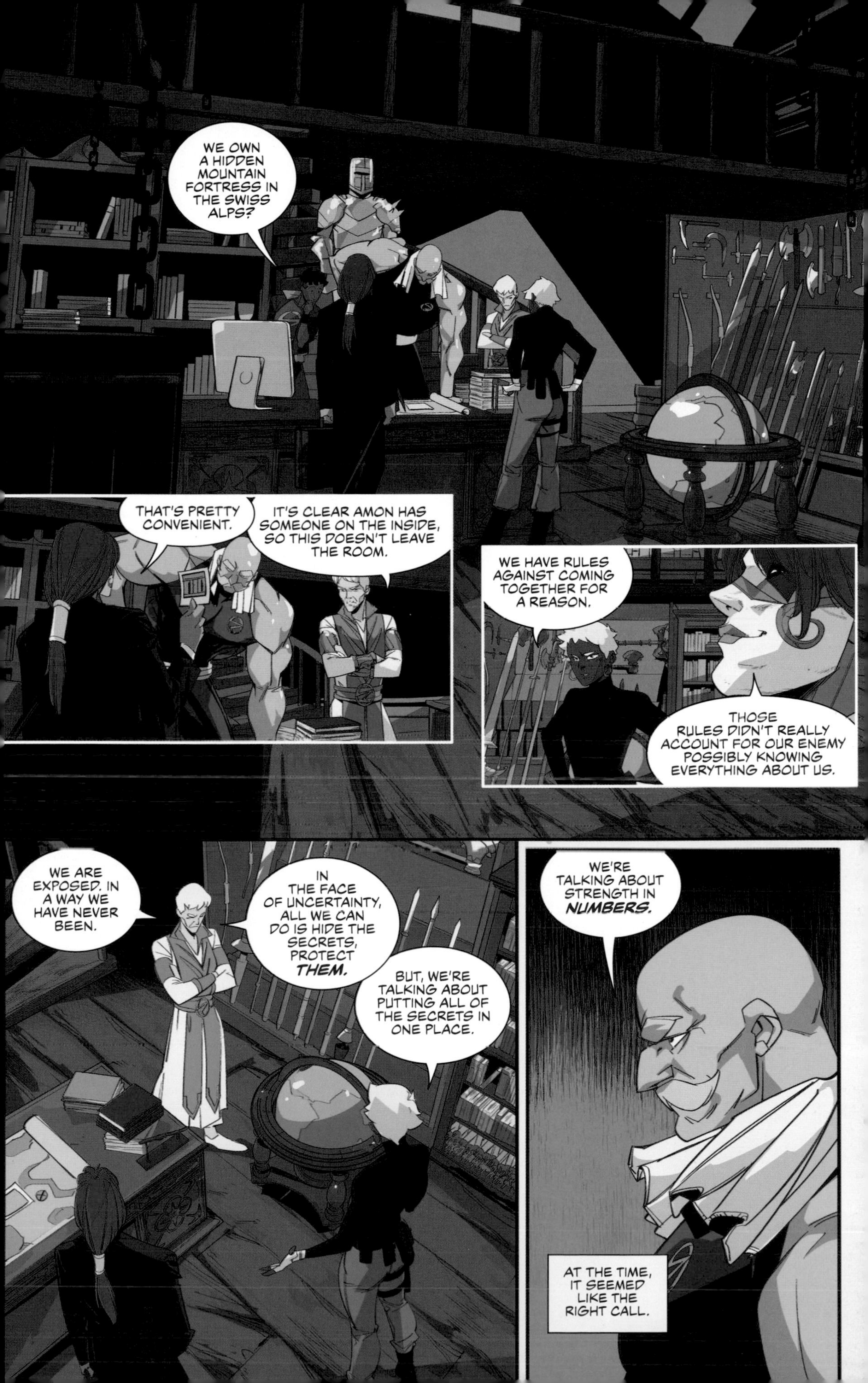
WE OWN A HIDDEN MOUNTAIN FORTRESS IN THE SWISS ALPS?
THAT'S PRETTY CONVENIENT.
IT'S CLEAR AMON HAS SOMEONE ON THE INSIDE, SO THIS DOESN'T LEAVE THE ROOM.
WE HAVE RULES AGAINST COMING TOGETHER FOR A REASON.
THOSE RULES DIDN'T REALLY ACCOUNT FOR OUR ENEMY POSSIBLY KNOWING EVERYTHING ABOUT US.
WE ARE EXPOSED. IN A WAY WE HAVE NEVER BEEN.
IN THE FACE OF UNCERTAINTY, ALL WE CAN DO IS HIDE THE SECRETS, PROTECT *THEM.*
BUT, WE'RE TALKING ABOUT PUTTING ALL OF THE SECRETS IN ONE PLACE.
WE'RE TALKING ABOUT STRENGTH IN *NUMBERS.*
AT THE TIME, IT SEEMED LIKE THE RIGHT CALL.

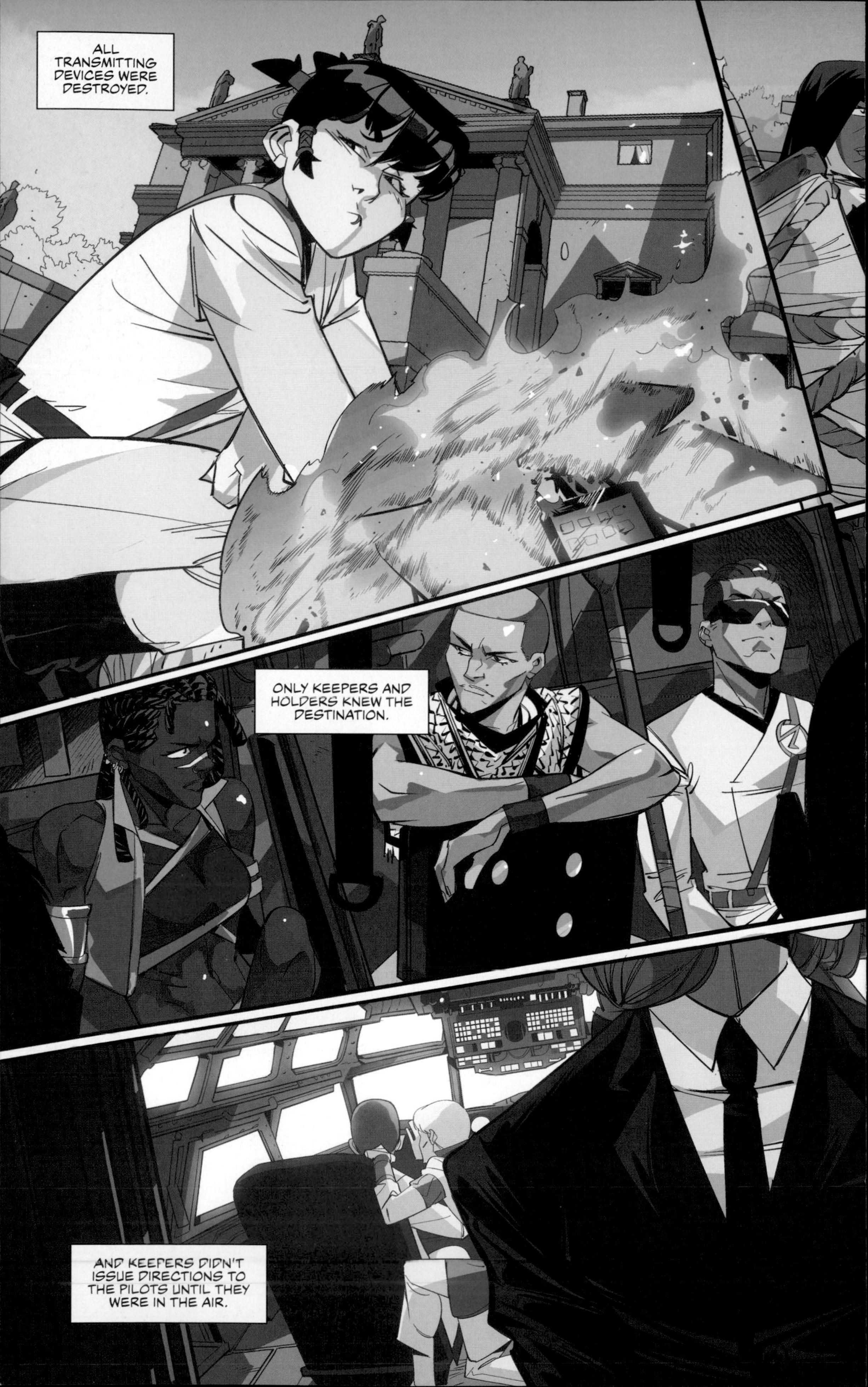
ALL TRANSMITTING DEVICES WERE DESTROYED.
ONLY KEEPERS AND HOLDERS KNEW THE DESTINATION.
AND KEEPERS DIDN'T ISSUE DIRECTIONS TO THE PILOTS UNTIL THEY WERE IN THE AIR.

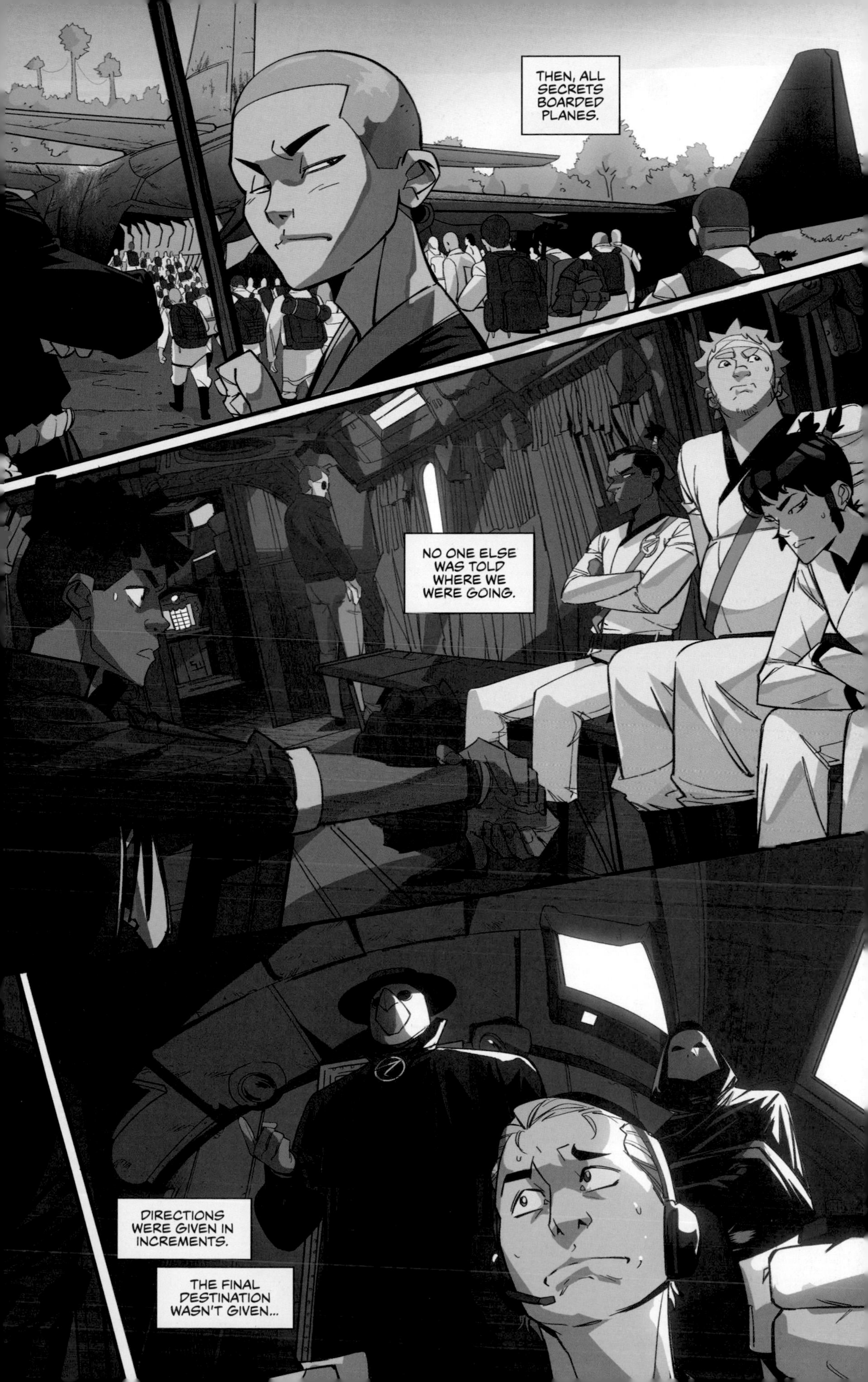
THEN, ALL SECRETS BOARDED PLANES.
NO ONE ELSE WAS TOLD WHERE WE WERE GOING.
DIRECTIONS WERE GIVEN IN INCREMENTS.
THE FINAL DESTINATION WASN'T GIVEN...

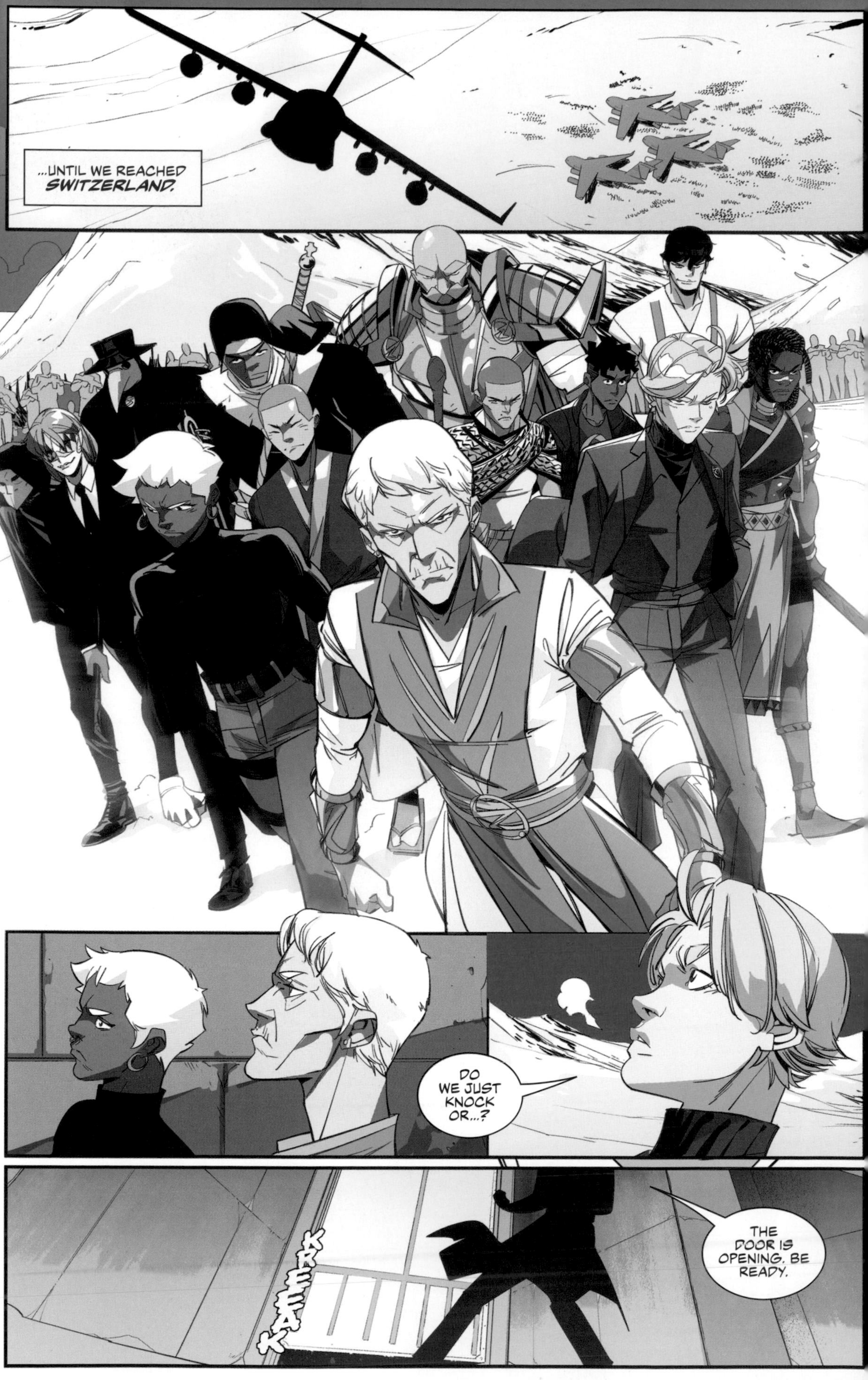
...UNTIL WE REACHED SWITZERLAND.
DO WE JUST KNOCK OR...?
KREEAK
THE DOOR IS OPENING. BE READY.

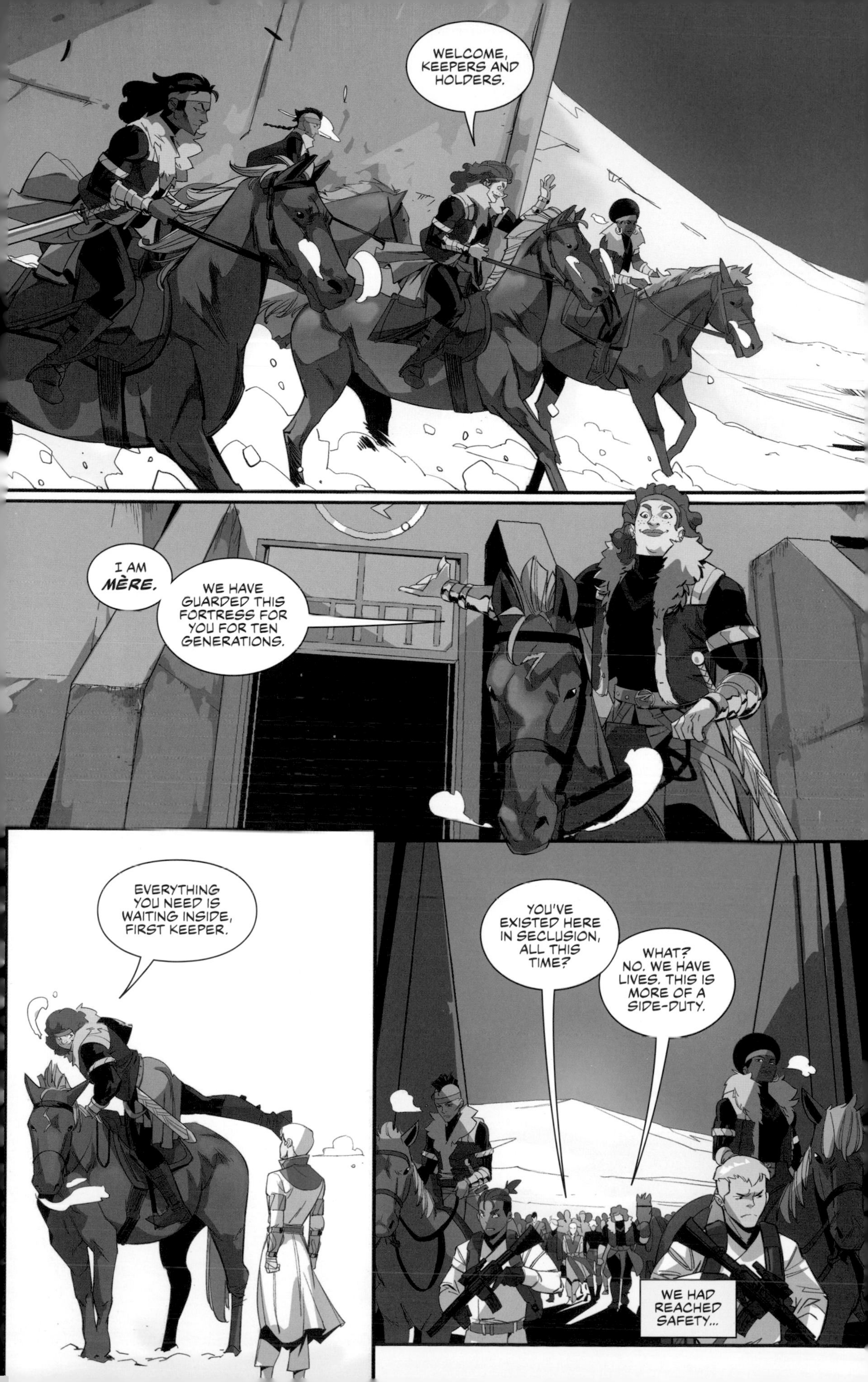
WELCOME, KEEPERS AND HOLDERS.
I AM MÈRE.
WE HAVE GUARDED THIS FORTRESS FOR YOU FOR TEN GENERATIONS.
EVERYTHING YOU NEED IS WAITING INSIDE, FIRST KEEPER.
YOU'VE EXISTED HERE IN SECLUSION, ALL THIS TIME?
WHAT? NO. WE HAVE LIVES. THIS IS MORE OF A SIDE-DUTY.
WE HAD REACHED SAFETY...

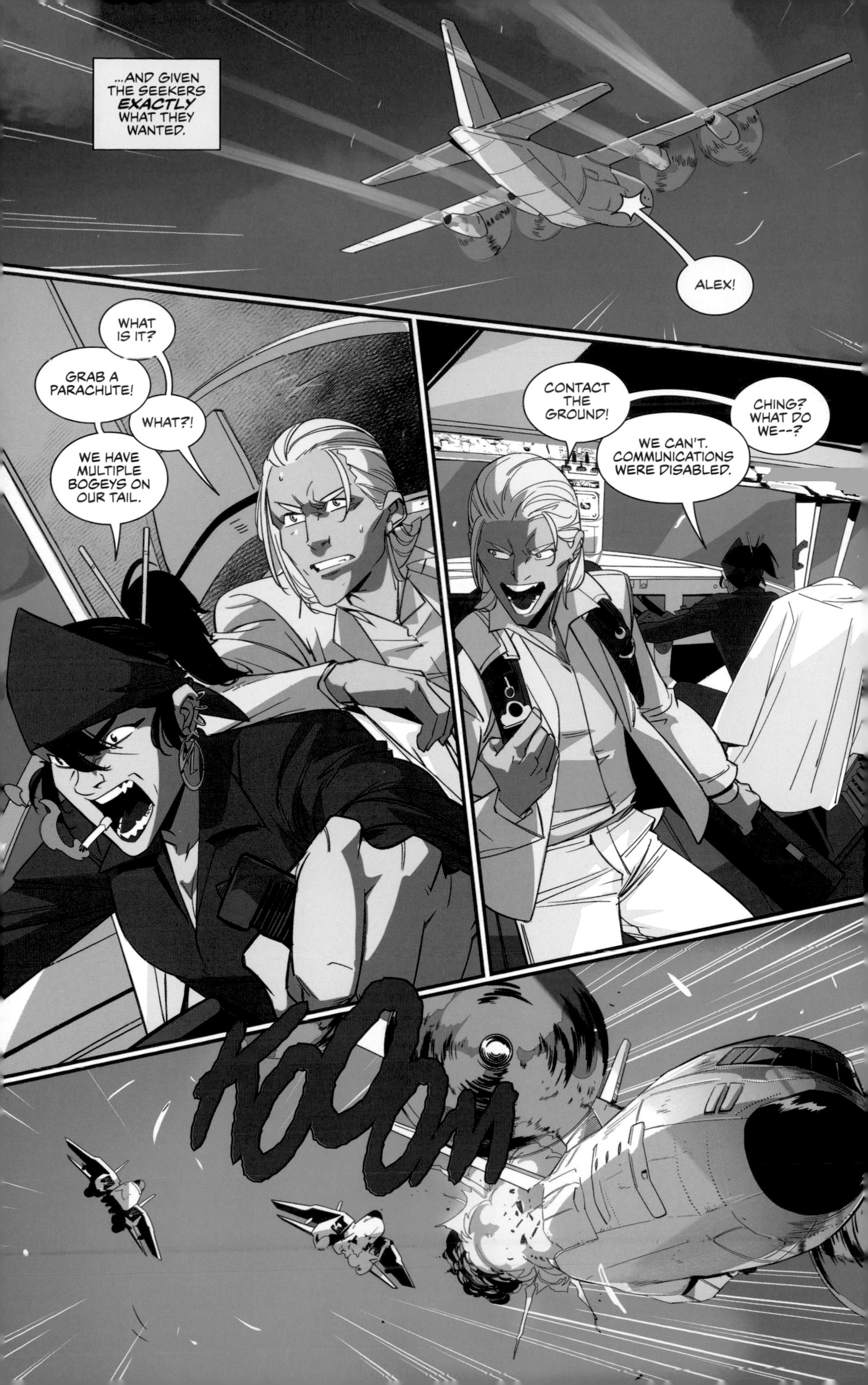
...AND GIVEN THE SEEKERS EXACTLY WHAT THEY WANTED.
ALEX!
WHAT IS IT?
GRAB A PARACHUTE!
WHAT?!
WE HAVE MULTIPLE BOGEYS ON OUR TAIL.
CONTACT THE GROUND!
CHING? WHAT DO WE--?
WE CAN'T. COMMUNICATIONS WERE DISABLED.
KOOM

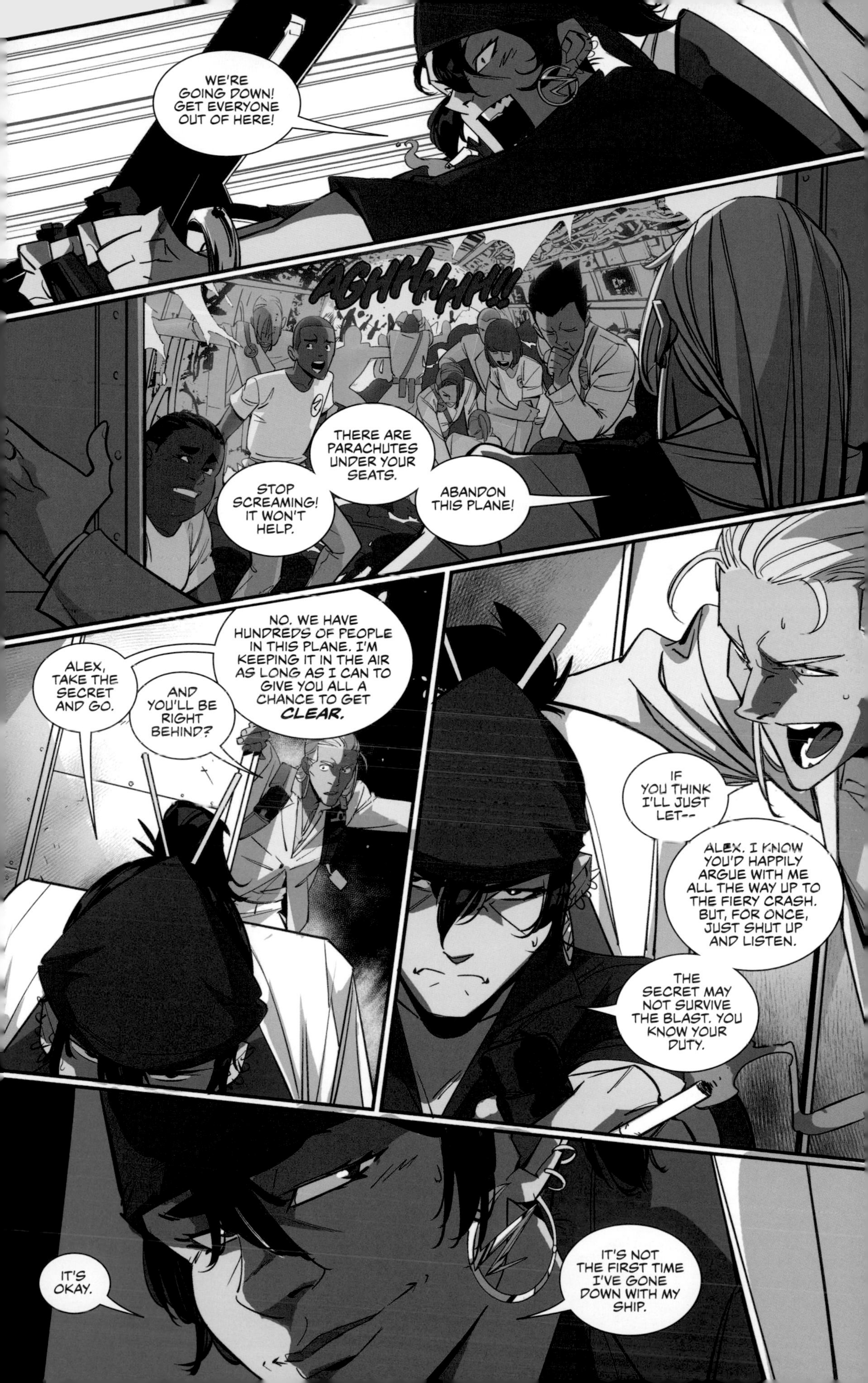
WE'RE GOING DOWN! GET EVERYONE OUT OF HERE!
AGHHHHHH!!
THERE ARE PARACHUTES UNDER YOUR SEATS.
STOP SCREAMING! IT WON'T HELP.
ABANDON THIS PLANE!
ALEX, TAKE THE SECRET AND GO.
AND YOU'LL BE RIGHT BEHIND?
NO. WE HAVE HUNDREDS OF PEOPLE IN THIS PLANE. I'M KEEPING IT IN THE AIR AS LONG AS I CAN TO GIVE YOU ALL A CHANCE TO GET CLEAR.
IF YOU THINK I'LL JUST LET--
ALEX. I KNOW YOU'D HAPPILY ARGUE WITH ME ALL THE WAY UP TO THE FIERY CRASH. BUT, FOR ONCE, JUST SHUT UP AND LISTEN.
THE SECRET MAY NOT SURVIVE THE BLAST. YOU KNOW YOUR DUTY.
IT'S OKAY.
IT'S NOT THE FIRST TIME I'VE GONE DOWN WITH MY SHIP.

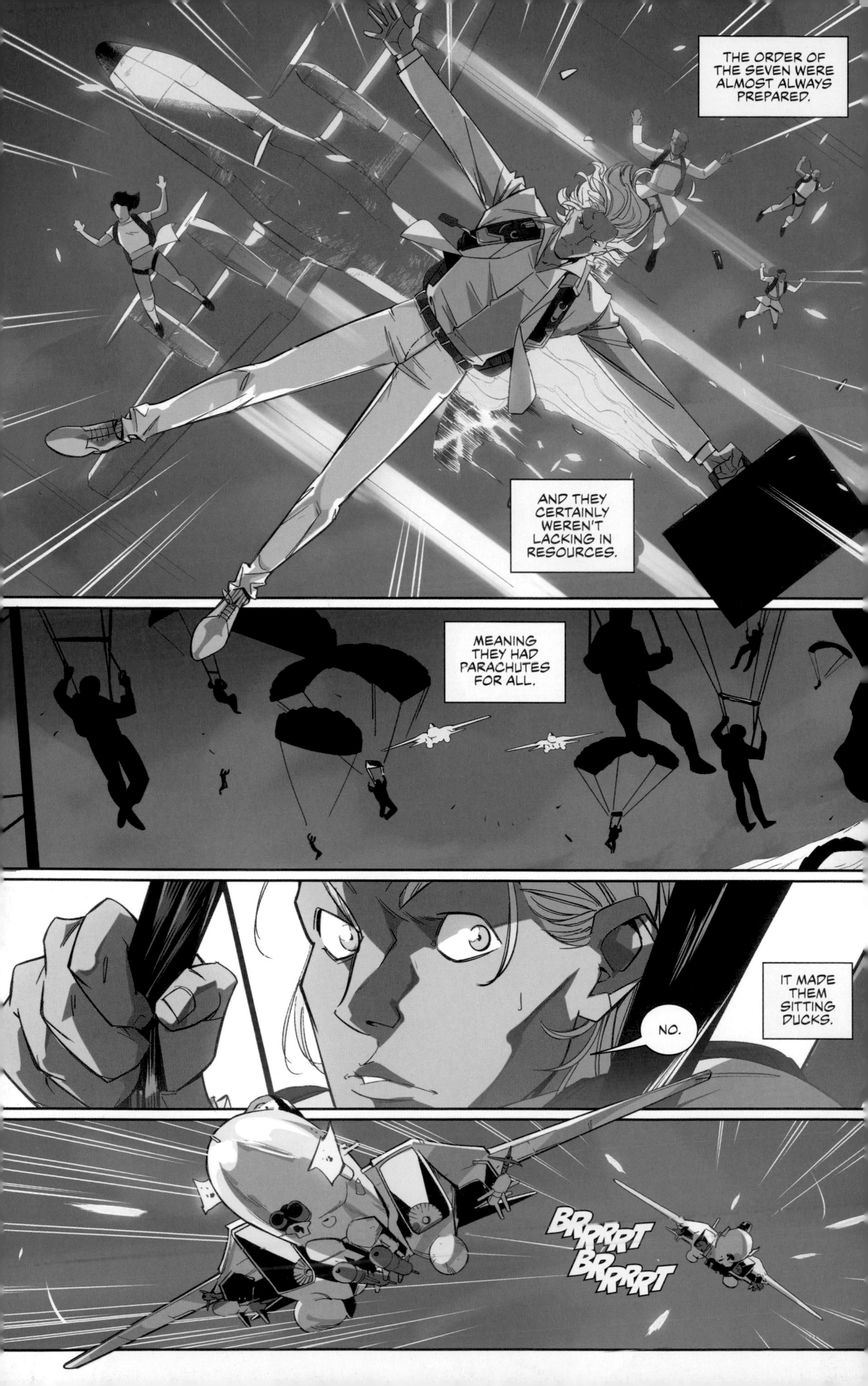
THE ORDER OF THE SEVEN WERE ALMOST ALWAYS PREPARED.
AND THEY CERTAINLY WEREN'T LACKING IN RESOURCES.
MEANING THEY HAD PARACHUTES FOR ALL.
IT MADE THEM SITTING DUCKS.
NO.
BRRRRT
BRRRRT

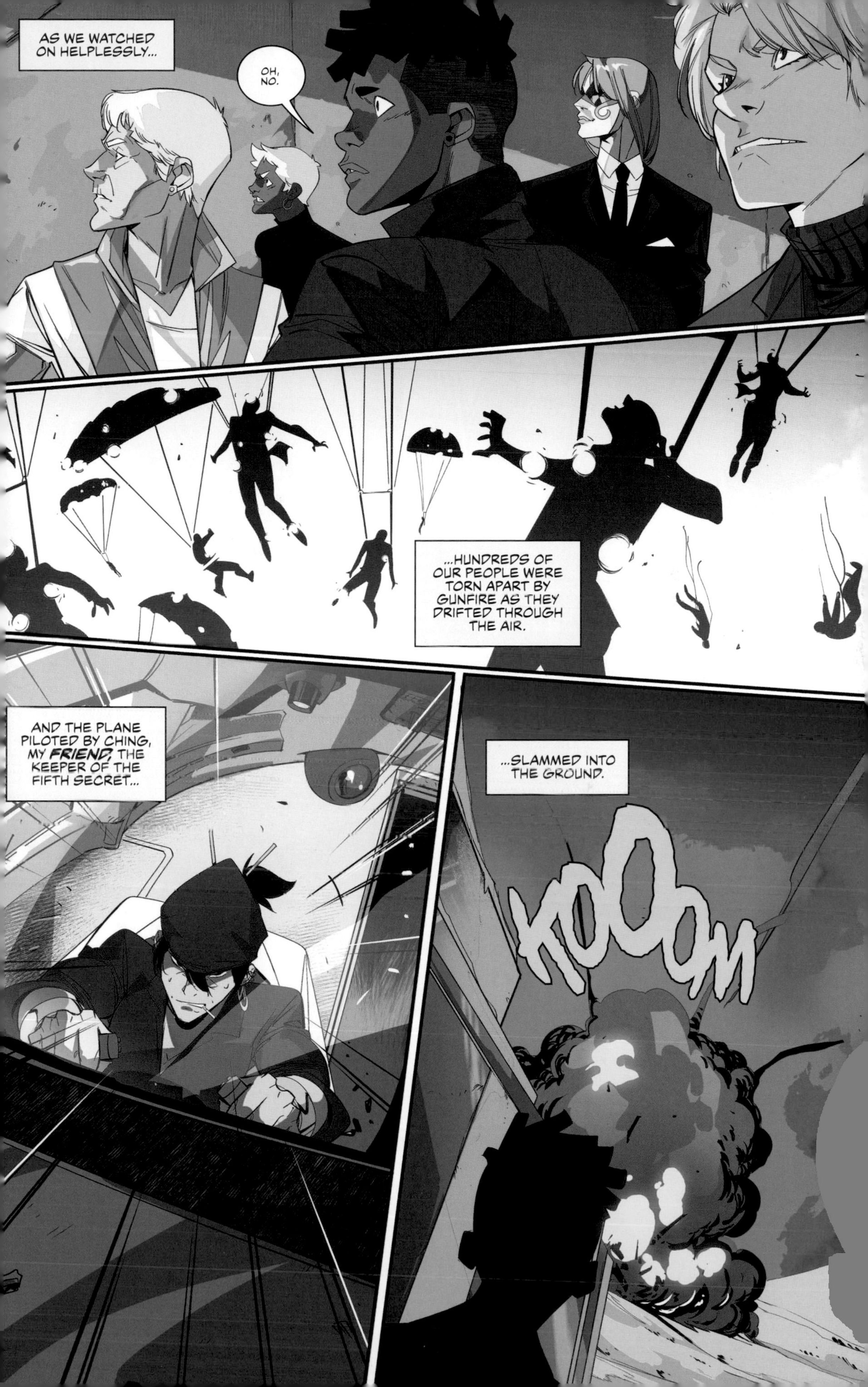
AS WE WATCHED ON HELPLESSLY...
OH, NO.
...HUNDREDS OF OUR PEOPLE WERE TORN APART BY GUNFIRE AS THEY DRIFTED THROUGH THE AIR.
AND THE PLANE PILOTED BY CHING, MY FRIEND, THE KEEPER OF THE FIFTH SECRET...
...SLAMMED INTO THE GROUND.
KOOOOM

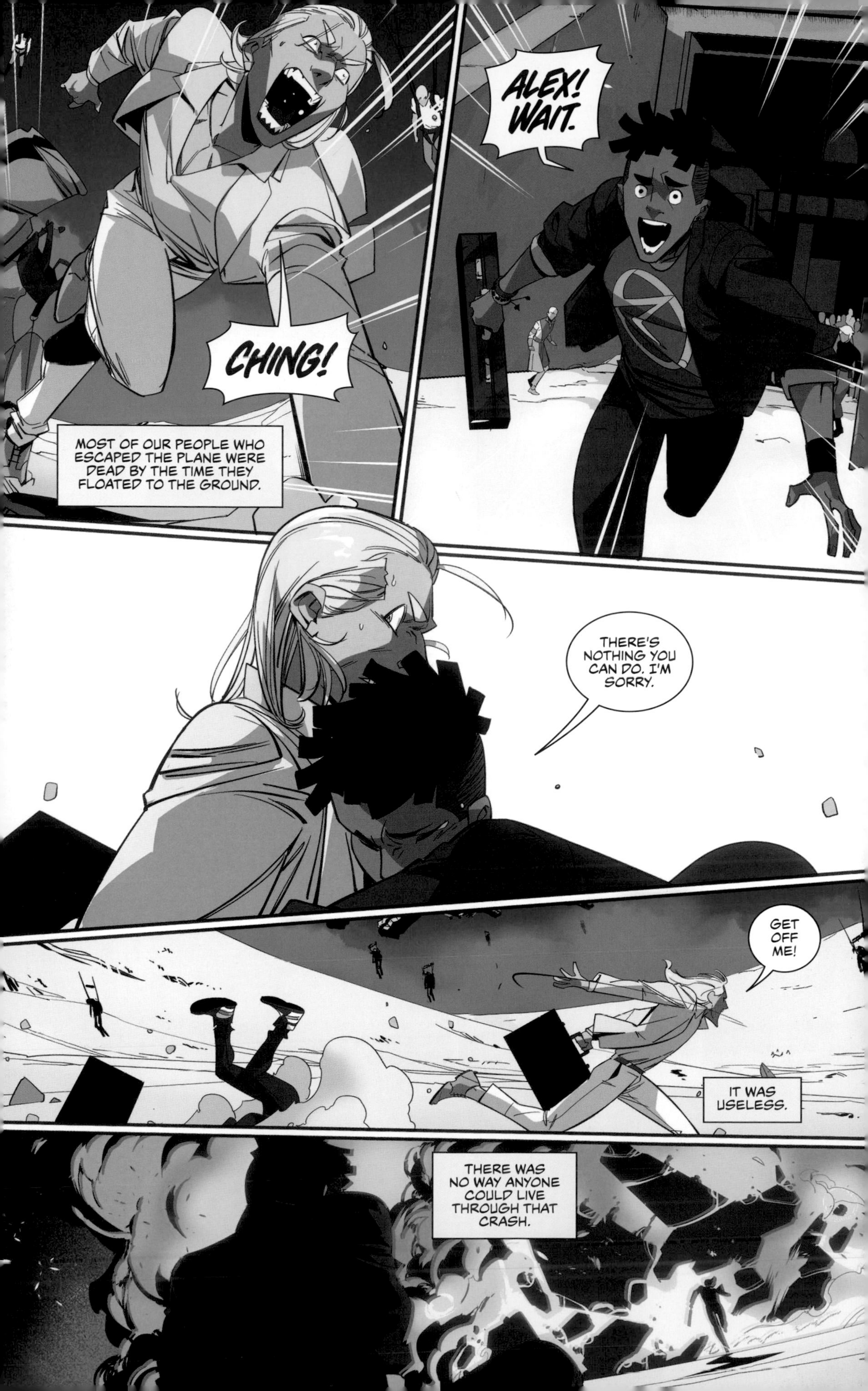

CHING!
MOST OF OUR PEOPLE WHO ESCAPED THE PLANE WERE DEAD BY THE TIME THEY FLOATED TO THE GROUND.
ALEX! WAIT.
THERE'S NOTHING YOU CAN DO. I'M SORRY.
GET OFF ME!
IT WAS USELESS.
THERE WAS NO WAY ANYONE COULD LIVE THROUGH THAT CRASH.

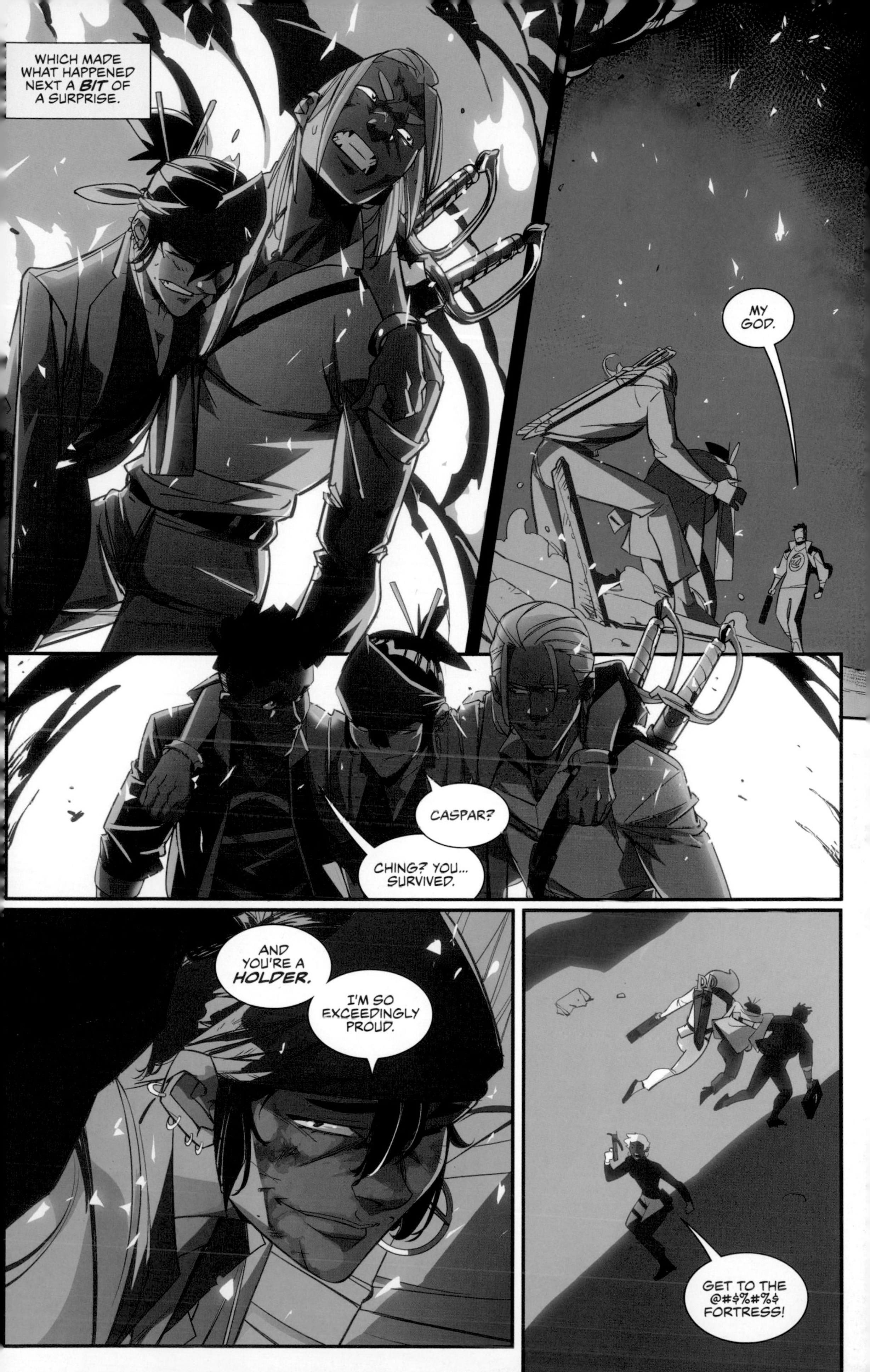
WHICH MADE WHAT HAPPENED NEXT A BIT OF A SURPRISE.
MY GOD.
CASPAR?
CHING? YOU... SURVIVED.
AND YOU'RE A HOLDER.
I'M SO EXCEEDINGLY PROUD.
GET TO THE @#$%#%$ FORTRESS!

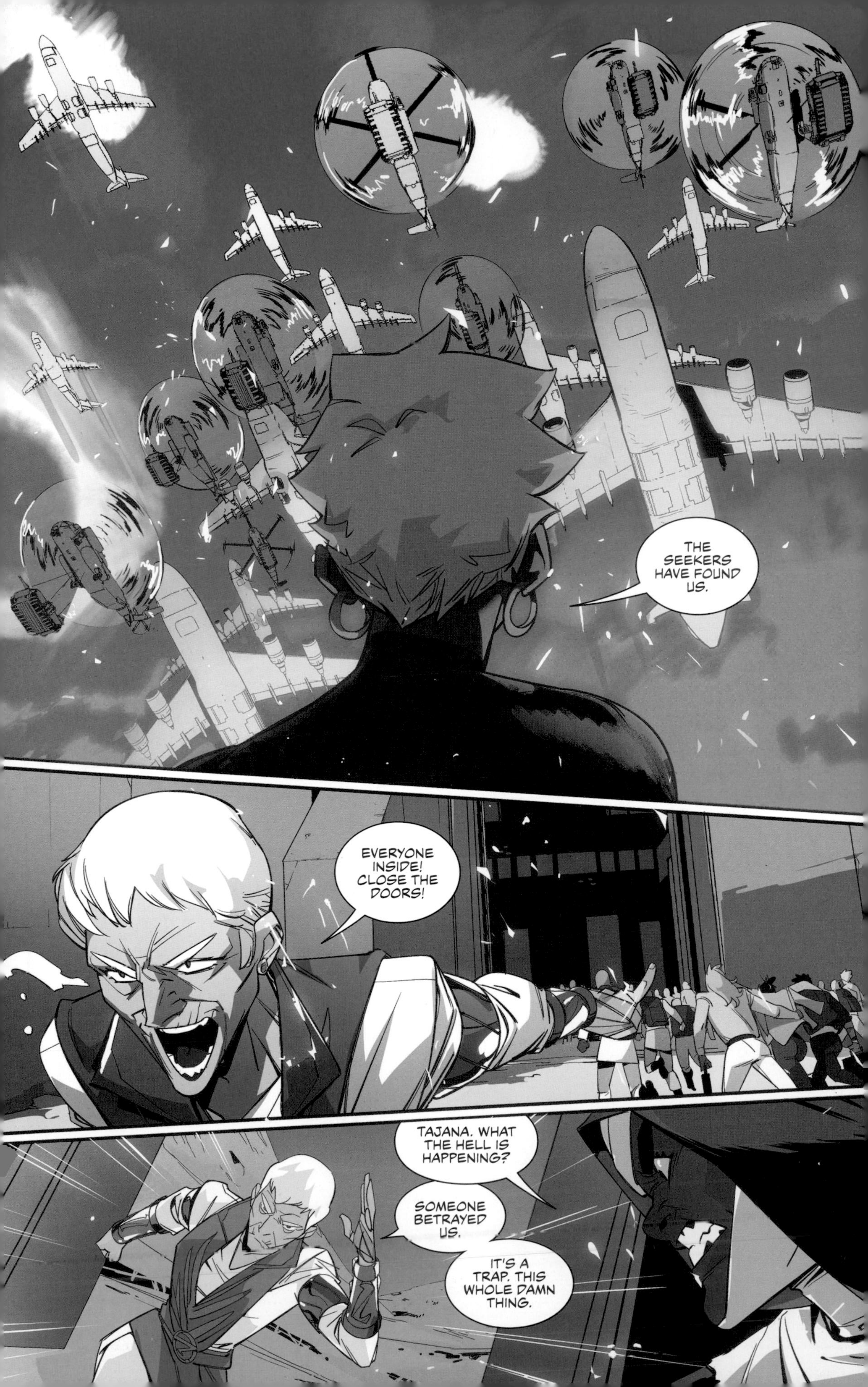
THE SEEKERS HAVE FOUND US.
EVERYONE INSIDE! CLOSE THE DOORS!
TAJANA. WHAT THE HELL IS HAPPENING?
SOMEONE BETRAYED US.
IT'S A TRAP. THIS WHOLE DAMN THING.

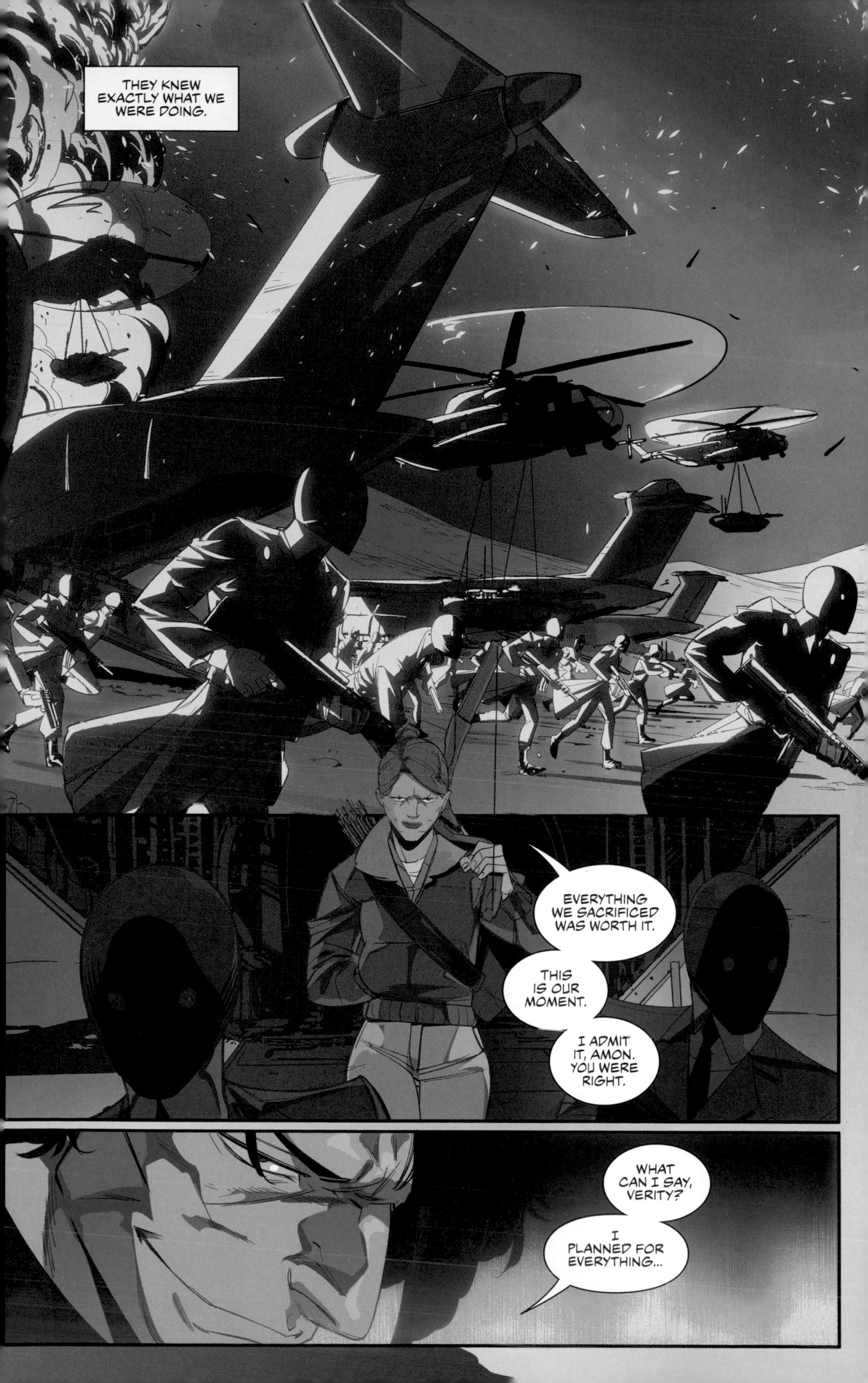
THEY KNEW EXACTLY WHAT WE WERE DOING.
EVERYTHING WE SACRIFICED WAS WORTH IT.
THIS IS OUR MOMENT.
I ADMIT IT, AMON. YOU WERE RIGHT.
WHAT CAN I SAY, VERITY?
I PLANNED FOR EVERYTHING...

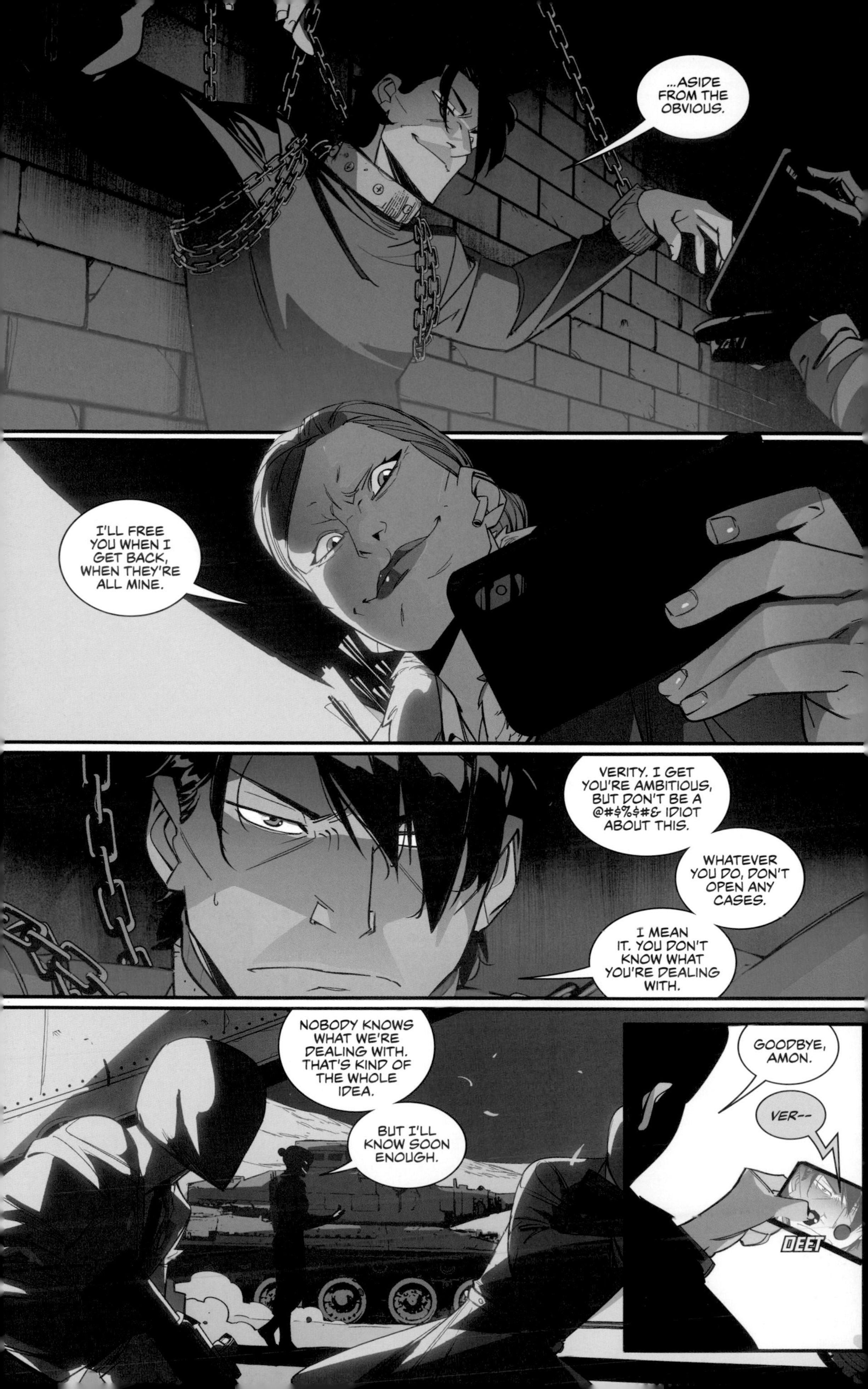
...ASIDE FROM THE OBVIOUS.
I'LL FREE YOU WHEN I GET BACK, WHEN THEY'RE ALL MINE.
VERITY. I GET YOU'RE AMBITIOUS, BUT DON'T BE A @#$%$#& IDIOT ABOUT THIS.
WHATEVER YOU DO, DON'T OPEN ANY CASES.
I MEAN IT. YOU DON'T KNOW WHAT YOU'RE DEALING WITH.
NOBODY KNOWS WHAT WE'RE DEALING WITH. THAT'S KIND OF THE WHOLE IDEA.
BUT I'LL KNOW SOON ENOUGH.
GOODBYE, AMON.
VER--
DEET

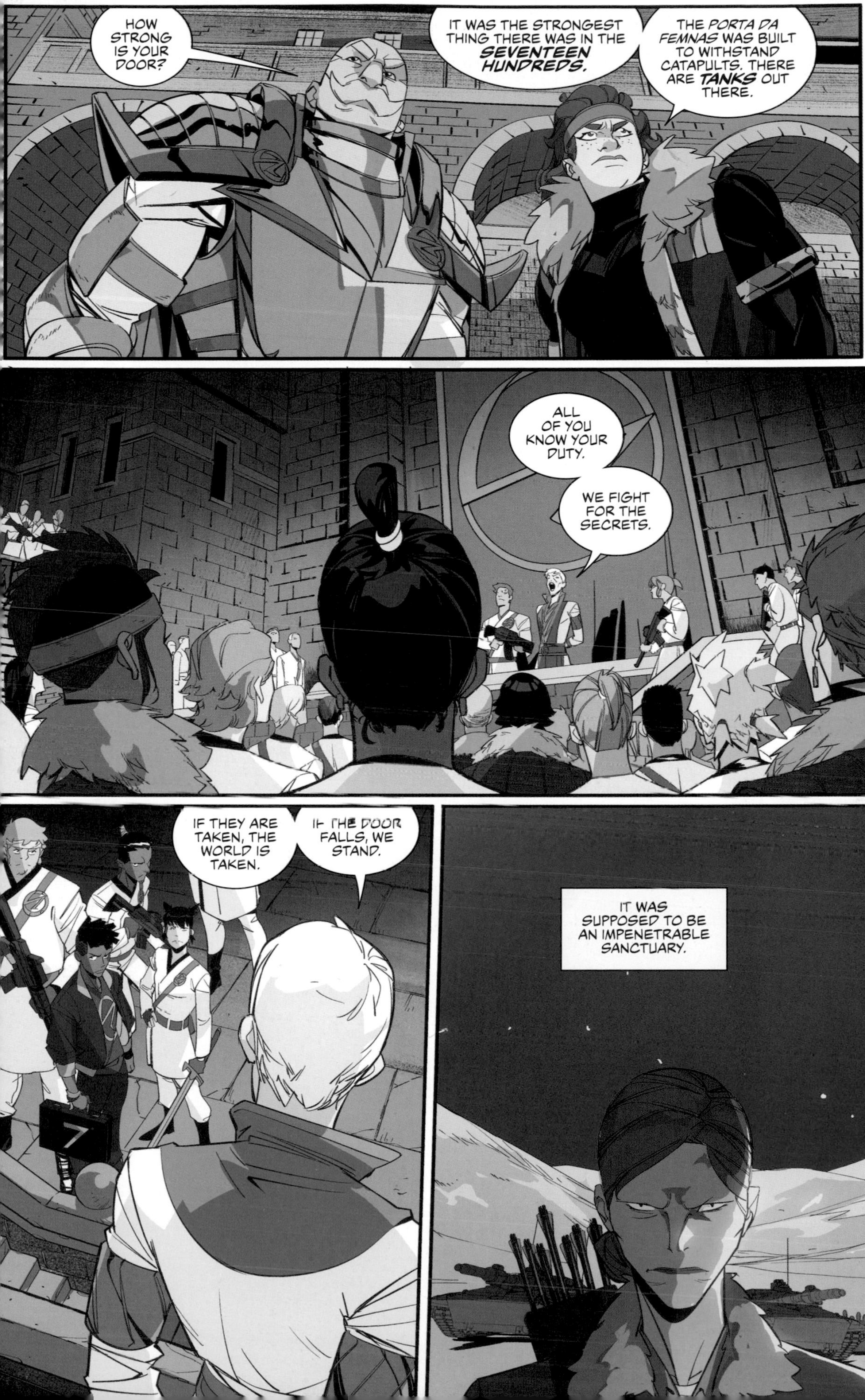
HOW STRONG IS YOUR DOOR?
IT WAS THE STRONGEST THING THERE WAS IN THE SEVENTEEN HUNDREDS.
THE PORTA DA FEMNAS WAS BUILT TO WITHSTAND CATAPULTS. THERE ARE TANKS OUT THERE.
ALL OF YOU KNOW YOUR DUTY.
WE FIGHT FOR THE SECRETS.
IF THEY ARE TAKEN, THE WORLD IS TAKEN.
IF THE DOOR FALLS, WE STAND.
IT WAS SUPPOSED TO BE AN IMPENETRABLE SANCTUARY.
7

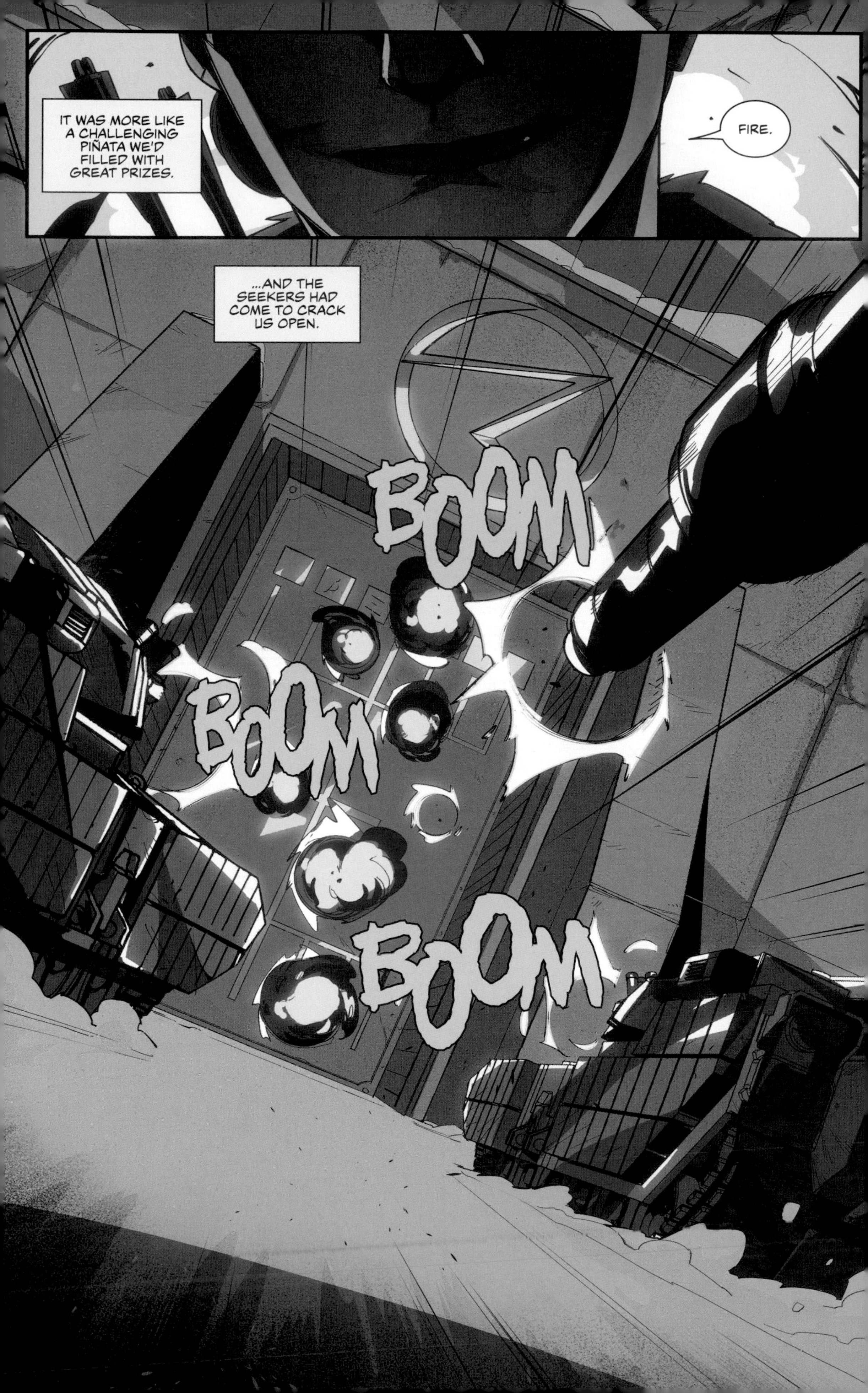
IT WAS MORE LIKE A CHALLENGING PIÑATA WE'D FILLED WITH GREAT PRIZES.
FIRE.
...AND THE SEEKERS HAD COME TO CRACK US OPEN.
BOOM
BOOM
BOOM

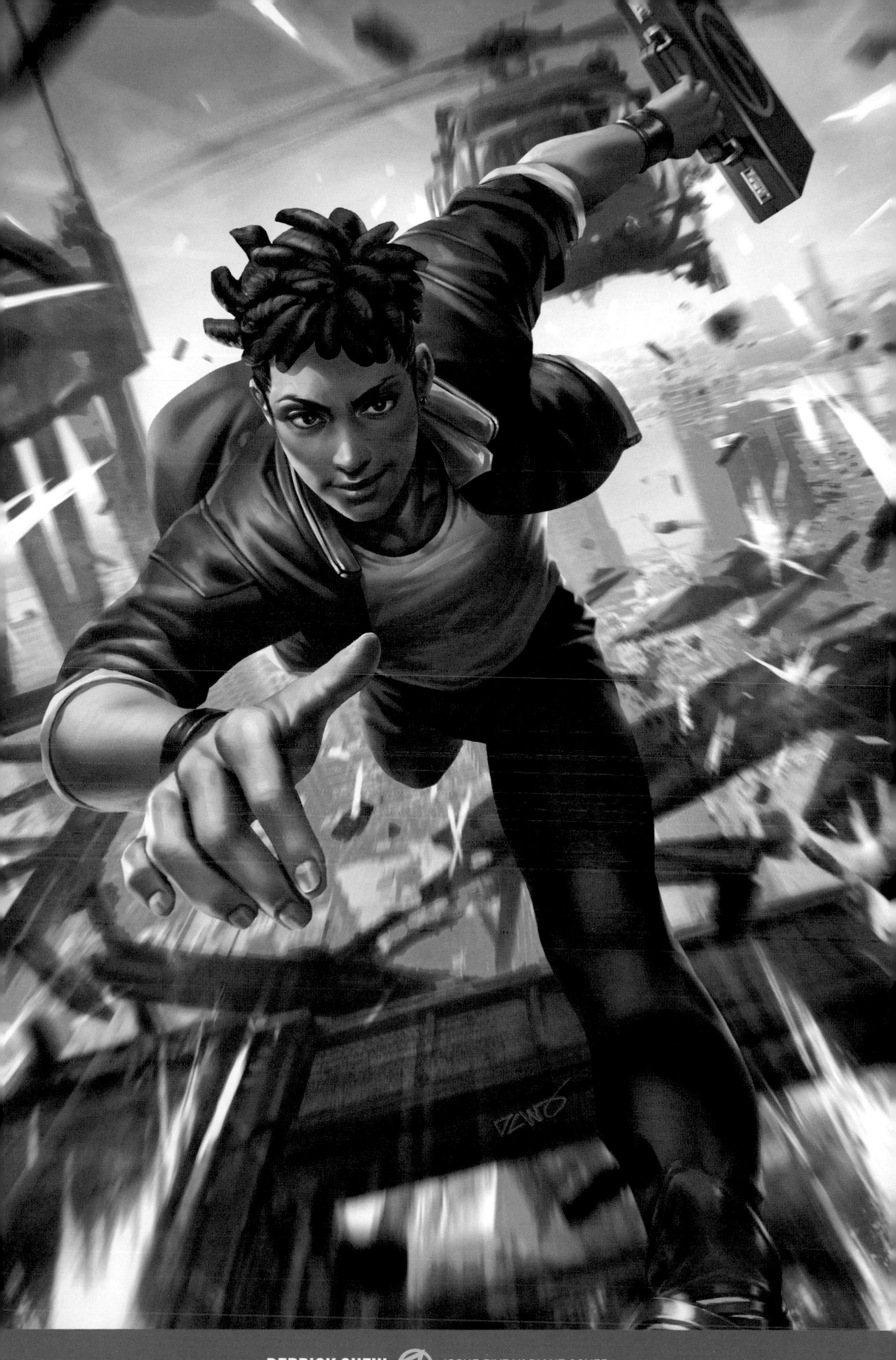

DERRICK CHEW ISSUE FIVE VARIANT COVER

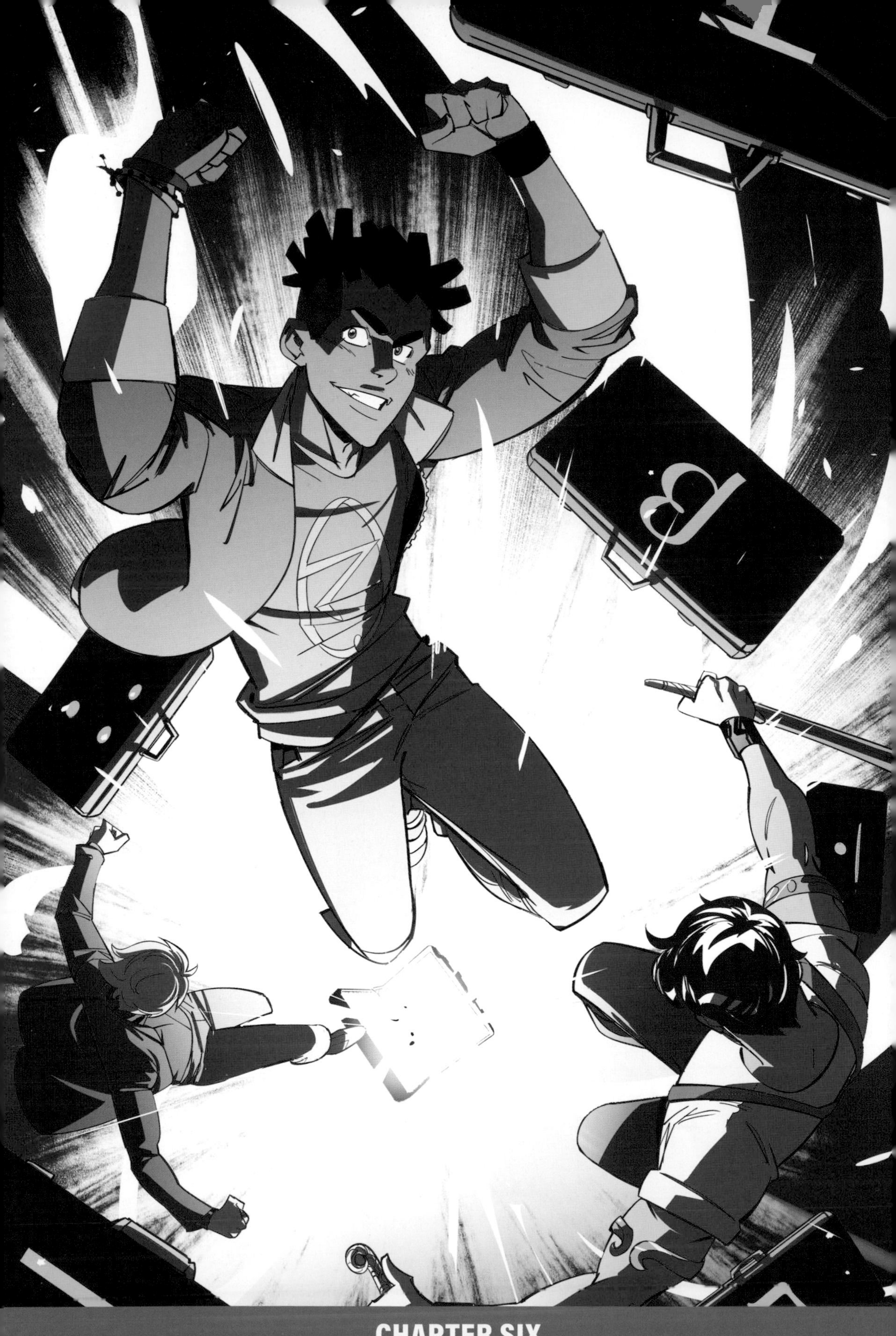

CHAPTER SIX

DANIELE DI NICUOLO ISSUE SIX COVER

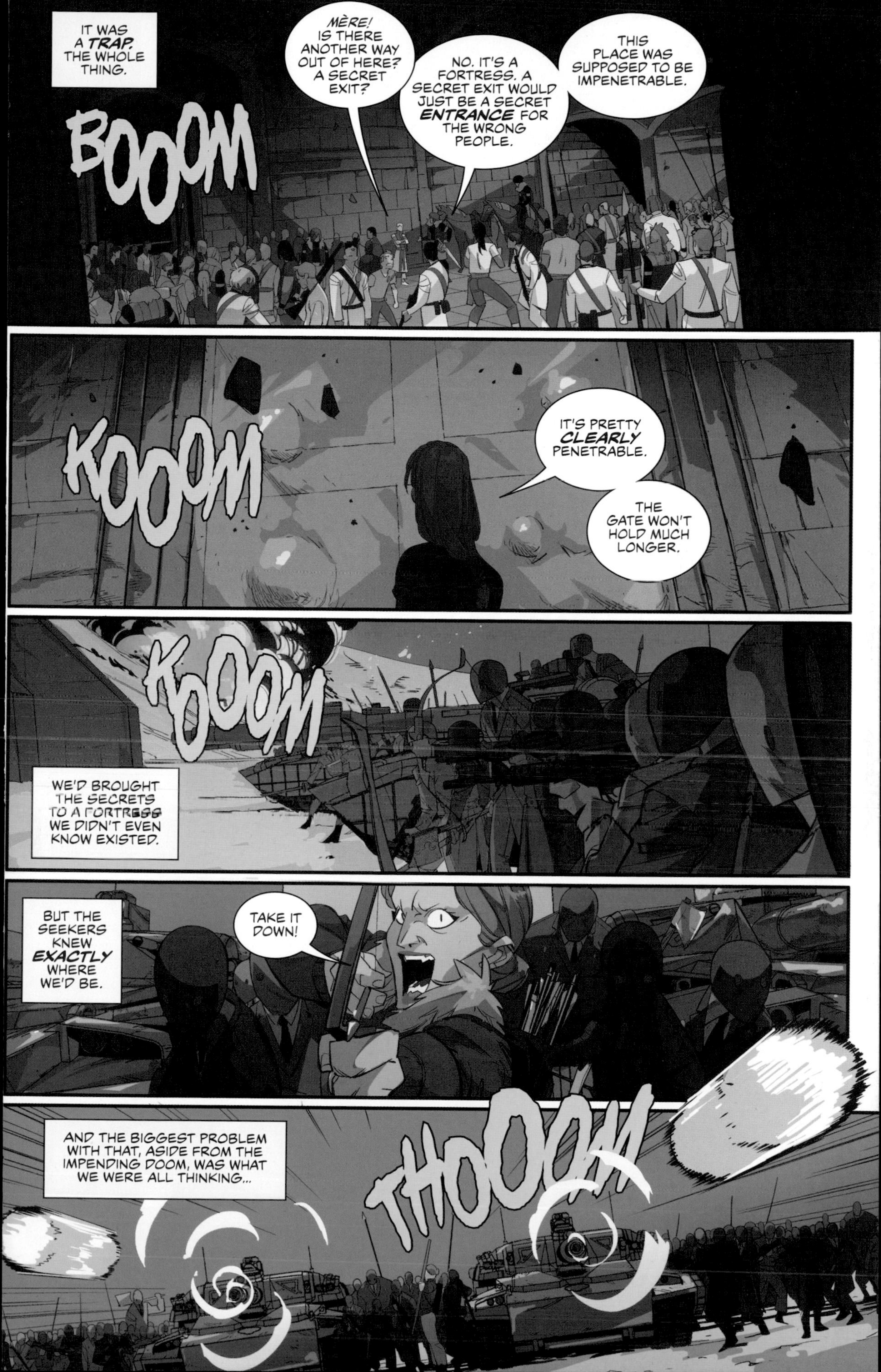
IT WAS A *TRAP.* THE WHOLE THING.
BOOOM
MÈRE! IS THERE ANOTHER WAY OUT OF HERE? A SECRET EXIT?
NO. IT'S A FORTRESS. A SECRET EXIT WOULD JUST BE A SECRET *ENTRANCE* FOR THE WRONG PEOPLE.
THIS PLACE WAS SUPPOSED TO BE IMPENETRABLE.
KOOOM
IT'S PRETTY *CLEARLY* PENETRABLE.
THE GATE WON'T HOLD MUCH LONGER.
KOOOM
WE'D BROUGHT THE SECRETS TO A FORTRESS WE DIDN'T EVEN KNOW EXISTED.
BUT THE SEEKERS KNEW *EXACTLY* WHERE WE'D BE.
TAKE IT DOWN!
AND THE BIGGEST PROBLEM WITH THAT, ASIDE FROM THE IMPENDING DOOM, WAS WHAT WE WERE ALL THINKING...
THOOOM

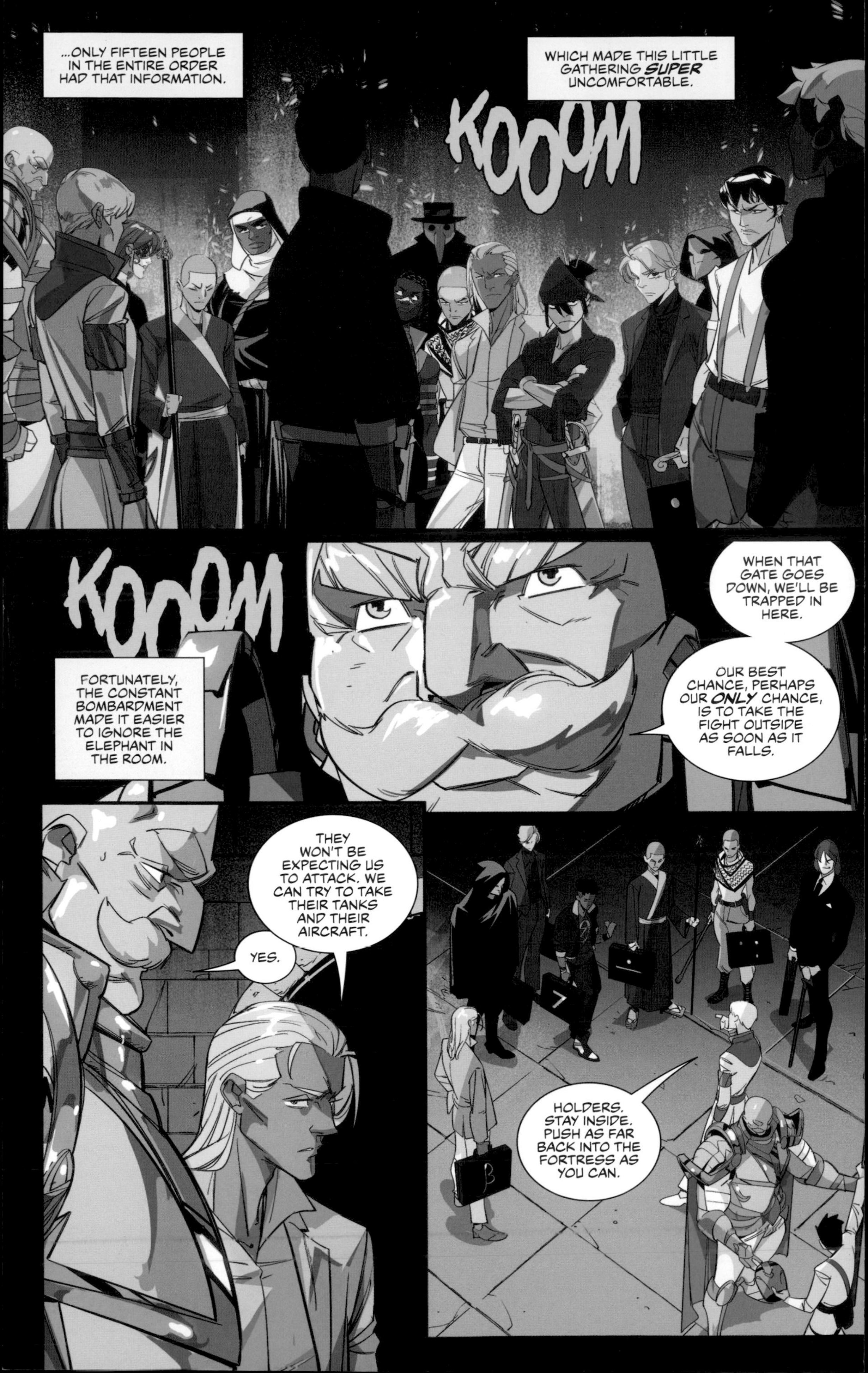
...ONLY FIFTEEN PEOPLE IN THE ENTIRE ORDER HAD THAT INFORMATION.
WHICH MADE THIS LITTLE GATHERING SUPER UNCOMFORTABLE.
KOOOM
KOOOM
FORTUNATELY, THE CONSTANT BOMBARDMENT MADE IT EASIER TO IGNORE THE ELEPHANT IN THE ROOM.
WHEN THAT GATE GOES DOWN, WE'LL BE TRAPPED IN HERE.
OUR BEST CHANCE, PERHAPS OUR ONLY CHANCE, IS TO TAKE THE FIGHT OUTSIDE AS SOON AS IT FALLS.
THEY WON'T BE EXPECTING US TO ATTACK. WE CAN TRY TO TAKE THEIR TANKS AND THEIR AIRCRAFT.
YES.
HOLDERS. STAY INSIDE. PUSH AS FAR BACK INTO THE FORTRESS AS YOU CAN.

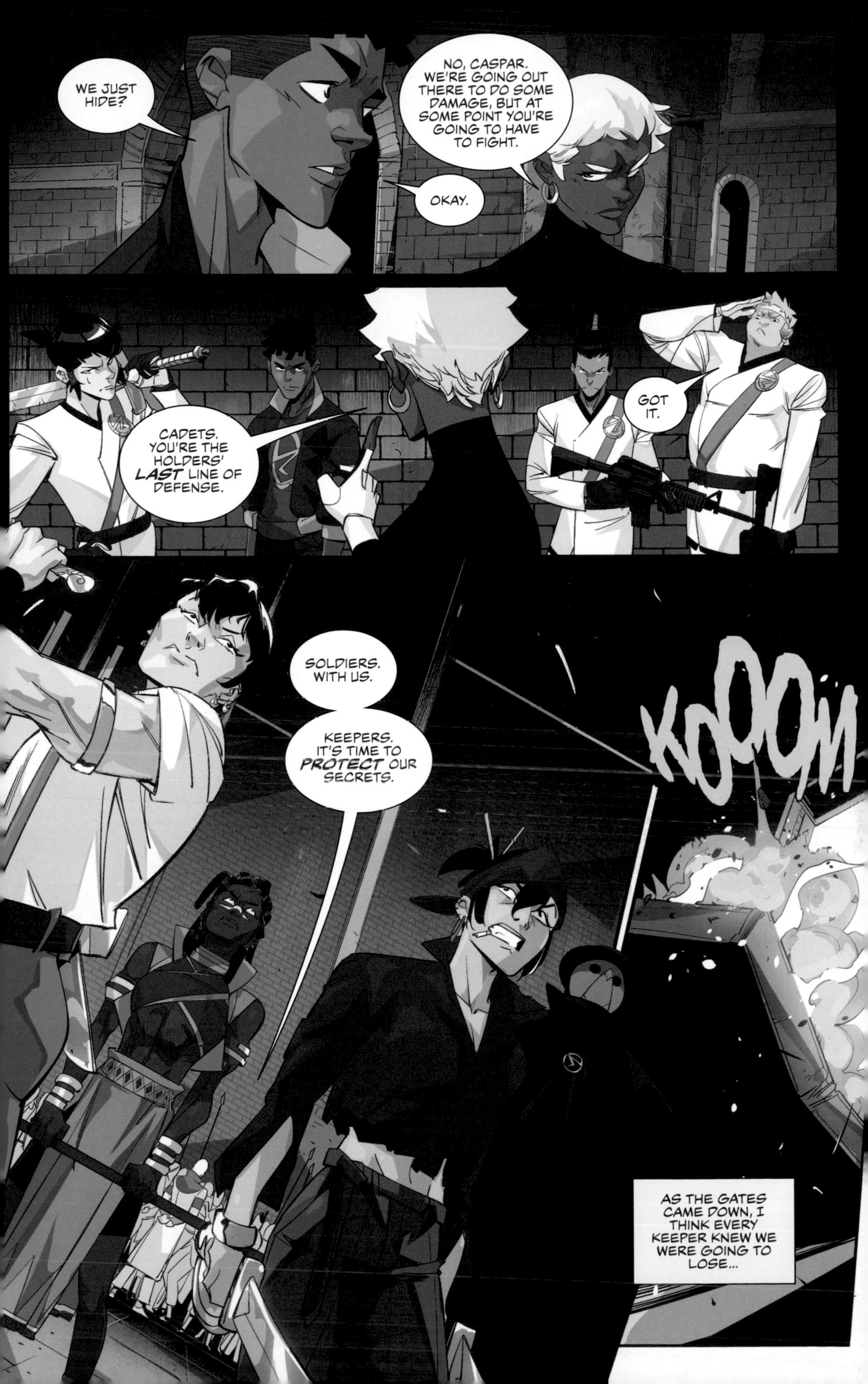
WE JUST HIDE?
NO, CASPAR. WE'RE GOING OUT THERE TO DO SOME DAMAGE, BUT AT SOME POINT YOU'RE GOING TO HAVE TO FIGHT.
OKAY.
CADETS. YOU'RE THE HOLDERS' LAST LINE OF DEFENSE.
GOT IT.
SOLDIERS. WITH US.
KEEPERS. IT'S TIME TO PROTECT OUR SECRETS.
KOOOM
AS THE GATES CAME DOWN, I THINK EVERY KEEPER KNEW WE WERE GOING TO LOSE...

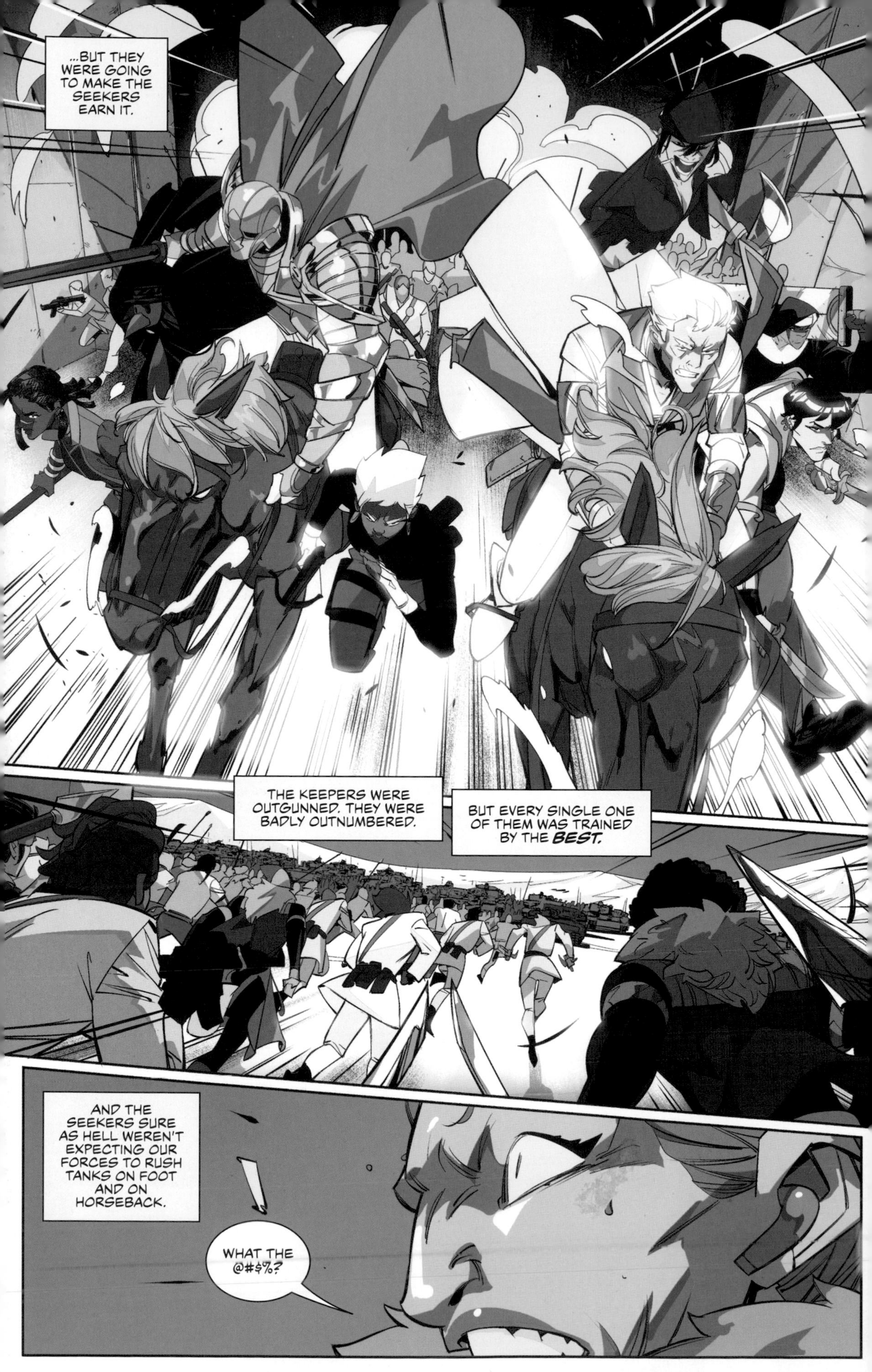
...BUT THEY WERE GOING TO MAKE THE SEEKERS EARN IT.
THE KEEPERS WERE OUTGUNNED. THEY WERE BADLY OUTNUMBERED.
BUT EVERY SINGLE ONE OF THEM WAS TRAINED BY THE BEST.
AND THE SEEKERS SURE AS HELL WEREN'T EXPECTING OUR FORCES TO RUSH TANKS ON FOOT AND ON HORSEBACK.
WHAT THE @#$%?

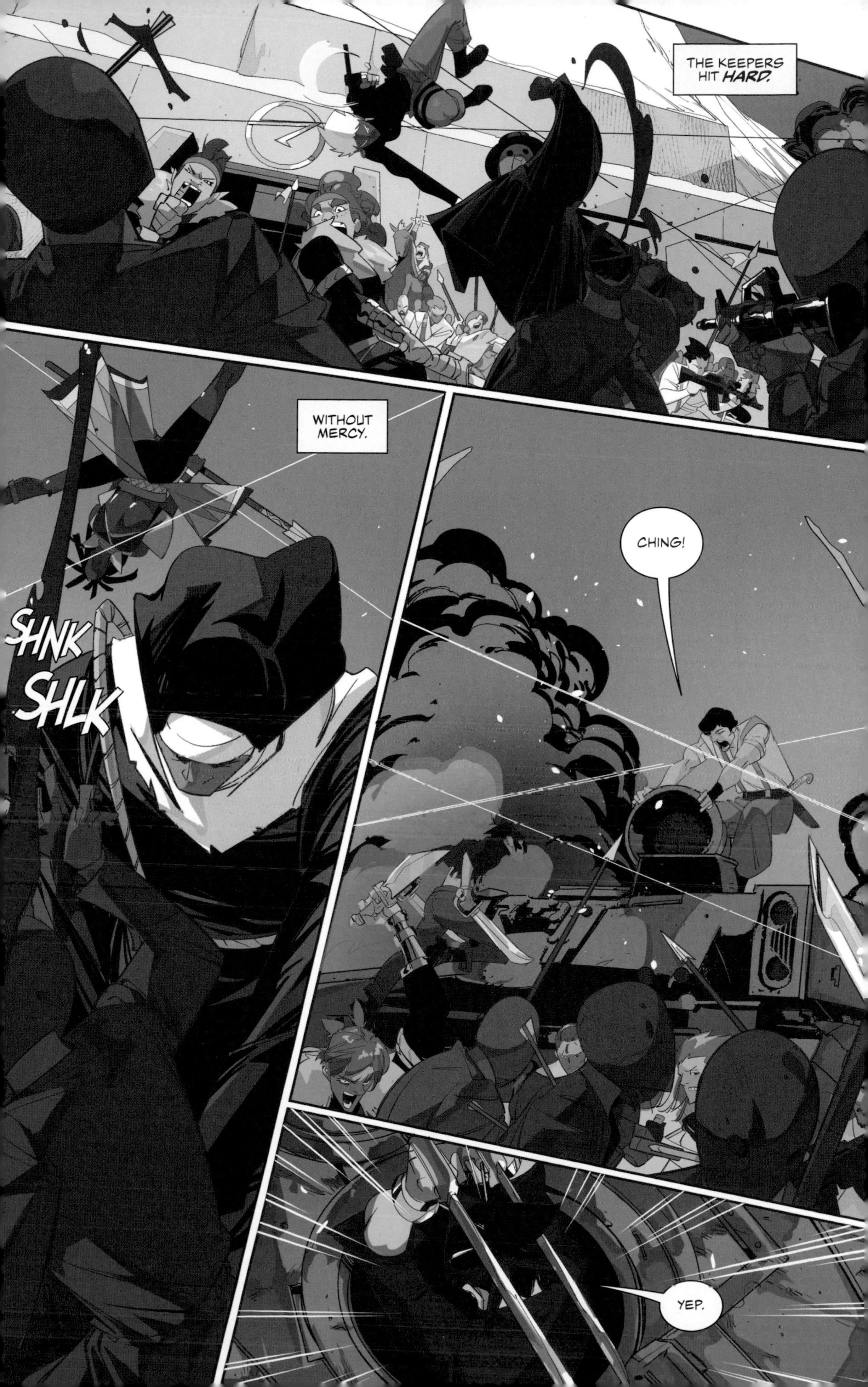
THE KEEPERS HIT HARD.
WITHOUT MERCY.
SHNK
SHLK
CHING!
YEP.

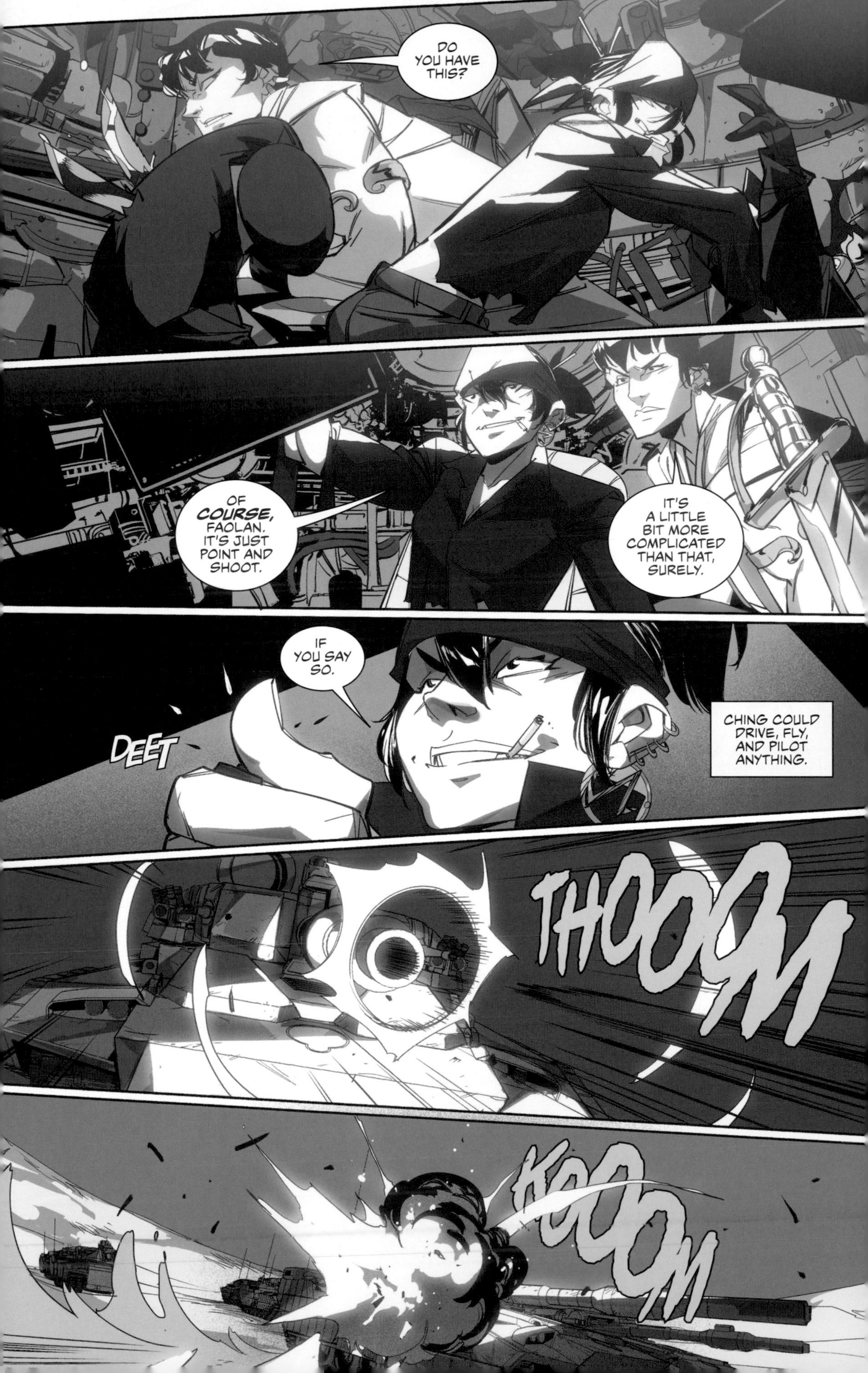
DO YOU HAVE THIS?
OF COURSE, FAOLAN. IT'S JUST POINT AND SHOOT.
IT'S A LITTLE BIT MORE COMPLICATED THAN THAT, SURELY.
IF YOU SAY SO.
DEET
CHING COULD DRIVE, FLY, AND PILOT ANYTHING.
THOOOM
KOOOOM

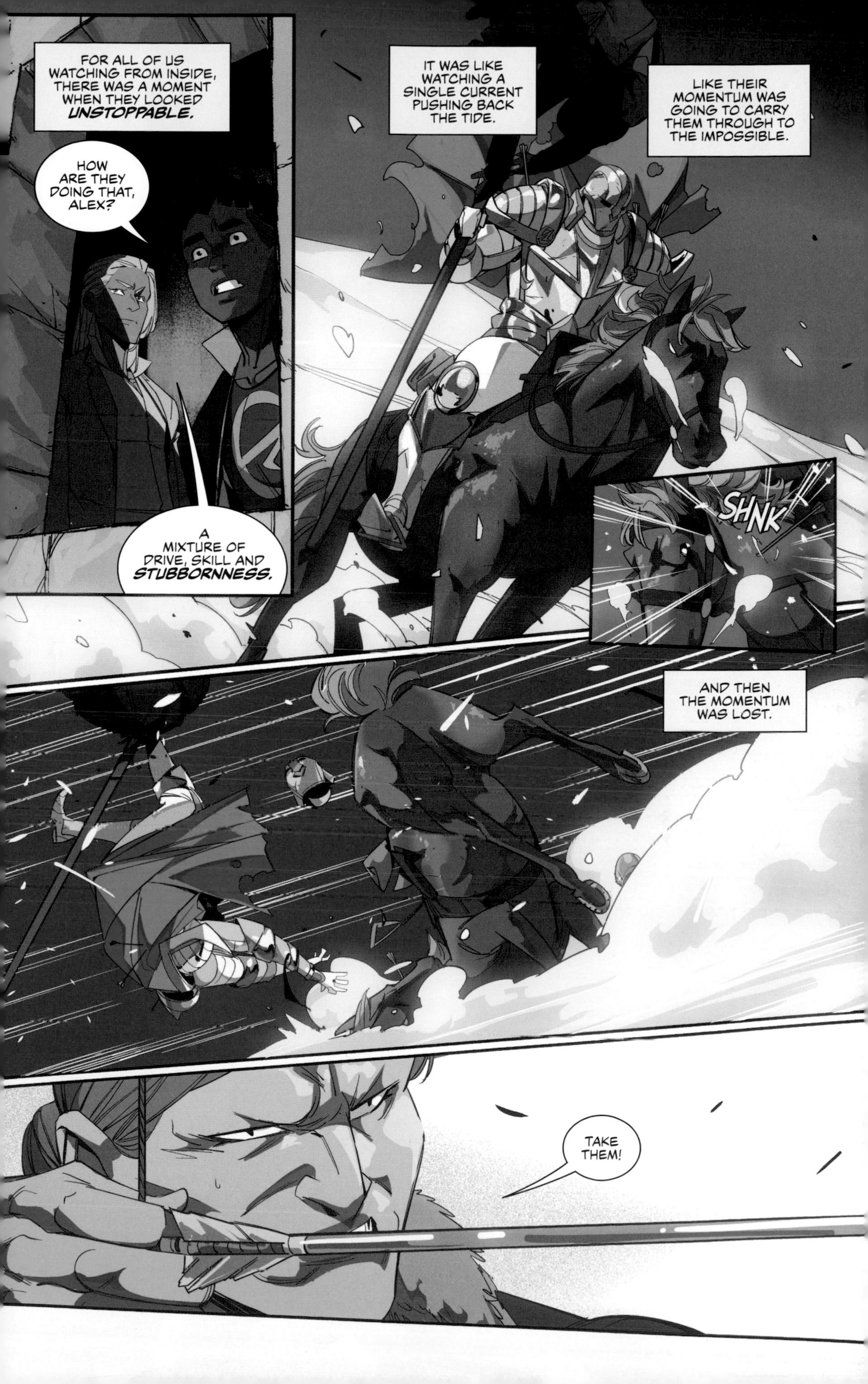
FOR ALL OF US WATCHING FROM INSIDE, THERE WAS A MOMENT WHEN THEY LOOKED ***UNSTOPPABLE.***
IT WAS LIKE WATCHING A SINGLE CURRENT PUSHING BACK THE TIDE.
LIKE THEIR MOMENTUM WAS GOING TO CARRY THEM THROUGH TO THE IMPOSSIBLE.
HOW ARE THEY DOING THAT, ALEX?
A MIXTURE OF DRIVE, SKILL AND ***STUBBORNNESS.***
SHNK
AND THEN THE MOMENTUM WAS LOST.
TAKE THEM!

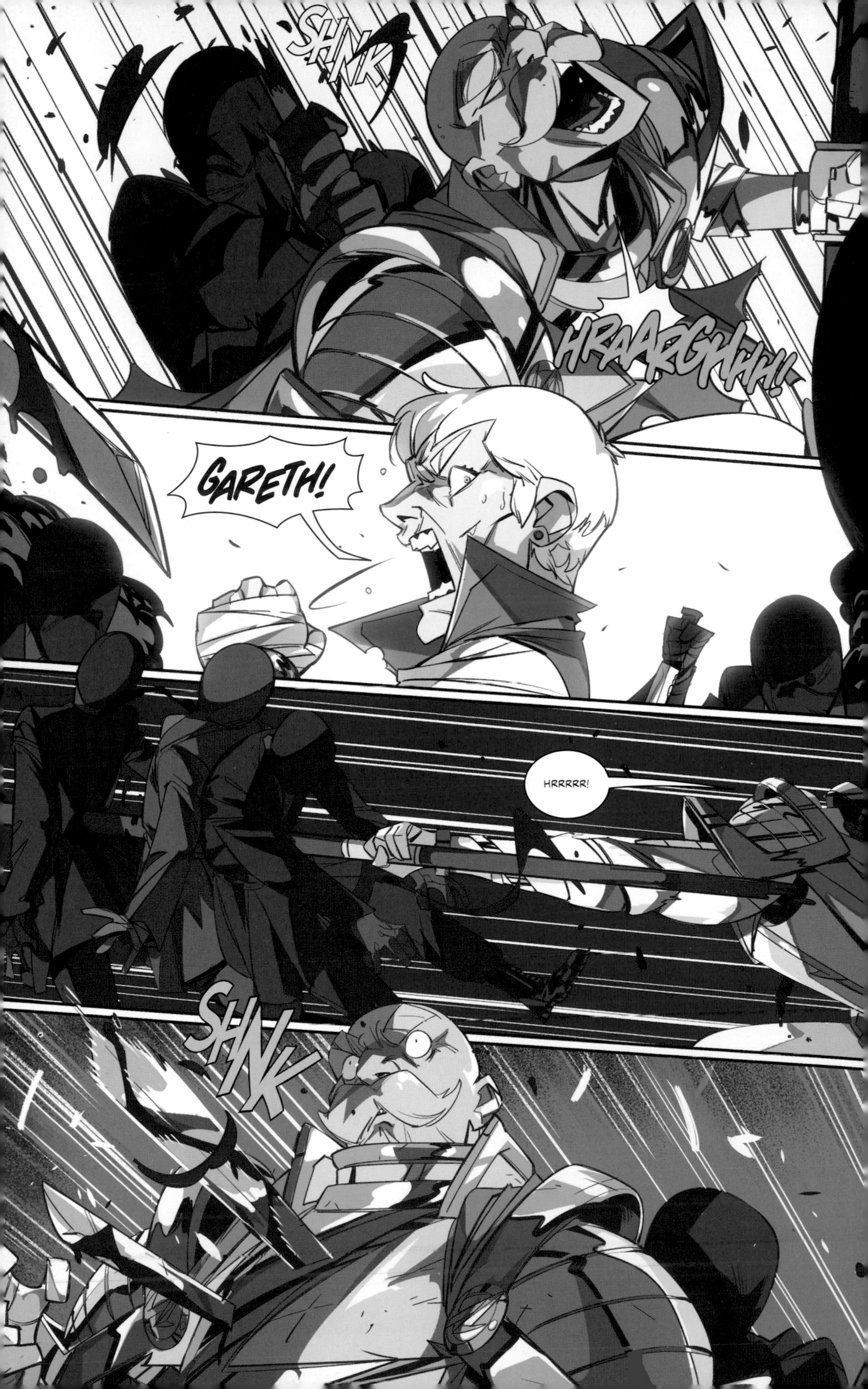
SHNK
HRAARGHHH!
GARETH!
HRRRRR!
SHNK

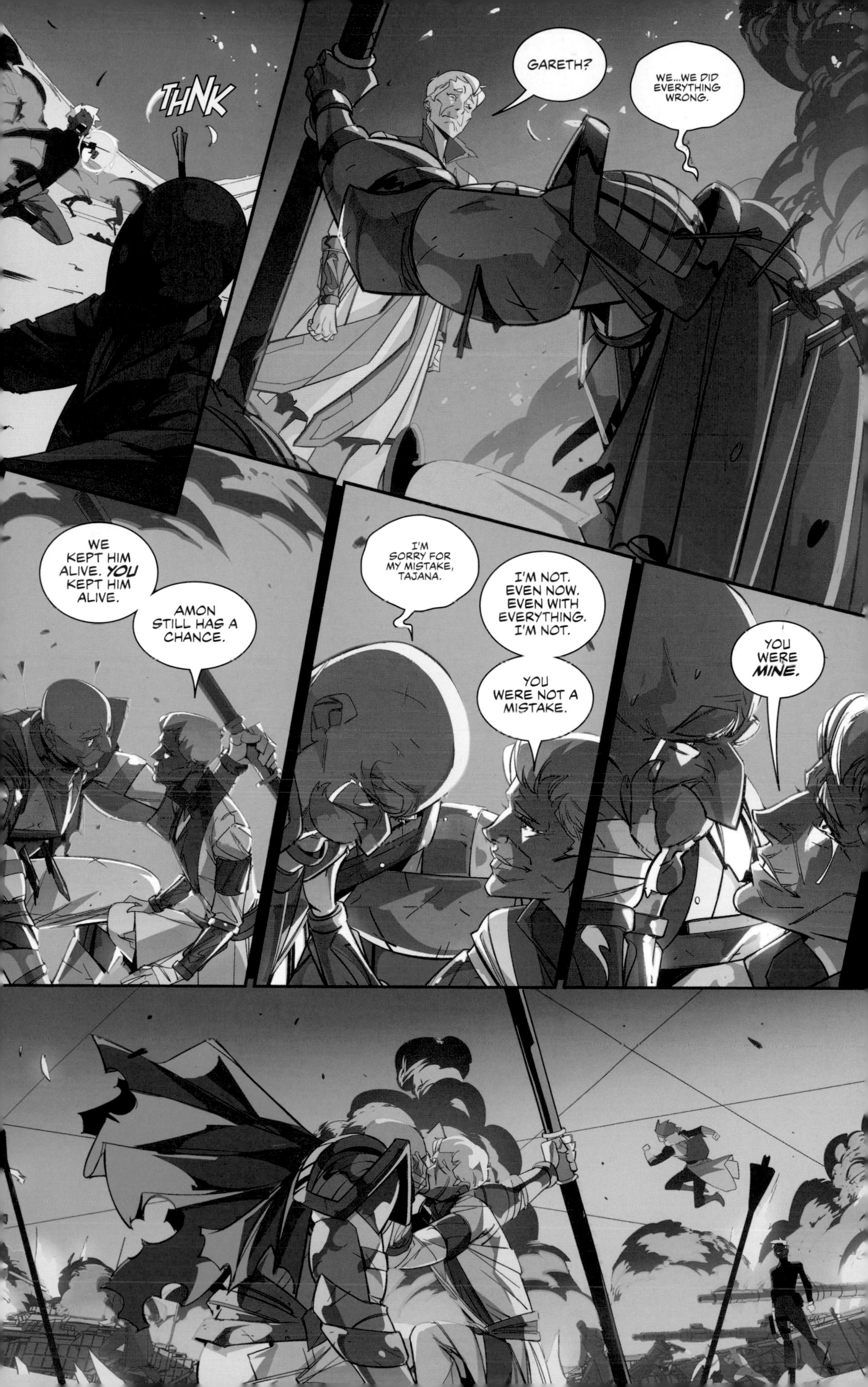
THNK
GARETH?
WE...WE DID EVERYTHING WRONG.
WE KEPT HIM ALIVE. YOU KEPT HIM ALIVE.
AMON STILL HAS A CHANCE.
I'M SORRY FOR MY MISTAKE, TAJANA.
I'M NOT. EVEN NOW. EVEN WITH EVERYTHING. I'M NOT.
YOU WERE NOT A MISTAKE.
YOU WERE MINE.

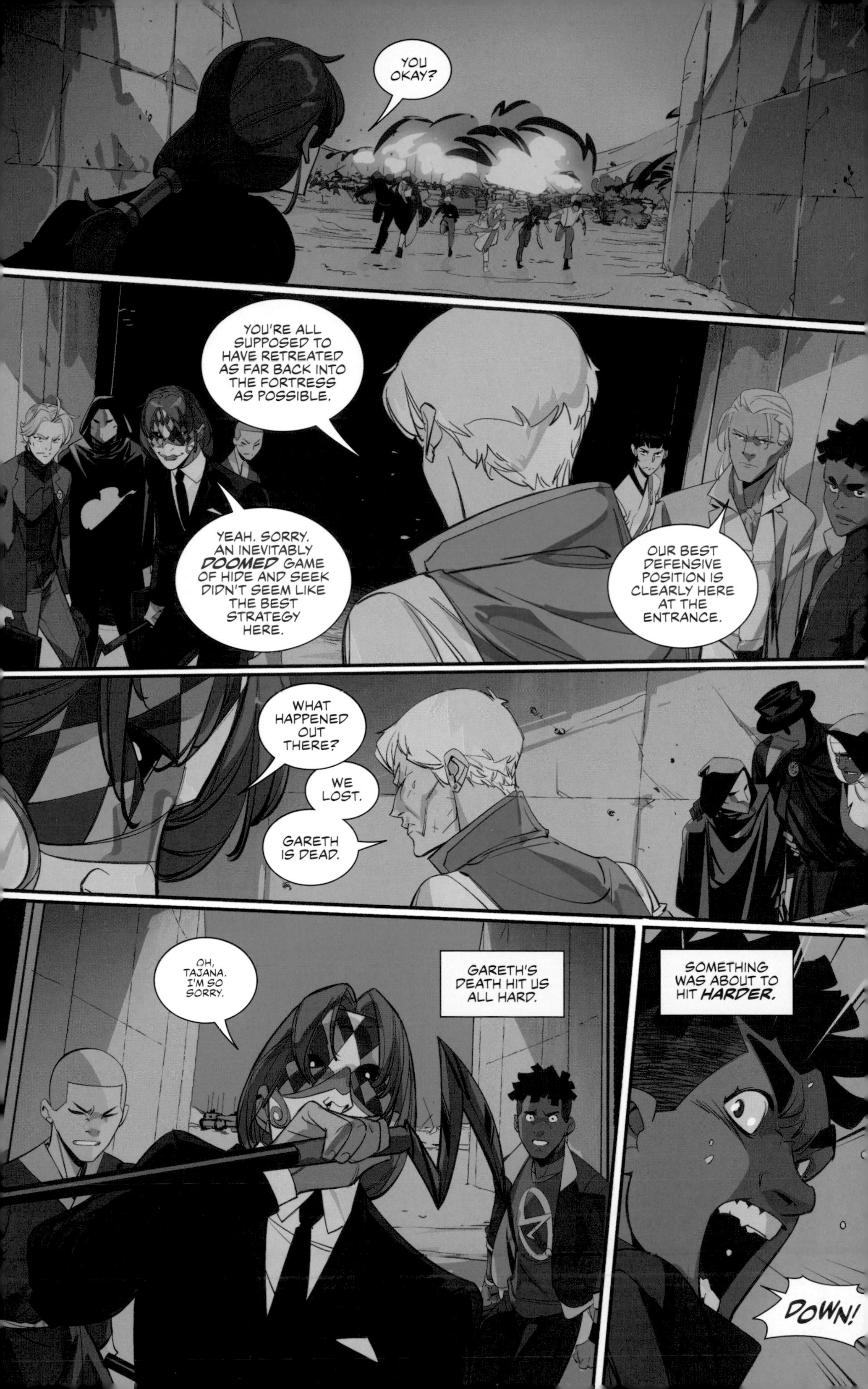
YOU OKAY?
YOU'RE ALL SUPPOSED TO HAVE RETREATED AS FAR BACK INTO THE FORTRESS AS POSSIBLE.
YEAH. SORRY. AN INEVITABLY DOOMED GAME OF HIDE AND SEEK DIDN'T SEEM LIKE THE BEST STRATEGY HERE.
OUR BEST DEFENSIVE POSITION IS CLEARLY HERE AT THE ENTRANCE.
WHAT HAPPENED OUT THERE?
WE LOST.
GARETH IS DEAD.
OH, TAJANA. I'M SO SORRY.
GARETH'S DEATH HIT US ALL HARD.
SOMETHING WAS ABOUT TO HIT HARDER.
DOWN!

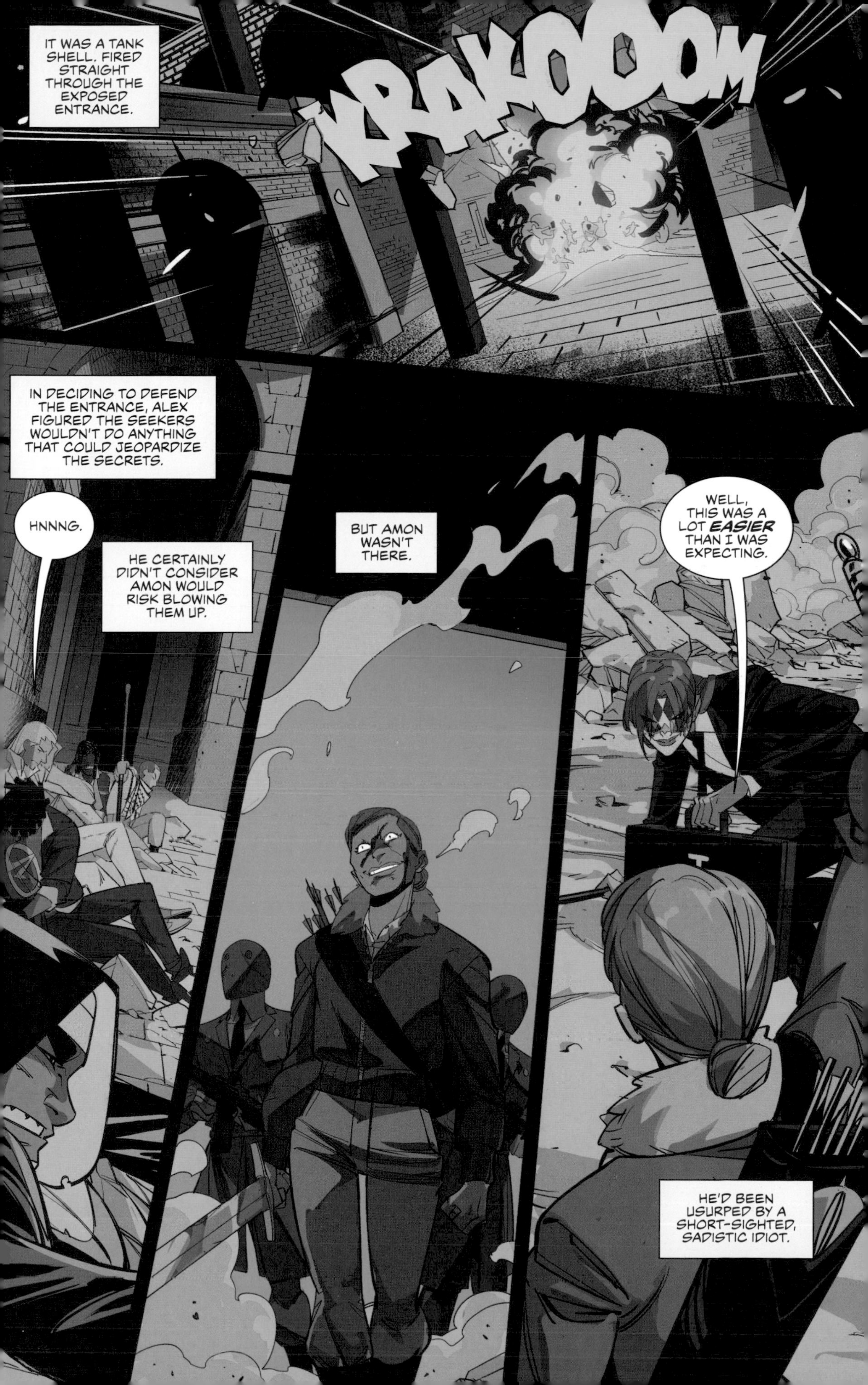
IT WAS A TANK SHELL. FIRED STRAIGHT THROUGH THE EXPOSED ENTRANCE.
KRAKOOOM
IN DECIDING TO DEFEND THE ENTRANCE, ALEX FIGURED THE SEEKERS WOULDN'T DO ANYTHING THAT COULD JEOPARDIZE THE SECRETS.
HNNNG.
HE CERTAINLY DIDN'T CONSIDER AMON WOULD RISK BLOWING THEM UP.
BUT AMON WASN'T THERE.
WELL, THIS WAS A LOT **EASIER** THAN I WAS EXPECTING.
HE'D BEEN USURPED BY A SHORT-SIGHTED, SADISTIC IDIOT.

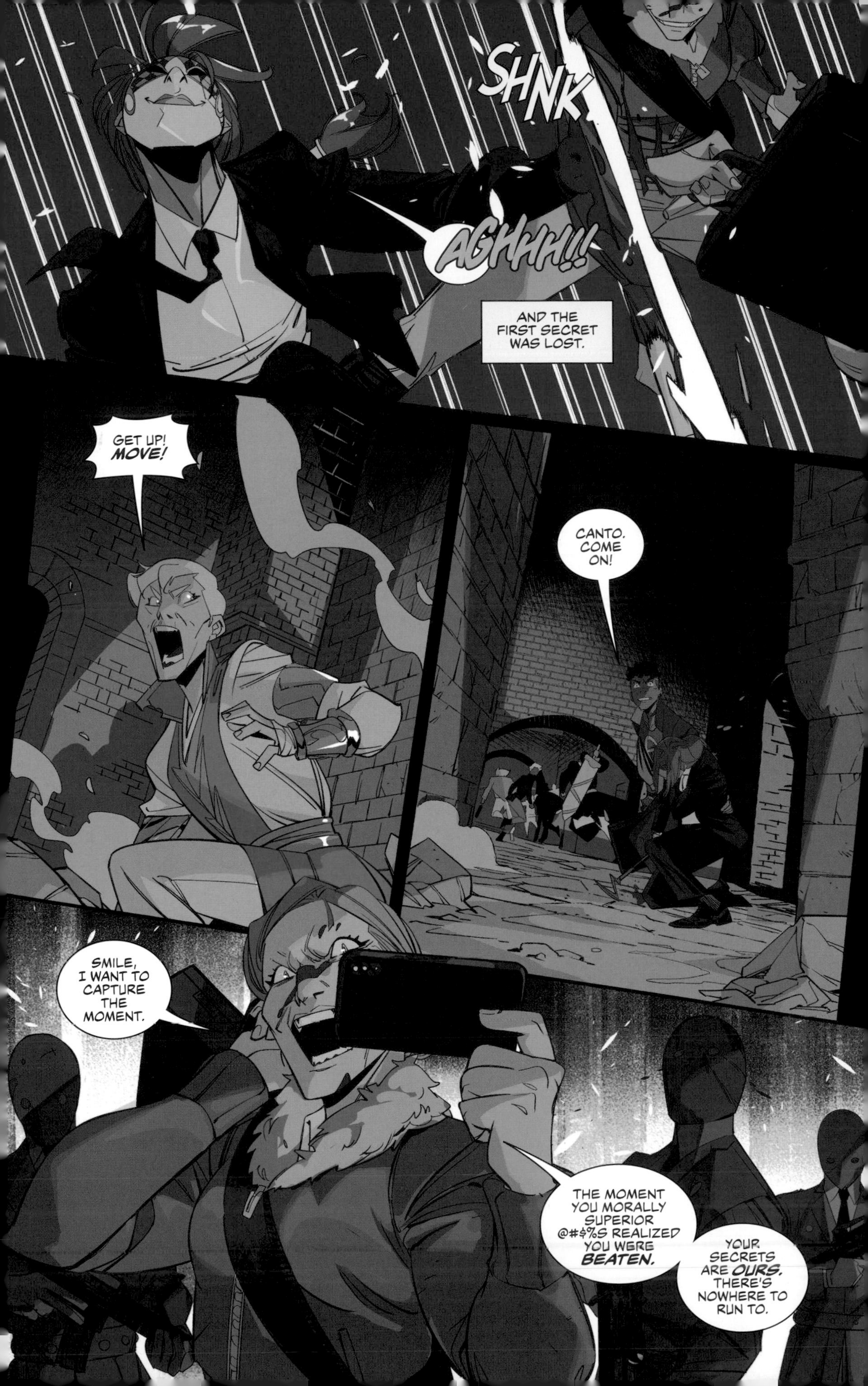
SHNK
AGHHH!!
AND THE FIRST SECRET WAS LOST.
GET UP! MOVE!
CANTO. COME ON!
SMILE, I WANT TO CAPTURE THE MOMENT.
THE MOMENT YOU MORALLY SUPERIOR @#$%S REALIZED YOU WERE BEATEN.
YOUR SECRETS ARE OURS. THERE'S NOWHERE TO RUN TO.

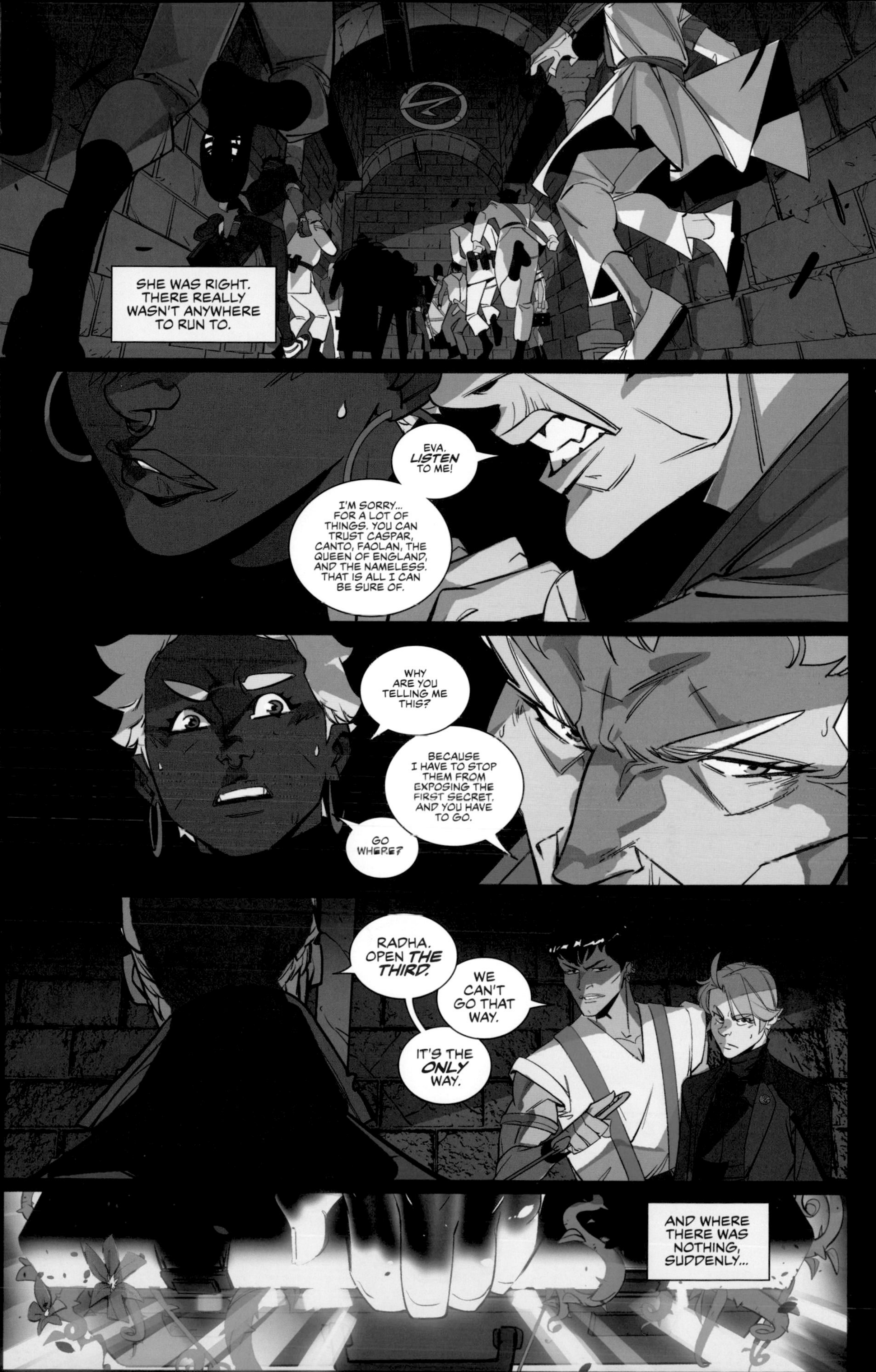
SHE WAS RIGHT. THERE REALLY WASN'T ANYWHERE TO RUN TO.
EVA. LISTEN TO ME!
I'M SORRY... FOR A LOT OF THINGS. YOU CAN TRUST CASPAR, CANTO, FAOLAN, THE QUEEN OF ENGLAND, AND THE NAMELESS. THAT IS ALL I CAN BE SURE OF.
WHY ARE YOU TELLING ME THIS?
BECAUSE I HAVE TO STOP THEM FROM EXPOSING THE FIRST SECRET, AND YOU HAVE TO GO.
GO WHERE?
RADHA. OPEN THE THIRD.
WE CAN'T GO THAT WAY.
IT'S THE ONLY WAY.
AND WHERE THERE WAS NOTHING, SUDDENLY...

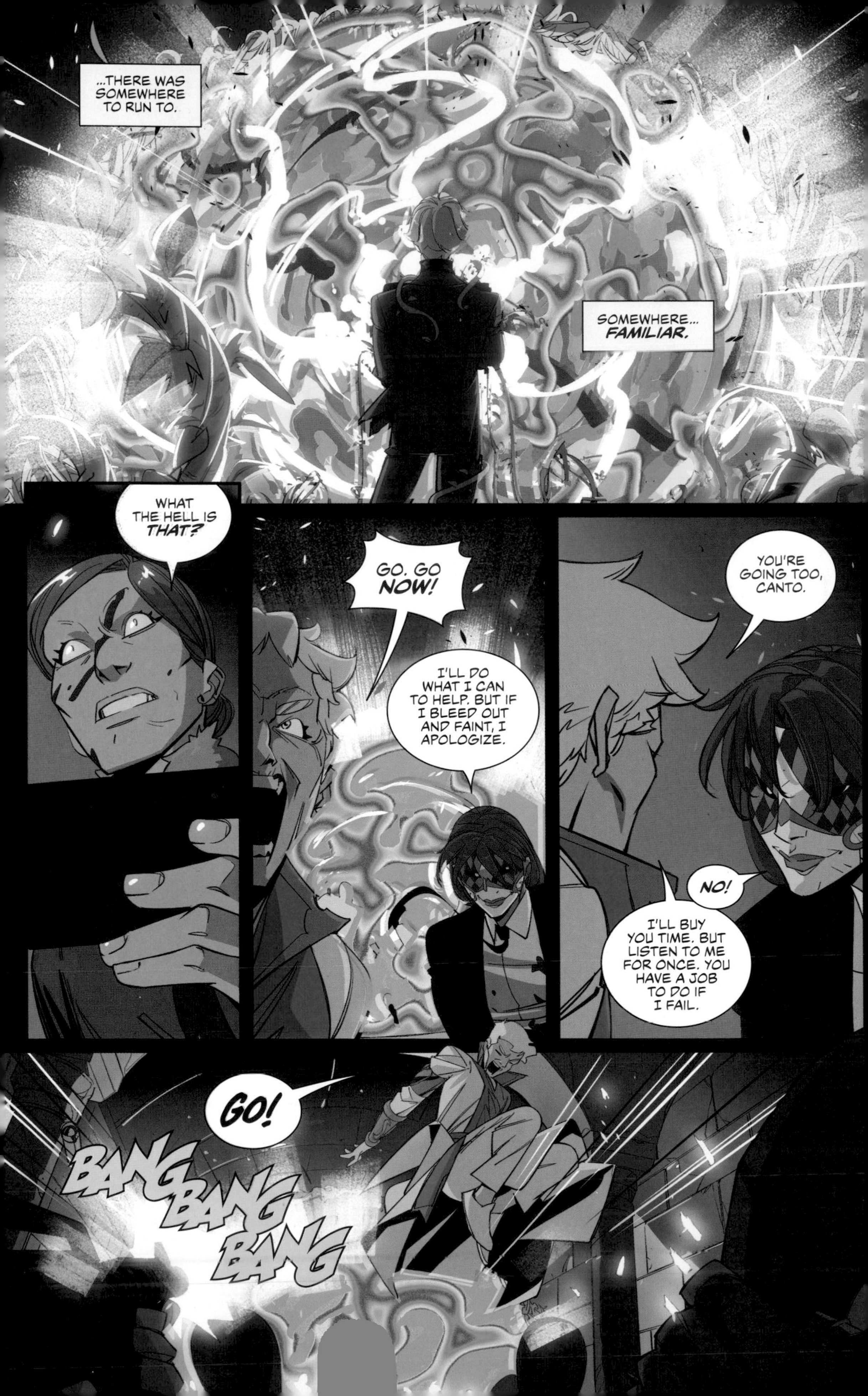
...THERE WAS SOMEWHERE TO RUN TO.
SOMEWHERE... *FAMILIAR.*
WHAT THE HELL IS *THAT?*
GO. GO *NOW!*
I'LL DO WHAT I CAN TO HELP. BUT IF I BLEED OUT AND FAINT, I APOLOGIZE.
YOU'RE GOING TOO, CANTO.
NO!
I'LL BUY YOU TIME. BUT LISTEN TO ME FOR ONCE. YOU HAVE A JOB TO DO IF I FAIL.
GO!
BANG BANG BANG

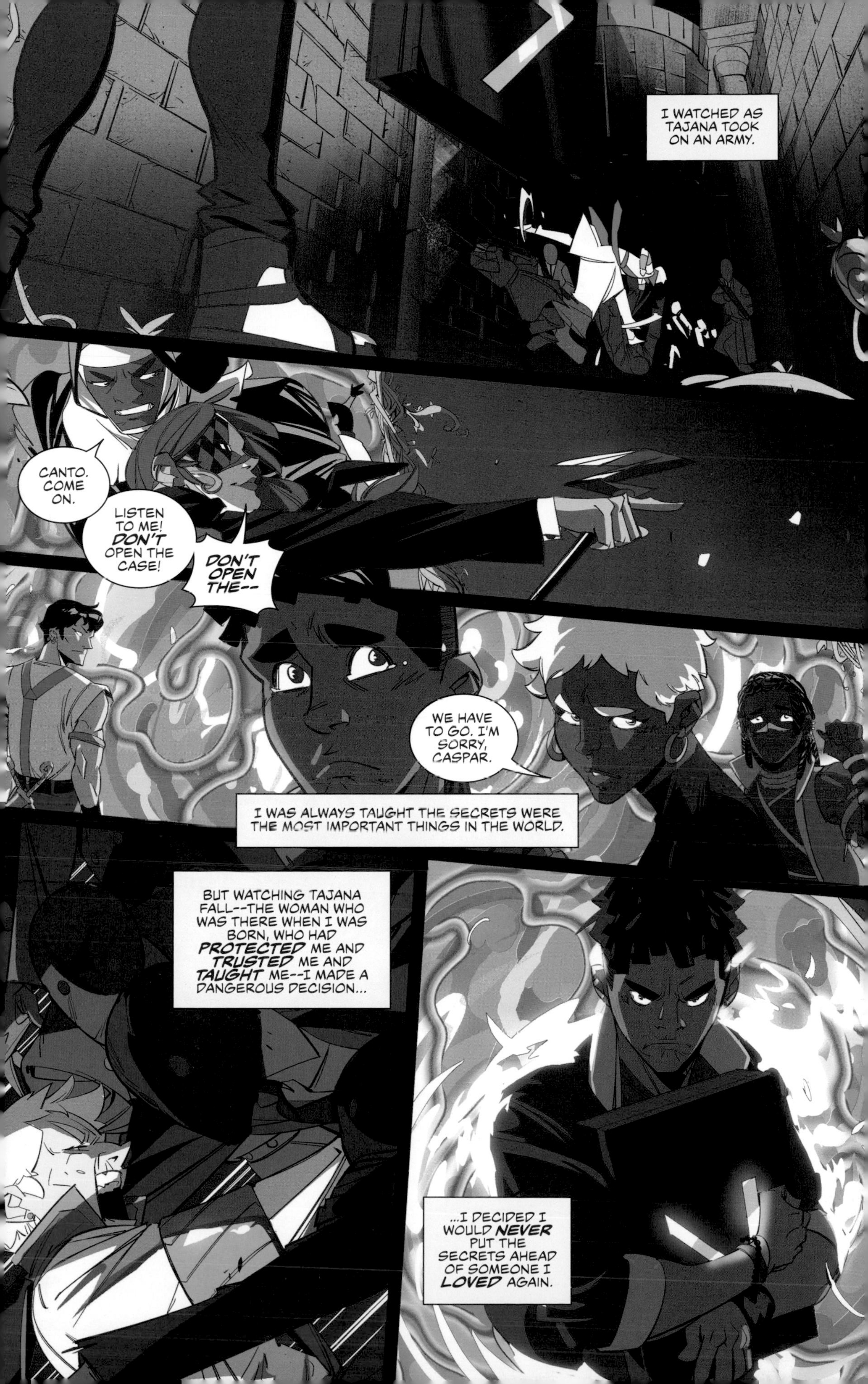
I WATCHED AS TAJANA TOOK ON AN ARMY.
CANTO. COME ON.
LISTEN TO ME! DON'T OPEN THE CASE!
DON'T OPEN THE--
WE HAVE TO GO. I'M SORRY, CASPAR.
I WAS ALWAYS TAUGHT THE SECRETS WERE THE MOST IMPORTANT THINGS IN THE WORLD.
BUT WATCHING TAJANA FALL--THE WOMAN WHO WAS THERE WHEN I WAS BORN, WHO HAD PROTECTED ME AND TRUSTED ME AND TAUGHT ME--I MADE A DANGEROUS DECISION...
...I DECIDED I WOULD NEVER PUT THE SECRETS AHEAD OF SOMEONE I LOVED AGAIN.

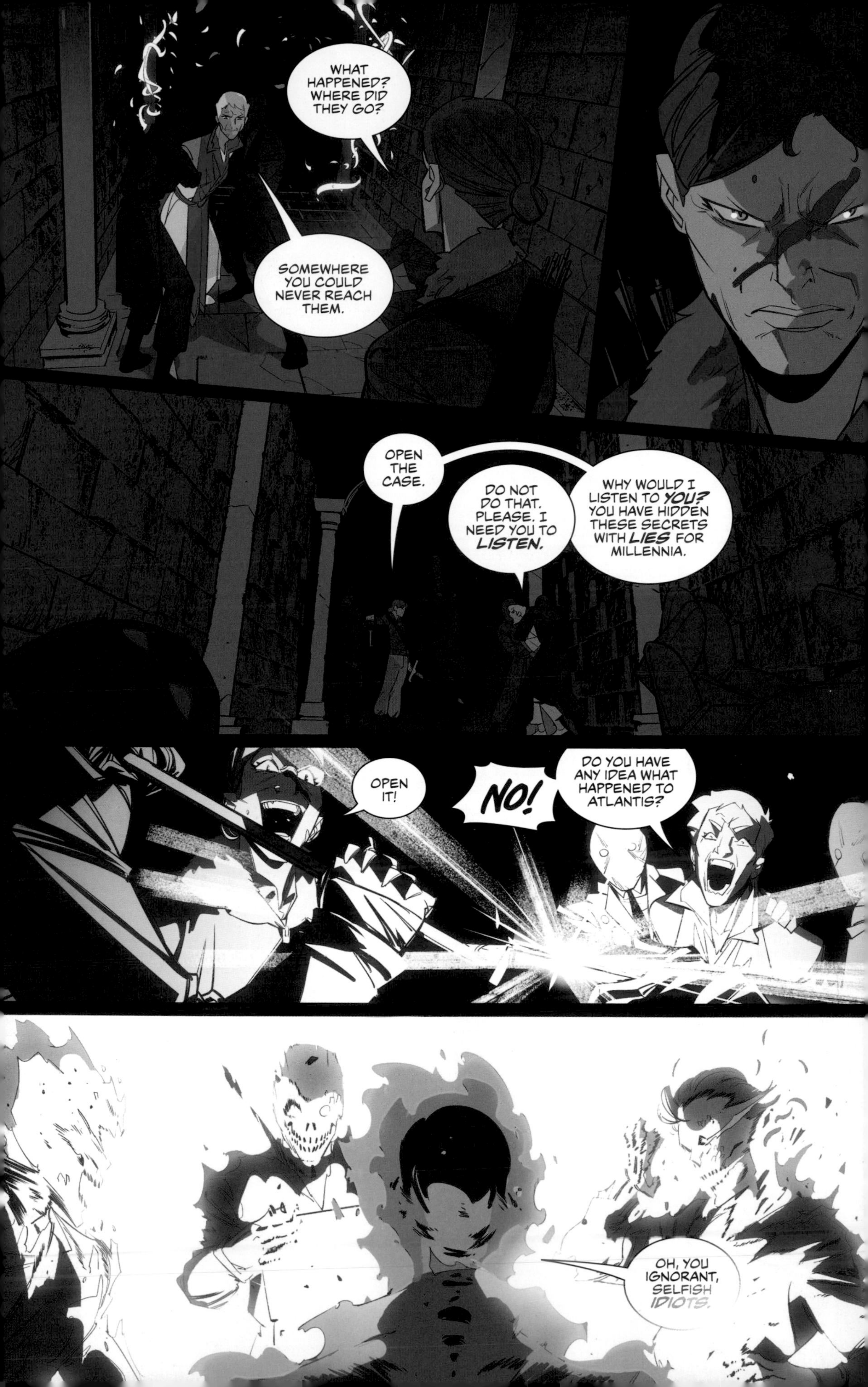
WHAT HAPPENED? WHERE DID THEY GO?
SOMEWHERE YOU COULD NEVER REACH THEM.
OPEN THE CASE.
DO NOT DO THAT. PLEASE. I NEED YOU TO LISTEN.
WHY WOULD I LISTEN TO YOU? YOU HAVE HIDDEN THESE SECRETS WITH LIES FOR MILLENNIA.
OPEN IT!
NO!
DO YOU HAVE ANY IDEA WHAT HAPPENED TO ATLANTIS?
OH, YOU IGNORANT, SELFISH IDIOTS.

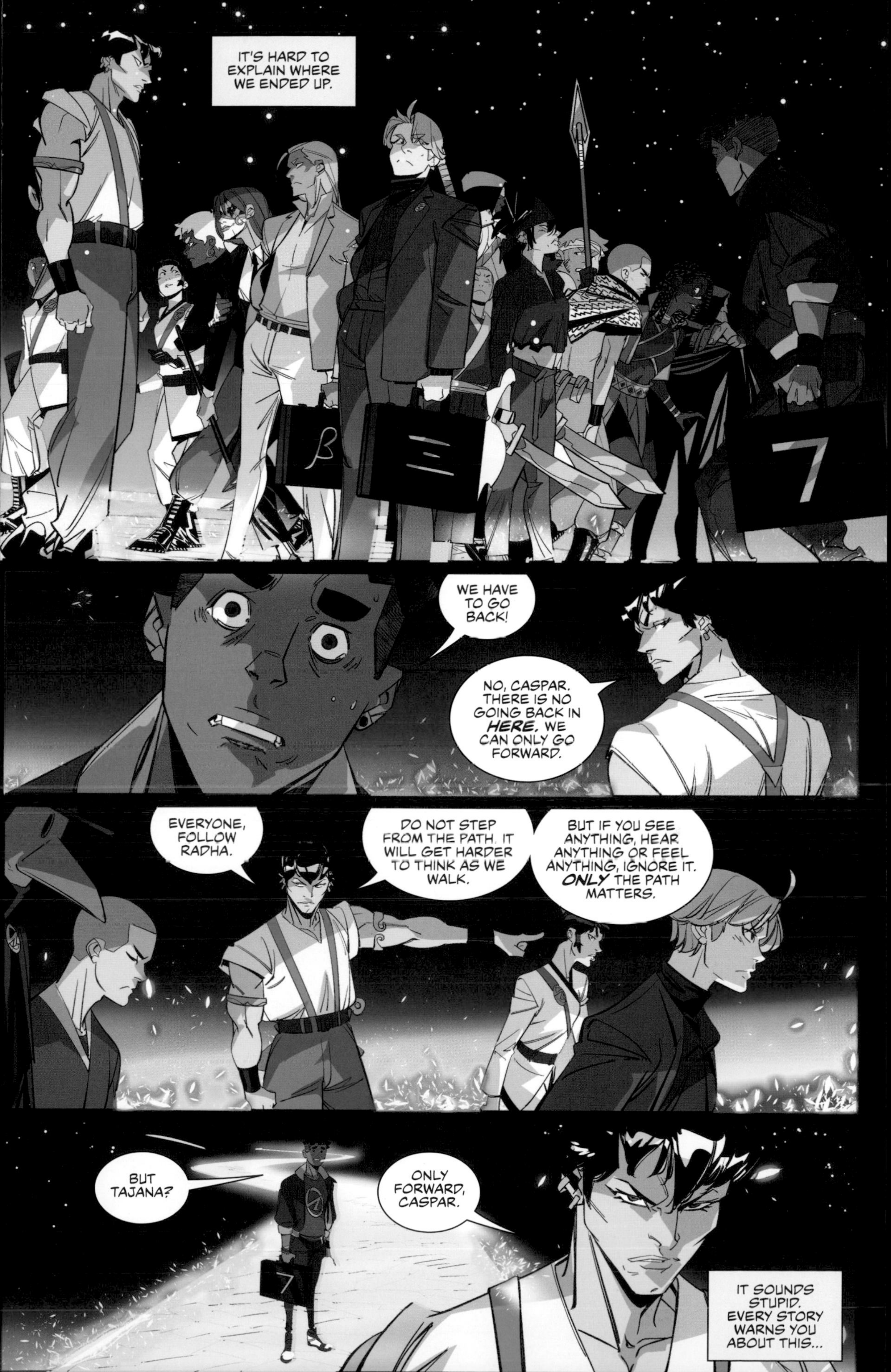
IT'S HARD TO EXPLAIN WHERE WE ENDED UP.
β
7
WE HAVE TO GO BACK!
NO, CASPAR. THERE IS NO GOING BACK IN ***HERE.*** WE CAN ONLY GO FORWARD.
EVERYONE, FOLLOW RADHA.
DO NOT STEP FROM THE PATH. IT WILL GET HARDER TO THINK AS WE WALK.
BUT IF YOU SEE ANYTHING, HEAR ANYTHING OR FEEL ANYTHING, IGNORE IT. ***ONLY*** THE PATH MATTERS.
BUT TAJANA?
ONLY FORWARD, CASPAR.
IT SOUNDS STUPID. EVERY STORY WARNS YOU ABOUT THIS...

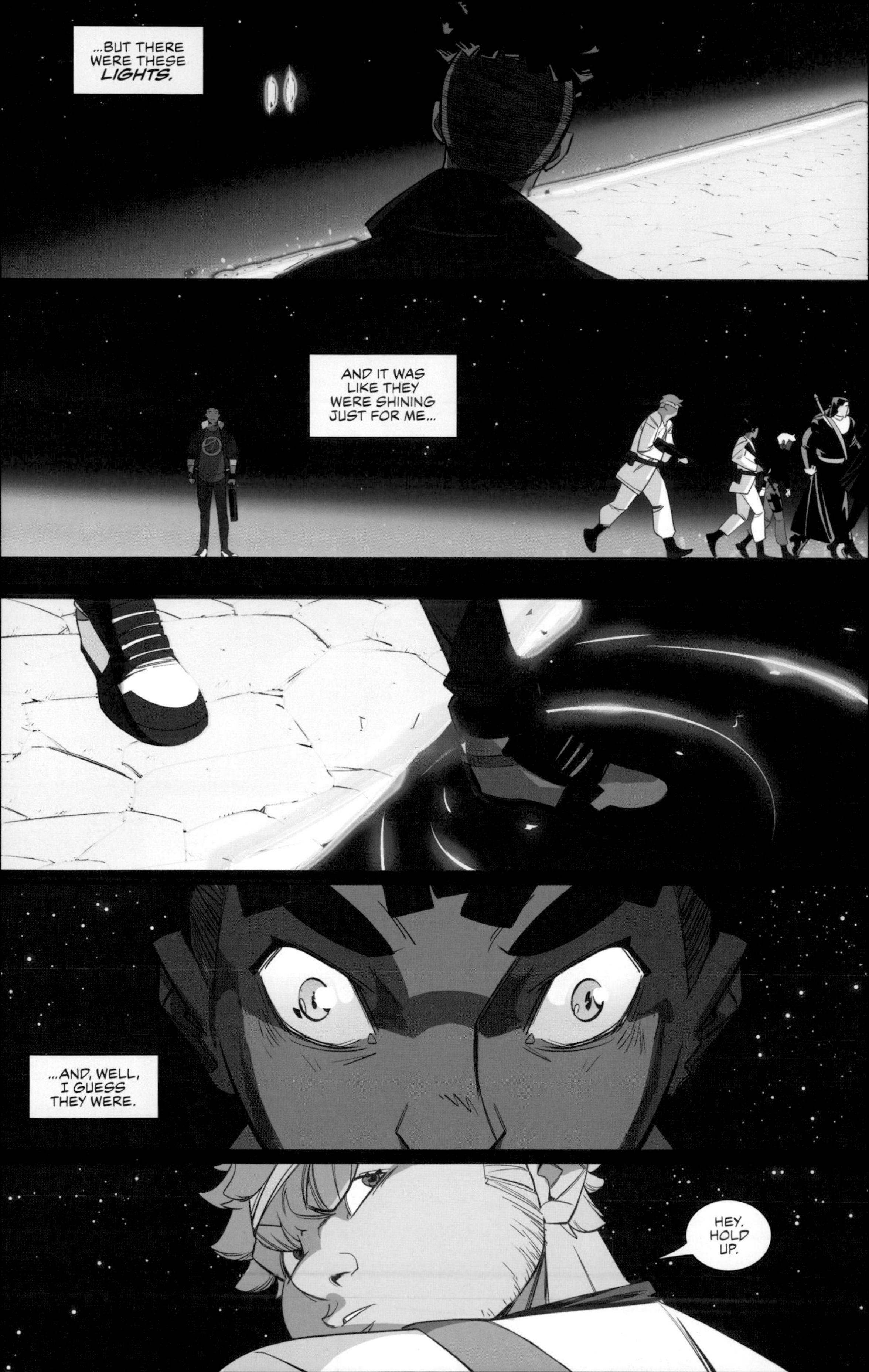
...BUT THERE WERE THESE LIGHTS.
AND IT WAS LIKE THEY WERE SHINING JUST FOR ME...
...AND, WELL, I GUESS THEY WERE.
HEY. HOLD UP.

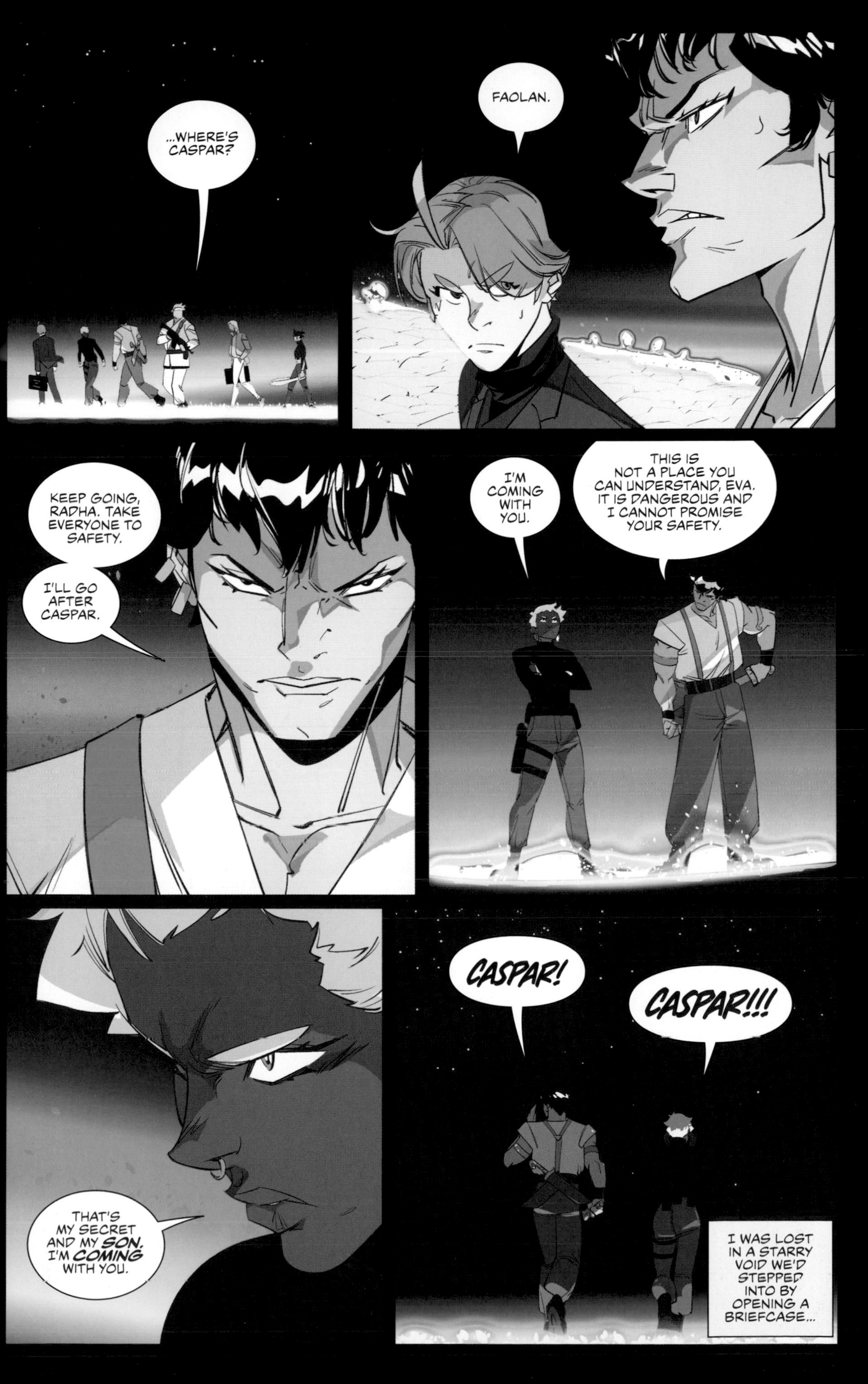
...WHERE'S CASPAR?
FAOLAN.
KEEP GOING, RADHA. TAKE EVERYONE TO SAFETY.
I'LL GO AFTER CASPAR.
I'M COMING WITH YOU.
THIS IS NOT A PLACE YOU CAN UNDERSTAND, EVA. IT IS DANGEROUS AND I CANNOT PROMISE YOUR SAFETY.
THAT'S MY SECRET AND MY SON. I'M COMING WITH YOU.
CASPAR!
CASPAR!!!
I WAS LOST IN A STARRY VOID WE'D STEPPED INTO BY OPENING A BRIEFCASE...

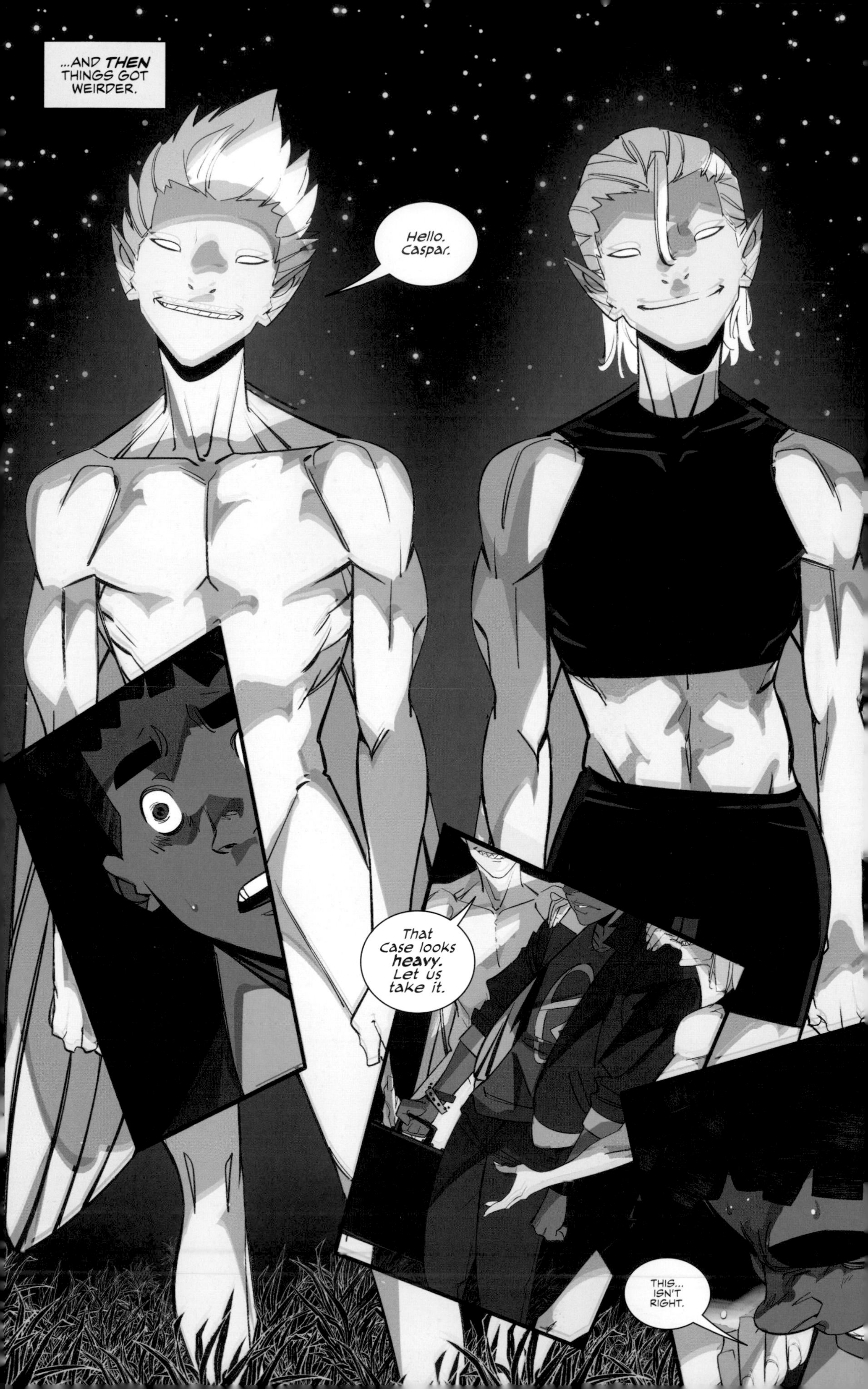
...AND **THEN** THINGS GOT WEIRDER.
Hello. Caspar.
That case looks **heavy.** Let us take it.
THIS... ISN'T RIGHT.

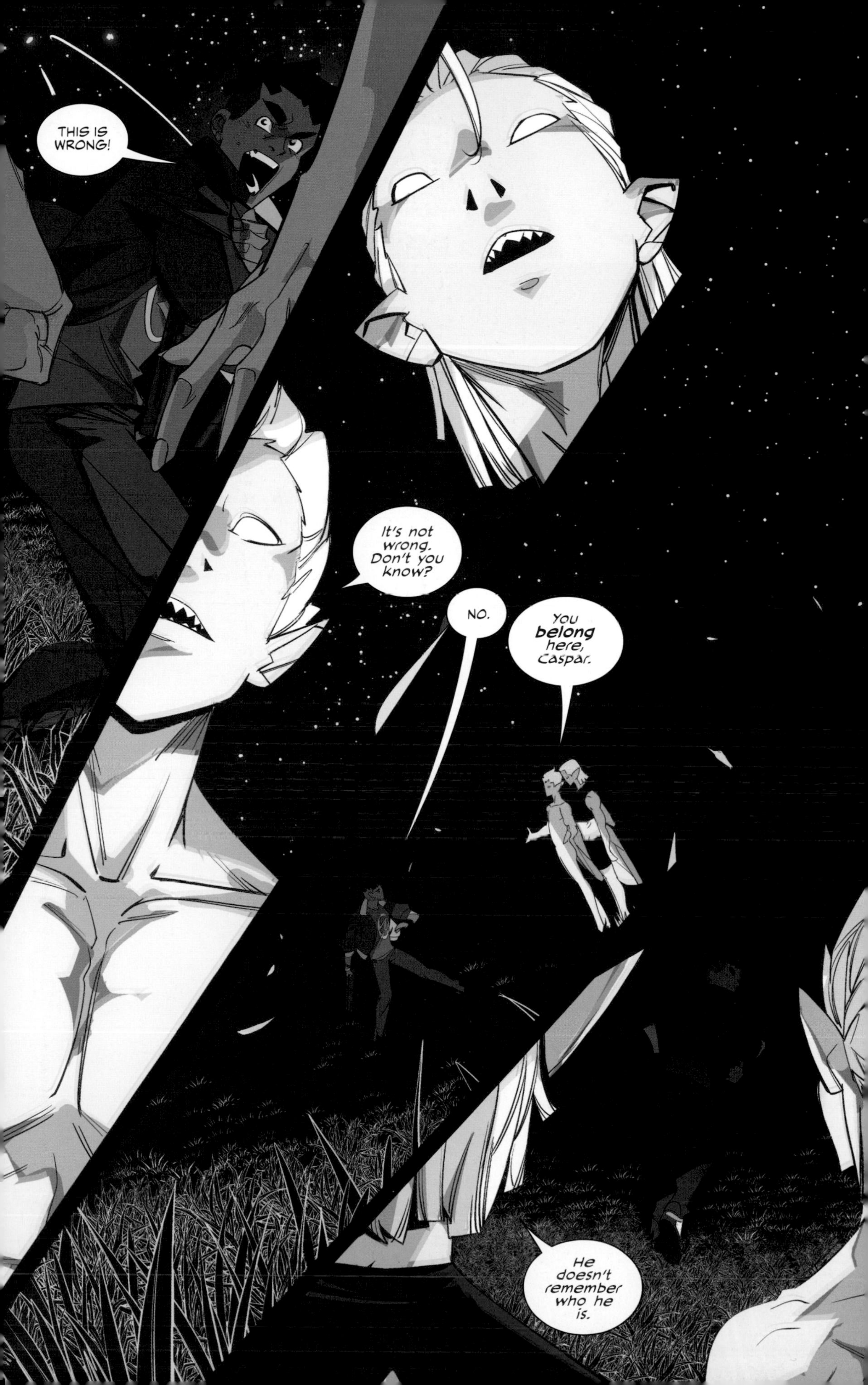
THIS IS WRONG!
It's not wrong. Don't you know?
NO.
You **belong** here, Caspar.
He doesn't remember who he is.

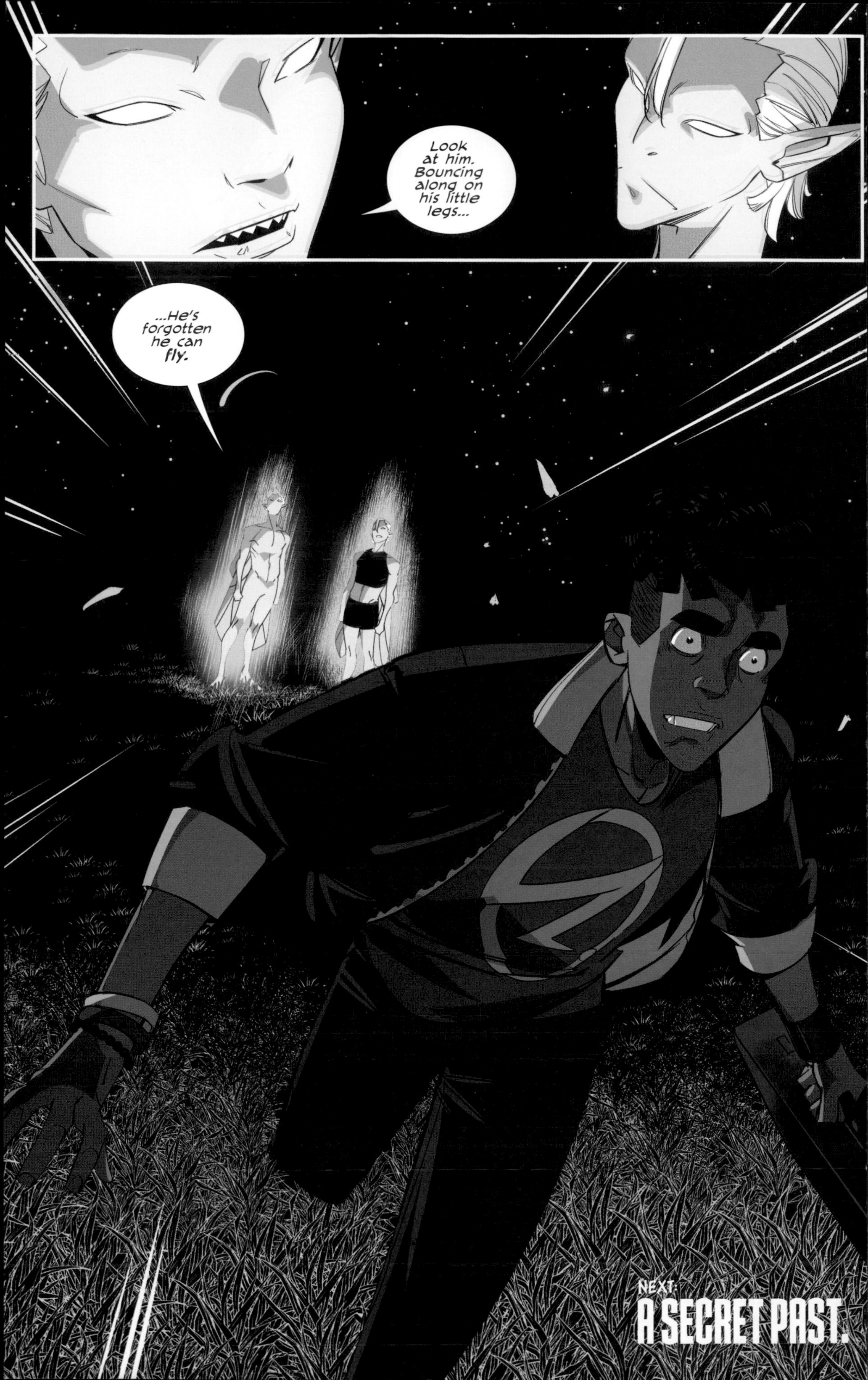
Look at him. Bouncing along on his little legs...
...He's forgotten he can fly.
NEXT:
A SECRET PAST.

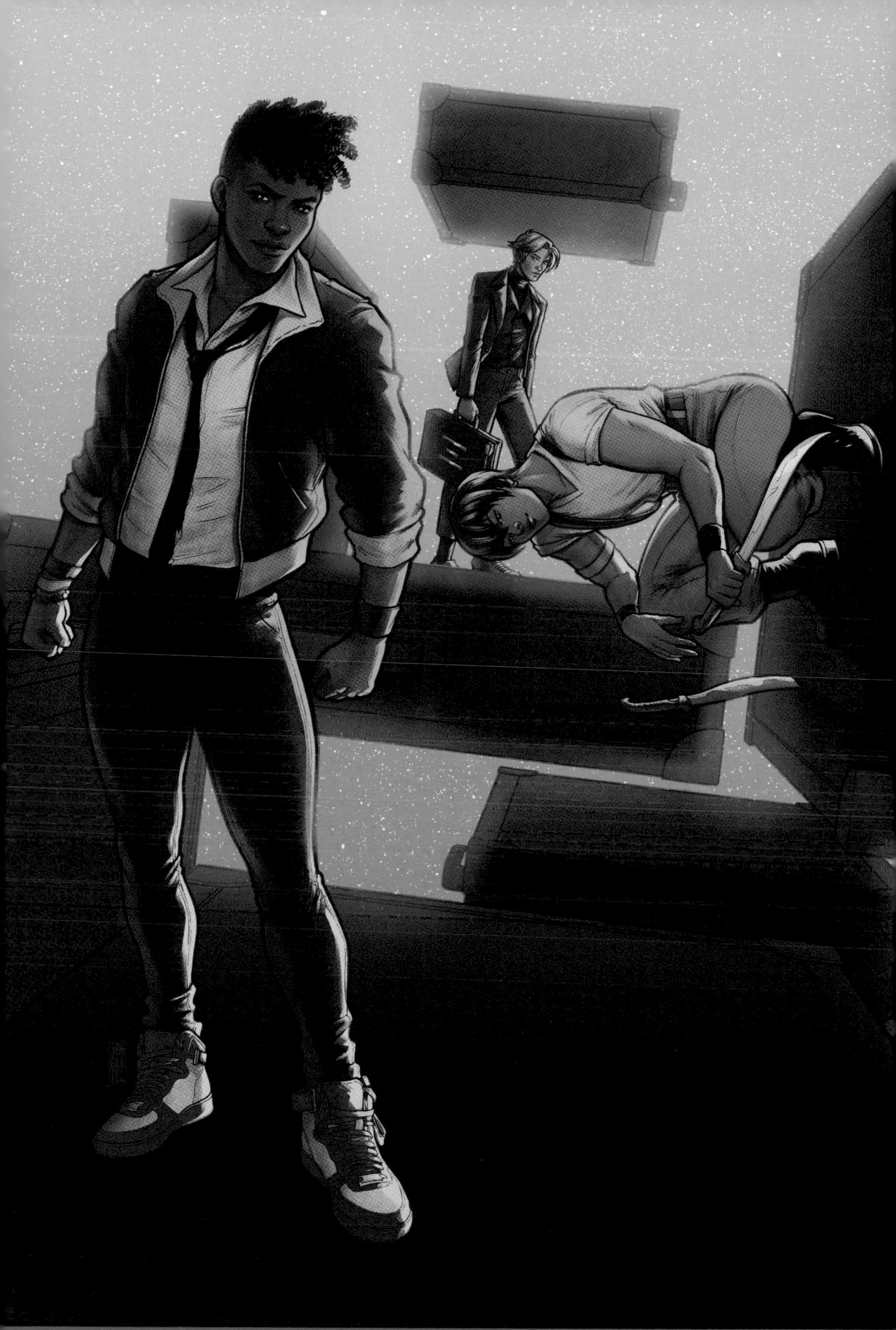

JEN BARTEL ISSUE SIX VARIANT COVER

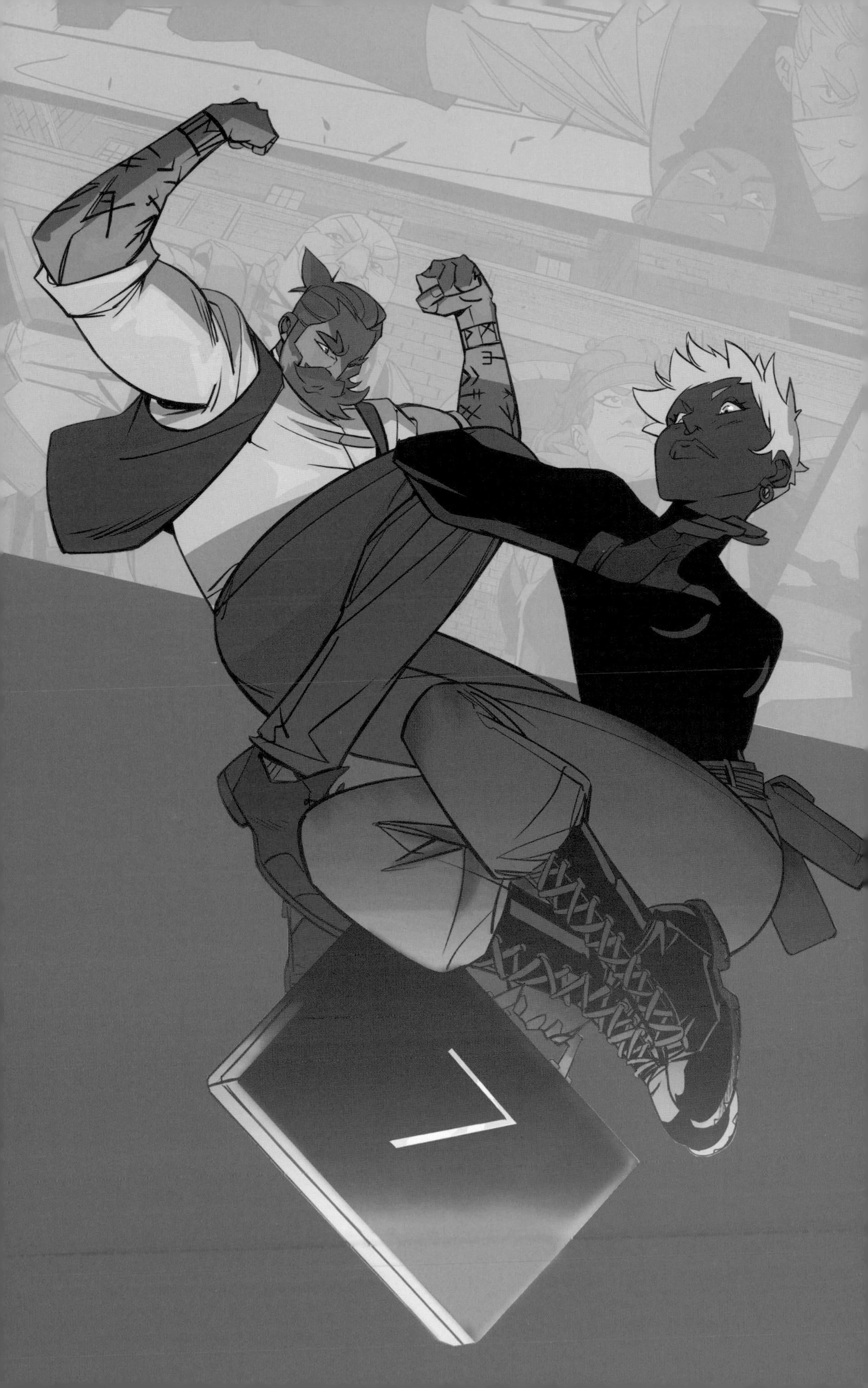

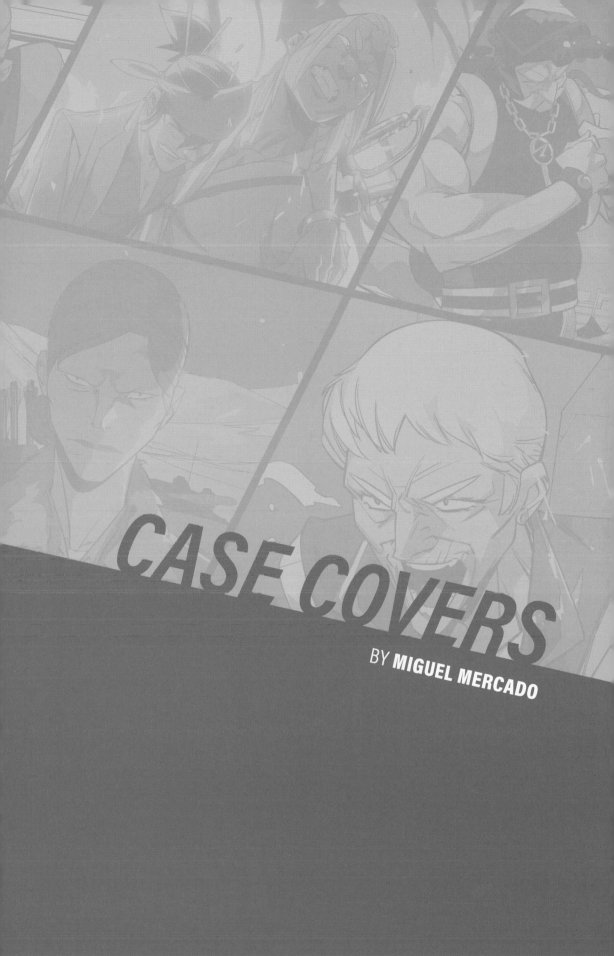

CASE COVERS

BY **MIGUEL MERCADO**

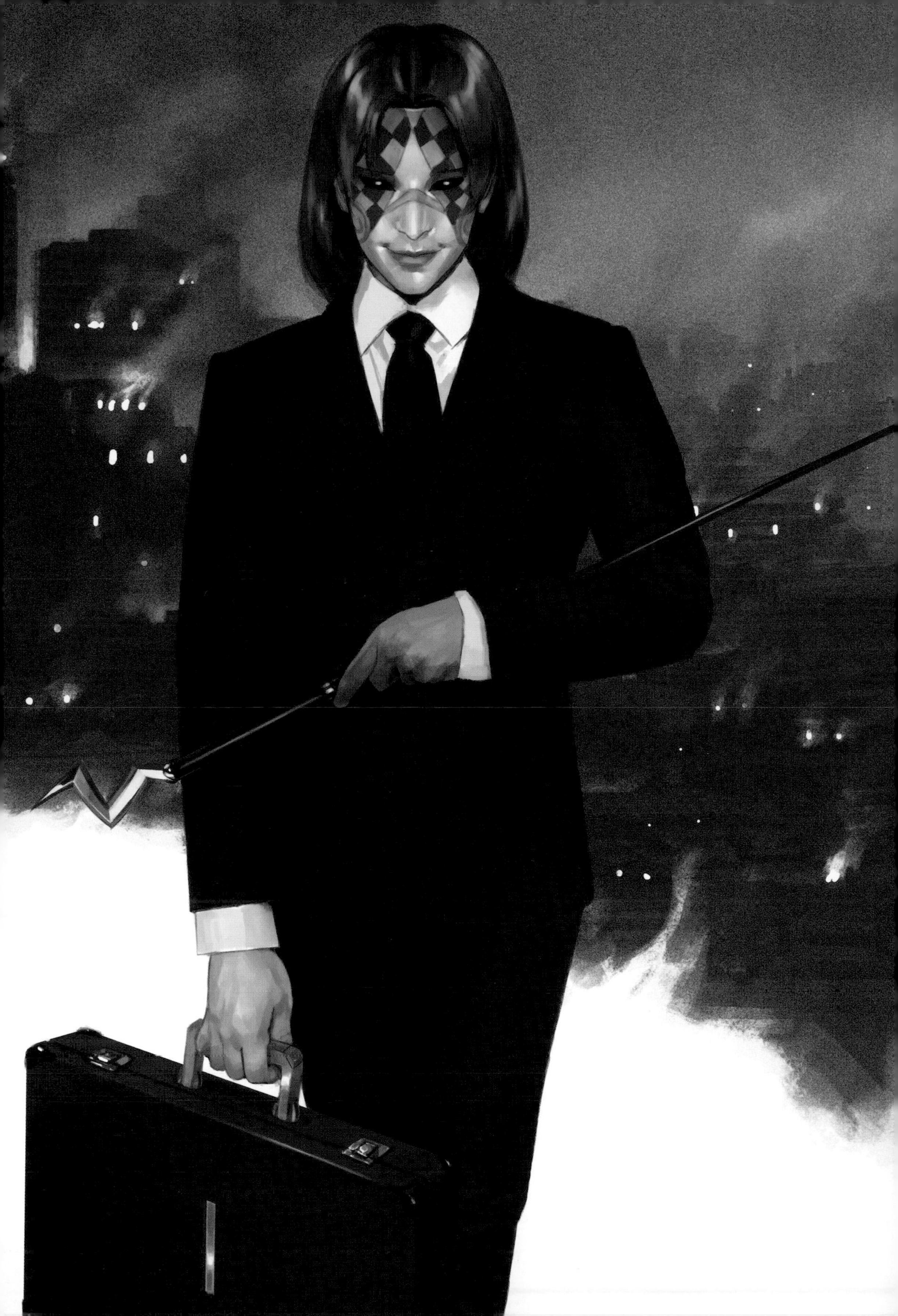

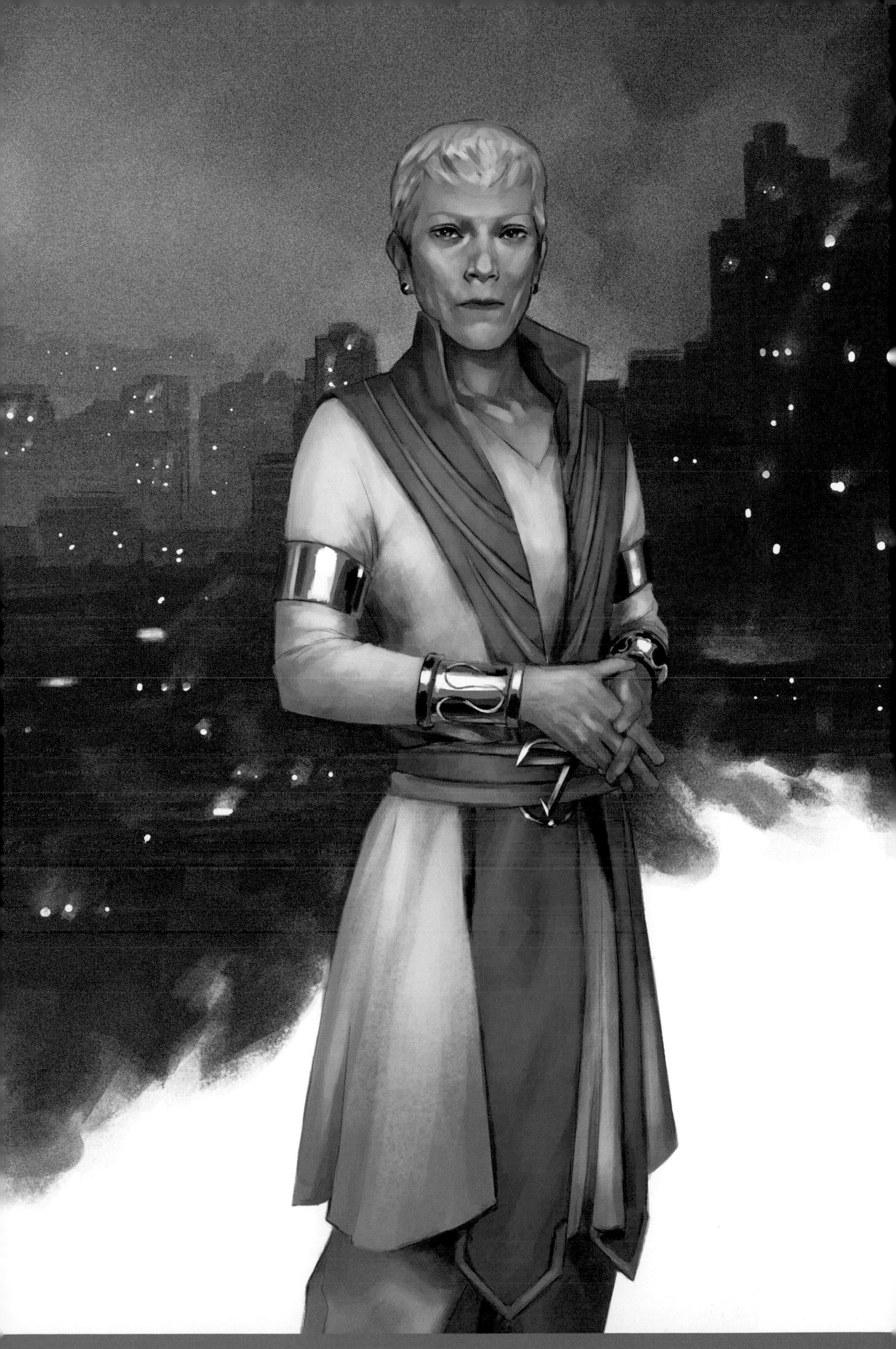

TAJANA CASE ONE KEEPER

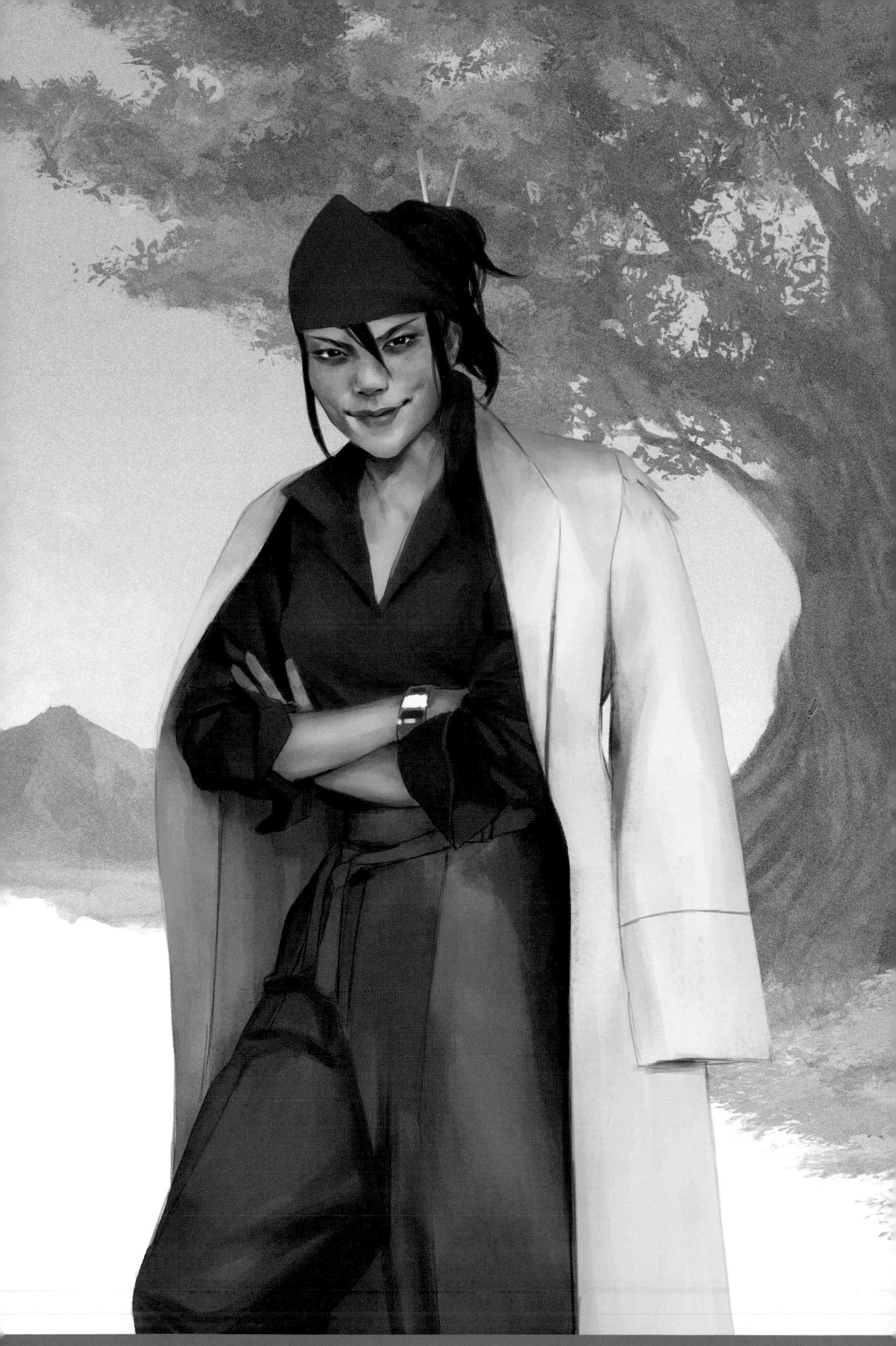

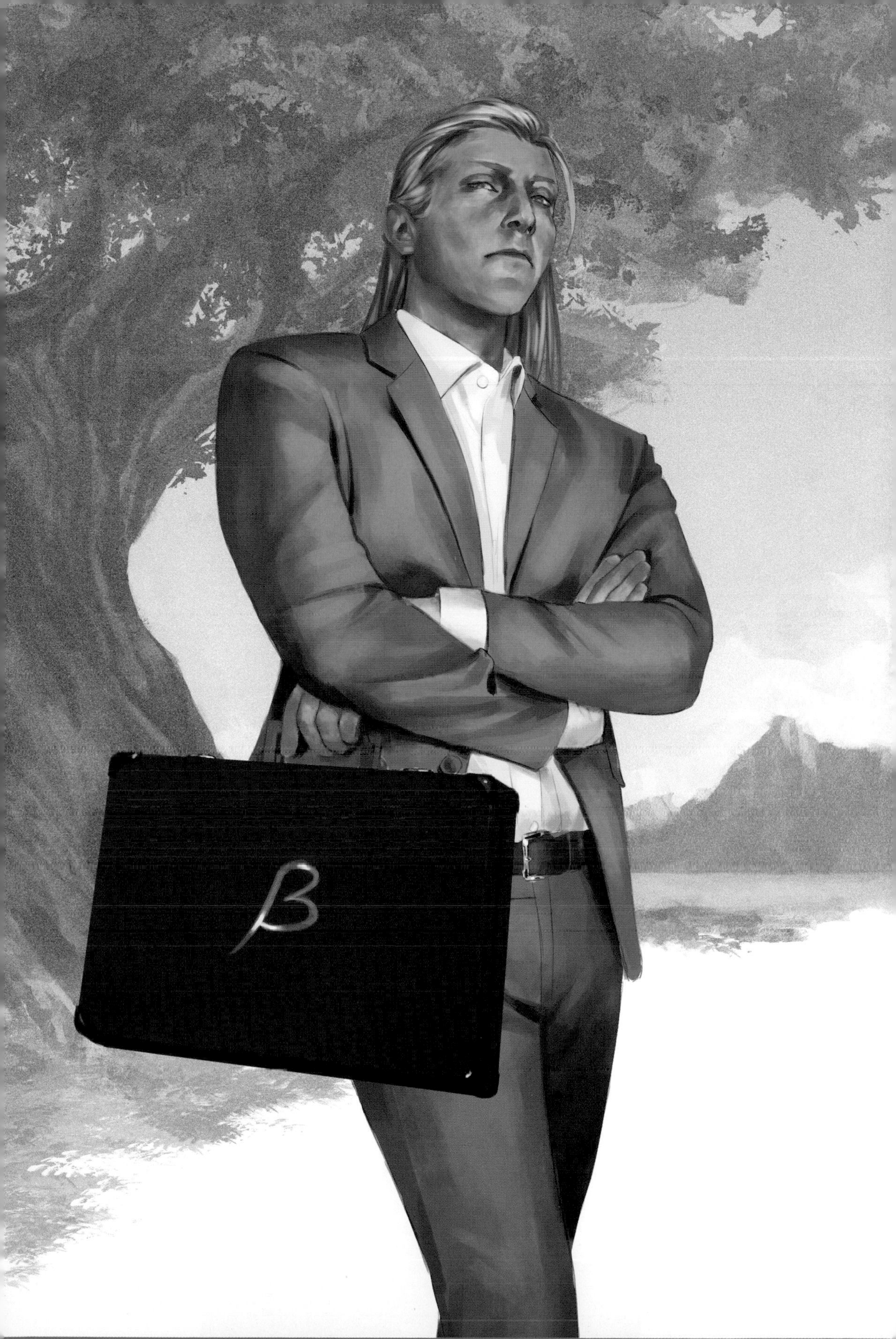
β

ALEX CASE TWO HOLDER

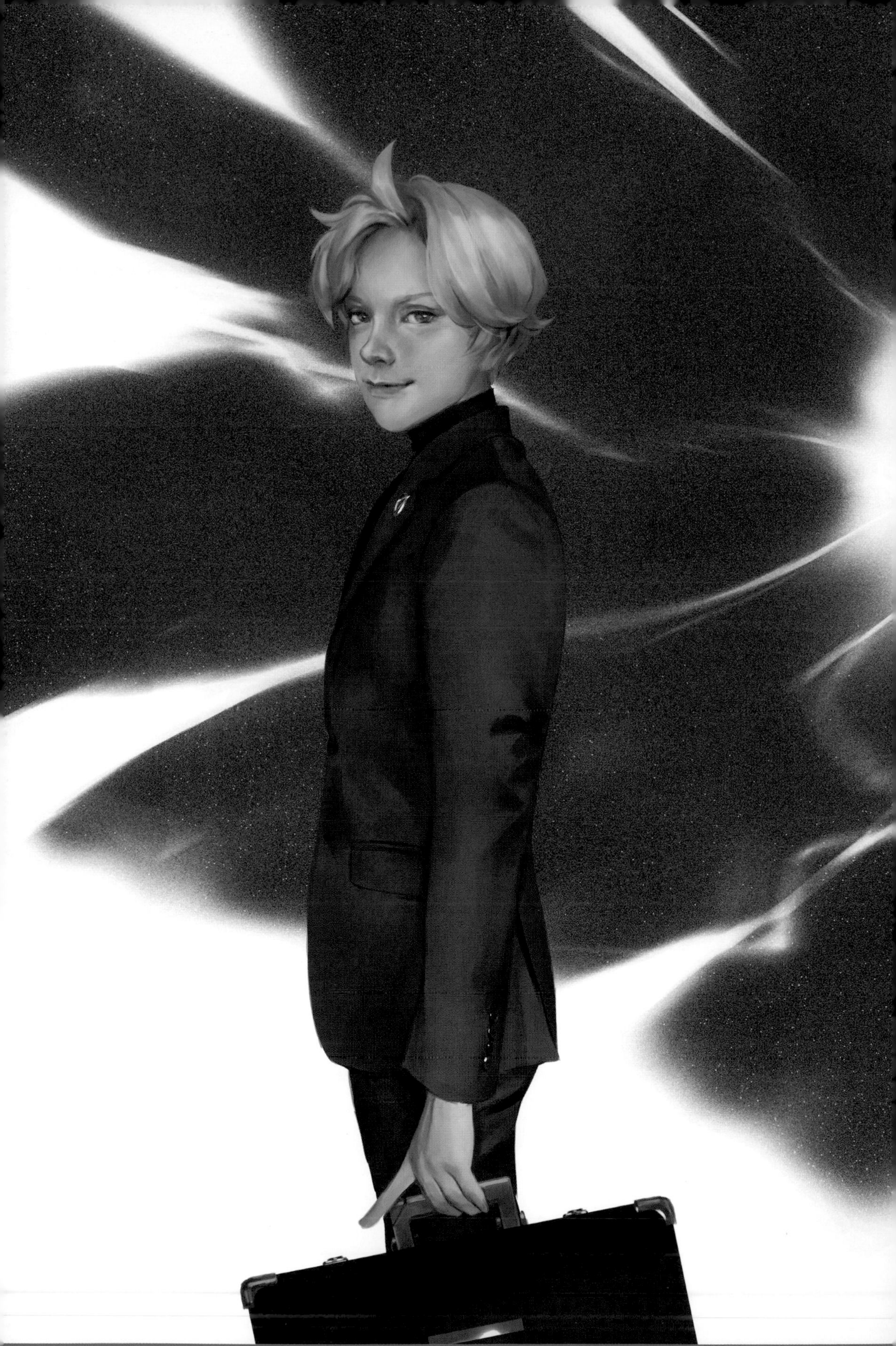

RADHA CASE THREE HOLDER

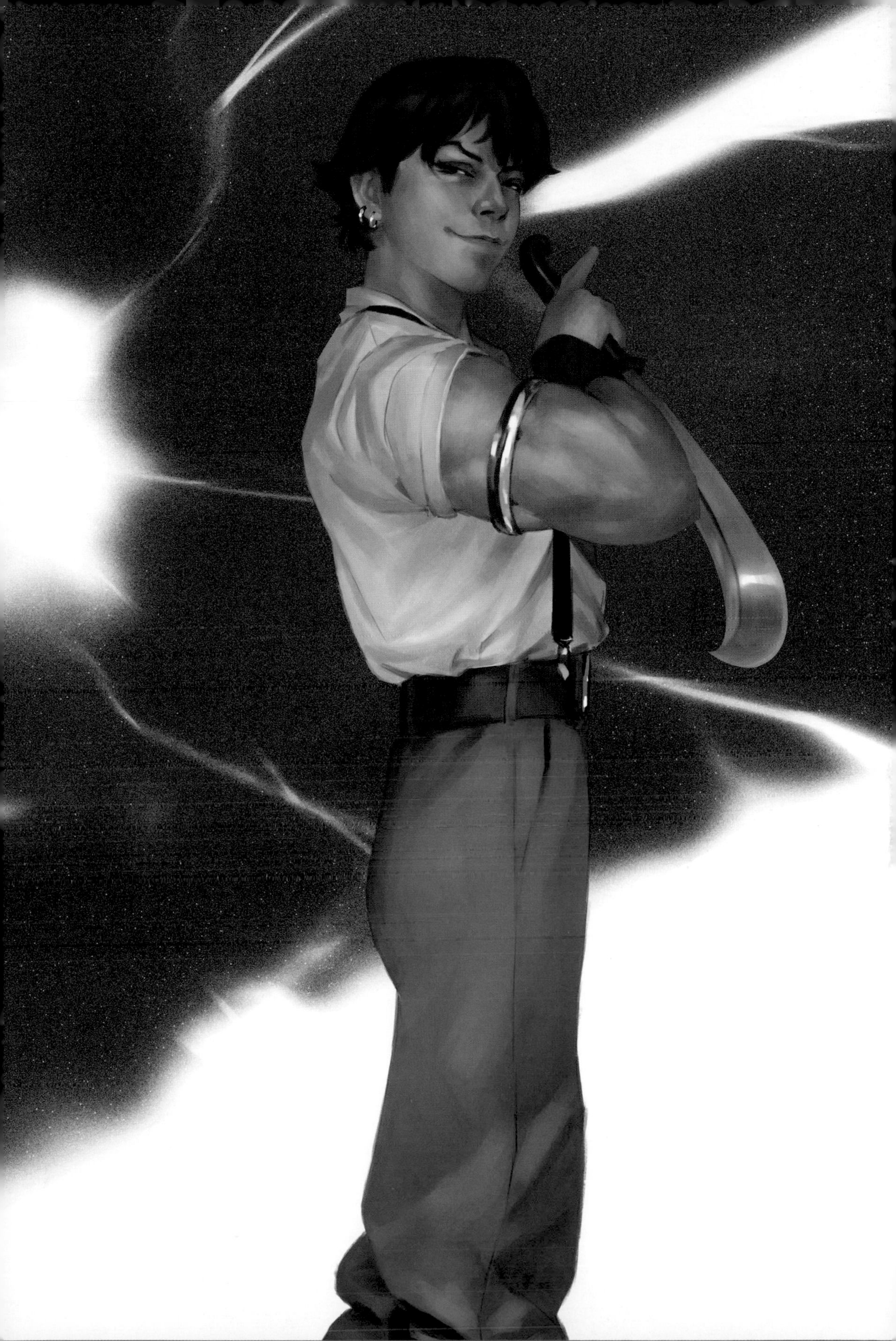

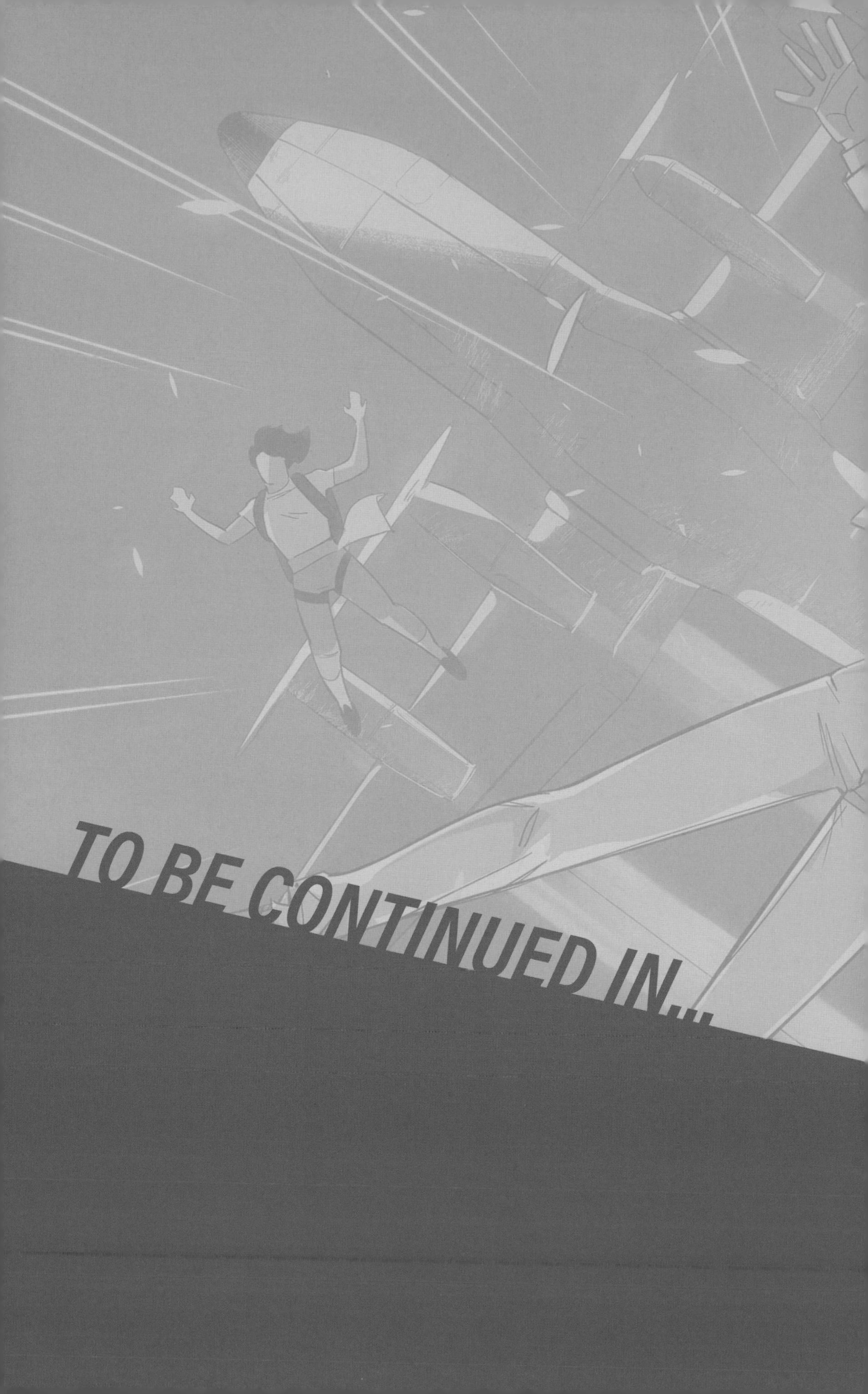
TO BE CONTINUED IN...

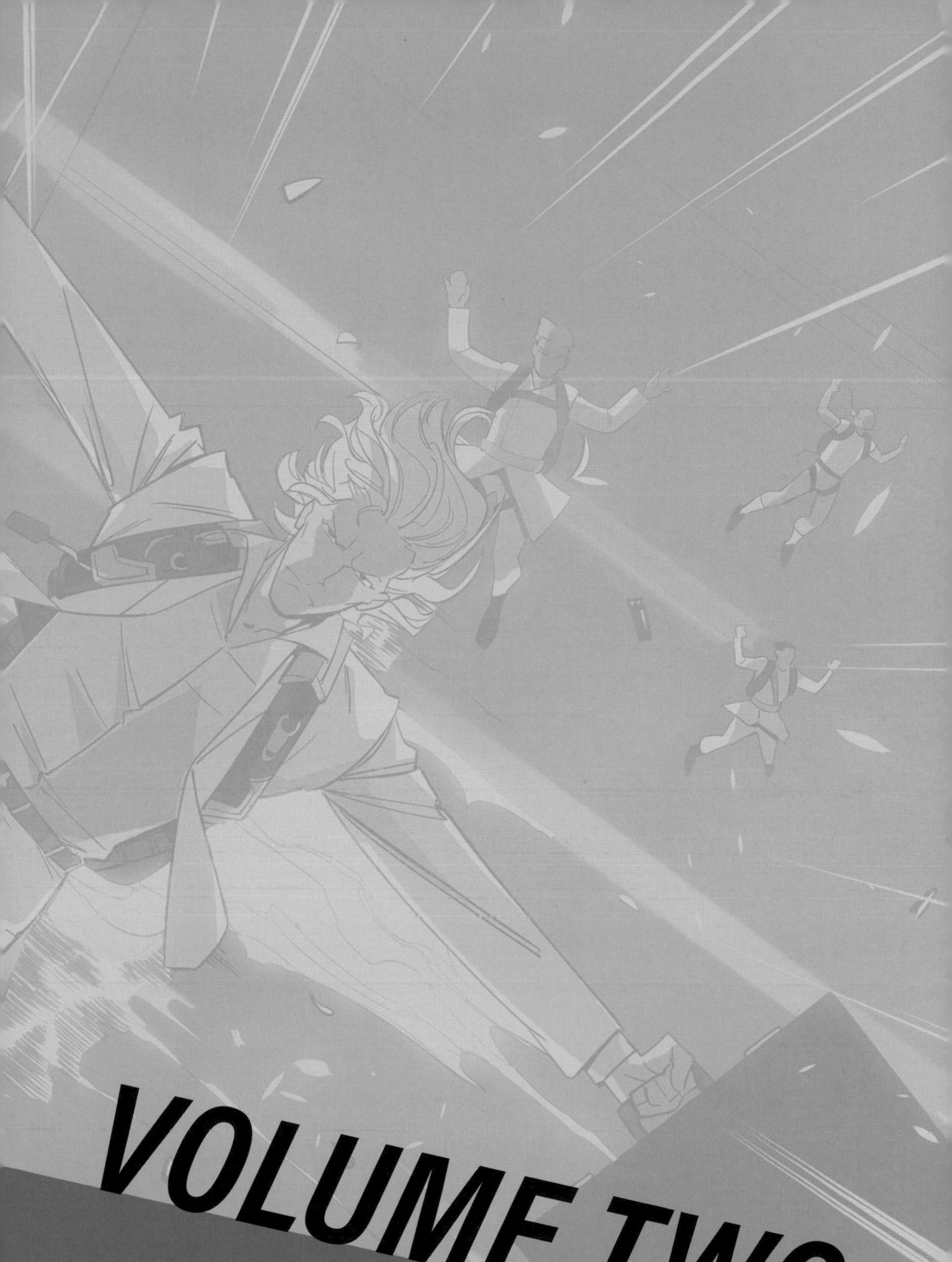

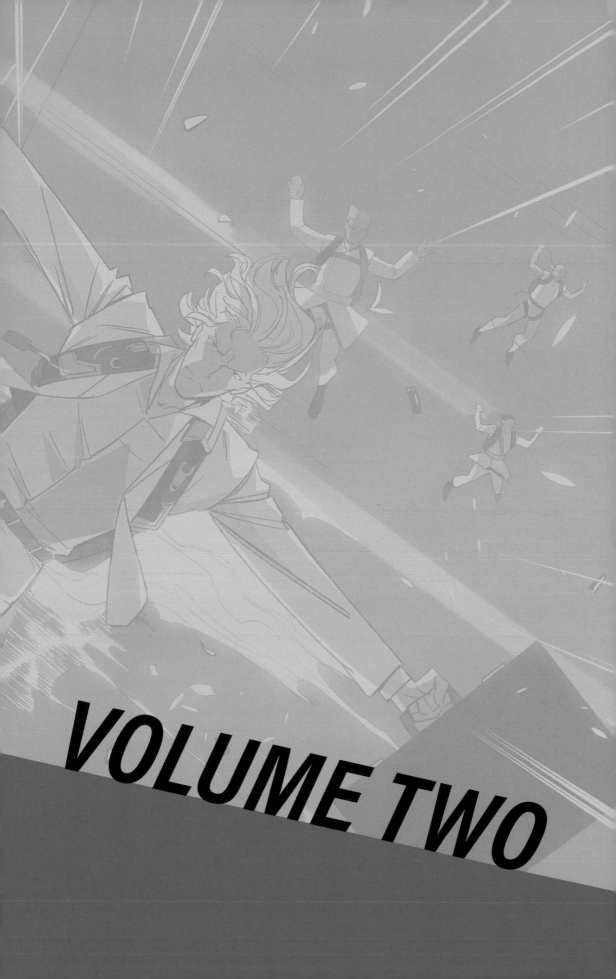

VOLUME TWO

WRITER

Tom Taylor is a #1 *New York Times* bestselling author and a multi-award winning playwright and screenwriter.

For DC Comics, after years spent writing the bestselling *Injustice* series, Taylor is currently the writer of the smash-hit *DCeased* series and the relaunched *Suicide Squad*. For Marvel, he has recently written *Friendly Neighborhood Spider-Man* and *Star Wars: Age of Resistance*, with more to come.

Over the past ten years, he has been the writer on such titles as *X-Men: Red*, *Justice League/ Power Rangers*, *All-New Wolverine*, *Batman/Superman*, *Iron Man*, *Earth 2*, *Green Lantern Corps*, and many *Star Wars* titles.

Taylor is the co-creator, head writer and executive producer of the BAFTA-nominated television series, *The Deep*, based on his graphic novels of the same name with artist James Brouwer, published through BOOM!.

The three seasons of *The Deep* screen in over 140 countries, including on Netflix in the US.